A History of

Monmouthshire

**FROM THE COMING OF THE NORMANS INTO WALES
DOWN TO THE PRESENT TIME**

by

Sir Joseph Alfred Bradney

Volume 2
Part 2

The Hundred of Trelech

ACADEMY BOOKS
1992

Sir Joseph Bradney's *History of Monmouthshire* was
originally published in twelve parts between 1904 and
1933. This facsimile edition reprints the whole of
Bradney's work, rearranged in nine parts, with the printed
area of each page slightly reduced from the original
impression.

This fifth volume comprises Volume 2
Part 2 of the original edition (1913) together with the indexes
and corrections to the whole of Volume 2, originally issued
separately in 1914.

A History of Monmouthshire
Volume 2
Part 2
The Hundred of Trelech

This edition first published in 1992 by Academy Books Limited
Copyright: Academy Books Limited

British Library Cataloguing in Publication Data:
Bradney, Sir Alfred Joseph (1859-1933)
A History of Monmouthshire from the coming of the Normans into Wales
down to the present time.
Volume 2 Part 2
The Hundred of Trelech
1. Monmouthshire
1. Title
942.99
DA 670.M7
ISBN 1 873361 16 5

Printed by:
Hillman Printers (Frome) Limited
Handlemaker Road
Marston Trading Estate
Frome
Somerset
BA11 4RW

Published and distributed by:
Academy Books Limited
35 Pretoria Avenue
London E17 7DR

Direct sales enquiries to:
Telephone: 081 521 7647
Facsimile: 081 503 6655

The Hundred of Trelech.

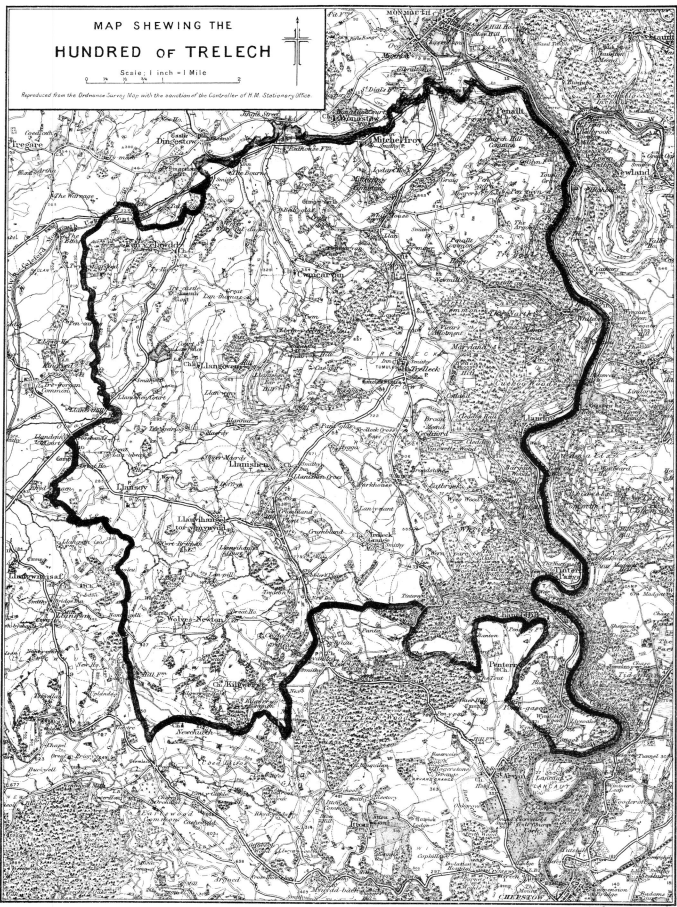

MAP SHEWING THE

HUNDRED OF TRELECH

Scale; 1 inch = 1 Mile

Reproduced from the Ordnance Survey Map with the sanction of the Controller of H.M. Stationery Office.

A History

OF

Monmouthshire

FROM THE COMING OF THE NORMANS INTO WALES
DOWN TO THE PRESENT TIME.

BY

JOSEPH ALFRED BRADNEY, C.B., M.A., F.S.A.

VOL. II.—PART II.

The Hundred of Trelech.

LONDON:
MITCHELL HUGHES AND CLARKE, 140 WARDOUR STREET, W.
1913.

The following Parishes are in the Hundred of Trelech.

———◆———

TRELECH.

PENALLT.

MITCHEL TROY.

CWMCARVAN.

PEN-Y-CLAWDD.

LLANGOVEN.

LLANDOGO.

LLANSOY.

LLANFIHANGEL-TOR-Y-MYNYDD.

WOLVESNEWTON.

CILGWRWG.

LLANISHEN.

TRELECH GRANGE.

TINTERN PARVA.

CHAPEL HILL.

List of Illustrations in Part II. of Volume II.

The

Hundred of Trelech.

◆

Trelech.

TRELECH means *stone-town*, taking its name from the three druidical stones which have for centuries been objects of note.[1] By modern writers, unaware of the meaning, the place is often written Trelleck. The parish occupies high ground, none of it being less than 500 feet above sea-level, and the highest point, the Beacon Hill, being just over 1000 feet. It is divided into Trelech town, which includes the village and 556 acres nearly in a circle around it, the remainder being known as Trelech parish.

The area is : Trelech parish 5001 acres of land and two acres of water, Trelech town 566 acres. The rateable value in 1815 was : Trelech parish 1459*l.*, Trelech town 761*l.*; in 1911, Trelech parish 2445*l.*, Trelech town 498*l.*

The population has been as follows :—

Year	1801	1811	1821	1841	1861	1871	1881	1891	1901
No. of Inhab. Trelech parish	536	568	756	1022	863	824	752	755	682
Trelech town	102	121	138		128	125	124	119	90

The number of houses is shewn thus :—

Year.		Inhabited Houses.	Uninhabited Houses.	Building.
1861	Parish .	180	6	3
	Town .	29	—	—
1871	Parish .	194	5	—
	Town .	28	1	—
1881	Parish .	179	19	—
	Town .	26	4	—
1891	Parish .	169	22	—
	Town .	25	3	—
1901	Parish .	167	11	—
	Town .	17	2	—

Until the year 1810 a large portion of the parish was unenclosed (and some continues still unenclosed), the act for which enclosure is referred to farther on. Moor game was fairly plentiful, and Charles Heath in 1810[1] relates that they had recently been all destroyed, the last *pack* that remained having been killed by a notorious poacher,[2] who sold the birds at Bristol for a high price. The inn till recently called the *Cocket*, but now the *Grouse*, bears testimony to this effect, Cocket being presumably for *cochiad* (a moor cock). In the inquisition of 1677 quoted further on this inn appears as *Le Gocquet*.

It is also certain that grouse were here, whimberries growing in abundance. Heath also says that the inhabitants kept large numbers of goats on the open land—as many as seventy in a flock.

Trelech being situated on high ground, the source of several brooks is found in the parish. The Great and Little Angidy (Anghiti Fawr, Anghiti Fach), often referred to in the *Liber Landavensis*, rise here. The former starts from the well at Higga ; the latter from Crumlin, and joins the larger brook half a mile below Trelech Grange, eventually entering the Wye at Tintern. The Gwenffrwd or Whitebrook rises at the Five trees on the main road between Monmouth and Trelech, where the four parishes of Trelech, Penallt, Mitchel Troy, and Cwmcarvan meet, and forming the northern boundary of the parish enters the Wye at the village of Whitebrook. The Catbrook (Cad-ffrwd, *the battle stream*) starts at the Park-house and enters the Wye at Tintern Parva. The Olwy rises half a mile above the town of Trelech, where it is but a very small stream, and after passing through Llandenny and the outskirts of Usk enters the river Usk at Llanllowel.

At the Nine Wells are said to be that number of separate springs, close together. There is also the remains of a bathing-place, reputed as of Roman origin, and from here runs a small brook which enters the Wye above Coed-Ithel.

[1] Some writers have asserted that Trelech means *Three Stones*. In order to have this meaning it would have to be *Tair llech* in modern Welsh, but it appears that anciently llech was masculine, and therefore Tri-llech (*three stones*) would be admissible. (*Vide Book of Llan Dâv*, p. 370.)

[1] *Excursion to Tintern Abbey*, 1810.

[2] The poacher was one Job Jones (or Williams), known as *Job the Outlaw*, who kept an inn at Cleddon. He used also to raid the deer in the Forest of Dean. (*Vide Border Counties' Worthies*, 1880, by Enoch Gibbon Salisbury, first series, p. 117.) Mr. Salisbury was once M.P. for Chester.

One mile south-west of the town is an earth-work called the Gaer (*fortress*), 700 feet above sea-level, near which is a spring called Ffynnon-y-gaer, whence the small brook known as Nant-y-gaer flows for half a mile before joining the Angidy Fawr. In the charter granted by William Marshall to Tintern abbey this brook, which is there stated to rise at Ffynnon-y-gaer, is called the Aranell; and in the survey of the manor, quoted further on, appears as Gortherchryd. At the cross-roads one mile south of the town known as Trelech Cross stands the base of an ancient cross.

The stones, or *meini hirion*, from which the place derives its name, stand in a field on the south side of the town. It is generally considered that they are of druidic origin, and therefore of remote antiquity, but from their position it is probable that they never formed part of a circle such as Stonehenge, nor are there any remains of other stones indicating that there was a group of stones here. By the inhabitants they are called *Harold's Stones*, in allusion to a victory which king Harold is said to have had here over the Welsh, and this idea is commemorated on the sun-dial described further on. The stones are the local conglomerate of the district known as pudding-stone, and were probably dug out of the ground in the immediate locality. They stand in a straight line, and each is out of perpendicular. Their size is—

    (1) 8 ft. 10 in. high by 2 ft. 18 in. round the base.
    (2) 10 ft. 4 in. high by 2 ft. 9 in. round the base.
    (3) 14 ft. 2 in. high by 4 ft. round the base.

The distance between the first and second is five yards; between the second and third six yards.

HAROLD'S STONES.

The town of Trelech was formerly much larger than it now is, and, similar to Grosmont, has become reduced till it is nothing more than a village. It is possible that the Romans had a station here; and archdeacon Coxe[1] considers this to have been the case, being of opinion that the cinders found about Trelech were of Roman origin. There is a field on the farm of the Cross Hands, where under the surface is a covering of cinders from two to three feet in depth. Nathan Rogers[2] in 1708 mentions the cinders left by the bloom-works, but does not seem to imply that they were Roman, though he obviously implies that there were no iron-works there then.

The road entering the town from the direction of Monmouth has traces of paving on it, and this road, instead of as now turning round by the east end of the church, anciently continued a straight course, as will be seen by the plan, on the west side of the church joining the existing road, where are also traces of paving, further on. On the western side of this roadway from the church to Tump Terrett can be traced the site of houses, this evidently having been a street of the town.

Edward Lhwyd, the antiquary,[1] about 1695, says that it is a market town, and had a mayor for its chief officer, but now is reduced to a poor inconsiderable village. He also says that the mount, of which more will be found further on, is called Twyn Tirret. This information was supplied by Charles Hutchins the vicar. *Tirret* is probably for *turret*, and refers possibly to a small tower built on the top. There are still several stones on the summit, but these are said to be the remains of a summer-house erected by the Rumseys.

There are two inns in the town, the *Crown*, so called probably from the king being patron of the

1 *Tour in Monmouthshire*, 1801, p. 323.
2 *Memoirs of Monmouthshire*, 1708, p. 34.

1 *Parochialia*, being a summary of answers to parochial queries. Printed for the Camb. Arch. Assoc., 1911.

living, and the *Lion*. The former was attached to the estate of the Rumseys until it was recently purchased by dr. Lachlan. The latter belonged to colonel Morgan-Clifford as part of his estate of Pant-glas, and was sold by him to mr. George Griffin Griffin.

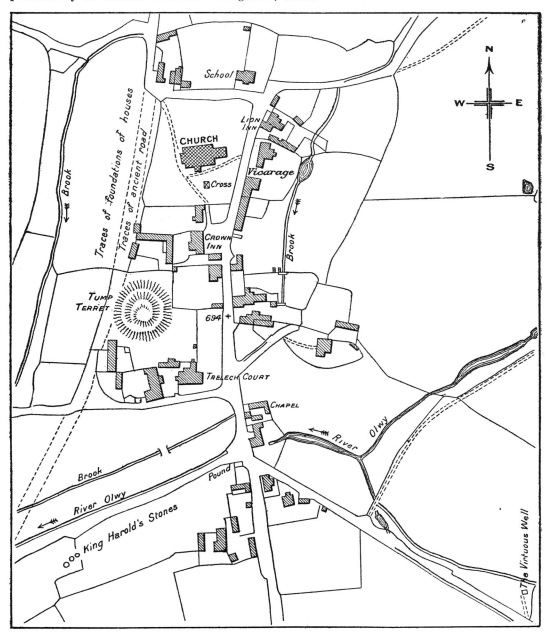

PLAN OF THE TOWN OF TRELECH.
Scale, 25 inches = 1 mile.

𝕿𝖍𝖊 𝖒𝖆𝖓𝖔𝖗.

The manor of Trelech was part of the great lordship of Usk, being a portion of the possessions which Robert, earl of Gloucester, obtained with his wife Mabel, the daughter and heir of Robert fitz-Hamon, the conqueror of Glamorgan. William, 2nd earl of Gloucester, left a daughter and heir Amice, who married Richard de Clare, earl of Hertford, who thus in right of his wife became also earl of Gloucester. This earl died in 1206, whose great-great-grandson Richard, earl of Gloucester and Hertford, was killed at Bannockburn in 1314. At his death he was seized of (with other property) the town of Trelech of the yearly value of 23*l*. 11*s*. 11¼*d*., and the manor of Trelech 26*l*. 7*s*. 10*d*.[1] Leaving no issue, his sister and coheir Elizabeth, wife of John de Burgh, earl of Ulster, had the lordships of Usk, Caerlleon, and Trelech. Their son William de Burgh left a daughter and heir Elizabeth, who married Lionel Plantagenet, duke of Clarence, 3rd son of Edward III. Of this marriage there was an

---

1 Close Rolls, Edward II., 1313—18, p. 131.

only daughter Philippa married to Edmund Mortimer, earl of March, who died in 1381. Their son Roger, 4th earl of March, left only daughters to have issue, of whom Anne married Richard Plantagenet, earl of Cambridge, 3rd son of Edmund, duke of York, the brother of John of Gaunt. Their son Richard, duke of York, was father of king Edward IV., whose daughter Elizabeth married king Henry VII., who thus became lord of Usk and Trelech. By Henry VII. these lordships were granted to William Herbert, 1st earl of Pembroke of the second creation. The earls of Pembroke owned these lordships until Charlotte, only child of Philip, 7th earl of Pembroke, married Thomas, viscount Windsor of Ireland. He died in 1699, and his son Herbert, 2nd viscount, sold Usk and Trelech to Robert, lord Clive, the subduer of India. Lord Clive died in 1774, and Usk and Trelech were sold by his son Edward, 2nd lord Clive, to Henry, 5th duke of Beaufort.

At the sale of the 9th duke's property in 1900 his grace's estates in Trelech, consisting mostly of woods referred to in the decree quoted further on, were purchased by the Crown, but the manor of Trelech (of mere nominal value) was purchased by mrs. Tweedy of Monmouth. The total amount of land purchased by the Crown from his grace in this neighbourhood comprised 5333 acres, of which 2850 acres are wood, lying in the parishes of Trelech, Penallt, Llandogo, Tintern Parva, Chapel Hill, St. Arvans, and Newchurch East. This property is now administered by the commissioners of woods and forests.

Cae-garw (*the rough field*), a farm of 224 acres on the borders of Llanishen parish, 800 feet above sea-level, belonged to the duke of Beaufort, and was sold in 1901 to lieut.-colonel Crompton-Roberts. Some thirty cottages, with land attached from eight acres to half an acre, comprising in all about ninety acres, were sold in most cases to the occupiers.

The following is a survey of the manor of Trelech made 19 October, 1677, Philip Herbert, 7th earl of Pembroke, being the then lord :—

Trellick Dominium. Inquisitio ibidem capta apud Le Gockquet in parochia de Cumcarvan in comitatu Monomuthensi xix° die Octobris anno regni Domini Caroli secundi, Dei gratia Angliæ, Scotiæ, Galliæ et Hiberniæ regis, fidei Defensoris, xxix°, annoque Domini 1677, coram Herberto Evans milite, Gulielmo Herbert, Gulielmo Kemeys et Thomâ Herbert, armigeris, Edwardo Ryder et aliis.

Recordatur quod per examinationem tenentium predictorum et diversorum aliorum credibilium testium et per sacramentum Johannis Catchmayd, Johannis Rosser, Gulielmi Thomas, Gulielmi Powell, Mauricii Jones, Johannis David, Walteri George, Johannis Edmonds, Johannis Phillips, Johannis Williams, Johannis Jones, Thomæ Jones et Thomæ Roberts, qui jurant, dicunt et presentant ut sequitur (viz.)

Imprimis. To the first article they find and present as well by their own knowledge as also according to the evidences given them that the circuits, mears, bounds and limits of the said manor and lordship of Trellick do extend and lie in manner and form following (that is to say).

First beginning at Whitebrook's Slip in the parish of Landoggo and county aforesaid, and from thence down the river Wye (leaving the said river on the left hand), to a place where is the ruins of an old house called the White House right over against Biggsware, and from thence to a place formerly called Monks Cross near the Carn, anciently belonging to the said White House, and thence directly up the hill through the lands of Sir William Catchmayd, knight, called the Coney Geare,[1] to a place where anciently a gate stood called by the name of Coleway's Gate, and from the said gate along the hedge that divideth the lands of the said Sir William Catchmayd and the said Earle's Bargain called the Cookoes,[2] leaving the said hedge on the left hand, unto an ancient tenement of the said Sir William Catchmayd where George Howell lately inhabited and now in the possession of one James Madley, and from the said tenement along the hedge of the said Bargains called the Cookoes unto a tenement held by Edward Perkins, gent., by the lease from the said Earle of Pembroke in the possession of the said James Madley, and adjoining to the lands of the Right Honourable Henry, Lord Marquis of Worcester, Lord President of Wales, called the Church Grove, late in the tenure of Thomas Catchmayd, fishmonger, and now held by lease by John Powell and Edward Hopkins, and so along the upper hedge of the said Church Grove to the upper end of the corner thereof adjoining to the waste ground of the Right Reverend Father in God, the Lord Bishop of Landaff, called Landogoa, leaving the said waste ground also on the left hand, and from thence directly up an ancient causeway there, being in divers parts and places thereof covered with grass and overgrown with wood, to a place called the Resting Stone, and from thence down along the broad way there called the Wainway unto the bargains of the said Earl called Cardithalls[3] bargains, leaving the said bargains on the right hand, and from thence directly down the brook called Sundrasses brook unto the river of Wye aforesaid unto a place called Lawrence Bead, being an ancient mear stone which lieth upon the bank of the said river of Wye within the parish of Tyntarn, and which divideth the fishing of the said Earle of Pembroke and the said Lord Marquis of Worcester, and from the said Lawrence Bead to a great stone that lieth upon the bank side of the said river of Wye near to a wear there called or known by the name of Ashwear, and from that stone to another stone that lieth in the street there between the houses of the Lord Marquis of Worcester and Henry Probert, esq., and from thence to a bridge called the Slansk bridge ; all which said last-mentioned mear stones do lie but a small distance asunder each from the other and do divide the parishes of Chappel Hill and Tyntarn. And from the said bridge directly upon an ancient brook or watercourse that divideth between the wireworks called by the name of Angebrook,[4] and so leading up the said brook (leaving it on the right hand) until you come to another brook called Blackbrook, leaving the same on the left hand, until you come to a place where anciently a stone bridge had stood overthwart the same brook, and from the ancient stone bridge directly up the hill there into the great highway[5] that leadeth from Chepstow towards Trelleck to a mear almost over-

1 Conigre (coningeria), a rabbit warren. A house has recently been built here by mr. Rooke, which bears this name.
2 The Bargains and Cuckoo's woods still retain their names.
3 Coed-Ithel.
4 This is the Angidy Fawr referred to on p. 129.
5 This ancient highway runs parallel to the present road, on the west side, from Tintern Cross to the *Fountain* inn.

grown and covered with grass and earth that it can hardly be discerned, which said last mear stone divideth the parishes of Trelleck and the Grange. And so up along the adjoining ancient highway upon the Wenarth[1] hedge (leaving the said hedge on the left hand), and so along the same highway that leadeth towards Trelleck's Grange, where sometime Edward Phillips dwelt, until you come to a house called Llillweathy,[2] which lieth upon a crossway leading from the said Llillweathy towards Trelleck's Grange aforesaid. And from the said Llillweathy along the great highway that leadeth to the Gelly Lloyd,[3] and from the said Gelly Lloyd along the lane there that leadeth to the house of one John David until it cometh to the great brook called Gorther-chryd,[4] and down the same brook (leaving the said brook on the left hand), leading to another cross-brook[5] that leadeth up to a little well adjoining the brew-house late of Andrew Lewis,[6] gent., and from the said well straight along the hedge there that divideth between the said parishes of Trelleck and the Grange, leaving the said hedge on the left hand, until it cometh to a certain brook[7] which leadeth over-thwart the lands of the said Marquis of Worcester, and thence up the highway that goeth from Trelleck to Lanyshen, and from the said highway directly along to Lanishen's cross which standeth upon the crossway that leadeth towards the Grange and Lanishen, and so from the said cross directly down the lane that leadeth to a little brook, and thence to the house of the heirs of Evan Harris, late of the parish of Lanishen aforesaid. And from the said house of the said Evan Harris straight along the lower hedge of the common called Lanishen's Meend (leaving the said hedge on the left hand) unto a parcel of land called Tyry Glynn,[8] near unto the house where George Jones lately dwelt and now John Jones inhabiteth. And from the said Tyry Glynn directly down the hill there to the brook called Oleway, and from the said brook straight up the hill there leading to a place where a great high oak lately stood and now a young oak standeth, right over against the house of [blank], where the said John Jones now dwelleth and wherein the said George Jones lately dwelt, which young oak standeth near unto the said place where the said great high oak lately stood. And from the said young oak along the lower hedge of the Meend and common there called Graige Coed Garth (leaving the said hedge on the left hand), and so to the house where David Evans lately dwelt and now Alice Waters inhabiteth. And from the house of the said Alice Waters along the hedge of the said Meend last mentioned to a place called Penylan, and from Penylan by the Gadder directly down the brook there called Llymmon, and so to a chappel there called Lanthomas chappel adjoining to the said brook (leaving the said brook and chappel on the left hand), and from the said chappel down the small brook still unto the house of Hugh Stephen and to a parcel of land there called the Cay Clift adjoining to the said house, and thence directly up to the house of William Lucas and to the lands of Abraham Williams, gent., called Fawith Deeon,[9] and from thence directly through the grounds of the said Abraham Williams unto a mear stone in the lane which divideth between the parishes of Cumcarvan and Penyclauth, which said last-mentioned lane or highway leadeth from the town of Monmouth towards the town of Usk. And from the said mear stone down the said lane or highway to Crofty Lloyd,[1] and from thence up the King's highway leading from the said town of Monmouth towards Ragland as far as a place called Coydy Vedow,[2] and so to a little stream there which lieth in the said Coyd y Vedow and homage of Tyre Newith,[3] holden under the lordship of Usk, and adjoining to a parcel of wood of John Phillips of Talavan, gent. (leaving the said stream on the left hand), and from thence down the said wood to a little rivulet or small stream[4] that runneth down the ruins of a water grist mill[5] erected by Sir Charles Jones, knight, deceased, now in the possession of Thomas Jones, gent., his under-tenants or assigns. And from thence down the said stream last mentioned (leaving the said stream on the left hand) unto a place called Pont y Stank,[6] which said little brook or stream divideth between the duchy of Lancaster and the manor or lordship of Trelick, and from the said Pont y Stank to the brook or river of Trothey.[7] And from thence down the said brook called Trothey (leaving the said brook on the left hand) to a parsonage mead of Mitchelltroy, crossing the river Trothey there, to the burgage late of Thomas Tyder, gent., and now the lands of the said Lord Marquis of Worcester, which said burgage is within this said manor or lordship, and there crossing the river again (and leaving the said river on the left hand), and so from thence to a place called Millhome,[8] and from thence down along Trothey side to the middle of the stone bridge near Troy House, upon which the letter P is cut in the stone in the wall in the side of the said bridge, and so directly down the said river of Trothey to the mouth thereof where Trothey emptieth itself into the river of Wye aforesaid, and from the mouth of the said river of Trothey down the said river of Wye (leaving it still on the left hand) to Saint Dennis Chappell,[9] and so to a passage or ferry adjoining to the said chappell that crosseth the river of Wye, and so from thence down the said river of Wye to Whitebrook Slipp aforesaid, the place where it first began.

The manor of Trelleck comprises the parishes of Trelleck, Penalt, Mitchelltroy, Cumcarvan, Langoven, Pen y Clawdd, Lanishen, Llanvihangell tor y monidd, Woolvesnewton, Killgorrugg, Tyntarn, and part of Landogo and Dingestow, and most part of Trelecks Grange.

The lord's bailiff summons the tenants to attend the assizes for the county of Monmouth, quarter sessions, coroners' inquests, etc., and gathers all merciaments and fines, and accounts for the same at the lord's audit holden at Cardiffe.

The court leet is holden on the next Friday after Michaelmas, and on the next Friday after Low Sunday; and a court baron monthly on Fridays only for actions to 3li. 11s., except in harvest.

---

1 Now the Wenallt.

2 This must be at or near the present *Fountain* inn.

3 Now the Gelli, only a barn, one mile north of Trelech Grange church.   4 Now called Nant-y-gaer.

5 The Angidy again.   6 This is Higga, *vide* p. 145.

7 This is the brook referred to above as Gortherchryd, or as now Nant-y-gaer. In the boundaries of Tintern abbey it is Aranell.

8 The Glyn farmhouse is half a mile due north of Llanishen church.   9 Ffawydd-duon (*black beeches*).

---

1 Crofft-y-lloi (*the field of the calves*), on the Monmouth and Raglan main road, 3½ miles from Raglan.

2 Coed-y-fedw (*the birch wood*).

3 Tir-newydd, now called by its English equivalent *Newland*.

4 This is the brook Whechan.

5 Tregaer mill, near Cefn-garw.

6 Pont-y-stanc (*the bridge of the mill stank*), just below the mill referred to.

7 Where the brook Whechan enters the Trothy below Parc Grace Dieu.

8 This would be Wonastow mill, close to Mitchel Troy.

9 This is referred to under Penallt.

The reeve collects the homage rents.

The fishery belongs to the lord; but Henry Probert, esq., of Pantglase, son and heir of Sir George Probert, knight, deceased, hath a right of fishing from a certain crabtree growing upon the English shore of the river Wye between Brockware and Lynware, and from there to a certain stone below Tyntarn church called Lawrence Bead, which said stone divideth the fishing of the said earle and the said Marquis of Worcester. Tenants bordering on the Wye have the right of fishing with angles and wheels over against their own lands and gravels.

The lord has waifs, estrays, deodands, felons' goods, treasure trove, wrecks, goods of outlaws, and felons fugitive. No customary tenant can for felony or treason forfeit his lands to the lord, for that custom is becoming a proverb—"Though the father go to the bough, the son may go to the plough."

The lord hath three water grist mills—one called Whitebrooks mill, in the possession of Charles Young as tenant to Thomas Catchmayd of London, fishmonger; one other called New Mill on the common of Penalt in the possession of Philip Young, as tenant to the said Thomas Catchmayd; and the other called Trepuscodlin mill in the possession of Richard Pinns, as tenant to John Catchmayd, gent., situate in the parish of Newchurch.

Wyeswood chase belongs to the lord, from the highway leading from the Devawden towards Monmouth to the river Wye, and from the washing-place on the Wye under Penalt church to the highway leading from Tyntarn Abbey towards Trelleck Grange.

The warren is enjoyed by Dame Magdalen, widow and relict of Sir George Probert, knight, deceased.

Coed y Vedow is claimed by Mr. John Ayleworth.

Quarries of millstones leased to Edward Perkins, gent. But the tenants may get millstones for their own use.

The burgesses paying rent to the lord of this manor for the borough of Treleck are aggrieved in regard they have not their charter renewed, which is humbly referred to the lord of this manor or lordship and his officers, that the same with the priveledges hereunto belonging may be restored to them as formerly the same have been.

Among the tenants are the following :—

Mr. Edward Perkins, a freeholder in Penalt.
The heirs of Thomas Evans, for the Lloysey lands.

Customary Rents of Whitebrook, Homage of Penalt :
Margaret Delahay, widow, for the Bannut tree hom.
Sir William Catchmayd, knt.
Thomas Catchmayd.

Penalt freeholders :
Dame Magdalen Probert, widow, for the lands of Edward Herbert, yeom.
William Kemeys, esq., for the lands in Edward Probert's possession.
Kedgwin Hoskins.
Edmund Dixton.

Penalt Customary holders :
Mrs. Thomas Jones of Dingestow.
Ann Jones, widow.
Thomas Jones, gent.
Walter Morgan.
William Adams, gent., for part of Maes Mynith.
William Adams of Monmouth, gent.
Elizabeth Richards, for Maes Mola.
John Hugh.

Maud Hugh.
John Stubbs.
Richard Hoskins, for Cae pen dyre.

Hallemote tenants in Mitchelltroy :
Mrs. Haldwick.
The heirs of William Morgan, esq.
John Ayleworth, late Thomas Edmonds.
William Thomas, for John Watkins' lands.
James Appletree, for a tenement and lands late the Bayley, and for his own land.
Mr. Philip Jones.
Mr. James Tyler.
Mr. Henry Cadogan.
Catchmayd Tyler.
John Phillips of Tallavan holds lands worth 30s. yearly and pays no chief rent.

Customary holders in Cumcarvan :
The heirs of Philip Jones, esq., for Borne's lands.
Bayley Glase.
Perthee.
Morgan Pask.
Cumbuchan.
The Glanne farm, William Kemeys, esq.
Whitehouse farm, do.
Thomas Gwynn's farm, do.
The Coom. The Unnis. Ffoosey Booley.
Maes y Velin. Loyn y Gare. Tyre Singlas.
Thomas Jones, gent., for Craig y dorth farm.
Walter Evans, gent., for William Brown's farm.

Freeholders in Cumcarvan :
James Appletree, sen., for lands of the Marquis of Worcester.
Edward Bevan, gent.
Walter Evans, gent.
John Watkins.
Catherine Phillpott.
Cae Perwith. The Kayn.

Tyntarn, Free and Customary :
Henry Probert, esq., for the fishing of Lynware.
Edward Fielding, esq.
The heirs of William Haynes.
Mr. Delahay, lands called Moore well.

Homage of Penarth Golley :
Edmund Hoskins, Fishpool and Trepuscodlin and Penty Gellen.
Sir Herbert Evans, knt., Caerwen.
Edmund Jones, esq., lands in Lanishen in the tenure of Blanch Jones.
Mr. Andrew Lewis.

Customary lands called Pontsayson :
The Borough rent.
Mr. George Catchmayd, 200 acres.
Edward Nicholas, gent.
John David Hopkin.
Zachary Babington, clk.
Mr. Henry Lewis.
Mary Gwynne, widow.
Richard Haynes.
Edward Harris of Lanishen.
Thomas Gwynne.
Cae pull y dynn. Gwyrlod kenoll y dre.

Encroachments :
In Trelick.
Jane Blower.
Ann Haines, widow.
Walter Hugh.
Elizabeth Williams.

Anthony Watkins.
Walter Morgan of ffreedeon, gent.
Morgan Keath.

In Landogo.
 Mrs. Mary Perkins, the Hill Grove, formerly called
  the Lower Bricks Snapp, adjoining her grove
  called the Orles.
 Nicholas Williams, gent., Badham's Gate in Tyntarn.
 John Kingston, in Landogo.

A large portion of the manor was unenclosed, and was known, as it still is, by the name of **Wye's Wood.** The chase of Wye's Wood was the subject of a lawsuit in 1581, owing to an attempt by the earl of Pembroke to enclose the same. The award is given below, by which it will be seen that the woods of the Glasgoed and Gwehelog, near Usk, were also included. The decree seems to imply that the earl was to have sole property in the wood called the *Old Park.* This, however, the earl did not enclose, and it remained open till 1810, when by act of parliament all the common lands were enclosed and allotted.

[1]To all true Chriſtian people to whome this pᵣſent writing indented of Award ſhall come, The right honᵇˡᵉ Sʳ Thomas Bromly, knᵗ, Chancellour of England, William, Lord Burleigh, Lord Trea'r of England, & Sʳ William Mildmay, knt., Chancellor of her Majeſtyes Court of Excheqʳ, send greeting in oʳ Lord God everlaſting. Whereas by an order taken in the Queen's Ma'ts high Court of Chancery the tenth day of December last past before the date of theiſe pᵣſents, Between Walter Morgan Wolph[2] & others, Compl'ts, & the R't honᵇˡᵉ Henry, Earle of Pembroke, defend't, The matter in variance depending in the ſame Court of Chancery between the sᵈ Compl'ts & defend't was by the aſſents of the ſaid parties comitted to the hearing & determining of us the said Lord Chancellor, Lord Trea'r, and Sʳ Walter Mildmay, as by the same order more at large appeareth.

Now know ye that we, the said Lord Chancellor, Lᵈ Trea'r, & Sʳ Walter Mildmay, having throughly heard & examined the ſame cauſe & controverſies and the allegac'ons of the ſaid p'ties doe by theiſe p'ſents by & wᵗʰ the conſents of the ſaid p'ties order, adjudge and award between the ſaid partyes in manner and forme following:

ffirſt, that the ſaid Earle, his heyres and aſſignes, shall have, hold and enjoy in severalty for ever the Wood and ground comonly called or knowne by the name of the Old Parke, wᶜʰ the Compl'ts p'tend to be parcell of the fforeſt or Chaſe of Wifewood; Provided allwayes nevertheles that if it ſhall be thought good to Thomas Wifeman & Walter Morgan Wolph, esqʳˢ, at any tyme before the firſt day of December next, or upon theyr not agreeing therein, Then, if it be ſoe thought good unto John Popham, esqʳ, her Majeſtyes Attorney gen'all, that any part of the ſame woods called the Old Parke shall be allotted to or for part of the Eighteen Hundred Acres of Wood hereafter mentioned to be allotted to or for the ſᵈ Compl'ts or in allowance of any part thereof, That then ſuch part of the ſaid Old Parke ſhall goe to be imployed as they the ſᵈ Thomas Wifeman and Walter Morgan

Wolph, or in theyr default as the ſᵈ John Popham shall order or ſet downe, And that then alſoe the ſᵈ Earle, his heyres & aſſignes, to have ſoe much land and wood in recompence thereof in the ſᵈ woods called Wifewood out of the ſᵈ Eighteen hundred acres to be allotted to the ſᵈ Compl'ts as the ſᵈ Thomas Wifeman and Walter Morgan Wolph, or in theyr default as the ſᵈ John Popham ſhall order or ſett downe.

And wee doe alſoe order & award that the ſᵈ Thomas Wifeman & Walter Morgan Wolph ſhall appoynt & ſet forth unto the ſᵈ Compl'ts Eighteen hundred acres of wood & wood ground out of the ſᵈ Wood & Wood grounds called Glaſcoed, Gwehelwg, and Wifewood, ſn the Bill of Compl't and anſwer of the ſᵈ partyes remaining of Record in the ſᵈ Court of Chancery menc'oned, (that is to ſay) Six hundred & threeſcore acres out of the ſᵈ Wood called Glaſcoed and Eleven hundred and forty acres out of the ſaid Wood called Wifewood, in ſuch places of the ſᵈ Woods as unto them by theyr good diſcretions ſhall be thought moſt fitt and convenient.

Item, wee doe further order that the ſaid Compl'ts and theyr heyres, and other the Reſsiants within the ſᵈ Lordſhipps, ſhall & may have & enjoy for ever within the ſᵈ 1800 acres ſoe to be ſet forth as aforeſᵈ the ſeverall profits hereafter menc'oned, (that is to ſay) convenient Eſtovers, (viz.) fireboot, ploughbote, houſebote & hedgebote, and all other Eſtovers to be ſpent upon the ſᵈ ſeverall Tenem'ts within the ſᵈ Lo'pps & Mann'rs in the ſᵈ Bill & anſwer menc'oned; And alſoe that the ſᵈ Compl'ts, & theyr heyres and Reſiants aforeſᵈ, ſhall have the pawnage and herbage of the ſᵈ 1800 acres of wood and wood-grounds, and ſhall alſoe have, digge, & take lime ſtones for gooding theyr grounds, Wall ſtones to build & repayre theyr houſes & other neceſsary Roomes, and ſlateſtones for covering theyr houſes, within the ſᵈ 1800 acres, and ſhall alſoe have free liberty to make & erect Lyme Kills upon the ſᵈ 1800 acres for the burning of the ſᵈ Lyme ſtones, and for building & for lymeing the grounds of the ſᵈ ſeverall Tenem'ts.

And that within the ſᵈ 1800 acres the ſaid Earle and his heyres and aſſignes, and all others clayming any eſtate of inheritance in any of the ſᵈ Lordſhips from, by, or under William, late Earle of Pembroke, decea'd, father unto the ſᵈ now Earle, ſhalbe for ever excluded to take any manner of profitts, except Waifs, Strayes, felons goods, & other profitts that ſhall ariſe & come by reaſon of the libertyes and ffranchiſes of the ſaid Earle in the p'miſſes, And except ſuch amerciam'ts as ſhall hereafter be ſett upon any the Tennants and Inhabitants of the ſaid Mannors, Lordſhips, pariſhes or Townſhips for uſing any of the ſame profitts to them aſſigned, to the true intent and meaning of this preſent order and Award.

Item, wee doe further by theiſe p'ſents order and award that the said Earle and his heyres ſhall have, hold and enjoy for ever All the ſaid Woods and wood grounds called Glaſcoed, Gwehellocke, & Wifewood in ſeveralty, ſaveing the ſaid 1800 acres, And that the ſᵈ Earle and his heyres and aſſignes ſhall or may at his & theyr will & pleaſure encloſe, have, hold, and enjoy in ſeveralty all the ſaid Woods and wood grounds called Glaſcoed, Gwehellocke, & Wifewood (except the ſaid 1800 acres), Provided allways and oʳ full meaning, order, & award is, that this preſent article nor any thing therein conteined ſhall in any wiſe extend but to ſuch woods & woody grounds of Glaſcoed, Gwehellocke, and Wifewood where wood doth now grow, or heretofore hath growne, and been

---

1 From a copy of the original, made apparently about 1620, preserved among the documents of the borough of Usk, now in the Free Library of Cardiff.
2 Walter Morgan Wolph was of Wolvesnewton.

cutt down or fpoyled by any the Compl'ts and defend^t or any of them, and not to any the other Wafts within the f^d woods.

Item, wee doe further order and award that the faid Thomas Wifeman & Walter Morgan Wolph fhall appoynt, meafure, and fett forth out of the faid 1800 acres before menc'oned in feveralty unto every feverall Townfhip or parifh within the faid Lordfhip and Mannor [torn] quantity of wood and wood ground to ufe the f^d feverall profitts therein, the one in feveralty from the other, as by theyr good difcretions fhall be thought convenient and necefsary for every of the f^d Townfhipps or parifhes, Lordfhips and Mannors. And if they fhall not agree in fetting forth thereof before the faid firft of December now next enfueing, That then the faid John Popham, efq^r, her Ma^ts Attorney gen'all, fhall by his good difcretion doe the fame at his convenient leifure.

Item, wee doe further order and award by theife p^rfents that the tenants of the f^d Lordfhips or Mannors fhall appoint or nominate Two fufficient perfons of every parifh to bee the Woodwards for the f^d feverall parifhes & for the tenants and inhabitants thereof for fuch part of the f^d woods as fhall be afsigned to that Townfhip or parifh, wch faid Woodwards fhalbe chofen yeerly at the Leet holden next after the ffeaft of St. Michaell the archangell, and fhall in the fame Court take theyr corporall oathes before the Steward there faithfully and truly to execute their faid office and thofe things which fhall apperteyne to their charge, and truly to prefent the defaults of fuch as fhall not obferve this order. And the faid Woodwards fhall yeerly from time to time appoint what part of the faid woods fhalbe felled and cutt downe for the ufe of the f^d feverall Townfhips or parifhes, haveing fuch regard in rateing the quantity thereof, as after that rate the ffellett thereof may by good prefervation have continuance for ever, and the f^d Woodwards fhall alfoe, after the felling of the fame woods at the charges of the f^d feverall Townfhips or parifhes, caufe the fame woods & the Standells therein to be left to be inclofed & p^rferved according to the Lawes and Statutes of this Realme in that behalfe provided.

Item, wee doe further order, adjudge & award by theife p^rfents that if any of the Tennants or they heyres, or any Inhabitants within the f^d Mannors, Lordships, parifhes or Townfhips, fhall hereafter at any tyme breake or infringe any p't of this order, or fhall make fpoyle of the faid woods, or any p't thereof, contrary to the true intent & meaning hereof, that then fuch p'fon and p'fons foe offending fhall be amerced at the Court of the faid Earle to be holden within the faid Mannors and Lordships according to the quality of his or their offence.

And wee doe further order and award by theife p^rfents, That the f^d Earle of Pembroke & his heyres and afsignes fhall have & enjoy for ever one fourth p't of all the refidue of the Wafts & Comons fcituat, lying & being afwell within the reft of the fforeft or chafe of Wifewood, Glafcoed, & Gwehellog, as elfewhere within the f^d Mannors and Lordfhips of Ufke, Treleeck, & Carlion, to be inclofed & improved & ufed in feveralty by the faid Earle, his heyres and afsignes for ever.

And that the ffreeholders, Cuftomary Tennants, and Tennants by Coppy of Court Roll of the f^d Mannors or Lordships, fhall have the other three parts and refidue of the Wafts and Com'ons to be devided as aforef^d, to be ufed and occupyed in Comon

by & amongft them to take therein Limeftone, Slate-ftone, & Wallftone, and other the profitts aforef^d for ever, without any thing therein to be claymed or any improvem^t thereof, or of any p't thereof, hereafter at any tyme to be made by the faid Earle, his heyres or afsignes, except onely waiefs, ftrayes, ffellons goods, and fuch other ffranchifes, libertyes, and p^rheminences, as are before referved unto the faid Earle and his heyres out of the faid 1800 acres as is aforef^d. In witnes whereof wee the f^d Lord Chancellor, Lord Trea'r, & Sr Walter Mildmay, have to each p't of theife p^rfents fett o^r feales, geoven the 18th day of December 1581, & in the 24th yeare of the raigne of o^r Sovereigne Lady Elizabeth, by the grace of God, of England, ffrance, and Ireland Queen, defender of the ffaith, etc.

T. Bromley canc.   W. Burleigh   Wa: Mildmay
     (seal).   (seal).   (seal).

Edward Dyer ⎫ ex p'te Comit' Pembrokie
Tho. Wifeman ⎭   virtute warrant'.

W. Morgan Wolph.

By the reference to the *Old Park* in the above award it is evident that deer were at this period, and doubtless for many years later, preserved in the chase of Wyeswood. A reference to the *parker* occurs as early as 28 September, 1326, when Robert de Knytteley, parker of Trelech, received a pardon from the king for the death of John atte Wall.[1]

The place, one mile and a half south of Trelech town, marked in the new ordnance map as Purcas and in the 1830 map as Parkhurst, ought to be *Park-house*, the residence of the parker.

Until the year 1810 a large portion of the parish was unenclosed. In that year, 50 Geo. III., there was passed an act, the title and preamble of which are as follows :—

AN ACT FOR *Inclosing Land within the Parishes of* Trelleck, Penalt, Mitchel-Troy, Cwmcarvan, Landogo, Tintern *and* Lanishen *in the County of* Monmouth.

WHEREAS there are within the parishes of Trelleck, Penalt, Mitchel-Troy, Cwmcarvan, Landogo, Tintern, and Lanishen, in the county of Monmouth, several commons and waste lands, containing together by estimation four thousand two hundred acres or thereabouts :

And whereas the Most Noble Henry Charles, Duke of Beaufort, is lord of the manor of Trelleck, which extends over the whole of the said several parishes of Trelleck, Penalt, Mitchel-Troy, Cwmcarvan, such part of the parish of Landogo as is not within the manor of Landogo, Tintern, and part of the parish of Lanishen :

And whereas the Right Reverend the Bishop of Landaff claims to be lord of the manor of Landogo, which may extend into and over part of the parish of Landogo aforesaid, and into or over some or other of the several parishes beforementioned :

And whereas the King's most excellent Majesty, in right of his crown, is entitled to the presentation to the consolidated vicarages of Trelleck and Penalt :

And whereas the Reverend William Seys, Master of Arts, is vicar of the said consolidated vicarages, and as such is entitled as well to the great as to the small tithes arising within the said parishes of Trelleck and Penalt :

1 *Cal. Rot. Pat.*, Edw. II., 1324—27, p. 330.

And whereas the Reverend Richard Bohun Tomkyns is rector of the consolidated rectories of Mitchel-Troy and Cwmcarvan, and as such is entitled to all the tithes arising within the said parishes of Mitchel-Troy and Cwmcarvan:

And whereas the Reverend William Berkin Meackham Lisle, Doctor of Laws, is one of the prebendaries of Caire founded in the cathedral church of Llandaff, and as such prebendary is entitled to all the great and small tithes arising within the said parish of Landogo:

And whereas the Reverend Daniel Drape is rector of Tintern, and as such entitled to all the tithes arising within the said parish of Tintern:

And whereas the said Henry Charles, Duke of Beaufort, is entitled to the impropriate rectory of Lanishen, and to all the great and small tithes arising within the said parish of Lanishen:

And whereas an Act was passed in the forty-first year of the reign of His Present Majesty, intituled "An Act for consolidating in one Act certain provisions usually inserted in Acts of Inclosure, and for facilitating the mode of proving the several facts usually required on the passing of such Acts:"

And whereas the said commons and waste lands are in their present uncultivated state of little value to the persons interested therein, and it would be advantageous to them if the same were divided, and specific parts thereof respectively allotted to the several proprietors in proportion to their respective rights and interests therein, in order that such allotments may be inclosed and held in severalty; but such division and inclosure cannot be effected without the aid of Parliament:

May it therefore please Your MAJESTY, That it may be enacted . . . . that Thomas Fulljames of Hasfield Court in the county of Gloucester, Esquire, and his successor . . . . shall be and is hereby appointed the sole Commissioner for setting out, dividing and allotting the said commons and waste lands . . . .

David Davies[1] of Llangattock, Crickhowel, is appointed surveyor. It is enacted that all encroachments made above twenty years, for which no rent had been paid to the lord, are to be the property of the possessors. All encroachments made within twenty years, for which no rent had been paid, are to be allotted to the freeholder as part of the allotment to which he may be entitled. No person is to cut turf from the commons without leave from the commissioner, who may order ditches and watercourses to be made, and may stop up old roads and footpaths after new ones have been made. The commissioner is to award unto the said William Seys and his successors, vicars, to Richard Bohun Tomkyns, William Birkin Meackham Lisle, and Daniel Drape, in lieu of tithes, such part as shall be in the whole equal to one-seventh part of the said commons. Persons who are entitled to raise mill-stones, grinding-stones, and tiles are to be allotted part of the commons not exceeding 100 acres, they to continue paying to the lord the accustomed royalty. The overseers of the poor are to be allotted, Trelleck 3 acres, Penalt 3 acres, Mitchel Troy 3 acres, Cwm-

carvan 2 acres, Landogo 3 acres, Tintern 2 acres, Lanishen 1 acre. Such waste land as is necessary is to be sold to pay expenses. All lands allotted are to be held by such proprietors by the same tenure as the lands in respect of which the allotment was made. The said William Seys and his successors, vicars, are empowered to charge the allotments which shall be made to him with the money laid out in erecting buildings. All leases at rack or extended rents are to become void so far as such lease concerns any allotment of the common lands which shall be made. Beneficial leases are not to be affected. The commissioner has power to permit exchanges to be made. Persons considering themselves aggrieved may appeal to quarter sessions. The award when made, with maps, etc., shall be deposited in the parish church of Trelleck. Nothing in the act is to affect the right of the duke of Beaufort to all mines of coal, lead, copper, tin, iron, and all other mines, minerals, ores, stones, fossils and quarries of what nature or kind soever (except lime-stone, fire-stone, free-stone, pavement-stone, tile-stone, sand-stone, gravel and sand), within the said commons, he and his heirs and his lessees, agents, etc., to work all mines, etc., as fully and effectually as he might have done before the passing of this act, he making satisfaction or compensation for all damages; and may make, etc., such pits, etc., and erect any number of steam-engines for the use of such mines, etc. But nothing herein contained shall authorise the said duke to enter upon any part of the said commons so to be divided and allotted which shall be the dwelling-house, or other building, garden, orchard, lawn, pleasure ground, avenue, or plantation (except plantations of coppice woods), or within the space of one hundred yards of such dwelling-house, etc., for the purpose of searching for or working the said mines or minerals.

The Court and Castle.

Though the castle of Trelech occurs in court rolls there does not appear to have ever existed here any stone-built Norman castle. The mount called Twyn Terret or Tump Terret, which stands near the Court, was, there can be no doubt, a place of defence of the Welsh, an artificial hillock protected by stout wooden palisading. When this part of the country was conquered by the Normans they left the fortress of Trelech alone, not troubling to make a castle of it, as they did in more important places. This mount has sometimes been considered as the burial-place of the men who were slain in the supposed battle by king Harold, as commemorated on the sun-dial, which has become an historical and oft-quoted monument, though far from giving a true description of what it describes.

The castle is mentioned as the *fortalice of Trillec* when, on 4 February, 1263, a mandate was issued to Humphrey de Bohun, earl of Hereford, of the lands late of Richard de Clare, earl of Gloucester,

[1] David Davies was father of Thomas Davies of the Neuadd in the parish of Llanbedr, who was sheriff of Breconshire 1856. This latter gentleman was the agent of the duke of Beaufort's Breconshire estates. His son is mr. Thomas Augustus Browne Davies.

VOL. II. T

who died in 1262, to deliver to Maud, countess of Gloucester, the manor of Usk, the manor of Trelech with the fortalice, conveyed to her in dower.[1]

The court of Trelech was early occupied by a branch of the noble family of Seymour, some of whom became, after the usual Welsh fashion, known as Williams. The last Seymour living here seems to be John Seymour *alias* Williams, so called from his grandfather *William* Seymour, who was here in the early part of the seventeenth century. He died leaving only daughters to have issue.

[1] *Cal. Rot. Pat.*, Henry III., 1258—66, p. 242. *Fortalice* is thus used by the translator, but I have no means of knowing what the original word in Latin was.

Pedigree of the family of Seymour of Trelech.

Sir John Seymour, knt.=Jane, dau. to sir John Arundel, knt.

Sir John Seymour, knt.=Edith, dau. to John Talbot, esq.

William Seymour, esq.=Amice, dau. to John Dennis, esq.

Jonet, dau. to .... David of Rhiwperra.=David Seymour *alias* Williams of Trelech.=Mawd, dau. to Thomas ap Philip ap Thomas Gwilym Jenkin (Herbert). (Vol. I., p. 319.)

John Seymour *alias* Williams of Trelech.=Bridget, dau. to Reynold ap Hopkin Powell (Herbert) of Rhedyen. — Thomas ap John Philip of Trelech=Margaret.

Charles Williams *alias* Seymour ; s.p. — Sir Thomas Williams *alias* Seymour, knt.; s.p.	William Williams *alias* Seymour ; s.p. — Dorothy, mar. Richard Hyett.	Elizabeth, mar. Walter Jones of Dingestow, esq. He ob. circa 1602. (Vol. I., p. 56.)	Lucy, mar. George Morgan of Pencrug, esq. — *A quo* MORGAN de Pencrug.	Margaret, mar. John Cales of Tintern. — Ursula, mar. George Williams, son of William ap Edmund of Trevildu.	Mary, mar. 1st William Edmund, one of the guard 1614; 2ndly, Sir Richard Morgan, clk.	Ann, mar. John Roger of Llantarnam.

Pedigree of the family of Rumsey of Trelech.

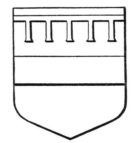

ARMS.—*Quarterly* : 1 and 4, *Arg., a fesse gu., a label of 5 points az.*; 2 and 3, *Az., a cinquefoil within a bordure erm.*
CREST.—*A talbot pass. az., armed and langued gu., ducally collared or.*

[*Vide* Vol. I., p. 384.]

JOHN RUMSEY, clk., fellow of Oriel College, Oxford, B.A. 1537, M.A. 1542; rector of Chalcomb, co. Somerset, 1554; son of William Rumsey of Bath.=Anne, dau. to Thomas ap David ap Philip Rhys of Usk, gent. Arms : *Gu., a lion ramp. arg.*

William Rumsey of Crickhowel, esq. — *A quo* RUMSEY de Crickhowel.	Walter Rumsey, of Usk, gent. Will dated 1606; proved 1609.=Elizabeth, dau. to John ap John Thomas.	Edward Rumsey of Usk, gent. Will dated 1613; proved 1615.=Eleanor.	Jane, dau. to William Blethyn, bishop of Llandaff. 1st wife.=Henry Rumsey of Usk, gent. Will dated 27 Sep. 1637.=Margaret, dau. to .... Baskerville of Pontrilas; living 1621. 2nd wife.	Margaret, dau. to Samuel Jones of Abermarlais, esq. 3rd wife.		

Walter Rumsey of Llanover, esq., the Welsh judge. — Vol. I., p. 384.	Cecil, dau. to William Morris of Graig-Olwy, gent.; widow of Walter Morgan of Llangattock Lingoed. 1st wife.=John Rumsey of Sudbrook, gent. Will dated 13 March 1637; proved 26 April 1638.=Barbara, dau. to .... Will dated 20 Jan. 1643; proved 7 March 1643. 2nd wife.	John Rumsey of Wolvesnewton, gent.; of Rhyd-y-maen in 1667. Will proved 1687.=Dorothy, dau. to .... Will dated 8 April 1703; to be buried in her mother's grave in Skenfrith church.	Cecily.	William Rumsey. — Edmund Rumsey. — Edward Rumsey.	Richard Rumsey of Usk, gent.=.... dau. to Lewis Morgan of Llangattock Lingoed and sister to sir Thomas Morgan, bart.		

Henry Rumsey[2] of Sudbrook, gent. Will dated 8 Feb. 1676; proved 1677.=Temperance, dau. to .... Will dated 29 Nov. 1681; proved 6 Dec. 1681.	Thomas Rumsey.	Henry Rumsey of Wolvesnewton, gent.; matric. Jesus College, Oxford, 17 March 1665⁄6, æt. 17; admitted to Gray's Inn 6 Feb. 1667.=Anne, dau. to .... Lewis of Higga and sister to HenryLewis, esq.	A dau., mar. .... Williams and had issue Morgan Williams.	Margaret, of Usk, spr. Will proved 1685. — Dorothy.		Colonel John Rumsey, of the Ryehouse plot.

2 By a mistake in Vol. I., p. 384, this Henry Rumsey is made to be a son of Henry Rumsey of Usk.

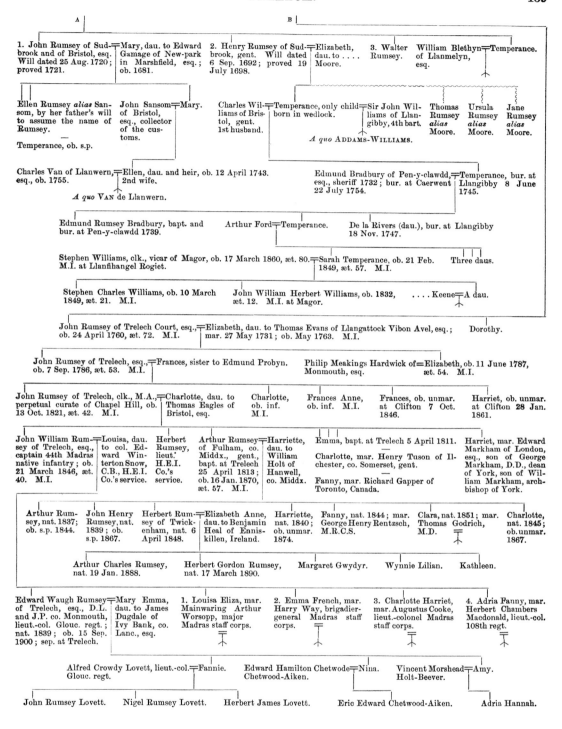

A | B |

1. John Rumsey of Sud⹃Mary, dau. to Edward
brook and of Bristol, esq. | Gamage of New-park
Will dated 25 Aug. 1720; | in Marshfield, esq.;
proved 1721. | ob. 1681.

2. Henry Rumsey of Sud⹃Elizabeth,   3. Walter   William Blethyn⹃Temperance.
brook, gent. Will dated | dau. to .... | Rumsey. | of Llanmelyn,
6 Sep. 1692; proved 19 | Moore. | esq.
July 1698.

Ellen Rumsey *alias* San-
som, by her father's will
to assume the name of
Rumsey.
—
Temperance, ob. s.p.

John Sansom⹃Mary.
of Bristol,
esq., collector
of the cus-
toms.

Charles Wil-⹃Temperance, only child⹃Sir John Wil-   Thomas   Ursula   Jane
liams of Bris- | born in wedlock. | liams of Llan- | Rumsey | Rumsey | Rumsey
tol, gent. | | gibby, 4th bart. | *alias* | *alias* | *alias*
1st husband. | | | Moore. | Moore. | Moore.

A quo ADDAMS-WILLIAMS.

Charles Van of Llanwern,⹃Ellen, dau. and heir, ob. 12 April 1743.
esq., ob. 1755. | 2nd wife.

A quo VAN de Llanwern.

Edmund Bradbury of Pen-y-clawdd,⹃Temperance, bur. at
esq., sheriff 1732; bur. at Caerwent | Llangibby 8 June
22 July 1754. | 1745.

Edmund Rumsey Bradbury, bapt. and
bur. at Pen-y-clawdd 1739.

Arthur Ford⹃Temperance.   De la Rivers (dau.), bur. at Llangibby
18 Nov. 1747.

Stephen Williams, clk., vicar of Magor, ob. 17 March 1860, æt. 80.⹃Sarah Temperance, ob. 21 Feb.   Three daus.
M.I. at Llanfihangel Rogiet. | 1849, æt. 57. M.I.

Stephen Charles Williams, ob. 10 March
1849, æt. 21. M.I.

John William Herbert Williams, ob. 1832,
æt. 12. M.I. at Magor.

.... Keene⹃A dau.

John Rumsey of Trelech Court, esq.,⹃Elizabeth, dau. to Thomas Evans of Llangattock Vibon Avel, esq.;   Dorothy.
ob. 24 April 1760, æt. 72. M.I. | mar. 27 May 1731; ob. May 1763. M.I.

John Rumsey of Trelech, esq.,⹃Frances, sister to Edmund Probyn.   Philip Meakings Hardwick of⹃Elizabeth, ob. 11 June 1787,
ob. 7 Sep. 1786, æt. 53. M.I. | Monmouth, esq. | æt. 54. M.I.

John Rumsey of Trelech, clk., M.A.,⹃Charlotte, dau. to   Charlotte,   Frances Anne,   Frances, ob. unmar.   Harriet, ob. unmar.
perpetual curate of Chapel Hill, ob. | Thomas Eagles of | ob. inf. | ob. inf. M.I. | at Clifton 7 Oct. | at Clifton 28 Jan.
13 Oct. 1821, æt. 42. M.I. | Bristol, esq. | M.I. | | 1846. | 1861.

John William Rum-⹃Louisa, dau.   Herbert   Arthur Rumsey,⹃Harriette,   Emma, bapt. at Trelech 5 April 1811.   Harriet, mar. Edward
sey of Trelech, esq., | to col. Ed- | Rumsey, | of Fulham, co. | dau. to | | Markham of London,
captain 44th Madras | ward Win- | lieut.* | Middx., gent., | William | — | esq., son of George
native infantry; ob. | terton Snow, | H.E.I. | bapt. at Trelech | Holt of | Charlotte, mar. Henry Tuson of Il- | Markham, D.D., dean
21 March 1846, æt. | C.B., H.E.I. | Co.'s | 25 April 1813; | Hanwell, | chester, co. Somerset, gent. | of York, son of Wil-
40. M.I. | Co.'s service. | service. | ob. 16 Jan. 1870, | co. Middx. | — | liam Markham, arch-
| | | æt. 57. M.I. | | Fanny, mar. Richard Gapper of | bishop of York.
| | | | | Toronto, Canada.

Arthur Rum-⹃   John Henry   Herbert Rum-⹃Elizabeth Anne,   Harriette,   Fanny, nat. 1844; mar.   Clara, nat. 1851; mar.   Charlotte,
sey, nat. 1837; | Rumsey, nat. | sey of Twick- | dau. to Benjamin | nat. 1840; | George Henry Rentzsch, | Thomas Godrich, | nat. 1845;
ob. s.p. 1844. | 1839; ob. | enham, nat. 6 | Heal of Ennis- | ob. unmar. | M.R.C.S. | M.D. ⹃ | ob. unmar.
| s.p. 1867. | April 1848. | killen, Ireland. | 1874. | | | 1867.

Arthur Charles Rumsey,   Herbert Gordon Rumsey,   Margaret Gwydyr.   Wynnie Lilian.   Kathleen.
nat. 19 Jan. 1888. | nat. 17 March 1890.

Edward Waugh Rumsey⹃Mary Emma,   1. Louisa Eliza, mar.   2. Emma French, mar.   3. Charlotte Harriet,   4. Adria Fanny, mar.
of Trelech, esq., D.L. | dau. to James | Mainwaring Arthur | Harry Way, brigadier- | mar. Augustus Cooke, | Herbert Chambers
and J.P. co. Monmouth, | Dugdale of | Worsopp, major | general Madras staff | lieut.-colonel Madras | Macdonald, lieut.-col.
lieut.-col. Glouc. regt.; | Ivy Bank, co. | Madras staff corps. | corps. | staff corps. | 108th regt.
nat. 1839; ob. 15 Sep. | Lanc., esq.
1900; sep. at Trelech.

Alfred Crowdy Lovett, lieut.-col.⹃Fannie.   Edward Hamilton Chetwode⹃Nina.   Vincent Morshead⹃Amy.
Glouc. regt. | Chetwood-Aiken. | Holt-Beever.

John Rumsey Lovett.   Nigel Rumsey Lovett.   Herbert James Lovett.   Eric Edward Chetwood-Aiken.   Adria Hannah.

The next proprietors of the court were the Catchmays. Christopher Catchmay, whose place in the
pedigree is not clear, left a widow Elizabeth, married to John Catchmay (brother of sir William
Catchmay of Bigsweir), who also resided here and
was living in 1683. Two of the children of Christopher Catchmay are buried in the church. The
will of Elizabeth, in which she is described as Elizabeth Catchmay the elder of the Court-house in the
town and parish of Trelleck, widow, was proved at
Llandaff 25 November, 1697. She makes no mention
of the estate, but refers to legacies left to her
children by her first husband Christopher Catchmay.

Soon after this John Rumsey, son of Henry Rumsey of Wolvesnewton, had the Court and resided here. Some account of the Rumseys has already been given[1] under Llanover, where Walter Rumsey, the Welsh judge and the most distinguished of his name, was seated. It is singular how the descendants of an English clergyman, the rev. John Rumsey, who on account of his marriage settled in Usk in the middle of the sixteenth century, increased and multiplied, spreading over this county and into Breconshire, owning several estates. In the Crickhowel valley they became very numerous and sent a branch to Longtown in Herefordshire, but owing to their large families several dropped into the lower walks of life. The name has of recent years become scarce, and their fertility in Breconshire and around Abergavenny seems to have exhausted itself.[2]

Henry Rumsey of Usk, ancestor of the branch settled at Trelech, a younger son of the rev. John Rumsey, made his will 27 September, 1637; proved at Llandaff.[3]

> Reparation of the cathedral church of Landaffe ij*s*.—reparation of the church of Uske xx*s*.—to my son John Rumsey all those my two mansion houses, orchards, gardens, etc., and freehold lands and tenements to the same house belonging, in the town of Uske—to my son Henry Rumsey the residue of my freehold lands in the parish of Lanbadocke, he to pay his two sisters Cecill Rumsey and Kate Rumsey, of which payment Thomas Morgan of Lanvedow, co. Monmouth, oweth me 50*l*., and my cozen Walter Rumsey of Lanovor, esq., oweth me 50*l*.—to my son Henry one mansion house wherein my father heretofore dwelt, one backside and garden situate in the town of Uske, and my freehold lands in Lanmartin and Byston—to my son Richard Rumsey one mansion house, one backside and garden in the town of Uske.

John Rumsey, then of Rhyd-y-maen, the son of the above Henry, purchased the Great-house at Wolvesnewton 11 May, 1663, from Rowland Morgan and settled there. He made his will in 1687 (P.C.C., Foot, 21), by which he left his property to his son Henry. This Henry, educated at Jesus College, Oxford, was a barrister and lived at Wolvesnewton, whose son John purchased or inherited Trelech Court, where his descendants resided till the death of John William Rumsey in 1846. His son was the late colonel Edward Waugh Rumsey, who at one time resided at Pilston and later at Rocklands in Goodrich, where he died in the year 1900, and was buried with his ancestors at Trelech. He left three daughters his coheirs.

The house is a building of no architectural features, and was apparently remodelled in the eighteenth century. Since the death of John William Rumsey in 1846 it has been let to a farmer and converted to the purposes of an ordinary farmhouse, and the gardens which surrounded Tump Terrett, or the mount, are things of the past. On Tump Terrett can be seen the foundations of a summerhouse, to reach which a circular path wound round the mount, which is planted on its sides with fir-trees. The stable looks as though it had once been a dwelling-house, and is entered by an arched doorway of the seventeenth century.

The only other residence within the limits of the town is that known as the Great-house, with but a very small amount of land belonging to it. In the eighteenth century a family named Hodges lived here, and it passed by the marriage of Amelia, daughter and heir of James Hodges, to the family of Winslow.

---

[1] Vol. I., p. 382.

[2] In the parish registers of Abergavenny many of the name appear in the eighteenth century.

[3] The date of probate is torn and cannot be read.

Pedigree of the family of Winslow of Trelech.

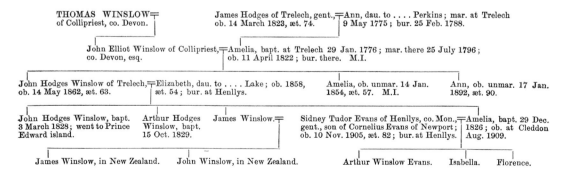

THOMAS WINSLOW=of Collipriest, co. Devon.

James Hodges of Trelech, gent.,=Ann, dau. to .... Perkins; mar. at Trelech ob. 14 March 1823, æt. 74. | 9 May 1775; bur. 25 Feb. 1788.

John Elliot Winslow of Collipriest,=Amelia, bapt. at Trelech 29 Jan. 1776; mar. there 25 July 1796; co. Devon, esq. | ob. 11 April 1822; bur. there. M.I.

John Hodges Winslow of Trelech,=Elizabeth, dau. to .... Lake; ob. 1858, ob. 14 May 1862, æt. 63. | æt. 54; bur. at Henllys.

Amelia, ob. unmar. 14 Jan. 1854, æt. 57. M.I.

Ann, ob. unmar. 17 Jan. 1892, æt. 90.

John Hodges Winslow, bapt. 3 March 1828; went to Prince Edward island.

Arthur Hodges Winslow, bapt. 15 Oct. 1829.

James Winslow.=

Sidney Tudor Evans of Henllys, co. Mon.,=Amelia, bapt. 29 Dec. gent., son of Cornelius Evans of Newport; | 1826; ob. at Cleddon ob. 10 Nov. 1905, æt. 82; bur. at Henllys. | Aug. 1909.

James Winslow, in New Zealand.   John Winslow, in New Zealand.

Arthur Winslow Evans.   Isabella.   Florence.

Pant-glas.

Pant-glas (*the green hollow*) was for many generations the chief seat of the ancient family of Probert, descended in the male line from Ynyr, king of Gwent.

The first to assume a surname was Walter Probert, who was sheriff in the years 1543 and 1555, though he was as often known as Walter Thomas Robert. His son George Probert figures as Siors Water (*i.e.*, George the son of Walter) in an elegy by Dafydd Benwyn on his death.

> Aeth eryr, haul a tharian
> Y Pantglas ym hob hynt glân.
> Maestr Siors mai eisiau drwy'r sir,
> Maeddwyd yr holl genedl meddir.
>
> . . . .
>
> Marw Siors ymroy sy rhaid,
> Mawr anhap, mawr i weiniaid,
> Llew Water canllaw ydoedd.
> Llew doeth dros yr holl wlad oedd,
> Hil Robert hael or hoyw barth,
> Waed rial bual barth.
>
> . . . .
>
> Y mae carw talh mewn côr teg
> An rhiolwr yn rhyleg.

> [*There went the eagle, sun and shield*
> *Of the Pantglas in every good way.*
> *Master George is missed throughout the county,*
> *The whole nation is distressed.*
>
> . . . .
>
> *That George is dead we might be resigned,*
> *A very great disaster to the poor,*
> *Walter the lion was their support.*
> *He was a wise lion over the whole country,*
> *The race of Robert the generous, gay, and alert,*
> *The real blood of the region of the bulls.*[1]
>
> . . . .
>
> *The tall stag is laid in the fair vault*
> *And our ruler is at Trelech.*]

At his funeral were the Morgans, preservers of Gwent (Y Morganiaid gaidwaid Gwent), and numbers of Herberts; also his wife Joan (Siwan) of the tribe of Warren. The poet further says that his son William will look after things.

The will is dated 2 August, 1577; proved (P.C.C., 20, Langley) 1578.

> To be buried in Trelegg church—to Jane my wife the moiety of my mansion house called Pantglas, with the moiety of the herb garden, for her life, and then to my eldest son, also lands called the Moors in Trelegg, and then to my son William Probert, also a parcel of land in Llangwm called Ynys Iarll, and after her to my son William—to Thomas Probert my 2nd son 10*l.* yearly—to George Probert lands called Penrose in Chappel Hill, lands in Llandogo, and lands in Llandenny, purchased of Thomas John Thomas, also to my son George lands in the town of Monmouth—to my wife Joane the half of my plate and of my cattle—to Ellinor my dau. 200 marks—to Dorothy my dau. 100 marks—to my sister Elizabeth Probert 50*l.*—to my sister Florence 20*l.*—Wm Probert my son and heir, ex'or—my cousin Thomas . . . . and my brother Charles Probert, overseers.

Of William, the eldest son of George Probert, nothing appears, except the mention of him in the poem. He married Anne, illegitimate daughter of William, 3rd earl of Worcester, and had issue Henry. This Henry Probert was sheriff in 1636, and, described as of *Pantglace*, made his will 15 July, 1663; proved (P.C.C., 88, Coke) 1669.

> To my parish church of Trelleg a pulpit cloth and cushion—my son sir George Probert, knt., to be sole ex'or; to him all my lands and goods except personal estate, this to him and my grandchild Mrs Jane Probert—to my grandchild Trevor Probert lands and house in the Moors, a mansion house in the parish of Christchurch, and my lands in Lancaut, Wiston, and Goldcliff—to my nephew Christopher Probert, gent., the Gayre for life.

Sir George Probert, son of the above Henry, was born about the year 1617, was admitted to Gray's Inn February, 163⁴⁄₅. He joined the king's forces when the civil war broke out, and was present at the siege of Oxford in 1643, when he was knighted. He and his father compounded for their estates in the sum of 134*l.* Though in his will he desires to be buried in the Temple church, he was, owing to his friendship with dr. Brabourn the vicar, buried in the chancel of Northolt, Middlesex, where is a monument with this inscription[1]:—

> Memoriae facrum D. Georgii Probert, militis, qui perantiquae familiae de Pantglafe in agro Monumethenfi tum rerum tum virtutum praeclarus heres, prorumpente nupero bello civili, ante retro omnia funettiffimo, fub piiffimi regis Caroli Primi fignis ftrenue militabat, ab eoque ad equeftrem ordinem circa annum 1644 evocatus eft. Demum a perduellibus per tria regna truculentiffime graffantibus multa diraque per 12 annos intemeratâ fide infractoque animo perpeffus, reduce auguftiffimo Carolo Secundo, Monmothiae Burgenfis remuneratus; toti honoratiffimae interioris domûs Parliamenti fenatui defiderantiffimus; patriae, propinquis & univerfim fingulis (quibus innotuit quam plurimis) chariffimus; Londini febre correptus, conftitutâ re familiari, fumpto S. Synaxeos viatico & pace ecclefiae acceptâ, integris ad extremum fpiritum fenfibus, piam efflavit animam Jan. 6, anno aetatis 60mo Salutis 1676-7. Ejus quod reliquum eft propter fummum amorem erga Gulielmum Brabourn S.S.T.D. hujus loci vicarium (qui ei 40 circiter annorum continuâ inviolatâque amicitiâ mœrens et uti par eft gratus fe profitetur aftrictum) in hâc ecclefiâ inhumatum fupremis votis reliquit; ubi jacet coram altare fub lapide Gyffordiano. Mœftiffima conjux Magdalena inclytiffimi D. Caroli Williams de caftro vocato Langybby in com. Monnumethenfi (a rebellibus in defectione nuperâ demolito), eq. aur.,[2] filia devotionis necnon gratitudinis ergo pofuit.

> [*Sacred to the memory of sir George Probert, knight, who, the illustrious heir both of the property and virtues of the very ancient family of Pant-glas in the county of Monmouth, on the late civil war, the most lamentable in comparison of all things before, breaking out, vigorously fought under the standard of the most pious king Charles I., and by him was raised to the order of knighthood about the year 1644. Afterwards, having undergone many dreadful things during twelve years by the ravages of the enemy throughout*

---

[1] The reference to the bulls is probably on account of George Probert's mother Dorothy, daughter of sir Christopher Baynham, whose arms were *Gu.*, *a chevron between 3 bulls' heads cabossed arg.*

[1] Lysons' *Environs of London*, iii., 311.
[2] Equitis aurati, *knight.*

the three kingdoms, his fidelity uncorrupted and his spirit unbroken, on the return of the most sacred Charles II. he was rewarded by being made burgess for Monmouth; most beloved by the whole council of the most honourable lower house of parliament; to his country, his neighbours, and universally to each of the very many to whom he was known, most dear; seized by a fever in London, his domestic affairs settled, provision for his journey being made and the peace of the church having been received, with his under-standing sound to the last breath, gave up his pious soul 6 January, in the 60th year of his age and of salvation 167⁶⁄₇. He left by his last will that his remains should be buried in this church on account of his great affection towards William Brabourn, D.D., vicar of this place (who with sorrow and dutiful grati-tude declares himself bound to him with the constant and unbroken friendship of about forty years); where before the altar under the stone of the Giffords he lies. His most sorrowing wife Magdalen, daughter of the most illustrious sir Charles Williams of the castle called Llangibby in the county of Monmouth (destroyed by the rebels in the late revolt), knight, out of devotion and gratitude placed this tomb.]

Pedigree of the families of Probert (Ynyr Gwent) and Morgan of Pant-glas and the Argoed.

ARMS.—PROBERT, *Per pale az. and sa., three fleur-de-lys or* (YNYR GWENT).
MORGAN, *Or, a gryphon segreant sa.*
CLIFFORD, *Chequy or and az., on a fesse gu. 3 cinquefoils arg.*

[For earlier descents *vide* Vol. I., p. 335.]

IORWERTH, 2nd son to Meurig ap Aeddan ap Sitsyllt,⊤ descended from Ynyr, king of Gwent.

Owen ap Iorwerth.⊤

Llewelyn ap Owen.⊤

Iorwerth ap Llewelyn⊤.... dau. to Rhys ap Bledri.   Meurig Goch⊤Angharad, dau. to sir Morgan ap Meredydd of Tredegar, knt.

Ievan ap Iorwerth⊤Elen, dau. to Roger ap Roger Stansio.

Howel ap Ievan⊤.... dau. to .... Robnet of Caldicot.   Gwilym ap Meurig Goch⊤Alice, dau. to Llewelyn ap Howel (from Bleddyn ap Maenarch).

Jenkin ap Howel⊤Jane, dau. to sir David Ballard, knt.

Robert ap Jenkin of Pant-glas, esq.,⊤Joan, dau. and   Elen, mar. Howel   Joyce⊤Hopkin ap Gwilym ap Meurig Goch. gent. usher to king Henry VII.; | heir to John ap   ap Rosser.   ⊥ was murdered.   Iorwerth.   *A quo* REYNOLDS de Llantrisant.

Thomas ap Robert *alias* Thomas Probert of⊤Jane, dau. and heir to William Herbert Fain (slender), youngest and Pant-glas, esq., 1509.   base son of William, 1st earl of Pembroke, K.G.

1. Walter ap Thomas ap⊤Dorothy, dau. to sir Christopher   2. William   3. John Probert=Blanche,   Alice, mar. Thomas Powell (Herbert) Robert *alias* Walter Pro-| Baynham of Clearwell, co. Glouc.,   Probert.   of Wentllwg. dau. to   of Whitchurch, co. Hereford, esq. bert of Pant-glas, esq.; | knt., by Joan, dau. to sir Thomas   ⊥ sheriff 1543 and 1555. | Morgan of Pen-coed, knt.   Moor.

George Probert of Pant-glas,⊤Joan, dau. to William   Charles Probert.   Christopher=.... dau. to James   Walter Jones of⊤Joan. esq. Will dated 2 Aug. 1577; | Worrall (or Warren) of   —   Probert of   ap Rosser of Llan-   Dingestow, esq. | proved 1578. | St. Briavels.   Anthony Probert.   the Argoed.   ddewi Rhydderch.   ⊥   *Vide* p. 56.

William Probert of⊤Ann, base dau. to Wil-   2. Thomas Probert.   Eleanor, mar. Francis Moor   Thomas Morgan of Hurst in⊤Dorothy, Pant-glas, esq. | liam, 3rd earl of Wor-   —   of Crick.   Lydney, co. Glouc., esq.; | ob. 1658. | cester, K.G.   George Probert.   ⊥   ob. 2 May 1664.

Henry Probert of Pant-glas, esq.,⊤Ann, dau. to Giles   William Morgan of Rumney, esq., 3rd son to sir William⊤Jane, dau. and heir. sheriff 1636. Will dated 15 July | Morgan of Pen-   Morgan of Tredegar, knt., by Elizabeth, dau. to sir Wil- | 1663; proved 1669.   A | crug, esq.   liam Winter of Lydney, knt.   ·B

A | B |

Sir George Probert of Pant-glas and the Argoed, knt.; built═Magdalen, dau. to | Edward Games.═Catherine═Edmund Jones of Buck-
the Argoed; knighted at Oxford 28 Sep. 1643; M.P. Mon- | sir Charles Wil- | 1st husband. | land, co. Brecon, esq.
mouth 1661—77; ob. 6 Jan. 167¾; bur. in Northolt church, | liams of Llangibby, | | 2nd husband.
Middx. Will dated 2 Jan. 1676; proved 14 Feb. 167¾. | knt.

Rachel, dau.═Henry Probert═Eleanor, dau. | 2. Trevor Probert═Mary, dau. to .... Somner, | Elizabeth, mar. Thomas | Anne, mar. 1st
to Thomas | of the Argoed, | to Henry | of Pant-glas, esq., | son of mrs. Somner, the | Williams of Monmouth. | William Tho-
Morgan of | esq., M.P. Mon- | Baker of | the last to live | eminent midwife. | — | mas of Mon-
Tredegar, | mouth 1698— | Abergavenny, | there; ob. s.p. | | Jane, mar. Charles Grif- | mouth, 2ndly
esq. 1st | 1700; sheriff | esq. | 1680. | | fith of Lan-yr-afon. | Thomas Riley
wife. | 1690. Will | | | Henry, æt. 4 in 1683. | | of London.
| proved 1719.

Henry Probert of═Hester, dau. to | George Probert. | William Morgan═Elizabeth. | Francis Jenkins═Rachel, bapt.═Thomas Clif-
the Argoed, esq.; | sir Roger Hill | — | (Gamage) of | Will dated | of Caerlleon, | at Monmouth | ford of New-
ob. s.p. 1727. Will | of Denham, co. | James Probert, | Coed-y-goras, | 27 Jan. | gent. 1st hus- | 16 March | port, esq.
dated 22 Nov. | Bucks, knt.; | ob. inf. | co. Glamorgan, | 1726. | band. | 1669. | Will dated
1726; proved 30 | mar. sett. 3 April | — | esq. | | | | 17 Aug. 1752.
May 1727. | 1700, had 3000l. | Rachel, ob. inf. | | | | | 2nd husband.

Francis Jenkins of Caerau in Newport, esq.,═Ann, dau. to Nathaniel Turner and | Thomas Clifford of Newport, esq.═Eliza-
bapt. at Caerlleon 2 Feb. 170¾; sheriff 1741. | sister of John Worthington Turner | Will proved 1 June 1756; left all | beth.
Will dated 3 July 1754. | of London, linendraper. | to his cousin Richard Morgan.

Edmund Blewitt, esq., eldest son of John Blewitt═Ann, only child and heir, bapt. at St. Woolos | Mary, only child.
of Llantarnam, esq. | 16 Dec. 1738. 2nd wife.

Ann, only child, died unmar.

William Morgan of═Elizabeth, dau. | 2. Henry | 3. Thomas Morgan of New-═Anne. | Rachel, mar. Wil- | Ann, mar. Wil- | Eliza-
Coed-y-goras, esq.; | to Lewis Tho- | Morgan. | port, attorney. Will dated | | liam Lambert of | liam Perkins of | beth,
sheriff co. Glamorgan | mas of Math- | | 7 Dec. 1745; proved 28 April | | Cardiff, gent. | Bristol, gent. | unmar.
1722; ob. 1752. | avern. | | 1748.

John Williams of═Elizabeth, | 2. Rachel, unmar. Will dated | John Thomas, son of═Ann. | Thomas Morgan. Henry Morgan.
Coed-y-goras, | eldest dau. | 15 June 1753, then of Mon- | John Thomas of Ffin- | — | —   —
maltster, in 1753; | and coheir, | mouth; left her real estate to | ffynnon in Llanedern; | William Morgan. Edward Morgan.
ob. 1780, æt. circa | ob. 1756. | her cousin Richard Morgan of | ob. 1777; bur. at
70. | | the Argoed. | Bristol.

John Chittenden of═Blanche, only | Frances, dau. to .... | Durbrow═William Morgan Thomas of═Rachel, dau. to David Thomas
Tooting, Surrey, | child, æt. 6 in | of Llanedern; bur. 24 June | | Pont-y-pandy, near Caer- | of Whitchurch. She mar. 2ndly
apothecary. | 1760. | 1792. 1st wife. | | phily; æt. 22 in 1781; bur. | William Lewis of Pant-y-
| | | | 6 Feb. 1827, æt. 67. | gwindy.

John William | Elizabeth | Evan Edwards of═Caroline, | A dau., mar. .... | Evan Prosser, clk., per-═Mary Anne, born 1806;
Chittenden, | and Eliza- | Caerphily, surgeon, | born | Banister. | petual curate of St. Mar- | mar. 1828; ob. 1834.
only son, born | beth, both | grandson of William | 1795. | — | tin, Caerphily, son of | Had issue Evan Thomas
29 Sep. 1778. | died young. | Edwards the bridge- | | Millicent, mar. | Roger Prosser of Por- | Prosser of Colchester,
| | builder. | | William Vachel of | thaml, co. Brecon, yeo- | chemist.
| | | | Cardiff, druggist. | man; ob. 1834.

Charles Probert of the Argoed, esq., sheriff 1721; | Eleanor; mar. sett. 16 Jan. 1705; ob. 28 March 1754,═Richard Morgan of Hurst, esq.,
ob. cœl. Will dated 20 July 1724; proved 1725. | æt. 71; bur. at Lydney. Will dated 8 May 1752. | ob. 5 Feb. 1716; bur. at Lydney.

Probert Morgan═Catherine; she was | Richard | Richard Morgan of═Abigail, | Thomas Mor- | George Morgan, ob. | Eleanor, mar. An-
of Hurst, esq., | living a widow at | Morgan, | the Argoed, esq., | dau. to | gan, captain, | 1719; sep. at Lydney. | drew Lewis of
eldest son, ob. | Hurst in 1779; | ob. Sep. | ob. 21 June 1782; | Thomas | ob. 1772, æt. | — | Amberley, gent.
1759, æt. 50. | ob. 15 July 1803, | 1706. | sep. at Lydney. | Phelps of | 57; sep. at | Magdalen, ob. unmar.
| æt. 72 (G.M., | | Will dated 9 April | Dursley, | Lydney. | 1743; sep. at Lydney. | p. 147.
| lxxiii., 697). | | 1779. | esq.

Thomas Morgan | Richard Morgan═Lois, dau. to .... Hoskyns | William Morgan of the Argoed, and of═Eliza Maria, dau. and in her
of Monmouth, | of the Argoed, | of Pantau; ante-nupt. sett. | Perrystone, co. Hereford, esq.; assumed | issue heir of John Lewis of
esq., ob. s.p. 29 | esq., sheriff 1795; | 31 Aug. 1793; sep. at Cam, | the surname of MORGAN-CLIFFORD in | Llantilio Crossenny, esq.;
April 1795. | ob. s.p. 10 Dec. | co. Glouc., 26 June 1815, | 1756, on inheriting the estates of his | mar. there 21 Jan. 1775.
| 1796. | æt. 53. | cousin Thomas Clifford, esq. | Will dated 1 Oct. 1814.

Morgan Morgan-Clifford of the Argoed, esq., lieut.═Sophia, dau. to Jonathan Willington of | William Morgan-Clifford of Perrystone, esq.,
12th light dragoons; ob. 14 Sep. 1814, æt. 34. | Rapla, co. Tipperary, esq. | ob. cœl. 22 Aug. 1850.

Henry Morgan-Clifford of Llantilio, the Argoed,═Catherine Harriet, dau. to | James Wallace═Fanny Eliza- | Philip James═Emily.
and Perrystone, esq.; succeeded to Llantilio on | Joseph Yorke of Forthamp- | Richard Hall | beth Mary; | Yorke, esq.,
the death of his cousin mrs. Taddy; colonel com- | ton, co. Glouc., esq.; mar. | of Ross, soli- | mar. sett. | colonel Scots
manding Royal Mon. militia; M.P. Hereford | sett. dated 11 Aug. 1834; | citor. | dated 6 May | Fusileer
1847—65; ob. 12 Feb. 1884, æt. 77; sep. at | sep. at Llantilio 3 March | | 1841. | guards.
Llantilio. M.I. | 1898.

Henry Somers Morgan-Clifford, only son, | James FitzWalter Butler, 24th lord Dunboyne in the peerage of═Marian, only dau. and
died at Merton College, Oxford, 25 Sep. | Ireland; assumed by royal licence the name of CLIFFORD- | sole heir; mar. 12 June
1856, æt. 20. | BUTLER 13 Nov. 1860; ob. 17 Aug. 1899. | 1860.

William Henry Brooke Peters of Harefield, co. Devon, esq.,═The hon. Rosalinda Catherine, only child;
major-general in the army. | mar. 30 April 1883.

Sir George rebuilt the Argoed in Penallt, and here he resided, his father, who lived to within about ten years of the son, living at Pant-glas.

The parish register of Northolt contains this entry:—

> Jan. 6. Sir George Probert, knt., of Penalt in the county of Monmouth, a most intimate friend of Dr Brabourne, vicar of this parish, died at Gray's Inn Lane in London, and was buried in the chancel Jan. 8, 167⁶⁄₇, by his own direction.

Sir George's will is dated 2 January, 1676; proved (P.C.C., 23, Hale) 14 February, 167⁶⁄₇, by Trevor Probert, esq., one of the executors.

> I give to my son Trevor Probert and Walter Morgan of Tredeeon, co. Monmouth, gent., the messuages, lands, etc., in trust as follows: All that farm, etc., in the parishes of Newland and Dixon in cos. Monmouth and Gloucester, now or late in the tenure of Edmond Tombes; all that farm late in the occupation of Walter Griffiths, sometime called Walter Griffiths' farm, in the parishes of Gwernesney and Lanvihangell Tor monith; all that farm, etc., in Langoven in the tenure of Walter Walters; all those messuages, etc., in the several tenures of John David, Moses Rogers, Jane Powell, Elianor Harry, widow, and others in Cumcarvan; all that farm, etc., in Mitchill Troy, heretofore in the tenure of Tho. George, now in the tenure of . . . . George, widow and relict of the said Thomas George; all that small tenement in the parish of Langwm, heretofore in the occupation of William Watkins and now or late of Tho. William or of me the said Sir George Probert; all that farm, etc., in Lanishen, now in the tenure of John Jones; also all those lands, etc., which I purchased of Jonas Morris and Morris Jenkins in the parish of Penalt, in my own occupation; and also all rents not settled on my son Henry Probert, esqr's marriage to be sold for the payment of my debts, and to pay as follows: my dau. Elizabeth 400li., my dau. Anne Thomas so much as shall make with what I have given her 300li., the overplus to Trevor Probert my son—all my goods to my wife dame Magdalen Probert—my said sons Henry and Trevor Probert, ex'ors.
> Witnesses: Jo. . . . ., Tho. Prichard, Stephen Walpoole, Moore Waters.

There is also a codicil dated 2 January, 167⁶⁄₇.

> My cousin Christopher Probert, his son Charles—to each of my grandchildren 10li. apiece at 21—to Moore Waters, my servant that attends me now in my sickness, 5li.—to my servant Walter Morgan 10li.—to each of my servants 40s.—to Henry Probert my son my watch—to Trevor my son my silver tobacco box and stopper—to my friends sir Trevor Williams, baronet, and major William Herbert, and mr. Thomas Prichard[1] rings of the value of 20s. apiece—to the poor of Penalt and Trelleck 40s. each parish—to the said mr. Prichard[1] for making my will 40s.—I desire my two sons to manage the farm at Lanvihangell, which I hold from his Majesty—to Jane Probert, youngest dau. of my cousin Christopher Probert, 5li.—to my brother Edmond Jones,[2] esq., a ring of 20s.—I desire to be buried in the Temple church, being a member of the Middle Temple—to

mrs. Jones who lives with my wife and her son of Brainford, and to my two dau's mourning rings of 20s. apiece—to my friends dr. Brabourne and his lady rings of like value.
> Witnesses: Tho. Prichard,[1] the mark of Anne Emerson.

Trevor Probert, the eldest surviving son of sir George, was the last of the family to live at Pant-glas. He died in 1680 without issue, since which time Pant-glas has been let to farmers. He was succeeded by his brother Henry, who made his will in 1719.

Henry, the son of the above Henry by his first wife, made his will 22 November, 1726; proved (P.C.C., 123, Farrant) 30 May 1727.

> My real estate, charged with 1000l., to be paid by my sisters Elizabeth Morgan, Rachel Clifford, and Eleanor Morgan to my wife Hester—10l. each, to buy mourning rings, to sir Roger Hill and his lady, to my brother Roger Hill and his lady, to my sister Edwin, and miss Lockey—legacies to servants—20s. to the poor of Penallt—20l. to the poor of Treleck—my cousin Rachel Wind 10l.—to Mary wife of Wm Rogers and Sarah her daughter, both of Trelech, the Penarth house and farm, or in lieu thereof 250l.—Wm Blower of Monmouth, gaoler, 5l.—estate given me by my cousin Henry Probert of Monmouth to my nephews Francis Jenkins and Thomas Clyfford—my brother-in-law Thomas Clyfford of Newport, gent.

This Henry dying without issue, and his half-brother Charles having done the same, the property became divided between the sisters Elizabeth, wife of Thomas Morgan of Coed-y-goras; Rachel, wife first of Francis Jenkins and then of Thomas Clifford of Newport; and Eleanor, wife of Richard Morgan of Hurst in Lydney. Pant-glas and the Argoed went to Eleanor, wife of Richard Morgan. Her son Richard resided at the Argoed, where he kept a pack of hounds, and was father of William Morgan, who by the will of his kinsman Thomas Clifford, proved 1 June, 1756, inherited all that gentleman's property, and though then under age assumed the additional surname of Clifford. His son was Morgan Morgan-Clifford, who purchased Perrystone in Herefordshire and removed there to reside. Dying in 1814, he was succeeded by colonel Henry Morgan-Clifford, who thus became possessed of Pant-glas, the Argoed, and Perrystone, with many farms. Colonel Morgan-Clifford was for many years a prominent figure in Monmouthshire and Herefordshire, and was M.P. for Hereford from 1847 to 1865 as a liberal. He was also in 1847 appointed lieutenant-colonel commanding the Royal Monmouthshire Light Infantry Militia, which post he resigned in 1853, and was from 1858 till his death in 1884 honorary colonel of the regiment.

In 1847 he succeeded, on the death of his cousin mrs. Taddy, to the estate of Llantilio, to which he removed from Perryston. The latter he sold in 1860 to mr. George Clive, who was for a time his colleague in the representation of Herefordshire. Colonel Morgan-Clifford, who was the last representative in unbroken *male* line of the Morgans of Tredegar,

---

[1] Thomas Prichard of Tre-Worgan in Llandenny, esq.
[2] Edmond Jones of Buckland, co. Brecon, esq., M.P., who died in 1683, married for his second wife Catherine, sister of sir George Probert. This marriage was omitted in the pedigree on page 42.

died at Torquay 12 February, 1884, and was buried with his wife at Llantilio. Their only child and heir, Marian, married the 24th lord Dunloyne. This nobleman assumed by royal licence in 1860 the additional surname and arms of Clifford.

Colonel Clifford sold Pant-glas to mr. George Griffin Tyler (afterwards Griffin), and the Argoed to mr. Richard Potter.

The descendants of Elizabeth, daughter of Henry Probert, who married William Morgan of Coed-y-goras, are given in the pedigree. Coed-y-goras, which is in the parish of Llanedern near Cardiff, has long since passed out of the family, after having been the subject of law-suits at the close of the eighteenth century, and the Morgans of that place are now represented only in the female line.

The Glyn formed part of the estates of the Proberts of Pant-glas, and descended with much other property to colonel Henry Morgan-Clifford. He sold the Glyn farm to James Richards.

Penarth also belonged to the Proberts, and was left by the will of Henry Probert of the Argoed, dated 22 November, 1726, to Mary, wife of William Rogers, and Sarah her daughter, both of Trelech. This Sarah married .... Davies of Portskewet, by whom she had two daughters and coheirs, Jane the wife of John Jones of Portskewet, mariner, and Sarah, the wife of William Morgan of Shirenewton, yeoman. John Jones and William Morgan, in conjunction with their wives, by indenture dated 30 October, 1790, released by way of mortgage all the messuage, lands, etc., called the Penarth House or farm to John Buckle of Chepstow, merchant, to the use of William Fisher of Llanvair Discoed, timber dealer. On 31 March, 1830, William Morgan (son of the above William Morgan) sold to James Richards. This now belongs to mr. Crompton Roberts.

A small farm called the Gelli or Gelli-lwyd also belonged to colonel Clifford. This he sold to William Hall.

Higga.

Higga is a curious corruption of Helyg (*willow trees*). That this is so is borne out by the boundary of Llanishen, as given in the *Liber Landavensis*, where the boundary is said to go to the willow-wood, the source of the Angidy Fawr.[1] The Angidy brook starts from the well at Higga.

The house is situated under the slope of a steep bank, on which are traces of ornamental gardens and grounds. Near by is an ancient circular pigeon-house, with a doorway of handsomely moulded stone. On the west side of the house is a large bathing-place, with steps leading into it, filled by a strong spring which comes out of the bank. This spring is referred to, as shewn above, in the *Liber Landavensis;* in the charter of William Marshall, earl of Pembroke, to Tintern abbey in 1223 as *fons qui vocatur*

caput Angedy ;[1] and in the boundaries of the lordship of Trelech in 1677 as the *little well adjoining the brew-house of Andrew Lewis, gent.*[2]—in each case as being the source of the Angidy brook.

Higga was long the seat of a family named Lewis, though from what Welsh sept they claimed descent I have not ascertained. Henry Lewis, called of Higga, esq., presumably son of Andrew Lewis mentioned in the boundary of 1677, made his will 1 June, 1733; proved (P.C.C., 243, Price) 7 September, 1733, by Edward Broughton[3] and Godfrey Harcourt.

> I desire to be buried in a private and decent manner, and that a dole may be distributed, the poor of Trelech to have a better share—to my wife towards rebuilding my mansion-house called Higga, the use of all my timber now piled up under thatch—all my mortgage lands, etc., in Kilgwrwg and Woolde Newton and that parcel called Cae funnon in Trelleg, by me formerly purchased from Andrew Nicholas, to Edward Broughton of Kington, co. Hereford, gent., during my wife's life, and also that messuage, etc., I purchased from George Thomas John in Trelleg, during the life of my cousin Maynard Roberts, now living with me at Higga—that messuage called Lan-y-nant in Trelleg and Lanyshen to said Edward Broughton for life of my said cousin—the above messuages and the Lloyne and Tyr y coydner, meadow in Lanishen, cottage in Tintern and estate in Tintern, which I purchased from John Vaughan, to my brother Thomas Lewis of Monmouth—to Robert Hughes of Trostrey, esq., and Lewis Harcourt of Danypark, co. Brecon, esq., all that capital messuage called Higga (excepting the messuage called the Ostrey[4]), after the decease of my wife, to my brother John Lewis of Amberley, gent.—my uncle Charles Gwillim, gent., dec^d—that messuage called the Ostrey and patch of ground called the Lower Meadow to my brother John Lewis and Thomas Lewis in trust to suffer my poor relations in Trelleg to inhabit the Ostrey—my bed, bedstead, and vallances in my room called the New Chamber at Higga to my wife Mary, and all standards left by my mother at Higga to be heirlooms—my father's Bible unto my brother John Lewis—my law books to my nephew Andrew Lewis—Edward Broughton[3] and Godfrey Harcourt of Wirewoods Green in Tyddenham, co. Gloucester, gent., to be ex'ors.

> Witnesses: E. Jones, John Thomas, Evan Morgan.

The will of Mary Lewis,[5] the widow of the above Henry, is dated 7 April, 1738, then of Llanarth; proved (P.C.C., 253, Seymour) 24 September, 1745, by Robert Berkeley.

> Poor of Trellegg 3l.—to mr. Ball the elder, minister of Trellegg, 1l. 1s.—to Henry Hall of Lanarth, gent., 2l. 2s.—to my loving sister Jane Davies of Clitha, widow, 1l. 1s., and to my loving sister Elizabeth, wife of my brother Thomas Lewis of Monmouth, mercer, 1l. 1s.—to my beloved niece Mary Berkley, wife of Thomas Berkley of Clitha, esq., all my rings and plate—to my goddau. miss Florence Jones, dau.

---

1 *Liber Landavensis*, p. 231 ; *Book of Llan Dâv*, pp. 242, 379.

1 *Vide* account of Tintern abbey.　　2 P. 133.
3 Edward Broughton was a medical man practising at Kington in Herefordshire. It is probable he was the son of .... Broughton of Kington by Lucy, daughter of William Jones of Llanarth. (*Vide* Vol. I., p. 307.)
4 The Ostrey, more properly Hostry (*hostilaria*), is a cottage situated on the road half way between the town and Trelech Cross.
5 I have not ascertained exactly who this lady was before marriage. (*Vide* pedigree of Davis and Berkeley, p. 115.)

of John Jones of Lanarth court, esq., 100*l.*—to my goddau. Margaret Probin, dau. of John Probin of Trellegg, tanner, 44*l.*, and 5*l.* 5*s.* due to me from her father—to John Rumsey of Trellegg, gent., 2*l.* 2*s.*—my beloved nieces Elizabeth and Mary, dau's of Thomas Berkley afores*d*—to Margaret Roberts, spr., now living with me, an annuity of 8*l.*, to be paid weekly by my nephew Robert Berkley of Clytha, gent.—my beloved niece Lucy Berkley, sister to s*d* Elizabeth and Mary.

Witnesses : Ann Holmes, Samuel Jones, William Powell.

Thomas Lewis of Monmouth, mercer, brother of the above Henry, made his will 2 June, 1743 ; proved (P.C.C., 271, Strahan) 22 September, 1748, by " Mary " Kane (wife of Clement Kane), the natural and lawful " daughter of the said deceased, William Watkins, " esq., sole executor, first renouncing, and Elizabeth " Lewis, widow, the relict of said deceased, renouncing " letters of administration."

To George Milborne of Wonastow, esq., and John Nourse of Weston under Penyard, co. Hereford, esq., all those mess's in Kilgorog and Wolves Newton, and Cae ffunnon in Trelleg formerly purchased by my brother Henry Lewis of Highga, esq., Lanynant, the Lloyne and Tyr y coed, cottage in Tintern, etc., and my two mess's in the town of Monmouth, upon trust to sell the same and pay to my ex'ors—William Watkins of Monmouth, gent., ex'or.

Witnesses : John Bulbrick, Will. Williams, James Prosser.

Andrew Lewis, on whom the estate of Higga was entailed by his uncle Henry, is in his will called of Amberley, gent. He was possessed of the estate of the Cwm in Welsh Newton and Llangunvil[1] in the parish of Monmouth. His will is dated 15 October, 1745 ; proved (P.C.C., 264, Edmunds) 3 September, 1746, by William Lewis.

Payment of my debts charged on estates of the Coombe and Langunville—the care and tuition of my son Henry Lewis to my worthy friend Jeremy Innis of Bristol, merchant, and my brother-in-law William Lewis of the same, boat-builder—whereas I am entitled to the reversion in fee in several mess's and lands at Coombe and Langunville on the death of my son without issue, I give these to Jeremy Innis and William Lewis to sell the same and pay my debts, the overplus to the three dau's of the s*d* William Lewis by my sister Susannah—whereas I am seized in reversion, in case my son die without issue, of a messuage, etc., at Amberley, of the yearly value of 60*l.*, rented by . . . . Jones, yeom., I give the same to my nephew William Lewis (son of the s*d* William Lewis and Susannah his wife), charged with 200*l.*—whereas I am entitled to lands in the colony of Virginia in America, I give the same to Jeremy Innis and W*m* Lewis on trust—residue to my s*d* sister Susannah and her children, the children of my late sister Mary, the late wife of m*r* John Williams, to be excluded from the benefit of my estate—Jeremy Innis and W*m* Lewis, ex'ors.

Witnesses : G. Tyndall, W*m* Lewis, William Bradley, jun*r*.

The first debt to be paid is 100*l.* to m*r* Daniel Baynton—to my cousin Elizabeth Hoskins, widow of my late cousin m*r* Edward Hoskins, dec*d*, 100*l.*, and to my cousin Anne Probyn, spr., dau. of m*r* John Probyn of Trellick, tanner, 100*l.*, chargeable on my estate at Amberley.

The last of the family was Henry Lewis, son of the above Andrew, who was a clergyman, though most of the family seem to have been catholics. This gentleman, who was possessed of considerable property, resided partly at Higga and partly at Bath, and on his death in 1794 a will was produced which was eventually declared a forgery. By this will mr. Lewis left his property to his father's first-cousin mrs. Mary Kane and her children; and concerned in this was, among others, sir John Briggs of Blackbrook.[1] One George Crossley was tried for the forgery on Monday, 22 February, 1796, at the Old Bailey sessions, the indictment being—

George Crossley, you stand indicted, etc., that Thomas Morgan, maternal heir-at-law of Henry Lewis, deceased, on the 29th of April, 35 Geo. III. [1795] and long before was seized of certain messuages in the parish of Trevegloes, co. Montgomery, as maternal heir of the said Henry Lewis, and that Sir John Brigges, late of the parish of Skenfrith, bart., Richard Holland, late of Skenfrith, yeoman, George Crossley, late of S*t* Martin-in-the-Fields, gent., and W*m* Austin, late of Bath, labourer, on the s*d* 29th of April did falsely forge a certain paper purporting to be the will of the said Henry Lewis, as follows :—

In the name of God, Amen. I, Henry Lewis of Hygga in the parish of Trellech, clk.—I give to Mary Kane of Monmouth, widow, one half of my freehold and copyhold estates, and after her to her dau. Frances Teresa Brigges, subject to legacies, viz.: £200 to Mary Kane and Grace Kane, two of the dau's of the said Mary Kane—to Lewis Brigges, son of the said Frances Teresa Brigges, £500— a yearly rent charge of £10 to each of my cousins Maria Williams and Grace Cornish of Bristol—to my cousin Susannah, wife of James Harman of Bristol, £1000—to my cozen Frances Rumsey of Trellech £300. Dated 10 Aug. 1791.

With intention to defraud the said Thomas Morgan.

The said Thomas Morgan died 29 April, 35 Geo. III. [1795].

Sir John Briggs, who was of Blackbrook in Skenfrith, did not appear. It is said he was afterwards apprehended (but I have met with no account of this) and committed to Hereford gaol, from whence he escaped by the aid of the catholics, and in his absence was condemned to death. Crossley at this trial was found not guilty.

William Austin was subsequently tried, and being found guilty was sentenced to death. While in Newgate gaol under sentence of death he confessed on 3 June, 1796, that one Jacob Isgar brought him the will ready made out and signed, and that after a stranger had drawn his pen over the name of Henry Lewis he, Austin, witnessed it; that he afterwards saw sir John Briggs and was apprehended; that the person who personated Henry Lewis was Richard Holland.

---

[1] Vol. I., pp. 26, 125.

[1] *Vide* Vol. I., p. 64.

Pedigree of the family of Lewis of Higga.

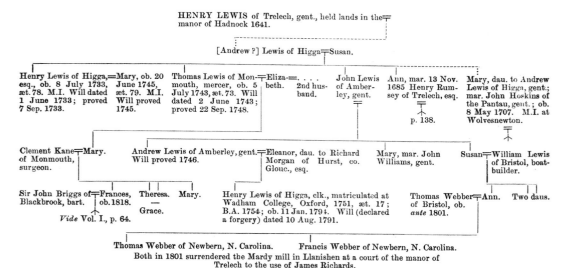

His death is thus recorded in the *Gentleman's Magazine*, 1795, vol. i., p. 83:—

> At Mrs Keene's,[1] Monmouth, where he was on a visit, in the 62^d year of his age, the Rev. Henry Lewis of Hyga, near Trelleck, Monmouthshire; a very singular and well-known character. Pofsefsing, by inheritance, a very handsome fortune which his parsimonious mode of life considerably increased, his relatives will come to the immediate pofsefsion of a large property. As he died intestate, the heir-at-law by the male line, who is married to a Mrs Read of Bristol, will inherit 600*l.* a year, and 140*l.* falls to Mr Morgan of Monmouth. Cash and notes to the amount of about 200*l.* were found in the house at Hyga.

Thomas Morgan, described in the indictment as the maternal heir of the rev. Henry Lewis, was the eldest son of Richard Morgan of the Argoed, whose sister Eleanor, wife of Andrew Lewis, was the mother of the rev. Henry Lewis. This gentleman's property was divided between the several heirs-at-law—Thomas and Francis Webber of North Carolina; Susanna, wife of James Harman of Bristol, pawnbroker; Mary Williams of Bristol, spinster, and her sister Grace Cornish of Bristol, widow. Milborne Williams of Bristol, surgeon, was admitted to certain lands as devisee of Mary Williams.

In 1848 William Page was the owner of Higga, the tithe map giving the area as 261 acres. It was purchased about 1875 by the late mr. Crompton-Roberts, whose second son, lieut.-colonel Crompton-Roberts, is now the owner of this and adjoining estates.

1 This should be mrs. *Kane's;* either his father's first-cousin Mary, wife of Clement Kane of Monmouth, surgeon, or one of their daughters.

Cleddon.

This place appears in the *Liber Landavensis* in the boundaries of Llandogo as Caletan, on whose banks near the river Wye bishop Oudoceus (Docheu) served God.[1]

Cleddon[2] belonged during the first half of the nineteenth century to John Chapman Roberts, a captain in the Royal Monmouthshire militia, who died 17 May, 1859, aged 81.[3] In 1870 it was sold by captain Roberts' executors to lord Amberley, the eldest son of earl Russell the Victorian statesman, who came here with his wife to reside. The estate comprised 87 acres, of which 63 were woods and plantations. Lord and lady Amberley were both possessed of views on life in strange discord to those of the simple-minded people among whom they settled, and strange stories are told of their proceedings and of the upbringing of their children. Lady Amberley died in 1874 and was buried in the garden, and lord Amberley died in January, 1876, being aged only 33, and was likewise buried in the garden, as was also one of their children. These bodies were subsequently removed by earl Russell, lord Amberley's father. Lord Amberley was a man of remarkably small stature, being only five feet in height, and his intellect was similarly contracted, though he wrote articles in magazines on many subjects and was the author of a book entitled *An Analysis of Religion.* The present earl Russell is the son of lord and lady Amberley.

1 *Liber Landavensis*, pp. 130, 147.
2 In *Tinterne and its vicinity,* by dr. Thomas, Cleddon is said to have been a cottage inhabited by Job Jones the poacher, referred to on p. 129.
3 Captain Roberts had been in the regular army, the 37th regiment; ensign 1800, lieutenant 1802.

After this Cleddon obtained further notoriety in being the residence of the marquis of B . . . ., son of the duke of M . . . ., and the countess of A . . . ., who ran away together and were the cause of a celebrated trial for divorce.

The next purchaser of Cleddon was mr. Arthur Bosanquet of the Bombay civil service, who came here in 1882. He was of the same family as that at Dingestow, being the son of Augustus Henry Bosanquet of Osidge in Hertfordshire, the son of William of London, banker, the son of Jacob, the eighth son of David Bosanquet, the first of the name to settle in England at the revocation of the edict of Nantes. By lord Amberley the place was called Ravenscroft, but mr. Bosanquet reverted to the old name of Cleddon, adding somewhat unnecessarily the suffix of *Hall*.

One of the few waterfalls, if not the only one, in the county is here, where the brook falls precipitously down the bank to Llandogo. This is known as Cleddon Shoots.

Lloisey.

Lloisey is probably a corrupted form of *llusi* (whinberries), which are plentiful in these parts. It was the residence of a family named Probyn. John Probyn, described as late of Loysey, gent., now of Mitchel Troy, made his will 15 May, 1762; proved at Llandaff 28 February, 1763.

> Several closes called Hopyards, Garthey bach or Little Gardens, and old orchard in the parish of Mitchel Troy to my son John Probyn and my son-in-law John Philpot—my grandson William Tyler—my three dau's Frances wife of John Philpot, Margaret Probyn, and Sarah Probyn.

John, son of the above John Probyn, is buried in the churchyard in 1805.

The Lloisey has for many years belonged to the rev. Henry Bolton Power, younger son of general sir Manley Power, K.C.B.

The estate of Nine Wells, taking its name from the ancient springs there, in 1848 comprised 123 acres and belonged to Mark Phillips. This now belongs to mrs. Margaret Price of Penmoel in Tidenham.

THE VIRTUOUS WELL.

The Virtuous Well.

Four hundred yards from the town on the left of the road to Cleddon is situated a well which is an object of interest to all visitors, more particularly because, with the stones and the mount, it is recorded on lady Probert's sun-dial. By the words below the representation of the well on the sun-dial it would appear that lady Probert discovered the well, or at all events discovered its properties—*Domina Magdalena Probert ostendit*. It consists of a circular pit enclosed with a wall with steps leading into it. On each side is a stone seat, and opposite the steps is an arch, from underneath which issues a strong spring of highly-coloured water of a chalybeate nature. On each side of the arch and on the opposite side are three more small wells of ordinary water, each of which is said to be a separate spring, though this is doubtful.

In the seventeenth century the well became the resort of people with various complaints, and Nathan Rogers, writing in 1708, says :[1]—

> .... *Treleg* wells, which of late years have been much frequented and have been found very medicinal, and of the nature of *Tunbridge* waters, flowing from an Iron-Oar mineral.

At the present time the well is in a bad state of repair and totally neglected.

[1] *Memoirs of Monmouthshire*, 1708, p. 34.

The Sun-dial.

The sun-dial, which has attained some celebrity, has been often described,[1] though not always with accuracy. It stands now inside the church at the west end of the south aisle, where, it is hoped, it will be for ever preserved. Until it was recently removed to the church it stood in the garden belonging to the school, to which place it had been removed many years ago from its original position, the exact location of which is uncertain.

THE SUN-DIAL.

It was erected by Magdalen, lady Probert, the widow of sir George Probert, in the year 1689, and commemorates the three chief objects of note in the town—Twyn Terrett, the stones, and the virtuous well. The upper block of the pedestal has the hours marked on each of the four sides, and on each face is a word forming the sentence—

HORA DIEM DEPASCIT EUNDO
(*the hour by going feeds the day*),

and underneath EUNDO is the date 1689.

The lower block of the pedestal has on the first panel a representation of Twyn Terrett, above being the words—

MAGNA MOLE
(*great in regard to the mount*),

and underneath—

O QUOT HIC SEPULTI
(*Oh! how many are buried here*),

signifying that the mount was a burial tomb.

On the next panel is a representation of the three stones, above being the words—

MAIOR SAXIS
(*greater in regard to the stones*),

and underneath—

HIC FUIT VICTOR HARALDUS
(*here Harold was the conqueror*),

alluding to a victory king Harold is supposed to have won here, and of which the stones were (erroneously) considered the memorial. The stones are inscribed 8, 10, 14, signifying their height in feet.

On the third panel is a representation of the virtuous well, with the words above—

MAXIMA FONTE
(*greatest in regard to the well*),

and underneath—

DOM. MAGD. PROBERT OSTENDIT
(*lady Magdalen Probert gives proof of it*).

The fourth panel is blank.

The sloping top is terminated at each end with a fleur-de-lys, and on each slope is an open book.

When the pedestal was removed from the school garden to the church it was discovered that the base was the ancient font inverted.

The School.

The first man, of whom there is any account, to keep school at Trelech was John Owen, who has attained fame as the author of a collection of Latin epigrams, first published in 1606 and subsequently translated into English and other tongues. He was a North Wales man of good family, educated at Winchester and New College, Oxford, where in 1590 he took the degree of B.C.L. On leaving Oxford in 1591 he kept school at Trelech, though it is not easily understood (unless, as it is said, Trelech was a much larger place than it now is) how an Oxford scholar came to settle here. In 1594 he was appointed headmaster of the grammar school at Warwick. The dedication of his epigrams is to Mary, the wife of Henry, 7th lord of Abergavenny, daughter of Thomas Sackville, earl of Dorset.

Zachary Babington, the vicar of Trelech, established a school here in 1691. This gentleman was a kinsman of Gervais Babington, who had been bishop of Llandaff from 1591 to 1595, when he was translated to Exeter, of the distinguished family long seated at Rothley Temple in Leicestershire.

By indenture dated 23 April, 1691, Zachary Babington granted to John Wyth and Benedict Edmonds a messuage lately converted into a school-house, with a parcel of land containing one quarter of an acre, in the town of Trelech near the churchyard, to the use (after the grantor's decease) of Henry Probert [of the Argoed], George Catchmayd, Henry Lewis [of Higga], and John Jones, and the vicar for

---

[1] *A Tour in Monmouthshire*, by archdeacon Coxe, 1801, vol. ii., p. 323; and many handbooks have adopted the description there found.

the time being, in trust, to employ the said premises as a school for teaching and educating gratis all such poor children as should from time to time be resident in the said parish of Trelech. He appointed Elizabeth George mistress of the school, and John Lawless, clerk, to be master after her death, the trustees to have power, in case of default of care in teaching or misdemeanour, to remove the master. He further purchased from Thomas Griffith of Llanover for 100l., on 16 March, 1 Jac. II. [1685], a piece of meadow-land called Gworlod Wenllan, containing six acres, at Llanwinny in Llangoven, and this he settled on the said trustees, the rents and profits of which were to maintain the school, after paying 6l. per annum to the said Elizabeth George, the residue to keep the school-house in repair, to buy books for the poorer children, and to buy one dozen of coal for the use of the school one month after Michaelmas yearly.

He also settled a piece of customary land in Nash containing nine acres *ad opus et usum sacerdotis sive lectoris qui divinas preces secundum ritum ecclesiæ perlegat populo in parochianâ ecclesiâ de Trelegg*, the rents to be paid yearly at the feast of the annunciation and of St. Michael by the trustees to such person sufficiently qualified as should perform the duty of lecturer by reading prayers in the church every Sunday, morning and evening, and also perform the duty of schoolmaster; but if the person selected by the trustees should not be admitted by the bishop to read prayers, then the rents should be paid to the schoolmaster and should not be had by the rector.

The school-house was the cottage which stands adjoining the lych-gate, and continued to be used as such till the year 1820, when the trustees sold the premises for 30l., and, with subscriptions of 100l. added, built a new school on what were known as the Clock-house lands.

TRELECH CHURCH.

The lands so called were, by indenture dated July, 1689, demised by Zachary Babington to Henry Probert and George Catchmayd, with the dwelling-house lately built by him, and a parcel of meadow containing two acres for 1000 years, at a peppercorn rent, upon trust to permit Morgan Holmes and Elizabeth his wife and their heirs to receive the rents for keeping the clock then affixed to the tower of the church in good going order. From about 1790 to 1820 the clock was out of repair, and so it was considered best to apply this charity to the school, and the new school was accordingly built on the land.

The Church.

No mention is made of the town or church in the *Liber Landavensis*, but the adjoining church of Trelech Grange appears under the name of *Trylec Lann Mainuon*.

The church is one of the largest and most handsome of the country churches in the county. It has the appearance of having been erected in the fourteenth century, and consists of a broad chancel and a nave lighted by clerestory windows, divided from two side aisles by five gothic arches. The chancel-arch and the arch at the west end are of great height, and are beautifully moulded. The tower is surmounted by a tall spire, an imposing object for many miles round.

The principal entrance is by a porch on the south side, on a stone of which is inscribed W. P. 1689, while the oak door, which is of great thickness, has the date let in lead of 1595.[1]

The pulpit is of oak, well preserved, bearing the date 1640. The communion rails are of oak, and have been left in their original position with two side rails, as well as the front one. They are of the period of the seventeenth century. At the west end are the arms of Charles II.: Quarterly, grand quarters: 1 and 4, Quarterly France and England; 2, Scotland; 3, Ireland. Underneath is—

16 C.R. 83.

There is a heap of moulded and carved stones collected from around the church by the late vicar. It has been suggested that these came from the abbey of Tintern.

CHURCHYARD CROSS.

The vicarage-house stands opposite the church, and though of comparatively modern appearance probably occupies the site of what has always been the residence of the vicar. There are no less than 450 acres of glebe, which was the apportionment of the common lands when the waste was enclosed under the act of 1810. There is no farmhouse on this land, which is let in portions to various farmers.

The advowson belonged to the priory of Chepstow, and at the dissolution of the monasteries seems to have come into the hands of William, 1st earl of Pembroke of the second creation. Philip, earl of Pembroke, presented to the living in 1660, and since that date the advowson was in the hands of the Crown until 1862, when it was ceded to the bishop of Llandaff by an order in council dated 5 February, 1862. Penallt was a chapelry under Trelech until the year 1887, when it was formed into a separate living.

There were till recently four ancient sepulchral stones in the church. One, of which a drawing

[1] Since this was written the door has suffered unnecessarily by being given a casing on the inside of narrow upright boards.

is given, was to be seen under the communion table, but the clergyman has recently had a block of stone placed under the table, completely burying this stone and the later one to Harry Tracy. It is probably a coffin-lid, on which is carved a wheel cross.

Scale, 1 inch = 1 foot.

The next has carved on it the figure of a person, the head resting on a cushion. This has recently been placed on the floor at the east end of the south aisle. It was before that standing up on end, having been moved from some other part of the church.

Scale, 1 inch = 1 foot.

There is also a stone, on which is carved a cross, in the chancel. Only part of it can be seen, the rest being hidden by the choir seats.

There is another stone, six feet long, standing at the west end of the south aisle. On it can be traced the outline of a floreated cross.

PATRON.	DATE OF INSTITUTION.	VICARS.
The king, by reason of the priory of Strignil, being in his hands on account of the war with France.	1 June 1359.	Benedict de Lanveir.[1]
. . . . .	. . . . .	John ap Gruffydd; resigned 1390 and appointed to Dingestow in exchange with Gregory ap David.[2]
The king, by reason of the temporalities of the alien priory of Chepstow, on account of the war with France, being in his hands.	30 Aug. 1390.	Gregory ap David, previously vicar of Dingestow; in exchange with John ap Gruffydd.[2]
. . . . . .	. . . . .	Howel ap Iorwerth; ratification of his estate 3 Feb. 1413.[3]
. . . . . .	. . . . .	Adam Johns, vicar in 1560, then non-resident in the diocese.[4]
. . . . .	. . . . 1611.	John Hughes, M.A. Oriel and Corpus Christi colleges, Oxford, D.D. 1621; a Cardiganshire man; also vicar of Tredynog; archdeacon of Hereford 1623; married at Mathern Aug. 1611 Isabel, daughter of Francis Godwin, bishop of Llandaff; died 6 June 1648.
. . . . .	. . . . 1620.	Henry Hackett, M.A. Hart Hall, Oxford; brother of Robert Hackett, rector of Mitchel Troy.
. . . . .	. . . . 1627.	Thomas Godwin, D.D. Christ Church, Oxford, son of Francis Godwin, bishop of Llandaff; also held livings in Herefordshire and was chancellor of Hereford.
. . . . .	. . . . 1639.	George Crump, B.D. Hart Hall, Oxford.
. . . . .	. . . . .	. . . . Simms, put in by the puritans but ejected at the restoration of Charles II.
Philip, 5th earl of Pembroke and Montgomery.	25 Dec. 1660.	Richard Meredith. His will (nuncupative) was made 20 Nov. 1669; proved (P.C.C., 80, Penn) 1 June 1670 by Ambrose Meredith. Vincent Edwards, gent., and his (testator's) sister Mary Edwards, and Ambrose Meredith, ex'ors—residue to his sister Mary Edwards and her children.
Charles II. . .	18 Jan. 16⁶⁸/₇₈.	Zachary Babington, M.A. Christ Church, Oxford, son of Zachary Babington of Lichfield, esq.
. . . . .	. . . . .	Charles Hutchins. His will is dated 1 May 1706; proved 9 Jan. 170⁴/₇. My nephew Thomas Hutchins of Gwern vawr, co. Brecon, my tobacco box—books in several languages to John, son of the said Thomas Hutchins—my sister Jane—my sister Elizabeth—my nieces Jane Davies and Sybil Davies—my nephew Thomas Davies—John Lawlis, clk.—Mr. Henry Lewis of Higga. (John Lawlis, lecturer in 1706.)
Queen Anne . .	9 June 1707.	James Ball, B.A. University College, Oxford, son of James Ball of Monmouth.
George II. . .	13 March 1753.	Peregrine Ball, M.A. Balliol College, Oxford, son of the previous rector; also vicar of Newland; died 1794.[5] (Howell Powell, lecturer and curate.) (Ezra Powell, lecturer and curate.)
The Lord Chancellor .	23 June 1795.	William Seys, M.A. Jesus College, Oxford, son of James Seys of Penrhos, esq.; resigned 1800.[6]
George III. . .	18 March 1800.	William Seys, M.A. Jesus College, Oxford, son of the previous vicar.
. . . . .	19 May 1842.	Charles Augustus Frederick Kuper, M.A. Merton College, Oxford, son of William Kuper of London, clk., who was tutor to . . . .; died 1887. (Stephen Parry, a Breconshire man, lecturer and curate for many years previous to 1848, when he died.) (From 1848 to 1871 William Bagnall Oakeley, curate.) (John Tyssyl Evans, curate in 1884.)
Richard, bishop of Llandaff.	. . . . 1888.	Henry Ardern Lewis, M.A. Hertford College, Oxford, son of Henry Lewis of Broughton near Manchester, gent.
Richard, bishop of Llandaff.	. . . . 1894.	Thomas Davies, M.A. Durham; previously rector of Henllys near Newport.

Monumental Inscriptions.

THE CHANCEL.

On the north wall:

In gratitude to the memory of Amelia, Late wife of John Elliot Winsloe, Esquire, Formerly of Collipriest, Devonshire, and Daughter of James Hodges, Esquire, and Ann his wife. She died on the 11ᵗʰ day of April 1822, aged . . years.

Near this place are Deposited the remains of James Hodges, Esq., of this Town. He died on the 14ᵗʰ day of March 1823, aged 74 years.

In memory of Amelia Winsloe of this Town, spinster, eldest sister of John Hodges Winsloe, who died on the 14ᵗʰ of January 1854, aged 57 years.

1 Cal. Rot. Pat., Edw. III., 1358—61, p. 212.
2 Ibid., Ric. II., 1388—92, p. 293.
3 Ibid., Hen. IV., 1408—13, p. 448.   4 Browne Willis.
5 The date of the institution of Peregrine Ball is from Notes and Queries. This vicar attained some fame as being the owner of the cradle in which Henry V. is said to have been nursed. (Vide Notes and Queries, 11 S., i., pp. 183, 253, 314.)
6 Vide his pedigree, p. 95.

Near this Place lie the Remains of Howel Powel, who was for many years Minister of this Parish. He died the 18th (?) of Jany 1787, aged 65 years.

Also of Mary his Daughter, who died the 24th of Octr 1766, aged 16 years.

And also of Rebecca Powell, Relict of the said Howell Powell. She died May 24th 1812, aged 96.

In a family vault in the churchyard are deposited the remains of the Reverend John Rumsey, Clerk, M.A., Son of John Rumsey, Esqr. He resided in this Parish for many years, where his active benevolence and charity gained him the respect and affection of all who knew him. He died 13th October 1821, aged 42 years.

> Si potuit fatum vitæ virtute repelli,
> Non jam plorarent hæc monumenta sibi,
> Divino multos lustravit lumine sanctos
> Palmifer in cœlo jam, velut astra, micat ! !

Also to the Memory of Charlotte Rumsey his wife, who died 15th October 1816, aged 37 years.

Immediately below the above monument:

To the memory of Herbert Rumsey, second son of the above named rev. John Rumsey, lieutenant of the Madras horse artillery. He died of cholera on the 6 of March 1830, aged 21.

Also of John William Rumsey, eldest son of the rev. John Rumsey, captain of the 44th regt. of Madras native infantry. He also died of cholera at Adamancottah 21 March 1846, aged 40. A monument erected at Trichinopoly by his brother officers testifies their respect for him as a soldier and a gentleman.

Also of Frances Rumsey, their aunt, who died at Clifton on the 7 October 1846.

Also of Harriet Rumsey, her sister, who died at Clifton on the 28 January 1861.

Also of Arthur Rumsey, youngest son of the above rev. John Rumsey, who died 16 Jan. 1870, aged 57.

On the east side of the chancel arch at the north end:

Near this Place are deposited the Remains of Elizabeth, wife of Philip Hardwick, Esq., of Monmouth, and sister to Iohn Rumsey, Esqr, of Trellick, who died Iune the 11th, 1787, aged 54 years.

On the east side of the chancel arch at the south end:

Near this Place are deposited the Remains of John Rumsey, Esq., whose Character is an Honour to his Family. He departed this Life the 7th Day of September, 1786, Aged 53.

Likewise of his Two Daughters, Charlotte and Frances Ann, who died Infants.

FLAT STONES IN THE CHANCEL.

HERE LYETH THE
BODY OF MARY THE
DAVGHTER OF CHRIS-
TOPHER CATCHMAY
ESQ. WHO DEPARTED
THIS LIFE THE 16TH
DAY OF MAY ANNO
DOMINI 1706.

HERE LYETH THE BODY OF
ELIZABETH YE DAVGHTER OF
CHRISTOPHER CATCHMAY
ESQ. & ELIZABETH HIS WIFE
DEPARTED THIS LIFE YE
.. TH DAY OF IANVARY ANNO
DOMINI 1729 AGED 81
YEARS.

Another Catchmay stone, of which the only words legible are CATCH .... GENT .... OF IANVARY 16 ..

....
James Ball
A.B. Minor Canon of
the Collegiate Church at
Bristol, Son of the Rev.
James Ball, Vicar of this
Parish, and Dorothy his
Wife, Died July 10th, 1739,
Aged 24 years.

HERE LYETH THE HONBLE
HARRY TRACY
OF TODIÑGTON, ESQR.
OBIIT 30 AUG. ANNO DNI 1699
ÆTATIS SVÆ 73.

At the top is a shield: *Or, an escallop in the chief point sa., between two bendlets gu., a crescent for difference.* Underneath the shield is the word *Resurget*.[1]

HERE
lieth the Body of
Elizabeth, the Relict of
John Rumfey, Efqr, who
died the 16th May 1763, aged 67.
Here alfo were depofited
the Remains of Hefter Evans.
fpinfter, her Aunt, & fifter
to the late Tho. Evans of
Langattock Vibonavel, Efqr.
Here alfo lieth Charlotte,
Daughter of John Rumfey,
Efqr, and Frances his wife
who died an Infant October
the 13th, 177 ..

In Memory of the
Rev. James Ball
died Decr 6th, 17 .., aged 76 years.[2]

HERE LIETH THE BODY OF CA ....
CHRISTOPHER PROBERT[3] OF THIS
PARISH, GENT., WHO DEPARTED
THIS LIFE THE 1 DAY OF FEB.
ANO DOM. 1676
AGED 57 YEARS.

At the top are the arms of Ynyr Gwent, borne by the Proberts of Pant-glas: *Per pale az. and sa., three fleur-de-lys or.*

---

[1] This stone has recently been covered by a stone platform placed to raise the communion table, and is no longer visible. Harry Tracy was the younger son of sir John, 1st viscount Tracy in the peerage of Ireland. His burial here is accounted for by the fact of his aunt Frances, sister of viscount Tracy, being the wife of sir Richard Catchmay of Bigsweir. His will, in which he is called Harry *alias* Henry Tracy of Trelech, esq., is dated 17 June, 1699, proved at Llandaff 14 September, 1699. He leaves to his two sisters 10l. apiece and the rest to his friend Henry Lewis of Hygay, who is made sole executor.

[2] This has recently been moved, and is now on the outside of the chancel door.

[3] It is probable that this Christopher Probert was a brother of sir George Probert.

HOWELL POWELL
died Jan. 18th, 1787.
REBECCA his wife
died May 24th, 1812.
MARY their daughter
died Oct. 24, 1766.
Also the REV.
EZRA POWELL
son of the above Howell
. . . . . .

FLAT STONES IN THE NORTH AISLE.

In memory of Benjamin & Joseph, sons of David & Margaret Williams. Ben. died May ye 4th, 1749, aged 14, Jo. Died May ye 17th, 1749, agd 7 Days.
George ye Son of David & Margaret Williams Died March 1, 1755, agd 4 yrs.

. . . . Margaret ye wife of George Morris, who died November ye 6, Anno Dom. 1737, aged 70 years.

In memory of Richard Bowen of this Town, who died January the 3rd, 1780, aged 52 years.
Also in Memory of Richard Bowen, son of the aforesaid, who died September ye . . 1806, aged 54 years.

Here lyeth the Body of
Henry Probert, Eſqr
ſon of Henry Probert, Eſqr
of the Argoed in the Pariſh
of Penallt, & Rachel Morgan
of Tredegar, who departed
this Life the eighth Day of
December 1726, aged 55 years.

IN THE CHURCHYARD.

An altar-tomb :
Here lyeth Henry Lewis of Hygay, Gent., obijt 8 July Anno Dom. 1733, ætatis suæ 78. Resurget.
Here lyeth Mary the wife of Henry Lewis, Gent., died the 20 Iune 1745, aged 79 (?) years.
Here also lieth the Body of John Rumsey of this Village, Gent., who was nephew to the said Henry Lewis. He died April 24th, 1760 (?), aged 72.

Sacred to the memory of John Probyn, formerly of the Loisey, Gent., who departed this life . . . . 1805.

An altar-tomb within high iron rails. On the north side :
Sacred | to the memory of | George Watkins,[1] esquire | a native of this parish | who died at his residence Trelleck Terrace, Pimlico | in the city of Westminster | on the 4th day of August 1841 | aged 59 years.

An altar-tomb within rails. On the top :
To the memory of | Joſeph Grimes,[2] Gent. | of Cledden Cottage in this Parish | and formerly Merchant of | the City of Briſtol, who died | the 8th day of Auguſt . . . . aged 43 years. | . . . . his wife, who . . . . 1822 . . . .

[1] George Watkins was the son of poor parents in the town of Trelech. He went into the service of a gentleman in London and did well.
[2] Joseph Grimes was a skinner in Bristol. His wife was Mary, daughter and coheir of William Williams (died 1793, aged 86) of the New-house in Llanvapley, yeoman, by Ann his wife (died 1780). The other daughters and coheirs were : Ann, married John Morris of Upton-on-Severn, yeoman, and had issue John Morris of Upton, cooper, only son, living 1793, whose wife was Sarah ; Elizabeth, married Matthew Watkins of Bryngwyn, yeoman, both living 1793. (From deeds.)

Penallt.

ENALLT means *the top of the wooded cliff*, a name descriptive of the parish, which covers a large extent of high ground situated precipitously above the river Wye, and much of it clothed with woods.

The parish contains 2375 acres of land and 24 acres of water, the latter being one half of the river Wye, which for two miles is the boundary between this parish and the county of Gloucester. The rateable value in 1815 was 1161*l.*, and in 1912, 1956*l.*

The population has been as follows :—

Year .	1801	1811	1821	1831	1841	1861	1871	1881	1891	1901
No. of inhab.	360	405	464	549	533	458	484	477	420	357

The number of houses have declined :—

Year.	Inhabited Houses.	Uninhabited Houses.	Building.
1861 . . .	109	5	0
1871 . . .	112	10	0
1881 . . .	103	18	0
1891 . . .	102	7	1
1901 . . .	94	15	0

There is no village, but there are many small proprietors who own their own dwellings with plots of land attached. Until the year 1810 a large portion of the parish was unenclosed, and by the act of that year, of which an account has been given under Trelech, those of the small copyholders (or cot-holders as they were called) who had had undisputed possession, without payment of rent, for over twenty years, became freeholders of the land they had encroached. Since then many of the others have purchased the freehold from the duke of Beaufort, so that there are an unusual number of small proprietors in the parish.

When coppice wood was valuable considerable employment was provided for the inhabitants in the converting of the wood into hurdles, hop-poles, brush handles, and hoops for casks ; but for various reasons the industry has declined.

In the valley of the Gwenffrwd near Whitebrook paper mills at one time flourished, and of recent years the ponds have found a new use in a trout farm which has been established. Another industry which flourished till recently was the cutting of mill-stones, both for grist and cider mills, the conglomerate stone which abounds forming excellent material. The grist mill-stones were known as Welsh stones, as opposed to those of composite manufacture, which were used in the mills for the production of fine wheat flour. The introduction of iron rollers driven by steam in flour mills has caused this industry to decline.

From the river Wye, 50 feet above sea-level, the ground rises steeply till at last it reaches, at Caecaws barn, the height of 844 feet, and at a point above the Graig wood, 600 yards north of Lydart, 863 feet. At a spot on the main road, two miles north of Trelech, the four parishes of Penallt, Trelech, Mitchel Troy, and Cwmcarvan meet, five trees having been planted to mark the place. This is known as the *Five Trees*, but only four remain, in the centre of which are the ruins of a building.

At Pen-y-garn is the base of a cross, and 150 yards further along the road south-west of this is another stone, which appears to be the block on which the base above mentioned rested. This latter spot is probably the original site of the whole.

On the road 600 yards due south of the church is another base of a cross. This is marked on the ordnance map as Cross Vermont.

At Croes-faen, near the entrance to the Argoed, there formerly stood a stone cross, but this some years ago was broken up and used in repairing the wall.

The Manor.

Penallt was included in the manor of Trelech, and descended in the same way. The principal part of the demesne lands were the woods sloping down to the river Wye. Edmund Mortimer, earl of March, who married Philippa, daughter of Lionel Plantagenet, duke of Clarence, built the bridge over the river Banne in Ireland with timber from Penallt, " causing divers Oakes of an extraordinary length to " be sent into Ireland from his Woods of Pennalt in " the Territory of Uske in Wales, wherewith he " framed a strong Bridge with purpose to set over " the River of Banne near to the Town of Kolle- " roth[1] . . . ."[2] He died in 1381.

The Argoed.

Argoed signifies *on the wood*, and is applied to places in woody districts. This has always been the chief seat and estate in the parish, and for several generations belonged to the family of Probert, of

---

[1] Coleraine.
[2] *The Baronage of England*, by sir Wm. Dugdale, vol. i., p. 149.

whom an account is given under Trelech. The house was built in its present form by sir George Probert, M.P. for Monmouth from 1661 to 1667, who resided here, while his father lived at Pant-glas. The latter place ceased to be the family seat at the beginning of the eighteenth century, the Argoed becoming the chief residence of the Proberts and their descendants the Morgans. From about 1800 till it was purchased by Richard Potter the Argoed was let as a farmhouse. This gentleman, who purchased the estate about the year 1865, was at one time chairman of the Great Western railway, and interested in many business undertakings. After his death the estate was put up for sale in 1892, comprising 438 acres—

	Acres.
Mansion and land in hand . . .	68
The Glyn (occupied by John Davies) .	150
The Bush and inn	26
Home farm	59
Lone Lane (Vaughan)	66
Lone Lane (John Herbert) . . .	10
Little Argoed (Thomas Phillips) . .	34
Other lands	—

The rent was stated to be 474l. per annum.

The mansion and the greater portion of the land was eventually purchased in 1897 by mr. Kyrle Chatfield, who now resides there.

The house has been much altered, and the only original part left appears to be the hall, a fine apartment containing a long table[1] with oak frame and spanish chestnut board, on which is inscribed—

April 9 1664

and initial letters which seem to be W Y or W I.

Over the front door is a fire-back, which has been removed from its rightful place in the hall fireplace. On it are the Stuart arms: Quarterly, 1 and 4, France and England quarterly; 2, Scotland; 3, Ireland; and the letters C. R. 1644 and G. P. This is considered to commemorate a visit Charles I. paid to sir George Probert. No record has been found of this visit, which, if it ever occurred, must have been in 1645. It might have happened on Sunday, 7 September, 1645, on the king's journey from Hereford to Raglan, when he paid his third visit to Raglan castle, or on Sunday, 14 September, 1645, when the king journeyed from Raglan to Monmouth on his way to Hereford.[2] But the king would have gone considerably out of the direct course to have done this.

The house is situated 700 feet above sea-level, and a feature of the place is the number and size of the sycamore trees that surround it. There are also remains of an avenue.

THE ARGOED.

Moorcroft.

The house now called Moorcroft has twice changed its name in recent years. It stands on the site of a small tenement called Cae-pwll-du (*the field of the black pit*), consisting in 1748 of two copyholds held under the lordship of Trelech (Herbert, viscount Windsor, being the lord) by John James and William Thomas. The property then comprised only three-quarters of an acre, with the usual rights of commonage. In 1781 William Powell of Monmouth, surgeon, was the owner, the property having been enlarged by the addition of a field called Ffort-las and comprising six acres, who sold in 1809 to George Evans, innkeeper. In 1821 an addition was made by the enclosure of several acres of common under the award of 1810. By his will in 1835 George Evans left the property, being then twelve acres, to his daughter and sole heir Sarah, wife of Henry Hatton.

In 1838, by this time comprising nineteen acres, the property was sold to Thomas Dyke of Croft-y-bwla for 650l. Thomas Dyke sold in 1843 to James Howell of Wandsworth for the same price, who in 1853 sold for 600l. to the rev. William Bagnall Oakeley. Mr. Oakeley, who was for many years curate of Penallt, changed the name from Pwll-du to

---

1 The table is no longer there. It was removed before 1897.
2 Pages 18, 19.

Snakescroft, the latter being the place near Bishop's Castle in Shropshire, from which his family derived. He pulled down the old cottage and built the present house, laying out the gardens and making it a complete residence. On being appointed lecturer at Newland in 1872 he removed there, selling Pwll-du, or Snakescroft, by this time comprising 27 acres, to mr. Charles Jeffreys. This gentleman resided there for a few years, and in 1883 sold it, having changed the name to Moorcroft, to the hon. Arthur Lowther Pelham, fourth son of Henry, 3rd earl of Chichester. Mr. Pelham has effected various improvements, and the black pit (*pwll du*), which gave its name to the place, is now an ornamental piece of water with gardens surrounding it.

A farm called the New-house comprises 80 acres of land, most of which was allotted in 1820 to . . . . Swift from the common, in accordance with the award of 1810. This was afterwards purchased by the rev. William Bagnall Oakeley.

————————

The Church-farm, about 100 acres, was part of the estate of the duke of Beaufort, and with Troy was sold in 1902 to Edward Arnott. Besides this the duke owned various cottages with small patches of land attached, amounting to 30 acres. These were for the most part purchased by the occupiers.

PENALLT CHURCH.

The Church.

The church has until recent years been a chapel under Trelech. It is mentioned in a list of churches printed in the appendix to the *Book of Llan Dâv* as paying annually, along with Trelech, 15*d.*, of which two parts were due to the bishop and one part to the archdeacon. The date of this list appears to be of the time of king John, 1199—1216.

By an order in council dated 15 September, 1887, mr. Richard Potter of the Argoed was instrumental in getting the parish separated from Trelech, and since then Penallt has had a resident vicar. He also built the vicarage-house.

The situation of the church above the river Wye, 400 feet above sea-level, makes it a conspicuous object. It stands on a bank sloping eastwards, in which direction the floor has a gradual fall. Up

to the year 1886 the edifice retained the features of the seventeenth century, with a large gallery on the north and west sides of the nave, high oak pews, an oak pulpit, reading desk, and clerk's pew, of which only the pulpit has been spared to remain. It consists of nave and chancel, and on the south side is an aisle separated from the nave by handsome fluted pillars and connected with the chancel by a passage, apparently an addition to the original building. In the chancel are remains of steps leading to the rood-loft, and these remained intact until the alterations in 1886. Up to this date the chancel was lower by one step than the nave, but the floor was then raised. At some time previous to this date the roof was lowered somewhat, so that a small clerestory window at the east end of the nave no longer looks into the church. The pulpit was fortunately preserved, is of the seventeenth century, and finely carved. The communion rails are of oak, with the lettering—

I R   C W   1743.

The door by which the church is entered is of considerable thickness, and has carved on it—

ANNO 1539

In the tower is an oak coffer of great antiquity, hewn out of a solid tree. It is 5 ft. 9 in. long, 2 ft. high, and 1 ft. 9 in. wide.

Over the chancel are the arms of queen Anne after the union with Scotland : 1 and 4, ENGLAND impaling SCOTLAND; 2, FRANCE; 3, IRELAND.

The porch has on the ridge of the roof a sun-dial, and on the right-hand side of the door are the remains of a receptacle for holy water.

In the churchyard is the base of a cross with two steps, and a portion of the shaft.

Around the church there is but a small population, and mr. Oakeley in 1869 caused another church to be built at Pentwyn, a spot within reach of most of the inhabitants. This was dedicated to St. Mary.

The school was built in 1834, as appears by the inscription over the door—

> This School was built in 1834, the adjoining School Church was dedicated to the service of God January 28, 1869.

CURATES AND VICARS OF PENALLT.

Stephen Parry, curate, died 1848.
William Bagnall Oakeley, 1850—80.
John Tyssul Evans.
First vicar, 1887, Reginald Philip Goldney, B.A. Christ's College, Cambridge.
1908, Martin Fawconer Harper.

Monumental Inscriptions.

ON THE NORTH WALL OF THE CHANCEL.

In memory of Thomas C. Rosser of his Majesty's Royal Navy and son of William & Sarah Rosser, late of this Parish. He died at Port-Royal, Jamaica, on the 23rd day of November 1832, aged 28.

Near this place lyeth
the body of Iohn Hoskings
Deceased the 15th of
February 1635 & for
Ever gave a parcel of
ground to this Church
& Poor of this parish
& for the true performance
There of put in trust ofesers
Tho' Hoskings
Iohn ap Iohn
Christopher edwards
Rowland Iohn.

The parcel of ground above-named | is situate at Cross Vane, in y⁸ parish | at y⁸ top of y⁸ Lone Lane, is bounded on | y⁸ North by y⁸ s⁸ Lane, on y⁸ South | East & West almost entirely by y⁸ | Argoed Lands, in shape oblong from | E. to W., in measurement 5ᵃ 1ʳ 8ᴾ.

To the memory of William James, who departed this Life August y⁸ 22ⁿᵈ, 1800, Aged 64 years.
Also Margaret James, who departed this Life Apˡ y⁸ 15ᵗʰ, 1804, Aged 68 years.

ON THE SOUTH WALL OF THE SOUTH AISLE.

In memory of Elizᵗʰ y⁸ Daughter of Wᵐ & Ann Edwards of the Passage, who died 2ⁿᵈ April 1790, Agᵈ 27 yʳˢ.
Also Ann the Wife of Thoˢ Frost, Daughter of John & Ann Stephens, died 17 Jan. 1805, Æt. 25 yʳˢ.
Also Ann Stephens, who died Decʳ 22, 1813, Aged 2 years.

The following is on the south wall near the ground, but is blocked by a pew :
Underneath lies the Remains of . . . . Davis of this Parish, who Departed this life on the . . of Novʳ 1809 . . . . A husband kind, a father dear . . . .
Also here lieth . . . . wife of the above-named . . . .

ON THE SOUTH SIDE OF ONE OF THE ARCHES.

Underneath lie the Remains of Martha and James, son and daughter of John and Elizabeth George, late of Mitcheltroy. Martha died in 1757, Aged 2 years. James died in 1769, aged 8 years.
Also John George, who died June 6ᵗʰ, 1796, aged 70 years. Elizᵗʰ his wife died May 14ᵗʰ, 1788, aged 59.

ON THE WEST WALL OF THE SOUTH AISLE.

Erected to the memory of Jane the wife of Paul Thomas of this Parish, who departed this Life Febʳʸ the 4ᵗʰ, 1814, aged 43 years.

FLAT STONES.

Inside the communion rails, in roughly-cut letters :
HER RESTETH THE BO
DY OF DORETY THE WIF
OF LEWIS YE
VANCE OF READ
BROOKE WHO
DEP'TED THE
9TH DAY OF IA
NVARY 1643.

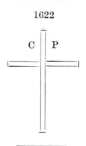

1622

C   P

In memory of William Probyn, who died 11ᵗʰ Octʳ 1812, aged 16 years.

FLAT STONES IN THE CHANCEL.

. . . .

WHO DEPARTED
THIS LIEF THE THIRD
DAY OF MAY IN THE
YEAR OF OUR LORD
GOD 1673.

Here lieth the Body of William Iones, who departed this Life the 10th day of October Anno domini 1729, aged 5 years.

Also in memory of Jane the wife of William Jones of this Parish, who dyed March ye 19th, 1753, aged 50 years.

James Edwards of the Passage died ye 2nd of July 1777, æt. 88.

Here lyeth the Body of William the son of Thomas & Jane Evanes, who dyed June ye 4th, 1754, aged 6 years.

Here lieth the Body of Ann ye Daughter of Philip & Ann Young, who Died the 20 (?) of March 1767, aged 4 years.

Also James their son, who Died the 22 May 1767, aged 2 years.

Here lyeth ye Body of Mary ye wife of Thomas Rowland, who departed this life y^e . . of November 1707.

Also here lyeth ye Body of Mary ye wife of Thos Probyn, who dyed March ye 28th, 1732, aged 48 years.

Also here lyeth ye Body of the above Thomas Probyn, who departed this Life 30th day of July 1740, aged 55 years.

HERE LIETH THE
BODEY OF MORIS
IOHN WILLIM WHO
DESEASED THE 14
DAY OF MAY AD
1642.
Here lieth the bo:
dy of Mary the
wife of Ionas Moris

. . . .

In memory of Iames Edwards, who died November ye 1, 1708.

Also in memory of Elizabeth Edwards, who died January the 20th, 1749, aged 90 years.

Also in memory of William Edwards of this parish, who Died ye 20 April 1763, æt. 43.

Hear lieth ye Body of Thos Rowland, who died the 18th day of August Anno 1738.

Also in memory of Mary ye Wife of Thos Rowland, who dyed February the 9th, 1752, Aged 76 years.

Here lyeth the Body of Mary Phillips of this Parish, who died Novr the 15th, 1738, aged 80 years.

Also here lieth the Body of Patient the Wife of Phillip Phillips, who Died the 16 day of May 1772, Aged 41 years.

Also in memory of Philip Philips, Died 11th July 1790, aged 70 years.

Here lieth ye body of William ye son of Iames and Blancs Iones, who died March ye 12, 1739, aged 18 yeres.

Here lieth the Body of Iane ye Daughter of James and Ann Edward of this Parish, who died April ye 27th, 1733, aged 2 years & 5 months.

Also in memory of Mary the wife of Phillip Phillips & daughter of James & Ann Edwards of this parish, who dyed feb. ye 3^d, 1755 (?), aged 37 yea^{rs}.

Also in memory of Ann the wife of Iames Edwards, who Died the 12 June 1769, aged 83 years.

Also In^o Stephens, died . . . . 1788, æt. 38 y^{rs}.

Here lieth ye body
of Iames Iones and
Blancs Iones who
died March ye 12
1739
aged 18 years.

Mourn not for me my
parencs dear I am
not ded but sliping
here.

FLAT STONES IN THE NAVE.

In memory of IOHN PERKINS, who died April the 26th, 1821, aged 72 years.

Also Frances wife of the above John Perkins, who died Octr 28th, 1827, Aged 51 (?) years.

Here lieth the Body of John Davies of this Parish, who died March the 2^d, 1779, Aged 58 years.

Here lieth the Body of Ann Dixon of this Parish, who died April the 11th, 1777, Aged 67 years.

. . . . wife of John Richards, who died November the . . aged 68 years.

Also Tho. Richards, who died . . Jany 1804, Aged 69 years.

Here lyeth ye body of Jane ye daughter of George & Sarah Kingstone, who dyed Jany ye 26th, 1733.

Here lieth the Body of John Prichard of this parish, who died Dec. . . 1763, aged . . . .

FLAT STONES IN THE SOUTH AISLE.

Here lyeth the Body of Thomas Williams of this parish, who died March ye 5th, 1748, aged 51 years.

Here lieth the Body of Charles ye son of Phillip Young of y^s parrish of penalltt, who departed this life November ye 13, 1722.

Here lieth the Body of Iohn Phillips, who departed this life the 8th day of Jany anno domini 1723.

Here lieth the body of Mary Young, who died Mar. ye 6th, 1732.

Also in memory of Esther the wife of William Jones of Redbrook, who died March ye 7th, 1750.

FLAT STONES IN THE PORCH.

Here lyeth the Body of Mary the wife of John Edwards, who departed this life the 19 day of January 1705.

Here lieth the body of Iohn Edwards of the glyn, who departed this life the 26 day of february anno domini 1728.

HERE LYETH THE BODY OF
THOMAS IENKYN DESE-
SED THE 14 DAY OF IANVARY
1641.

In Memory of John Martin of this Parish, who died June the 12th, 1793, Aged 48 years.

In Memory also of Ann the Daughter of John and Martha Martin, who died April the 12th, 1784, aged 4 years.

In Memory of Thos Martin of this Parish, who died . . August 1800.

There are four bells lettered thus :—

SIR GEORGE PROBERT KNIGHT WILLIAM JONES WID (?) C. W. 1662.

JOHN EDWARDES DAVID MATEN CVRCHWARDENS 1700.

PROSPERITY TO MY BENEFACTORS W E 1751.

THOS EVANS CHVRCHWARDEN W E 1751.

At or near Redbrook ferry stood formerly a church or chapel, of which nothing is now known, dedicated to St. Denis. Mention of it occurs in a lease from Henry, earl of Pembroke, to George Morgan of Itton, esq., dated 28 October, 36 Eliz. (1594), of one parcel of meadow ground in Penallt called Gworlod y cappell, containing four acres, in which meadow Christopher Probert claimeth about one acre on the south side and meareth to the river of Wye on the east and lands of William Edwards, lands of Hugh Dixton on the west, Cappell St. Denys on the north, the common on the south. It also appears in the boundaries of the lordship of Trelech.[1]

---

[1] Page 133.

Mitchel Troy.

MITCHEL TROY is called in Welsh *Llanfi-hangel Troddi* (the church of St. Michael on Trothy). The word Troy is taken from the river Trothy, on the bank of which the church is situated, derived from the Welsh word *troi*, to turn or twist. The word Mitchel has been considered by some to be a form of Michael. This, however, cannot be so, for *mitchel* is a form of *much* or *mickle*, and in this case is used to distinguish the parish from the important manor of Troy Parva. Similarly in Herefordshire are found Much Birch and Little Birch, and in Gloucestershire Mitchel Dean and Little Dean.

The parish contains 1970 acres of land and 15 acres of water. The rateable value in 1815 was 1967*l.*, in 1906, 1855*l.*, and in 1912, 1900*l.*

The population has been as follows :—

Year .	1801	1811	1821	1831	1841	1861	1871	1881	1891	1901
No. of Inhab.	220	250	305	375	383	385	382	339	265	268

The number of houses is shewn thus :—

Year.	Inhabited houses.	Uninhabited houses.	Building.
1861 . . .	85	3	0
1871 . . .	80	6	0
1881 . . .	71	5	1
1891 . . .	63	10	0
1901 . . .	65	4	0

Contrary to what is usually seen in this county, there is a small village surrounding the church, a noticeable object being the stocks standing near the entrance to the churchyard.

There is no manor called Mitchel Troy, but the parish is included in the manor of Trelech, which was part of the great lordship of Usk.

The main road from Monmouth to Raglan, which runs through the parish of Mitchel Troy for four miles, was constructed under an act of parliament, dated 18 May, 50 Geo. III., cap. 97 (1810), entitled—

An Act for enlarging the term and powers of three Acts of his late and present Majesty, for repairing several roads therein mentioned leading to, through and from the town of *Monmouth*, and for making a new piece of road to communicate therewith.

The recital refers to an act of the 28 Geo. II. for repairing and widening several roads leading to, through, and from the town of Monmouth ; a similar act of 17 Geo. III. enlarging the terms of the previous one ; another act of 33 Geo. III. enlarging the terms of the two previous acts—

And whereas the trustees acting in the execution of the said acts have borrowed several sums of money on the credit of the tolls thereby granted, which still remain unpaid ; and whereas the present road leading from *Trothey bridge* in the parish of *Mitchel Troy* to *Ragland* is very much out of repair, incommodious and dangerous for travellers, and it would be of public utility if power were given to make a new road from *Trothey bridge* aforesaid to *Ragland* aforesaid, etc.

The remainder of the act is merely formal, and it may be concluded that the road was made shortly after this date, 1810.

What the old road was like can only be conjectured, but it is certain that it was a twisting and narrow lane, in places worn very deep into the clay, similar to the lanes in the neighbourhood. The new highway was made on the track of the old one in some places, but most of it is an entirely new road.

The piece of road from Monmouth to the Trothy bridge referred to above was made in the early part of the eighteenth century, and is described further on.

Troy Parva.

The manor of Troy Parva was held of the lords of Usk by half a knight's fee, and is first mentioned as having been the seat of sir Alexander Catchmay, one of the companions of Hamelyn the conqueror of Over Gwent. He left an only daughter and heir, Jane, married to sir Alan Scudamore, whose son sir Titus Scudamore is styled lord of Troy and Bigsweir. His descendant, sir John Scudamore of Kentchurch, who married the daughter of Owen Glyndwr, was lord of Troy Parva in 1425.

In 1314, among the knights' fees in Wales belonging to Gilbert de Clare, earl of Gloucester and Hertford, is a moiety of a knight's fee in Little Troy, held by John Martel, of the annual value of 50*s.*,[1] and also the manor of Troy, of the annual value of 19*l.* 1*s.* 5¼*d.*

Adam of Usk mentions Philip Scudamore of Troy, who in 1411, with other gentlemen associated with Owen Glyndwr, was taken by the captain of Powis castle and drawn to the gallows at Shrewsbury and hanged, his head being set up on the bridge there.[2]

By the time of Henry VII. it had passed out of the Scudamore family, and was the seat of sir William Herbert, an illegitimate son of William, 1st earl of Pembroke. It is somewhat uncertain how the

---

[1] Close Rolls, Edw. II., 1313—18, p. 137.
[2] *Chronicon Adæ de Usk*, 1377—1421, 2nd ed., 1904, p. 118.

Herberts obtained this manor and also Wonastow,[1] but according to the Welsh pedigrees sir William ap Thomas, father of the earl of Pembroke, had it with his concubine Cary Ddu (*Caroline the Black*), who is called heiress of Troy. Thomas, illegitimate son of sir William ap Thomas, resided at Troy after serving in the French wars under Richard, duke of York, and Humphry, duke of Gloucester. On his death without issue Troy must have gone to his half-brother the earl of Pembroke, who bestowed it on his illegitimate son sir William Herbert. This sir William was possessed of much property, as is seen by his will dated 15 March, 152¾; proved 15 April, 1524.

> My body to be buried in the south side of the new chapel which I builded lately in the parish church of Monmouth,[2] my ex'ors to cause a tomb of marble to be made over my grave with images of me, Margery my first wife and Blanch my now wife, and an epitaph to be made for me.[3]
>
> Blanch my wife to have my manors of Wonastowe and Saint Moghen [St. Maughan's], llanveyr mibon Owen, Trecapraghed, llansey [Llansoy], and Redmayn, and the capital messuage with appurt's called *litell Troye*, and all lands and tenements in those manors and litell Troye in the parish of Troye, for the term of her life, with remainder to the use of Charles

Herbert my eldest son, in default to Thomas my younger son, in default to Henry Somersett, knt., lord Herbert.[1]

To Thomas Herbert my younger son lands, etc., in Tregare in the lordship of Bergevenny, lands called Tere holl phos (?), lands, etc., called Tere pipe in the lordship of Grosmont, in default to Charles my son.

A priest to pray for the soul of my wife and child, and for the souls of Will'm late earl of Huntingdon, Charles now earl of Worcester, and Henry Somersett, knt., now lord Herbert.[1]

Blanch my wife to have the tenement I lately builded in Chepstow, after her to Thomas my son in fee tail, in default to the said Charles, in default to the said Blanch and her heirs.

To the said Thomas the house in Chepstow by the street leading from the parish church towards the key [quay].

To Richard Herbert, my natural son, the tenement called Tere lloyvos[2] in the lordship of Whitecastle.

The said Blanch and the said Charles to have all my cattle and household goods at Litell Troye.

Being present William Ryddall,[3] sergeant at the lawe; James ap Jones; Thomas ap Jones; Sir Stevyn, parson of Troye.

Proved by Charles Herbert personally present and Dame Blanche, relict, in the person of Richard Watkin, notary public, procter in the cathedral church of St. Paul's.

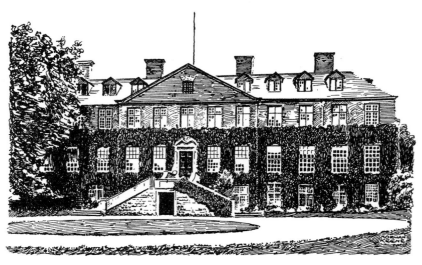

TROY HOUSE.

Sir William was succeeded by his son sir Charles, who was steward and receiver of the estates of the duchy of Lancaster, and in 1553 M.P. for the county. Shortly before his death, which occurred between 1552 and 1557, he was in trouble for being behind-hand in paying up the proceeds, in consequence of which his property was seized. He was buried in

the chapel built by his father. His will is dated 23 April, 1552; proved 20 January, 155⅞.

> I, Charles Herbert of Troye, knight.
>
> The manors of Wynastowe and St. Mogans, being of the clear yearly value of 40 marks, to Edward Herberte and William Herberte of Colbroke, esquires, to be sold for payment of my debts, who have entered bandes, together with Xtofer Baynham, William Herbert of St. Julian's, John Hayley, Edwarde Herberte, John ffrye, and Roger Williams, gent., for payment thereof.

---

1 About the year 1278 the manor of Wonastow was held by Alice, daughter and heir of John Marmyon, by quarter of a knight's fee (Duchy of Lanc. papers).

2 This chapel no longer exists, or is merged in the present edifice, but it can be seen in the view of the church in Vol. I., p. 11, as it was in 1684.

3 There are no remains of this tomb now.

---

1 Afterwards 2nd earl of Worcester.

2 Llyfos in the parish of Llantilio Crossenny.

3 William Rudhall of Rudhall in Herefordshire died 1530.

The capital house of Troye, with park, domaines, and other lands, etc., in the parishes of Michel Troye, Comcarvan, Monmouthe, and Penault, to Johane Herberte my eldest daughter, in default to Watkin Herberte my base son, in default to Thomas Herberte my brother.

All lands in the parish of Tregaere to the said Watkin Herberte, in default to Johane Herberte my eldest dau.

Touching the manors of Wynasto and St. Moghans, if the said debts can by other means be discharged, then the said manors with the house of Wynasto to the said Johane Herbert my eldest daughter, in default to the said Watkin Herbert, in default to Thomas my brother.

All implements, etc., in my capital house of Troye to the use of Johane Herberte my eldest dau., except such stuff as Dame Cecill Herberte my wife did bring with her.

Item that Dame Blanche Herberte, widow, my mother, shall have that part of my said capital house of Troye wherein she now liveth for the term of her life, and after to the said Johane Herberte.

I give my farm called Newe Grange in the Moor[1] to Dame Blanche Herberte, widow, my mother, and after to Dame Cicill Herberte my wife.

As to certain plate, in case the said plate be spent at the time of my decease, then the lands bequeathed to the said Johane shall be chargeable to satisfy the ex'ors of Sir George Bainham.

To Dame Cicill Herberte my wife all my sheep, etc.

To Watkin Herberte my base son 20 milch kine.

The residue to Dame Cicill Herberte my wife, Edward Herberte of Montgomerie and William Herberte of Colbroke, esquires, whom I make my ex'ors.

Lady Cecil, the widow of sir Charles Herbert, survived him thirty years. She was the daughter of sir John Gage, and married first (marriage settlement dated 15 November, 19 Henry VIII.) sir George Baynham of Clearwell. At the time of making her will, dated 28 June, 1585, proved 8 July, 1585, she was residing in Bristol.

I, Dame Cicely Harbert, otherwise Bayneham, of the city of Bristol, widow.

To my son George Bayneham 150l. for his relief, to be delivered into the hands of my son Thomas Baynham, paying 15l. by the year to the said George—my dau. Philippa Bayneham—my dau. Jane—my dau. Mary 100 marks, and besides 200 marks which was given her by her late father Sir George Baynham, knt., deceased—my dau. Anne Sturley[2] 100l., to be delivered into the hands of Sir Anthony Sturley, knt.; if she die then to the children of the said Anne—I forgive Sir Anthony Sturley,[3] my son-in-law, 100l.—I forgive my son Thomas Bayneham 100l., and I give to his dau. Cicely, my goddau., 100l.—my dau. Alice Brayne—my dau. Dorothy Williams, wife of Roger Williams[4]—my dau's Philippa

Bayneham and Jane Bayneham, ex'ors[1]—Sir John Yonge, knt., overseer.

[Signed] D'ne CECILIE BAYNEHAM.

Witnesses: Jo. Yonge, Charles Harbert, gent., John Webbe.

The debts contracted by sir Charles Herbert were paid, and the property was restored to his two daughters, his coheirs. Of these, Joan, to whom Troy was devised in the will, married George ap James ap Watkin of Llanddewi Rhydderch,[2] who served the office of sheriff of the county in 1562 and resided at Troy. Elizabeth, sometimes called Blanch, married Oliver Lloyd of Leighton in Montgomeryshire. These two ladies were at law with one another as to the estates, but with what result I do not know, except that some time afterwards Troy was sold by Charles James (the son of George ap James) to Edward, 4th earl of Worcester.

It will be noticed in the will of sir Charles Herbert that Wonastow was left to his daughter Joan if the debts could be by other means discharged. This perhaps could not be done, for sir Thomas Herbert, sir Charles' brother, was shortly after in possession of, and seated at Wonastow. He was sheriff in 1560 and 1572, and was possessed of considerable property, Parc Grace Dieu and the Beaulieu, being abbey lands granted by the king. Wonastow from this time ceased to be attached to Troy and became a separate estate, descending to its present possessor, sir Henry Pilkington, in unbroken succession, though going two or three times by female descent.

Edward, the 4th earl of Worcester, who, as seen above, purchased Troy about the year 1600, was succeeded by his eldest son Henry, created marquis of Worcester, the defender of Raglan castle. Sir Thomas Somerset, K.B., the next brother of the marquis, resided at Troy, and was skilled in gardening and the cultivation of fruit. Being "a compleat "gentleman of himself everyway delighted very "much in fine gardens and orchards,"[3] and his present of apricots and other delicacies to king Charles I. during one of his visits to Raglan castle much pleased the monarch. Sir Thomas was created viscount Somerset of Cashell in Ireland, and left an only daughter Elizabeth, who devised Badminton, which had been purchased by her father, to Henry the 1st duke of Beaufort.

The next resident at Troy was sir Charles Somerset, K.B., a younger brother of sir Thomas, who died there in December, 1665.

After this, Raglan being in ruins, and Badminton, the seat of the dukes of Beaufort, being situated in Gloucestershire, Troy became the residence of the dukes of Beaufort when visiting Monmouthshire.

The western portion of the mansion was the abode of the chief steward or agent of the estates. John Curre, steward to the first duke, resided here,

---

1 This is the Grange of Magor.

2 Anne, daughter of lady Cecil by her first husband, was the wife of John Strelly.

3 Joan, daughter of lady Cecily, was the wife of sir Anthony Strelly, knt., brother of John.

4 Of Llangibby.

1 All the children of lady Cecil were by her first husband sir George Baynham.

2 Vide Vol. I., p. 284.

3 Apophthegmes of the earl of Worcester, 1650.

and dying in 1685 was buried in Mitchel Troy church. John Burgh, referred to later on, also resided here, as did his successors, until mr. Osmond Arthur Wyatt removed to the house called Gibraltar about 1877. Troy then became the residence of lieutenant-general Edward Arthur Somerset, C.B., son of general lord Robert Somerset, younger son of the fifth duke. Lieutenant-general Somerset had a distinguished career, serving throughout the Crimean war, and holding afterwards important military posts. From 1868 to 1873 he was member of parliament for West Gloucestershire.

CHIEF STEWARDS OF THE DUKES OF BEAUFORT.

John Curre, died 1685.
Charles Price, son of Rees ap David of Penllyn, co. Glamorgan; died 1703, aged 79; buried at Badminton, where is his monument.
John Burgh, died 1740.

Robert Blandford.
Silas Blandford.
Zouch Turton, died 1814.
 Lewis Richards, under-steward, died 1807.
Arthur Wyatt, died 1833.
 James Richards, under-steward, son of the above Lewis Richards; died 1841.
Osmond Arthur Wyatt, son of the above Arthur Wyatt.
William Verinder, previously under-steward.
Edward Longworth Lister, major Royal Monmouthshire Engineer Militia, died 1896.
Samuel Hood Cowper Coles, resigned 1911.
 Francis Hobbs, under-steward.
Francis Hobbs, previously under-steward, 1912.

At the sale of the estates of the duke of Beaufort in 1901 Troy was put up by auction, but was not sold. It was some time afterwards purchased, together with the advowson of the church, by mr. Edward Arnott for the sum of nearly 50,000l. The estate was comprised as follows:—

Tenant.	Description.	Quantity. A.	R.	P.	Rent.
In hand	The mansion, gardens, orchards, meadows, etc.	29	2	18	
	Woods:—				
	In Mitchel Troy:				
	The Graig, the Orles,[1] Troy Park, the Livox	136	0	21	
	Longstone	3	2	19	
	Cochsida	3	1	12	
	Pwllydeon[2]	31	0	15	
	Lydart Orles and the Graig	24	0	12	Estimated value
	Roadway	0	0	28	575l. per ann.
	In Penallt:				
	The Livox	4	3	4	
	Ditto	0	0	25	
	In Wonastow	0	0	35	
	In Monmouth and Dixton Hadnock	114	2	25	
	Total	347	2	18	
	Farms:—				l. s. d.
Aaron Smith	Troy and Longstone	334	3	2	300 0 0
John Williams	Lydart	177	2	22	180 0 0
.... Jones	The Church farm	108	2	2	105 0 0
Herbert Probert	The Square	73	3	10	60 0 0
John Davies	The Red House	165	3	25	188 0 0
In hand	The Hill	98	0	12	168 0 0
Walter Haskins	The Church farm, Penallt	101	1	28	68 0 0
The sub-agent	The Elms	7	0	39	45 0 0
Mrs. Stead	Lands and buildings	31	0	28	25 0 0
Isaac Jones	Land at Dingestow station	40	0	3	49 0 0
Mrs. Stead	Ditto ditto	14	1	15	22 0 0
Michael Moxham	Milbrook	10	0	36	35 0 0
Mrs. Stead	Troy lodge	15	3	23	30 0 0
John Williams	Meadows	19	3	34	Let with the farm.
Aaron Smith	Meadows	44	0	35	Let with the farm.
James Vaughan	Cottage	0	2	38	0 1 0
Various	Cottages and lands	66	3	32	159 16 0
Ditto	Ditto ditto	11	1	25	2 7 9
		1669	3	23	2012 4 9

The house that stood on the site of the present mansion in the time of the Scudamores in the fifteenth century could have been but a small one and of no great importance. The first house of any size or distinction was erected by sir William Herbert, illegitimate son of William, 1st earl of Pembroke, in the latter part of the fifteenth century. The mansion, as it is now, appears to be the building of three distinct periods. The oldest portion is that on the south, nearest the farmyard. This is probably a part of sir William Herbert's house, and the door by which the house is entered from the yard, after passing through a small walled garden, may be the original front entrance of sir William's mansion.

---

1 Orles is the local word for alders.
2 This word ought to be Pyllau-duon (the black pits).

The next in point of age appears to be the central portion containing the main stairs, while the north front to the width of the suite of state rooms was erected probably in the time of Charles II. This front has been said to be the work of Inigo Jones, who died in 1657, but it would be hardly likely to have been built before the destruction of Raglan castle, and from that event till the return of Charles II. nothing of this kind would be done. It is most likely that this front was built by Henry, the 1st duke, who built Badminton at great cost, and would need, as Raglan was destroyed, a residence in Monmouthshire appropriate to his dignity and wealth. A picture of Troy, apparently painted about 1680, hangs at Badminton, shewing this front of the house with an avenue of a double row of elms to the river Monnow. The principal entrance to the mansion is approached by a handsome double flight of steps, so that the chief or state apartments are on the first floor. The hall is in the centre, with the state dining-room on the left, and on the right a suite of withdrawing-rooms. The stairs are very broad and occupy a large square behind the hall, running from the bottom to the top of the house. The balusters are of handsome oak of the time of Charles II. At the west end is the entrance to that part occupied from time to time by the agent. On the south side, facing the yard, is the ancient doorway referred to above, and westward from this is another door, the two opening into a private garden surrounded by a high wall. On the south wing is a clock turret containing an ancient clock which strikes on a bell, on which is the date 1607. There were several portraits hanging on the walls, but these on the sale of the estate were removed to Badminton. An object of much interest, which has also been removed to Badminton, was an ancient cradle considered to be the cradle in which king Henry V. was nursed. Heath, in his *Account of Monmouth*, 1804, describes with care a cradle then in the possession of a mr. Whitehead at Hom-brook, Frenchay, Bristol, which was looked upon as being Henry's cradle. This had previously belonged to the rev. Peregrine Ball, vicar of Trelech and Newland, whose ancestor was said to have been employed as the rocker of the cradle.[1] As Heath's description applies to the cradle which was at Troy, it may be that the one so described eventually found its way to Troy. It was 3 ft. 2 in. long, 1 ft. 8 in. wide at the head, 1 ft. 5¾ in. at the foot, and 1 ft. 5 in. deep.

Of gardens and pleasure-grounds there is not much left. These seem to have covered what is now the orchard on the south-east side of the mansion. From here there was a path leading to an ancient gateway opening on to what is known as the duchess's garden. This gateway has been to some extent filled up with soil by the action of water. Beyond this can be traced the remains of a large extent of pleasure-grounds on the bank of the Trothy, once laid out with paths and shrubs but now a wilderness of trees and bushes. On a bank above is a curious square building of the seventeenth century, measuring inside 8 ft. by 8 ft., with a narrow door and a small window in each pine-end of the roof. The kitchen garden, which is on the western side of the roadway to the farm, has a handsome doorway.

The most ancient approach to Troy was by the roadway which still exists on the south side of the kitchen garden, leading from the main road to Trelech just above the residence called the Elms. A single row of elms lines one side of this roadway, and it can be imagined that there was once another row on the other side. Another approach was made later to Troy by a drive on the north side of the kitchen garden, reaching the main road at the junction of the roads to Raglan and Trelech, and the cottage in the angle was built as a lodge for the gate-keeper. The present main road from the Cinder-hill to Troy was made by John Burgh, the duke's steward, in the early part of the eighteenth century. Previous to this the road out of Monmouth by the Cinderhill turned to the right over the bank under Gibraltar, descending again to the bridge over the Trothy, from whence it continued along the track to be seen a few yards on the left of the present road towards Trelech. John Burgh, who was the only gentleman in the neighbourhood to keep a coach, caused the present road from Troy, by what is now Troy station, to the Cinderhill to be made for the convenience of his equipage, which could not get up the steep hill by Gibraltar. This, when the coach-road to Raglan was made in the eighteenth century, was improved, and became the main road.

I have met with no account of a deer-park beyond the reference to the park in the will of sir Charles Herbert, 1552 (p. 163), but seeing that the fields above Troy are still called Troy-park there can be no doubt but that a deer-park formerly covered this ground. It will be observed that the land on this slope is divided into square fields with straight hedges, implying that the fields were enclosed in comparatively recent times, and that the hedges are not nearly as ancient as the twisting fences usually seen on land that has been enclosed for centuries.

The farmhouse and buildings are, as is usual in ancient demesnes, close adjoining to the mansion and on the south side. Some of these buildings are of great antiquity, and there are three ancient archways to the yards. Besides the farm premises there are stables and accommodation for the duke's horses and carriages, and for the numerous retinue that used to accompany their graces on their occasional visits to Troy. The farm has always been one of the best and largest in the district, and when corn was grown produced heavy crops.

The occupiers of the farm have been :—

Thomas Morgan, in 1748.
William Morgan, son of the above.
James Yarworth,[1] in 1800; afterwards of Tre-rhiw.
Robert Jones, from about 1833 to 1850.

---

[1] *Vide* p. 152.

[1] For his pedigree, *vide* Vol. I., p. 107.

Edmund Jones, son of the above, from about 1850 to 1863, when he left for Cwrt-Brychan.

James Evans Hale and Ferdinand Hale, brothers.

Aaron Smith, died 1905.

Alfred Edwin Jones, son of Amos Edwin Jones of the Priory, son of Amos Jones, who was brother of the above Robert Jones. Mr. Jones is a magistrate for the county, and was mayor of Monmouth in 1905 and 1911.

As the descendants of Thomas Morgan, the occupier of Troy farm in 1748, have continued in a respectable position in the county, I give the pedigree. Many of them were catholics, and still conform to that faith. Their attachment to the catholic church arose from the marriage of Elizabeth, wife of William Morgan, whose father Thomas Powell is said to have married a catholic lady.

Pedigree of the family of Morgan of Mitchel Troy.

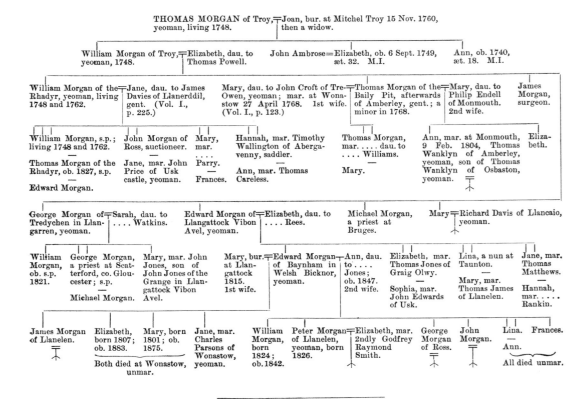

John Burgh, referred to previously, steward of the estates of the dukes of Beaufort, was a man who exercised considerable influence in the county, being manager of the property during the minority of the third duke.

On the death of William Bray, M.P. for the boroughs, in 1720, mr. Burgh announced his intention of standing for the seat without having taken the precaution of obtaining the consent of the duke, who was then but thirteen years of age. Finding that the duke was supporting brigadier-general the hon. Andrews Windsor (a younger son of the third earl of Plymouth), who had been previously defeated by Bray,[1] he withdrew, and Windsor was returned

unopposed. The following letters shed a curious light on the subject :—

(From James Powell[1] to Philip Cecil[2] of Llanover.)

Dr Phill,

I am ordered in the name of his Grace ye Duke of Beaufort to acquaint you that Mr Burgh his steward has presumed to set up Burgefs for Monmouth contrary to his knowledge or consent or his interest. So he ordered me to acquaint you to desire yu stick by him and all his other ffreinds, & desires yu vote for Brigadeer Windsor, for whom his Grace & Mr Morgan of Tredegar votes. You are desired to show this to

---

1 The author printed in 1906 the poll of this election, which was declared 12 March, 1715. The number of votes polled was—Bray 1028, Windsor 944.

1 I am uncertain as to what James Powell this is. I think he must have been the one of the name living at Mynachdy, who died in 1762, aged 80. For his pedigree vide Vol. I., p. 105; his tombstone, ibid., p. 118.

2 For his pedigree vide Vol. I., p. 82.

Mr Giles Meredith[1] & other his Grace's ffreinds, & desire their concurrence there to his Grace, & with service to you & other his ffreinds, & I am with service to y^u & y^{rs}, Dr Phill,

Y^{rs} affectionately,
28 April, 1720.   JAS. POWELL.

[Endorsed :] Philipp Cecill, Esqr, att Lanover in Monmouthshire, these.

(From Trevor Webb[2] to the hon. James Bertie.[3])

Hon^d S^r,

This morning I resev^d your Com'ands from Mr Ayskew in relation to the Election at Monmouth, which I shall be sure to obey, but I am sorry to acquaint your Hon^r that his Grace has given Brig^r Windsor Letters of Recommendation to the Gentlemen of Monmouthshire to engage their votes & interest for him. The Dutchefs of Grafton[4] having sent for his Grace, and there he wrote joyntly with her unknown to me, tho I waited on their Lordships to the Dutchefs of Grafton's house. But returning home his Grace acquainted me with what he had done. I then spoke so much to his Grace on that subject that he was angry with me. His Grace and my Lord Noel[5] are very well and gives their servis to your Hon^r.

I am, with great respect,
Y^r Honour's most dutyfull and obedient humble
                                   TREVOR WEBB.
April ye 29th, 1720.

(From Edward Kemeys of Bertholey to John Burgh.)

Worthy S^r,

I proposed the afair I mentioned to you to Mr Lewis Morgan, butt have not yet his resolution. He seems, however, inclined to cultivate a good understandeing with his neighbours by whatt I can learn. I hear nothing of Mr Morgan of Tredegar. In case he shoulde not concerne himself, which I see hitherto noe likelyhood he will, you will stand faire for a good number of the Newport men. Sr Charles[6] is nott yett returned from his Glamorganshire expedition.

I am, S^r,
youre very humble Servante,
                              EDWARD KEMEYS.
Cardiff, May 1st, 1720.

I have one thing to remarke to you, viz., that my Lord Duke's friends have always used the *Ship* and noe other house att Newport, the young woman who

now keeps itt hath as good if nott better accommodations than any of the other Inns, her ancestors have been sufferers for their Loyallty, and her grandfather dyed a nonjuror, nor will any of the other Inns receive you in case an Election should att any time happen in Newporte.

E. K.

To John Burg, Esquire, att Troy house neare Monmouth, post payd 0 . 0 . 3^d.

(From John Burgh to sir Charles Kemeys, bart.)

S^r, I perceive my Lord Duke of Beaufort has writ to desire your interest for Brigadeer Windsor at ye ensueing Eleccon for this town, and ye reason given is that I stand without his consent or knowledge. His Grace being but 13 yeares of age and under guardianship, I did not think he w^d so soon attempt ye managem^t of his own affaires, but y^t the consent and direction of his Guardians was sufficient. But since his Grace is prevailed upon to think himself better able to judge of his affaires and interest in this country than I am, I think myself obliged to return you my most hearty thanks for ye civilitys you have been pleased to shew and exprefs to me on that occasion, and to tell you that I will not farther concern myself in ye Elec'on. Your pardon for this trouble will add to ye obligac'ons already conferr'd upon

S^r,
Y^r most obed^t humble Servt,
                                 J. BURGH.
Monm^o, 2^d May, 1720.

(From the hon. James Bertie to John Burgh.)

London, 14th May, 1720.
Dear Captⁿ,[1]

I am as much surprised at y^r usage about ye Election of Monmouth as y^u can be, & really believe if Mr Dennison had not unluckily been employ'd about his Election at Oxford the Duke had not been perswaded, contrary to his own interest, into writing such a letter as y^u sent me a copy of. I am sure y^u can't think I have been well used in this affair, but what has been done is by a lady,[2] who I think ought to have had a greater respect for her br's memory than to have acted ye part she has. For ye future I shall endeavour to keep the young L^d as much as is in my power from her Grace since I find she is so ready wth her insinuations to their prejudice, & as y^u have hitherto been so kind to assist me, & I think I have constantly follow'd y^r advice & approv'd it in ev'y respect, so I shall for the future always beg the favour y^t y^u will continue y^r assistance. I desire y^u will give my service to y^r family, & believe me to be, as I really am,

Y^r most humble Servt,
                                 JA. BERTIE.

To John Burgh, Esqr, at Troy, near Monmouth.
Fr. Ja. Bertie.

In 1722 John Burgh purchased from viscount Windsor the lordships of Newport, Caerlleon, and Abercarn, and about the same time the manor of Park Lettice, Llanover. He must have been a wealthy man. He died in 1740, and is buried in the

1 Giles Meredith was sheriff of the county in 1713. For him and his family *vide* Vol. I., pp. 371, 372.

2 I conclude that Trevor Webb was a son of captain Charles Webb, who married 30 September, 1712, Elizabeth, daughter of sir Hopton Williams, 3rd baronet. The only son of this marriage that I have a note of is Hopton Williams Webb, appointed rector of Goitre 1 March, 174⅝ (*vide* Vol. I., p. 422).

3 The hon. James Bertie was 2nd son of James, 1st earl of Abingdon. He married Elizabeth, only daughter and heir of George, 7th lord Willoughby of Parham, by whom he had the manor and estate of Stanwell in Middlesex, where he resided. His lineal descendant is the present earl. John Burgh may have been related to James Bertie, for one of his sons is called Bertie Burgh.

4 The duchess of Grafton was aunt to the young duke of Beaufort. She was lady Henrietta Somerset, daughter of Charles, marquis of Worcester (who died before succeeding to the dukedom), and sister of Henry, 2nd duke.

5 Lord Charles Noel Somerset, younger brother of the duke of Beaufort.

6 Sir Charles Kemeys of Cefn-Mabli, bart.

1 I have not found in what regiment John Burgh was a captain.
2 The duchess of Grafton, above mentioned.

churchyard of Mitchel Troy, where is a handsome monument, which has been allowed to get into bad repair. His will is dated 14 April, 1740; proved (P.C.C., 204, Browne) 17 October, 1740.

> I desire to be buried in the churchyard of Monmouth, or Michell Troy if I happen to die at Troy—to my son Henry all the right I have in a farm called Woolestone's Grange, co. Glouc., in the tenure of mr. John Berrow—to my son William the farm called the Pillhouse, co. Glouc., in the tenure of mr. Thomas Williams—to my son Bertie the farm called the Dayhouse, co. Glouc., in the tenure of mr. Richard Williams—to my son Ashburnham the farm in Penrose, co. Mon., late in the tenure of John Smart, except the part I purchased from James Kenard, all which farms I hold of Henry, duke of Beaufort—I desire that whatever may be owing of 1200*l*. I promised my dau. Mary on her marriage with William James Musgrave may be paid her—to my dau's Levina, Lydia, Elizabeth, and Anne 1200*l*. each—my servants Penelope Perryman[1] and Richard Angle—the estate I purchased of James Kennard in Penrose and the residue of my estate I bequeath to my son Henry, he ex'or.
>
> [Signed] J. BURGH.

Witnesses: Mary Gough, Gil. Hearne, E. Jones.

---

[1] The will of William Perryman (nuncupative) was proved at Llandaff 6 December, 1732. Sick of the small-pox, whereof he died two days after—to his son 10*l*.—to each of his two dau's 5*l*.—to his wife Penelope Perryman the residue. The parish registers have—William Perryman, bur. 20 Aug. 1750; M*rs* Perryman, bur. 6 June, 1758; John Jones Baryman of Monmouth, bur. 14 Jan. 1803.

John Burgh was succeeded in his estates by his second son, the rev. Henry Burgh (the eldest son John having died without issue in the father's lifetime), who in 1744 was living at Penrhos in the house now known as Penrhos-farm.[2] By his wife Mary, daughter and coheir of Godfrey Harcourt of Wirewood's Green, he had a son Charles Henry, who died without issue in 1778, and a daughter Mary, the wife of colonel Thomas Johnes of Hafod Ychtryd in Cardiganshire. This gentleman, who with his wife had a large fortune, represented Radnorshire in parliament from 1780 till 1796, and Cardiganshire from 1796 till his death in 1816. He was a man of parts, translated Froissart, built a magnificent gothic mansion at Hafod in 1785, in which were stored a most valuable library, and in a cottage near had a printing press, from which were issued many of his works. He was also colonel of the Cardiganshire militia and lord lieutenant of the county. As an agriculturist he was an authority on farming, and planted annually an immense number of larch trees, an example which was followed by many other landowners in the district. In 1807 his mansion, with nearly the whole of the library, was burnt, but he rebuilt it at great cost and formed another library. His only child, a daughter, dying unmarried before her father, the Monmouthshire property reverted to the representatives of mrs. Johnes' mother.

---

[2] *Vide* Vol. II., p. 86.

Pedigree of the family of Burgh.

ULYSSES BURGH, bishop of Ardagh in Ireland.

John Burgh of Troy, esq., steward to the duke of Beaufort; ob. 25 April 1740, æt. 67; bur. at Mitchel Troy. M.I. Will dated 14 April 1740; proved 17 Oct. 1740.—Lydia, dau. to Henry Clark of Moulsey, co. Surrey, esq. | William Burgh, at Limerick in 1719.

James Burgh of Stanwell, Middlesex; bur. there 1739.=Mary, dau. and coheir to John Cotton, esq.; bur. 1735. | Thomas Burgh, bur. at Badminton. | Mary, mar. William James Musgrave. — Lavinia, mar. at Mitchel Troy, 23 Sep. 1740, John Melksum, clk. | Lydia, mar. 1745 captain John Jones of the Tump at the Pitt, Llanarth, younger son of John Jones of Dingestow, esq. (p. 57). | Anne, mar. at Mitchel Troy, 23 Sep. 1740, William Norris, clk. | Elizabeth, mar. Hugh Penry of Llwyn-cyntefn, co. Brec., esq.; ob. 1789, æt. 82. M.I. at Monmouth.

1. John Burgh, bur. at Badminton. | Henry Burgh, clk., of Penrhos in 1744, after of Monmouth; bur. at Mitchel Troy 5 June 1765.=Mary, dau. and coheir to Godfrey Harcourt[3] of Wirewood's Green near Chepstow, esq.; bur. at Mitchel Troy 20 May 1786. Will proved 1786. | William Burgh of Chepstow, gent. Will proved 1788.=Mary. | Bertie Burgh. | Ashburnham Burgh of Llanarth, esq., in 1771.

Charles Henry Burgh, ob. s.p.; bur. at Mitchel Troy 6 March 1778. | Mary, bur. at Mitchel Troy 21 June 1751. | Lydia Anne, bur. at Mitchel Troy 29 Oct. 1759. | Maria, ob. s.p. bur. at Mitchel Troy 11 April 1782.=Colonel Thomas Johnes of Hafod Ychtryd, co. Cardigan, M.P.; ob. 1816. | Mary, mar. Nicholas Blanning of Chepstow; of Caerlleon in 1799. | William Burgh, bap. at Llanarth 27 March 1765.

Maria Anne, ob. inf. *vitá patris.*

---

[3] In Vol. I., p. 80, a mistake s made in the pedigree of Harcourt. Of the children of Godfrey Harcourt, Lewis Harcourt had two daughters—Amy, married Richard Gwillim of King's Capel, co. Hereford, and had issue Thomas Harcourt Gwillim of Westhide, co. Hereford, clk.; Mary, married William Powell of Llanelly, co. Brecon, clk. Charles Harcourt (son of Godfrey) had issue as there given. Godfrey Harcourt (son of Godfrey) was of Wirewood's Green near Chepstow (will proved 1758), had issue James Harcourt, M.D.; Margaret; Mary, married Henry Burgh, clk.; Anne, married Edward Williams of Llangattock Court, co. Brecon, and had issue as in Vol. I., p. 80; Amy, married John Powell of Llanhamlech, co. Brecon, and had issue Thomas Harcourt Powell, who died unmarried in 1835; Frances.

Lydart.

Lydart, though so called now-a-days, would be more correctly written Llwydarth (llwyd garth, *grey ridge*), descriptive of the situation. As by the following will the testator leaves money for the poor of Llwydarth it is possible that there was here a small village. At present there is only the gentleman's house, the farmhouse, and one cottage.

Walter James, described as of Mychel Troy, made his will 17 April, 1581; proved 5 April, 1582 (P.C.C., 13, Tirwhitt), by Richard Windor, notary public, proxy for Henry James, the executor named in the will.

> I desire my ex'ors to give 10*s.* for me amongst the poor dwelling at Loydarthe—my goods to be divided in three parts; one part I give to my brother Harry James, the second part to my brother William James, and the moiety of the third part to my sister Margaret, the remaining moiety to my sister Alice—my wife is sufficiently provided for—ex'or, my brother Harry James.
>
> per me prenominatum Walterum James.

Lydart, with much other land in Mitchel Troy, Cwmcarvan, and Trelech, was in the seventeenth century the property of William Morgan, esq., of Pencrug in the parish of Llanhenog. Some of this land, if not all, seems to have come to him by the marriage of his grandfather George Morgan of Pencrug with Lucy, daughter and eventual coheir of John Seymour *alias* Williams of Trelech. His will is dated 20 October, 1661, proved (P.C.C., 48, Mico) 20 March, 166⅚, by which he divided his estates between his seven daughters and coheirs, viz., Anne, wife of Herbert Evans[1] of Neath, esq.; Jane, wife of Walter Evans of Llangattock Vibon Avel, esq.; Elizabeth; Dorothy,[2] afterwards wife of William Kemeys of Kemeys, esq.; Cecil, afterwards wife of Christopher Perkins of Pilston, esq.; Margaret, afterwards wife of Edward Kemeys of Bertholey, gent.; Mary. To his eldest daughter Anne he left Pencrug. To his youngest daughter Mary, who died in 1663, aged 16, he leaves—

> My free and customary lands in Cumcarvan, Micheltroy, and Penallt, now in the possession of sir George Probert, knt., William Richard, John Watkin, Charles Tyler, and Philip William of the Vedow, my freehold land in Trelleck in the possession of John David Hopkin, together with a house in Trelleck, late in the possession of Charles Browne.

To his daughter Jane, wife of Walter Evans, the latter being under 21 years of age, he leaves—

> That messuage in Micheltroy in the possession of John Robert, and my freehold land there bought from Christopher Tyler, my customary lands there now in the possession of the said John Robert, James

Appletree, and Abell Tingell, my customary lands in Cumcarvan in the possession of William Browne, William Young, John Powell, John Evans, Walter Thomas, John Jayne, upon condition that the said Walter Evans within one year after he attains to the age of 21 settle his chief mansion-house in Langattock Mibon Avell, now in the possession of James Evans, gent., and freehold there to the amount of 100*l.* per annum, for the said Jane Evans his wife, and shall settle all his estates in cos. Monmouth, Hereford, and in the city of Bristol, upon the heirs of the said Jane.

The property above mentioned was left by Thomas Evans (son of Walter Evans and Jane Morgan), by his will dated 1730, to his second son Kingsmill Evans, a bencher of Gray's Inn and a practising barrister residing at Hammersmith. The latter accordingly became seated at Lydart, and to him are probably due the handsome fir and other trees now in full maturity. It is also highly probable that the present house was built by this gentleman, a comfortable residence in the style then usual, and the stables, kitchen-garden, and the park wall all appear to be of the same date. The original residence was what is now the farmhouse, which has since been sold and added to the estate of Troy.

Kingsmill Evans died in 1762, and was succeeded by his eldest son Kingsmill, who, being an officer in the First Foot Guards and afterwards colonel of the regiment, let Lydart in 1766 to Richard Willis, who had married his sister Anne. Mr. Willis remained here for ten years, and after this colonel Evans resided here occasionally when on leave from his military duties. He was severely wounded at the battle of Lincelle in Flanders on 18 August, 1793, and died therefrom a few weeks afterwards. His son Kingsmill, a captain in the First Foot Guards, succeeded to Lydart, and in 1806, on the death of miss Jane Clarke, inherited the mansion and estate of the Hill in the parish of Walford, to which he removed.[1]

Lydart was sold about the year 1817 to mr. Thomas Oakley, who was induced to come to this part of the country by his relationship to mr. Attley, who some time previously had settled at the Leys in Ganerew. Thomas Oakley was the third son of Richard Oakley of Snakescroft in the parish of Bishop's Castle in Shropshire, representing a branch of the ancient family of Oakeley of Oakeley. The estate of Snakecroft was inherited by Robert Oakley, the elder brother of Thomas, but by family arrangement became vested in Thomas Oakley. It eventually came to his sons, the rev. William Bagnall Oakeley, Richard Henry Oakeley, and the rev. James Oakeley,[2] who in the year 1862 sold it for 6143*l.* to Beriah Botfield, M.P.[3]

By the marriage of Thomas Oakley with Elizabeth, daughter of Joseph Pearce, their descendants

---

[1] Herbert Evans was knighted in 1674. Mary his daughter and eventual sole heir married sir Humphrey Mackworth, knt., from whom descends sir Arthur Mackworth, bart., the present owner of Pencrug.

[2] In Vol. I., p. 47, a mistake is made in making the wife of William Kemeys of Kemeys to be Dorothy, daughter of William Evans of Llangattock. She was as stated above.

[1] For details of the families of Evans and Clarke *vide* Vol. I., pp. 47, 48.

[2] It will be noticed that some of the family prefer the spelling of *Oakley*, others *Oakeley*.

[3] Information of the rev. William Bagnall Oakeley.

represent the ancient families of Lewis (Wallis) of Llanddewi Rhydderch[1] and Morgan of Lanrhymny, and many other Welsh stocks of Gwent. Some portraits of Lewis and Morgan hang at Lydart.

The farmhouse of Lydart, which is presumably the ancient residence, was not purchased by mr. Oakley, but with the land on the upper or eastern side of the old road descended to the rev. Henry Bolton

Power, who some years ago sold it to the duke of Beaufort. This now belongs to the trustees of the late mr. Arnott.

A considerable alteration was made to the road about the year 1830, when it was diverted from its original course. The ancient road can be traced through Lydart farmyard, where there are remains of paving known as *Lydart causeway*, following the wall which forms the boundary of the Lydart demesne.

---

1 *Vide* Vol. I., p. 285.

Pedigree of the family of Oakeley of Lydart.

The arms of OAKELEY of Oakeley are *Arg., on a fesse between 3 crescents gules as many fleurs-de-lys or*, but this family have borne *Gu., 3 snakes nowed in a triangular knot arg.*, which is the coat of Ednowain ap Bradwen, founder of the fifteenth noble tribe of North Wales.
PEARCE, *Az., a mural crown between 2 lions passant in chief, and in base as many cross-crosslets fitchée or*.

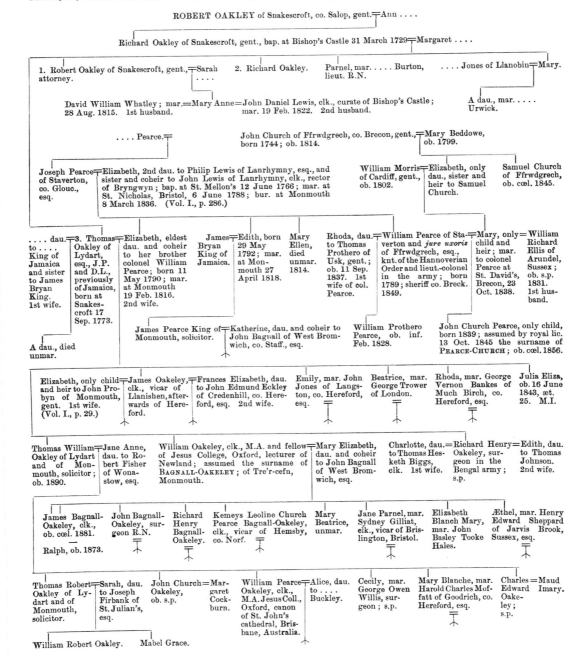

The house in the village on the south side of the road opposite the school, now called the Church-farm, was formerly the residence and estate of a branch of the Catchmays, from whom it descended to the Tylers. Catchmay Tyler died about the year 1690, and his descendants resided here for the next hundred years. Since this time it has been let to a farmer, and later was sold to the duke of Beaufort and included in the estate purchased by the late mr. Arnott.

The Tylers were a family of long standing in the parish. James Tyler held customary lands at Lydart in 1570; John ap John *alias* Tyler was buried at Mitchel Troy in 1636. The earliest will of the name I find is that of Mary Tyler of Cwmcarvan, widow,[1] dated 2 February, 1624; proved at Llandaff 25 February, 162⅘.

Towards the reparation of the cathedral church of landaff iiij*d*.—to Sissill Sheppard one cow called Mousy[2] coloured browne red—to Mary Sheppard one heifer called Silver coloured browne red—to James Sheppard one cow coloured red called Rauny—to Mary Tyler one cow called Rossie[3] coloured red and white—to Richard Tyler one heifer coloured yellow called Melly[4]—to Sibill Tyler all my goods, she sole ex'trix.

An inventory is attached to the will, the total value being 19*l.* 5*s.* 4*d.*

𝔓𝔢𝔡𝔦𝔤𝔯𝔢𝔢 𝔬𝔣 𝔱𝔥𝔢 𝔣𝔞𝔪𝔦𝔩𝔶 𝔬𝔣 𝔗𝔶𝔩𝔢𝔯 𝔬𝔣 𝔐𝔦𝔱𝔠𝔥𝔢𝔩 𝔗𝔯𝔬𝔶.

ARMS.—*Vert, on a bend arg., between 6 passion nails or, 3 crescents gu.*[5]

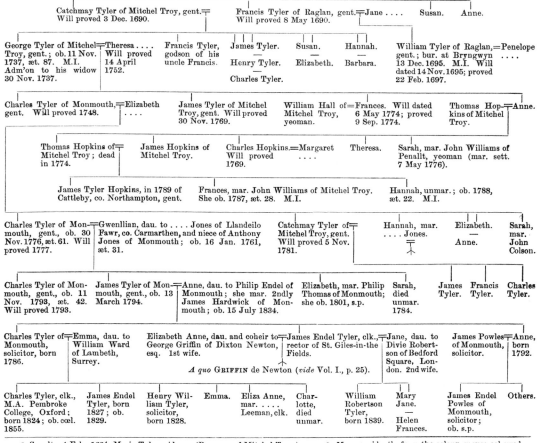

JAMES TYLER of Mitchel Troy, gent., living 1640=Dorothy, dau. to John Rosser of Tregaer.

Catchmay Tyler of Mitchel Troy, gent. Will proved 3 Dec. 1690.

Francis Tyler of Raglan, gent.=Jane .... Susan. Anne. Will proved 8 May 1690.

George Tyler of Mitchel Troy, gent.; ob. 11 Nov. 1737, æt. 87. M.I. Adm'on to his widow 30 Nov. 1737.=Theresa .... Will proved 14 April 1752.

Francis Tyler, godson of his uncle Francis.

James Tyler. — Henry Tyler. — Charles Tyler.

Susan. — Elizabeth.

Hannah. — Barbara.

William Tyler of Raglan, gent.; bur. at Bryngwyn 13 Dec. 1695. M.I. Will dated 14 Nov. 1695; proved 22 Feb. 1697.=Penelope ....

Charles Tyler of Monmouth, gent. Will proved 1748.=Elizabeth ....

James Tyler of Mitchel Troy, gent. Will proved 30 Nov. 1769.

William Hall of Mitchel Troy, yeoman.=Frances. Will dated 6 May 1774; proved 9 Sep. 1774.

Thomas Hopkins of Mitchel Troy.=Anne.

Thomas Hopkins of Mitchel Troy; dead in 1774.

James Hopkins of Mitchel Troy.

Charles Hopkins.=Margaret .... Will proved 1769.

Theresa.

Sarah, mar. John Williams of Penallt, yeoman (mar. sett. 7 May 1776).

James Tyler Hopkins, in 1789 of Cattleby, co. Northampton, gent.

Frances, mar. John Williams of Mitchel Troy. She ob. 1787, æt. 28. M.I.

Hannah, unmar.; ob. 1788, æt. 22. M.I.

Charles Tyler of Monmouth, gent., ob. 30 Nov. 1776, æt. 61. Will proved 1777.=Gwenllian, dau. to .... Jones of Llandeilo Fawr, co. Carmarthen, and niece of Anthony Jones of Monmouth; ob. 16 Jan. 1761, æt. 31.

Catchmay Tyler of Mitchel Troy, gent. Will proved 5 Nov. 1781.

Hannah, mar. .... Jones.

Elizabeth. — Anne.

Sarah, mar. John Colson.

Charles Tyler of Monmouth, gent., ob. 11 Nov. 1793, æt. 42. Will proved 1793.

James Tyler of Monmouth, gent., ob. 13 March 1794.=Anne, dau. to Philip Endel of Monmouth; she mar. 2ndly James Hardwick of Monmouth; ob. 15 July 1834.

Elizabeth, mar. Philip Thomas of Monmouth; she ob. 1801, s.p.

Sarah, died unmar. 1784.

James Tyler.

Francis Tyler.

Charles Tyler.

Charles Tyler of Monmouth, solicitor, born 1786.=Emma, dau. to William Ward of Lambeth, Surrey.

Elizabeth Anne, dau. and coheir to George Griffin of Dixton Newton, esq. 1st wife.=James Endel Tyler, clk., rector of St. Giles-in-the Fields.=Jane, dau. to Divie Robertson of Bedford Square, London. 2nd wife.

James Powles of Monmouth, solicitor.=Anne, born 1792.

A quo GRIFFIN de Newton (*vide* Vol. I., p. 25).

Charles Tyler, clk., M.A. Pembroke College, Oxford; born 1824; ob. cœl. 1855.

James Endel Tyler, born 1827; ob. 1829.

Henry William Tyler, solicitor, born 1828.

Emma.

Eliza Anne, mar. .... Leeman, clk.

Charlotte, died unmar.

William Robertson Tyler, born 1839.

Mary Jane. — Helen Frances.

James Endel Powles of Monmouth, solicitor; ob. s.p.

Others.

---

1 Sepulta, 4 Feb., 162⅘, Maria Tyler, vidua. (Par. reg. of Mitchel Troy.)
3 Rossie, Rosey.
2 *Mousy*, evidently from the colour, mouse-coloured.
4 Melly, from *melyn*, the Welsh for yellow.
5 The nails must originally have been *tiler's* nails, adopted from the surname, and developed later into *passion* nails.

The Wern (*the alders*) belonged in 1736 to James Powell, who with Martha his wife, at a court of the manor of Trelech on 2 December, 1736, surrendered it to the use of William Paske, to the use of Thomas Warner, Elizabeth his wife, and their heirs. In 1748 Thomas Warner surrendered the same to Thomas Morgan[1] and Joan his wife for life, remainder to their son William Morgan and Elizabeth his wife, remainder to William Morgan, jun. (son of the said William Morgan). In 1762 William Morgan (son of Thomas Morgan) and Elizabeth his wife, and William Morgan their son, and Thomas Williams surrendered the Wern, with closes called the Wern, the Upper Graig, the Middle Graig, Cefn-y-wern, Gworlod sladock, and Cae Saeson bach, in the tenure of Evan Young, to the use of George Catchmayd in trust for the said Thomas Williams for life, remainder to Mary Tanner in fee.

In 1775 a mortgage-deed was executed between Philip Stead of the 1st part, John Mills of the 2nd part, Mary Tanner, widow, and David Tanner

her son of the 3rd part, John Hopkins[1] of the 4th part, by which John Hopkins advances 4000*l*. on this and other property. In 1800 the Wern and Cae Saeson were sold by the executors of sir John Hopkins for 720*l*. to Lewis Richards of Troy.

On Mitchel Troy common, now enclosed, is an ancient house known merely by the name of the Commin,[2] long the residence of a family of Davis. Walter Davis of this place was father of John Davis, rector of Grosmont 1746, which he resigned in 1772 on being appointed vicar of Monmouth. His son Duncombe Pyrke Davis succeeded his father as vicar of Monmouth in 1798. On the death of Duncombe Pyrke Davis in 1815 this small estate, together with a large farm called the Hill in Grosmont, became the property of his relative in the half-blood Joseph Pyrke, formerly Watts. The Commin has recently been sold by Duncombe Pyrke to . . . . Denston.

As the Pyrke and Davis families are closely connected with this county I give their pedigree.

---

1 *Vide* pedigree, p. 166.

1 Afterwards sir John Hopkins, knt. (*vide* Vol. I., p. 129).

2 A Common is called by Welsh people *Commin*.

Pedigree of the families of Pyrke of Little Dean and Davis of Mitchel Troy.

ARMS OF PYRKE.—*Arg., on a fesse sa. 3 mullets of the field, a canton ermines.*

RICHARD PYRKE of Mitchel Dean⊤Joan, dau. to John Aylway.

Thomas Pyrke of Little Dean, gent.⊤Deborah, dau. to Richard Yate of Arlingham, esq.; ob. 9 Feb. 1662. M.I. Abenhall

Nathaniel Pyrke of Little Dean, esq., ob. 28 Oct. 1715, æt. 62. M.I. Abenhall.⊤Mary, dau. to sir Duncombe Colchester, knt., by Elizabeth, dau. to sir John Maynard, knt., serjeant-at-law; bapt. at Abenhall 29 April 1662; ob. 22 Nov. 1738, æt. 76. M.I. Abenhall.

William Rowles of Cockshut in Newnham, gent.⊤Mary.

Thomas Walter of Stapleton, co. Glouc.⊤Mary.

Thomas Pyrke of Little Dean, esq.⊤Dorothy, dau. to Richard Yate of Arlingham, esq.

Duncombe Pyrke of Bristol, gent.⊤Elizabeth, dau. to William Gwillym of Langston, co. Hereford, esq.

Nathaniel. — Deborah. Ob. infantes.

Jane⊤Rowles Walter of Stapleton, esq.

Walter Davis of Mitchel Troy, gent.⊤Elizabeth, ...

Thomas Pyrke, eldest son, matric. Pembroke College, Oxford, 1734, æt. 17; s.p. — Charles Pyrke, matric. Balliol College, Oxford, 1737, æt. 16, B.A. 1741; s.p.

Nathaniel Pyrke, ob. 10 Jan. 1748, æt. 31. — Maynard Pyrke; s.p.

Bridget; s.p. — Dorothy; s.p.

Nathaniel Pyrke; s.p.

Joseph Watts, clk., of the Hill in Grosmont, rector of Llangua 1734. 1st husband.⊤Elizabeth, in her issue heir to the Pyrkes. 2nd wife of John Davis.⊤John Davis, clk., D.D., rector of Grosmont 1746 to 1772, vicar of Monmouth 1772; born at Mitchel Troy 2 July 1720; matric. Queen's College, Oxford, 1739; D.D. 1769; ob. 1798.⊤Margaret, dau. to William Robinson, clk., rector of Mitchel Troy; mar. at St. Maughan's 17 Nov. 1746; ob. 31 Jan. 174¾, æt. 24. M.I. 1st wife of John Davis.

Joseph Watts of Little Dean, esq., assumed the name of PYRKE; matric. Balliol College, Oxford, 1759, æt. 18.⊤Charlotte, dau. to George Evans of Gray's Inn, esq.

Mary.

Thomas Leech⊤Elizabeth. of Monmouth. 1st wife.

Duncombe Pyrke Davis, clk., vicar of Monmouth 1798 to 1815; bapt. at Grosmont 21 April 1753; matric. Queen's College, Oxford, 1769, M.A. 1776; ob. 8 April 1815; bur. at Monmouth. M.I.

Dorothy, ob. 9 Dec. 1816, æt. 64. M.I.

Elizabeth, bap. at Grosmont 29 Sep. 1747; ob. 6 Feb. 1815, æt. 66. M.I.

Joseph Pyrke of Little Dean, esq., verdurer of the Forest of Dean, born 1774; ob. 1851.⊤Elizabeth, dau. to Thomas Apperley of Wootton, co. Glouc., gent.

George Pyrke, clk., rector of Whitchurch, co. Hereford, 1815; matric. Queen's College, Oxford, 1801, æt. 18; M.A. 1808; ob. 1852.

Duncombe Pyrke of Little Dean, esq., verdurer of the Forest of Dean, ob. 7 Dec. 1893.⊤Harriet Jemima, dau. to William Mairis, clk., vicar of Bishop's Lavington, co. Wilts.

Duncombe Pyrke of Little Dean, esq.⊤Susan, dau. to Thomas Evans of Gloucester, M.D.

The Church.

Of the foundation of the church there is no record, nor does it appear in the *Liber Landavensis*, but from its being called in Welsh Llanfihangel Troddi it is dedicated to St. Michael. The building consists of chancel, and nave with aisles on each side separated from it by handsome early-English arches. These arches and the tower at the west end are almost all that is left of the original church, for *the restoration* in the year 1876 was so thorough that the whole edifice with these exceptions was practically rebuilt. In the garden of the rectory-house can be seen several *rockeries* composed of dressed stones, which once formed part of the doorways and windows of the old church. For many years previous to 1876 the arches on the north of the nave had been filled up with masonry, thus forming the north wall of the church.[1] In this year the masonry was removed and the north aisle rebuilt on the old foundations. An inscription placed on the south wall in 1876 states that the church was built in 1208. There is nothing to shew how this date was arrived at, but it is probable that the church was built about that time by the Clares, lords of Usk and Trelech, and that the tower, so far as the ridge of the roof, was built at the same time. The portion of the tower above this was probably added later, a decorated window and the handsomely-moulded string-course pointing to the next century.

MITCHEL TROY CHURCH.

The tower is built of the local pudding-stone, some of the stones being of great size. At the south-west angle of the tower is a huge stone above five feet from the ground as hard as flint, on which is inscribed in runic letters—

✠ ORATE PRO GODEFRE
DO ET IOHANNE ✠

The date of this would probably be the twelfth or thirteenth century, and may refer to the persons who built the tower. Who Godfrey and John were has not been discovered. The inscription appears to have escaped any alteration or emendation, owing probably to the fact that it is cut in a stone full of flint-like pebbles, the whole being too hard for an ordinary tool to make any impression on. .

The churchyard is entered by a lych-gate, and close by are the ancient stocks.

For many years the ancient font, a massive stone without ornamentation, lay in the garden at Troy, whither it had been taken after one of the restorations of the church, its place being taken by a fanciful one of modern design. The old font has been recently brought back to its old place, and is now once more used for the purpose for which it was intended.

The shaft of the ancient cross remains in the churchyard mounted on a base, below which are three steps. The shaft is four-sided with chamfered edges, on which are devices of shields and ball-flowers alternately.

The advowson of the living was in mediæval times in the hands of the lords of Usk and Trelech. In 1314 the advowson of Troy, with the chapel of Cwmcarvan, was returned as the property of Gilbert de Clare, earl of Gloucester and Hertford and lord of Newport, who was slain in that year at Bannockburn. The yearly value was 30 marks.[2] In 1322 the living, with other churches, was conveyed by Hugh le Despencer and Eleanor his wife to Elizabeth, widow of John de Burgh. With the lordship of Trelech it passed to William, 1st earl of Pembroke of the second creation, and so to viscount Windsor,

---

1 In the eighteenth century this north aisle was called the Evans' aisle, from having been appropriated to the Lydart family.
2 Close Rolls, Edw. II., 1313—18, p. 137.

and with that lordship was purchased by the 5th duke of Beaufort. It was sold with the estate of Troy to the late mr. Edward Arnott.

Cwmcarvan has always been considered a chapelry to Mitchel Troy, and the two livings are still held by the same incumbent.

The old book of registers begins with the year 1590 and continues until 1717. It has been ill-cared-for, and at some subsequent period has been irregularly bound. But though considered to be of Mitchel Troy there is nothing in it to confirm this, and the entries seem mostly to belong to Cwmcarvan. In 1662 this note appears:—

Res memorabiles hujus parochiæ Comcaruanensis in hoc registerio insertæ pro tredecim annis aliquo inuidioso et impio casu perderentur.—Wᵐ Morris.

LYCH-GATE AND STOCKS.

PATRON.	DATE OF INSTITUTION.	INCUMBENT.
. . . . . .	. . . .	Henry Mocelot. An indult from the pope dated 30 June, 1349, that he is to have a canonry in the cathedral of Salisbury, notwithstanding that he has the church of Troy.[1]
The king, by reason of the custody of the lands and heir of Edmund Mortimer, the late earl of March.	11 Sept. 1382.	Adam de Usk *alias* Porter. On 13 May, 1382, during the minority of Edmund Mortimer, earl of March, tenant in chief, a grant by the king was made to Adam Porter, clerk, for his maintenance in the schools of Oxford of 100s. yearly from the issues of the lordship of Usk until presented to a benefice, as he had by grant of the said Edmund at the request of Philippa his consort. This was cancelled because he was presented to the church of Troy 11 Sept., 7 Ric. II. Adam de Usk was a famous person, cleric, and lawyer, born at Usk about 1360. He has left a chronicle of his doings, *Chronicon Adæ de Usk*.[2] He was buried in Usk church, where is a brass to his memory. Resigned Mitchel Troy 1385 on presentation to Babcary, co. Somerset, in exchange with Hugh Wacham.[3]
Ibid. . . .	21 Sept. 1385.	Hugh Wacham, previously parson of Babcary.[3]
. . . . .	4 April 1391.	Thomas Terry.[4]
. . . . . .	. . . .	Richard Dyer; resigned 1410 in exchange with Thomas Gybones.[5]
The king, by reason of the minority of the earl of March.	12 March 1410.	Thomas Gybones, previously parson of Rodmarton in the diocese of Worcester.[5]
. . . . .	9 Feb. 1411.	Robert Lyster, chaplain.[6]
. . . . .	. . . .	William Burley, parson of Troy; ratification of his estate 3 June, 1411.[7]
. . . . .	. . . . 1434.	William Dylowe.[8]
. . . . .	. . . .	Sir John ap Howel ap Ievan Fychan, rector in 1454.[9]
. . . . .	. . . .	Sir Stephen Vaughan, parson in 1524.
. . . . .	. . . .	Alexander Johns, in 1535.[10]
. . . . .	. . . .	John Williams, LL.B., rector in 1560; non-resident in the diocese.[11]

1 Cal. of Papal Reg., vol. iii., p. 326.
3 *Cal. Rot. Pat.*, Ric. II., 1385—9, p. 22.
5 *Ibid.*, Hen. IV., 1408—13, p. 169.
8 Harl. MS. 49, G. 10.
10 *Valor Ecclesiasticus.*

2 Edited by sir Edward Maunde Thompson, K.C.B., 2nd edition, 1904.
4 *Ibid.*, Ric. II., 1388—92, p. 391.
6 *Ibid.*, p. 279.   7 *Ibid.*, p. 238.
9 From a deed (MSS. of late Thomas Wakeman).
11 Browne Willis.

PATRON.	DATE OF INSTITUTION.	INCUMBENT.
. . . . .	. . . . 1602.	Nathaniel Baxter, B.D. Magdalen College, Oxford. Was a leader of the puritan divines and tutor to sir Philip Sidney. Before coming to Mitchel Troy he held livings in England, and was warden of New College in Youghal in Ireland. While at Mitchel Troy he wrote the poem by which he is best remembered, *Ourania*, 1606.
		(Richard Lace[1] was curate in 1602, afterwards vicar of Rockfield.)
. . . . .	. . . . 1611.	Robert Robotham, M.A. and D.D. Magdalen Hall, Oxford, a Buckinghamshire man ; also in the same year appointed to the rectory of Llangibby ; archdeacon of Llandaff 1607. He married Frances, daughter of Francis Godwin, bishop of Llandaff.
William, 3rd earl of Pembroke, K.G.	1 Feb. 162¼.	Robert Hackett, M.A. Wadham College, Oxford, a Gloucestershire man; died of the plague July, 1625.
William, 3rd earl of Pembroke, K.G.	4 Aug. 1625.	James Whitney, M.A. Brasenose College, Oxford, a Herefordshire man; also rector of Donhead St. Andrew's, Wilts.
Philip, 5th earl of Pembroke and Montgomery.	28 Dec. 1631.	John Hardwick, M.A. Brasenose and Oriel Colleges, Oxford ; married Mary, daughter of William Gough of Willersley, co. Glouc., esq.; died 1666. Will dated 14 June, 1665 ; proved (P.C.C., Drax, 113) 15 October, 1683, by Mary the widow.
		To my dau. Mary Hardwick the lands bought by me of Laurence Browne in Hewelsfield and the reversion of all my right to the lands and tenements in the parishes of Hewelsfield and Woollaston, co. Glouc., in the tenures of widow White, widow Clerke, Wm. Evans, and Richard Pyner, the same to be confirmed by Thomas Morgan of Hurste, my trustee, my said dau. to have as much plate and household furniture as her sister had—to my dau. Evans 20*l.* on 11 Nov. next out of rent due from mr. Curre, also to her the rent of the *Christian Acre* and the purchase-money when it is sold—my books to my dau's and my cousin Eustace Hardwick—the lease lands in Hewelsfield to the use of my wife and my dau's—my wife Mary ex'trix.
Philip, 5th earl of Pembroke and Montgomery.	10 April 1666.	Richard Meredith, M.A.; died 1669-70.
William, 6th earl of Pembroke.	25 Feb. 16⁶⁶⁄₇₈.	Richard Vaughan ;[2] in 1674 appointed vicar of Wonastow.
William, 6th earl of Pembroke.	1 May 1672.	William Morris, died 1701-2.
		(John Lawlis, curate in 1695.)
Charles Tooker, esq., *pro hâc vice.*	12 Aug. 1702.	William Catchmayd, M.A. Jesus College, Oxford, son of William Catchmayd of Monmouth, gent.; previously vicar of Chepstow; died 25 Sept., 1709 ; buried in the church. M.I.
Thomas, 1st viscount Windsor.	9 Dec. 1709.	Thomas Andrews, M.A. Queen's College, Oxford, son of George Andrews of Battersea, gent.; also from 1703 vicar of Llanover ; died 1714.
		(William Gwillym, curate in 1713.)
Thomas, 1st viscount Windsor.	18 Feb. 171⁴⁄₅.	Edward James, B.A. Jesus College, Oxford, son of Lewis James, clk., rector of Llanvetherine; also vicar of Abergavenny and Llantilio Pertholey, the latter of which he resigned on appointment to Mitchel Troy; died 1719.
Thomas, 1st viscount Windsor.	3 Nov. 1719.	William Robinson, M.A. St. John's College, Cambridge ; also rector of Llansoy; died 31 May, 1740, aged 44; buried at Mitchel Troy. M.I.
		(William Samwell, licensed as curate to Mitchel Troy and Cwmcarvan 28 Oct., 1743.)
		(John Davies, licensed as curate of Mitchel Troy and Cwmcarvan 7 July, 1745 ; afterwards rector of Grosmont and vicar of Monmouth.)[3]
. . . . .	12 Dec. 1745.	James Martin, B.A.; buried 1 March, 1782.
. . . . .	About 1782.	Robert Penny, D.D. Oriel College, Oxford, son of Robert Penny of Castle Cary, co. Somerset, gent.; also vicar of Badminton and rector of Cwmdu; died 31 July, 1809.
Henry Charles, 6th duke of Beaufort, K.G.	2 Nov. 1809.	Richard Bohun Tomkyns, LL.B. New College, Oxford, son of Thomas Tomkyns of Buckenhill, co. Hereford, esq.; resigned 1825 on appointment to Saham Toney, co. Norfolk; died 19 April, 1833.
Henry Charles, 6th duke of Beaufort, K.G.	. . . . 1825.	Henry George Talbot, M.A. Christ Church, Oxford, son of Charles Talbot, clk., dean of Salisbury, son of George Talbot, clk., vicar of Ginting, co. Gloucester, 3rd son of Charles, 1st lord Talbot of Hensol; died 10 March, 1867.
Henry Charles, 8th duke of Beaufort, K.G.	. . . . 1867.	Boscawen Thomas George Henry Somerset, M.A. Oriel College, Oxford, 5th son of lord William George Henry Somerset, clk., 6th son of Henry, 5th duke of Beaufort, K.G.; resigned 1874 on appointment to Crickhowel.
Henry Charles, 8th duke of Beaufort, K.G.	. . . . 1874.	Robert William Everett, St. John's College, Oxford, son of Thomas Ellis Everett, clk., vicar of Rockfield; died 1885.
Henry Charles, 8th duke of Beaufort, K.G.	. . . . 1885.	Henry Marriott Tomson Bidwell, previously vicar of Magor; resigned 1911 ; ob. 1912.
Trustees of the late Edward Arnott, esq.	. . . . 1912.	Edwin Arnott, B.A. Lampeter, son of Edward Arnott of the Garth, esq.

---

1 Richard Lace was a local man, and B.A. Jesus College, Oxford, 5 Feb., 159⁴⁄₅. The name would appear to be *Glas* (blue). The will of George *Glace* of Wonastow is dated 9 Feb., 1630 ; proved at Llandaff 16 Feb., 1631. To be buried in the church of Wonastow—cathedral church of Landaff vj*d.*—for tithes vj*d.*—to Elizabeth my wife 24 ewes towards discharging debt to Howell Nicholas—to my dau. Marrie George 2 acres of corn in Maes Teylin—to my son Phe' oats that grow on the land of the widow Hughes. Signum Georgij Glace. In presence of John Wm. Griffith, John Wm. John.   **2** For his wife *vide* p. 62.   **3** For his pedigree *vide* p. 172.

Monumental Inscriptions.

ON NORTH WALL OF CHANCEL.

In memory of The reverend Henry George Talbot, M.A., who during 42 years was rector of this parish with Cwmcarvon. He was the eldest son of the reverend Charles Talbot, B.D., Dean of Salisbury, and of the Lady Elizabeth Somerset, daughter of Henry, 5th Duke of Beaufort, K.G. He married Mary Elizabeth, daughter of Major General the honourable Sir William Ponsonby, K.C.B., and dying on the 10th day of March, 1867, at the age of 68 years, was buried with his wife and only daughter at Allhallows, St. Giles, in the county of Dorset.

In a stained-glass window close by :

In memoriam Filiæ unicæ desideratissimæ Elizabethæ G. Talbot, ob. 1855, æt. 18.

A modern brass :

In this Chancel rest the bodies of—

Charles Tyler, who died 29 Oct., 1717, aged 76.
George Tyler,   „   „   11 Nov., 1737,   „   87.
Elizabeth Tyler, „   „   7 June, 1762,   „   80.
Charles Tyler,   „   „   30 Nov., 1776, „   61.
Charles Tyler,   „   „   7 Nov., 1793,   „   38.
James Tyler,   „   „   13 Mar., 1794, „   40.
                and also of

Charles James, James Tyler, and George the infant children of James Powles of Monmouth and Anne his wife, only daughter of James Tyler.
To the Glory of God.
In memory of the above named
James Powles and Anne his wife
stained glass was placed in the East
window of this Chancel, A.D. 1873.

ON SOUTH WALL OF CHANCEL.

In the vault beneath are deposited the remains of Arabella Montagu, wife of Arthur Wyatt of Troy in this parish, Esq. She was the daughter of the Revd Willm Higginson, M.A., rector & lord of the manor of Gretworth in Northamptonshire, by Elizabeth, eldest daughter of James Montagu of Lackham House and of Alderton in the county of Wilts, Esq. She died 3rd October 1818, aged 37 years.

Also here rests the body of her husband, Arthur Wyatt, of whose endearing virtues his bereaved children make this inadequate record. He died the 8th of June 1833, aged 58.

In memory of Helen Montagu, third daughter of Arthur Wyatt and Arabella Montagu his wife, of Troy House in this Parish, born November 30, 1812. She died at Troy, March 10, 1844, and is buried in this church.

Also of Blanch Montagu, eldest daughter of the above Arthur and Arabella Montague Wyatt, born December 21, 1805. She died in London, October 20, 1846, and is buried at Kensal Green in the county of Middlesex.

To the memory of Emma Montagu, 4th daughter of the late Arthur Wyatt of Troy House in this parish. Born May 1st, 1816. She died at Tuebrook, Liverpool, Dec. 29, 1881.

Sacred to the memory of William Buck,[1] who died July xvth, MDCCCXXXIV, aged LXXV years.
Also of his widow Mary Ann Buck, who died Jan. v, MDCCCL, aged LXIV years.

---

1 He lived at Gibraltar in the parish of Monmouth.

A window has the following :—
In memoriam conjugis beatifsimæ Mariæ Talbot, ob. 1838, æt. 27.

ON WALL OF NORTH AISLE.

Iuxta
Deponuntur Cineres
WILLIELMI CATCHMAYD
A.M.
hujus Parochiæ
per spatium Septem
annorum Rectoris
ob. 25 Sept.
1709.

Arms below : *Barry of 6, a canton erm.*

IN THE EAST WINDOW OF NORTH AISLE.

Beneath the badge of the Prince of Wales' Regiment the arms : *Quarterly arg. and sa. 3 lions pass. guard. counterchanged, a spear or, headed ppr. in bend.* Crest : *A lion pass. guard. per pale arg. and sa. holding an anchor.*

In memory of Sydney Arthur Trower, 98th (the Prince of Wales) regt, as a token of esteem & affection by his brother officers, 19 Nov. 1878.

ON THE SOUTH WALL OF SOUTH AISLE.

A brass :

Sacred to the beloved memory of Lieutenant Cornwallis Jasper Trower, Royal Navy, H.M.S. Boadicea, fourth son of George S.[1] Trower, Esq. He was killed in action at the battle of Majuba Hill, Transvaal, 27 February, 1881, aged 26.

IN A WINDOW ON EAST END OF SOUTH AISLE.

In memory of Edward Oakeley Trower, Lieut. 75th Regt, who died Novr 7th, 1875.

ON THE WEST WALL OF SOUTH AISLE.

A brass :

To the glory of God and in loving memory of Edward William Henry Somerset,[2] Lieut. 1st Battn Prince Consort's own Rifle Brigade. Born January 25th, 1866. Died at Bareilly, India, March 20, 1890.

A brass :

To the glory of God and in loving memory of Evelyn, beloved wife of G. Caulfeild Browne, daur of Lt-General E. Somerset, C.B., died July 1st, 1883, leaving a son Evelyn, born July 1st, 1883. This tablet is erected by her sorrowing mother-in-law Honble Mrs Geo. Browne.

IN A WINDOW AT WEST END OF SOUTH AISLE.

To the glory of God and in loving memory of General E. A. Somerset, C.B., who died March 12th, 1886, this window is erected by his sorrowing children.

ON THE WEST WALL OF NAVE.

In grateful remembrance of the Christian virtues and parental tenderness of Ann, wife of James Hardwick and relict of James Tyler of Monmouth, who resigned her soul into the hands of our great Redeemer on the 15th day of July 1834, in the 76th year of her age.

---

1 Sydney.
2 Son of general Edward Arthur Somerset, C.B.

To the memory of Julia Eliza Oakeley, eldest daughter of Thomas Oakeley, Esqʳᵉ, of Lydart House, who died the 16ᵗʰ of June 1843, aged 25 years.

The following are in the tower, but were once in the church :—

In Memory of
Mary yᵉ wife of
William Tyleʳ
Daught of John
& Dorithy Probiⁿ,
who Died Decʳ
yᵉ 2ᵈ, 1760, aged
58 Years.1

In memory of Ja . . . . of this Parish, died 28 June, 18 . ., Aged 16 yʳˢ.

Also in memory of Margaret, Dautʳ of James Goodall by Mary his Wife, who died the 6ᵗʰ of February, 1812, aged 29 yʳˢ.

Also Benjamin Goodall, died Febʳʸ 6, 1818, aged 21 years.

In memory of Hannah Hopkin of this Parish, Spinster, who died May the 28ᵗʰ, 1788, Aged 22 years.

Also in memory of Frances, Wife of John Williams of this Parish, who died 7 Novʳ 1787, aged 28 yʳˢ.

FLAT STONES IN THE NORTH AISLE.

Here lyeth the body of Cornelius, the son of Francis & Ann Young of this Parish, who departed this Life April the 10ᵗʰ, 1794, aged 2 years and 11 months.

Near this place lieth the Body of Francis Young, who died 5 April, 1820, Aged 66 years.

Ann Young died 30 March, 1822, Aged 68 years.

Here lyeth the body of Mary, the wife of John Williams, who departed this life the two and twentieth day of Aprill anno domini 1705.

And here lyeth the Body of John Williams, who departed this life July the ninth day anno domini 1724.

Catherine Williams, died 7 December 1735, aged 84.
John Young, died 20 June 1785, aged 63.

Elizabeth, wife of John Ambros and daughter of Thomas Morgan of Troy, farmer, died 6 September 1749, aged 32.

Ann, daughter of Thomas and Jone Morgan, died 9 December 1740, aged 18.

FLAT STONE IN THE SOUTH AISLE.

HERE RESTETH THE BODY OF IOHN CVR [*broken*]2 GENT. HEE WAS BORN AT STVBBWOOD IN THE PARISH OF HVNGERFORD IN THE COVNTY OF BARKS, LATE OF TROY IN THIS PARISH, WHO DEPARTED THIS LIFE WITH CERTAINE HOPE OF THE RESVRREC TION THE 6 DAY OF IVLIE IN THE YEAR OF OVR LORD GOD 1685, IN THE YEAR OF HIS AGE 63.

---

1 John Probyn, gent., was of the Loisey in Trelech. The parish register has—4 Dec. 1760, Mary, wife of William Tyler of Carllion in our county.

2 The stone has been cut to fit the paving. The spelling ought to be Curre. This John Curre, who was steward to the 1st duke of Beaufort, is ancestor of the family long seated at Itton.

VOL. II.

CHURCHYARD.

An altar-tomb handsomely carved with marble coigns. On the north side :

IN MEMORY
OF JOHN BURGH, ESQ., WHO DIED APRIL
THE 25, 1740, AGED 67.
A Man of fingular Efteem both in publick and private Life, whofe ruling Paffion was to do good and whofe whole Conduct fpoke him The Generoufe, Humane, and Honeft Man.

On the south side :

He married Lidia, Daughter of Henry Clark of Moulfey in the County of Surrey, Efq., And had Iffue by her feven Sons and five Daughters, who died the 22 of April 1718 And lies Buried in the Chancell of Great Badminton in the County of Gloucefter, with John and Thomas their Eldeft and Youngeft Sons.

ON THE SOUTH OF THE CHANCEL.

A flat stone :

Gulielmus Robinson, A.M., in Parochiâ de Crosby Garret in Agro Westmariensi natus, Ecclesiæ Mitchel Troy & Lansoy in Comitatu Monumethensi Rector, Coll. S. Johannis apud Cantabrigien. Studiis academicis instructus. Vir ingenio summo, judicio accurato, facundiâ singulari, affabilitate & comitate, Nulli Secundus, Vitam innoxiam exegit, Opes neglexit & quam . . . . satis habuit, sub hoc tumulo quidquid erat mortale depos . . . . 31 Maii A.D. 1740, Ætat. 44.2 Hic jacet Margareta, Uxor charifsima Johannis Davis, Cler., filia Gul. Robinson, Obiit 31 Januarii A.D. 1747, Æt. 24.

Qua nihil majus meliusve terris
Fata donavere bonique Divi,
Nec dabunt, quamvis redeant in aurum
Tempora priscum.3

A flat stone :
In memory of Ann, wife of James Hardwick and relict of James Tyler, who died July 15ᵗʰ, 1831, in the 76 year of her age.

Also Charles Tyler, died 18ᵗʰ April 1851, Aged 64.

An altar-tomb :

Here
lieth Sarah the wife of John
Colfon and daughter of
Charles and Elizabeth Tyler
of Monmouth, who departed
this life Oct. yᵉ 9ᵗʰ, 1745
Aged 37 years.

---

1 The bill for making this tomb is as follows :—
Rece'd this 25ᵗʰ of Novʳ 1741 of Mʳ Henry Burgh One Hundred Pound one Shilling & sixpence for errecting a Tomb for his late Father in Mitchel Troy Churchyard, in full for carriage, stone, smith's work, & all other demands whatsoever. p' me Mich. Tidnell.

2 31 May 1740. William Robinson, rectʳ, dises'd, and was buried June yᵉ second (par. reg.). *Vide* pedigree, p. 172.

3 Horace, iv., 2, 33.

A A

An altar-tomb.   On the north side :

In memory of ANN, the wife of JAMES RICHARDS, who died y⁰ 2 of March 1801, aged 80 years.

Also JAMES RICHARDS, died Sept. y⁰ 14, 1802, aged 80 years.

On the top :

To the memory of ANN DOWDING, daughter of J. & A. Richards, died July 10th, 1834, aged 81 years.

_____

An altar-tomb.   On the top :

In memory of Jane, daughter of James and Ann Richards of this parish, who died April 29th, 1760, aged 10 years.

Also Maudlin, daughter of the above, who died May 4th, 1760, aged 5 months.

Also in memory of George Richards, son of the above named, who died April 25th, 1785, aged 28 years.

_____

An upright stone :

In memory of ELIZABETH, the wife of MATHEW Heydon of this Pariſh, who died Dec. the 12th, 1791, aged 35 years.

_____

ON THE WALL OF THE PORCH.

In
Memory of philip
Stead,¹ who died des-
ember the 13th
1736, Aged 67.

Life is Unsartain
And deth is so shuer
Sin is the wound
& Christ is the Cuer.

_____

¹ The family of Stead (pronounced *Steed*) has been long resident in this parish. 5 Sept. 1764, buried Thomas Stead, clerk of this parish 30 years (par. reg.).

A flat stone :

Here
Lyeth the Body of John
Appletree, who departed
this Life y⁰ 20th day of
february Anno Dom.
1733, Aged 36.
Here
Lyeth the Body of Anne
Harris of this Parish, widow,
shee died the 9th day of July
1751, Aged 70 years.
Also here lieth y⁰ Body of
Margaret, Sister to y⁰ above
Nam'd Ann Harris, who died
y⁰ 24th of Sept. 1761, Aged 71.
Also the Body of Jane, y⁰ Wife
of William Williams, who died
the 19th of Janʸ 1771, Aged 55.

_____

John Appletree, died 30 April 1743.
Mary his wife, died 29 January 1757, aged 74.
Francis Appletree, son of the above, died 25 December 1769, aged 63.

_____

James Appletree, died 9 April 1762, aged 16.

_____

Lydia, wife of John Power and daughter of Richard & Elizabeth Hills, late of Lympne, co. Kent, ob. 24 Feb. 1840, æt. 72.

_____

John Power of Wraheen, co. Kilkenny, Ireland, ob. 7 Aug. 1841, æt. 64.

_____

John Dowding, ob. 28 July 1834, æt. 73.

_____

ADDITIONS TO WONASTOW.

Although not in the parish now being dealt with, it may be desirable to here give an account of two farms in Wonastow, the particulars of which have come to hand since the first volume of this work was printed.

Worthy brook belonged in 1672 to John Hughes, who with Mary his wife, by indentures made 18 April, 1672, conveyed this estate to Edward Lewis. The latter, by his will dated 20 March, 1675, left it after the death of his (testator's) wife Joan (who afterwards married Thomas Blackbourne) to William Lewis. By indentures made 5 and 6 February, 1675, William Lewis, the devisee, and Martha his wife, Thomas Blackbourne and Joan his wife, granted the property in mortgage to John Morgan, who the next year became possessor. By indentures made 28 and 29 September, 1697, John Morgan, Rebecca his wife, and John Morgan their only son, mortgaged it for 350*l.* to Richard Bond. In 1708 Richard Bond and Elizabeth Taylor, widow (devisee of the last John

Morgan), sold the property for 950*l.* to Charles Harford, described as—

All that capital messuage called Worthy Brook with appurt's, and also those five closes of land called Gworlod uwch lawr y ty, with a sheep cot at the upper end thereof, the Trippen piece, Kae mawr, Cae yr greeg, Kae main, Gworlod ffrood, and all those seven parcels with ten acres of coppice wood called Tyre gwern y saint, situated in Wonastow between the lands of his grace the duke of Beaufort, the lands of William Jones, esq., and the highway leading from Dingestow's bridge towards Monmouth, theretofore in the possession of John Morgan the elder; and also that meadow called Gworlod ar lan Trothy in Wonastow and Llangattock Vibon Avel, and also that parcel of arable called Gworlod y ffrood in Wonastow.

Reference is made to a deed dated 9 March, 1692, by which John Morgan sold to John Symons—

All his iron cinders raised out of lands in the parish of Monmouth called Monnow, containing 3000 dozen bushels of cinders, redeemable on payment, etc.

In 1719 Charles Harford purchased the cinders from Symons and Elizabeth Taylor. By his will, dated 12 April, 1723, he devised the premises to his son Truman Harford. The latter, in his will dated 11 July, 1751, names his four sons, Charles, James, John, and Richard. In 1766 James Harford sold the premises to John Thomas in trust for William Morgan. Later Worthy brook was purchased by the owners of Wonastow.

New Wonastow belonged in 1760 to the duke of Beaufort. By indentures made 23 and 24 June, 1760, the earl of Lichfield and Norborne Berkeley, esq., devisees in fee of the then late duke of Beaufort, conveyed to John Thomas New Wonastow in trust for the above William Morgan and Elizabeth his wife. In 1773 William Morgan and Elizabeth his wife conveyed the same to Daniel Williams, who purchased for, or sold soon after to Charles Milborne of Wonastow, esq., or his daughter Mary, wife of Thomas Swinnerton, esq. New Wonastow continued hereafter part of the estate of Wonastow until it was recently sold with Worthybrook, under the small holdings act, to the county council by sir Thomas Pilkington.

The Harfords mentioned above as owners of Worthybrook were a quaker family settled in Bristol, whose origin was from Bosbury in Herefordshire. By the purchase of cinders by Charles Harford in 1719 they would seem to have had a forge on the Monnow close to Monmouth. Of the sons of Truman Harford, James, then of Bristol, in partnership with Jeremiah Homfray (afterwards sir Jeremiah Homfray), John Partridge of Monmouth, Richard Summers (whose daughter Anne was the wife of James Harford), Philip Crocker, Thomas Prichard the younger, and Samuel Harford (son of James Harford), established in 1796 the ironworks at Ebbw Vale, previously worked in a comparatively small way by Walter Watkins and Charles Cracroft. John founded the works at Nant-y-glo in 1795.[1] Some account of these works will be found under their respective parishes. As this branch of the Harfords were much connected with this county I give their pedigree.[2]

---

[1] Vol. I., p. 475.
[2] Further information will be found in *The Annals of the Harford Family*, 1909.

Pedigree of the family of Harford.

CHARLES HARFORD of Bristol.⊤

Charles Harford of Bristol, purchased Worthybrook ⊤ Rachel, dau. to John Truman. | Edward Harford ⊤ Elizabeth, dau. to Charles Jones, said to be grandson of Hugh Jones, bishop of Llandaff.
in 1718. Will dated 12 April 1723. | of Bristol.

A quo HARFORD of Falcondale, Blaise castle, etc.

Truman Harford of Bristol.⊤ Mary, dau. to .... Taylor of Baldock, co. Hertford. | William Lyne of Keynsham, co. Somerset ⊤ Mary.
Will dated 11 July 1751.

1. Charles Harford, under age in 1751. | 2. James Harford ⊤ Anne, dau. to Richard Summers. of Ebbw Vale, ironmaster; sold Worthybrook 1766. | 3. John Harford = Beatrice, dau. to John Harman. of Nant-y-glo, ironmaster, 1795; ob. s.p. 1816. | 4. Richard Harford of Keynsham, esq.; assumed by royal licence the name of LYNE 9 March 1820. ⊤ Grizel, dau. to .... Green. | Elizabeth, mar. John Harman. | Edward Lyne.

Thomas Harford ⊤ Mary, dau. to .... Biddle. of Limehouse, brewer. | Samuel Harford, at Ebbw Vale in 1796. | John Harford. | Mary. — Elizabeth. | Sarah. — Sophia. | Henry Harford of Keynsham, esq.; assumed by royal licence the name of LYNE 20 Dec. 1826. ⊤ Elizabeth .... | Charles Richard Harford. | Edwin Harford.

James Harford. | Truman Harford. | Edmund Biddle Harford. | Richard Summers Harford of Chew Magna. | Harford Lyne of Keynsham, esq., living 1908.

Cwmcarban.

WMCARVAN would be more correctly written Cwm Carfan, the valley of the Carfan brook that runs under the church and so through the centre of the parish into the Trothy.

The parish contains 3003 acres of land; the rateable value in 1815 was 1835*l.*, and in 1912, 1680*l.*

The population has been as follows :—

Year .	1801	1811	1821	1831	1841	1861	1871	1881	1891	1911
No. of Inhab.	177	279	293	301	315	332	321	240	215	258

The number of houses is shewn thus :—

Year.	Inhabited houses.	Uninhabited houses.	Building.
1861 . . .	65	10	0
1871 . . .	66	7	0
1881 . . .	54	11	0
1891 . . .	53	6	1
1901 . . .	55	5	0

Cwmcarvan formed part of the lordship of Trelech and descended in the same way. In the *inquisitio post mortem* of Gilbert de Clare, earl of Gloucester and Hertford, who was slain at Bannockburn, dated 18 August, 3 Edw. II. (1329), is, among much other property—

> Cwmcarvan and Leydarth [Lydart] 824½ acres held by Welsh customers, a water mill, etc.

In 1570 there were in Cwmcarvan 16 free tenants and 48 copyholders.

The parish slopes from the height of 800 feet, where it joins Trelech at the top of Cwm-bychan and Croes-Robert woods, in a northernly direction to the river Trothy, 100 feet above sea level. The brooks all run in the same direction. The Carvan rises at the Glanau, and flowing below the church on the eastern side divides the parish nearly in half. The Pencam rises in the woods above Cwm-bychan, and keeping below the church on the western side joins the Trothy below the Bourne. The Llymon rises near Pen-y-lan, and passing Llanthomas joins the Pencam at the Lower-house or Ty-isha. The Pinket rises at Upper Pen-y-clawdd, and before joining the Pencam, near the Bourne, runs parallel with the Pencam for half a mile, the two brooks being only separated by meadows about 200 yards wide.

There is the base of an ancient cross at the junction of the roads between Crofft-y-lloi and the church, and there is another, sexagonal in shape, half a mile south-east of the church in the lane leading to Cwm-collier.[1]

A prominent feature in the parish is the hill called Graig-y-dorth (*the rock of the loaf*). This rises to the height of 785 feet, and on the ordnance map is marked *Site of battle, A.D.* 1404. This refers to a battle won by Owen Glyndwr against the English, but the date is more probably 1402. It was in 1402 that Owen with a force of 30,000 men overthrew the castles of Usk, Caerlleon and Newport, and fired the towns, doing similarly throughout Wales.[1]

Cwmcarban Court.

The estate attached to this residence is the result of many purchases from small freeholders in the parish by James, Lewis, and James Richards, who were stewards to the dukes of Beaufort in the eighteenth and early part of the nineteenth century. The house occupies the site of a small farm-house called Ffos-y-bwla (*the ditch of the cattle*), and was built by James Richards about the year 1820. The first Lewis Richards is described as a coppersmith of Mitchel Troy, and his son Lewis was taken when a boy into the duke's office at Troy and rose to be steward of the duke's manors. His daughter Mary married .... Tucker and emigrated to America, as is shewn by the following appointment of her brother James as her attorney :—

> 30 July, 1753. Before me William Winter, notary and tabellion publick, by royal authority duly admitted and sworn, practising in Boston in New England, and witnefses, personally appeared Mary Tucker of Boston in the county of Suffolk and province of Massachusetts Bay, widow, and (as she declares) the only surviving daughter of Lewis Richards late of Mitchel Troy near Monmouth in Wales in the kingdom of Great Britain, coppersmith, deceased, who by these presents doth appoint her beloved brother James Richards of Mitcheltroy her attorney, etc. Mary Tucker [*L.S.*]. Witnesses : A. Francis, John Belcher [*L.S.*].

The affidavit of execution is signed by Abraham Francis of Boston, New England, mariner, and John Belcher, late of the same, mariner. Sworn at Bristol before John Clements, mayor, 24 September, 1753.

Ffoes-y-bwla (the site of Cwmcarvan Court) belonged in 1696 to John Jones of Llangarren, co. Hereford, gent. (described afterwards as living in

---

[1] Collier here means, not a man who raises pit coal, but a charcoal burner.

[1] *Nam* [Owenus] *totam Walliam cum ejus marchiâ, triginta millium de cavernis exeuntium consortio stipatus, omnia partium castra, inter quae de Usk, Carlyon et Nuportu, subvertit ac oppida succendit.*—Chronicon Adæ de Usk, 1377—1421, 1904, p. 78.

the city of London 6 June, 1696), who surrendered a parcel of land so called containing 3 acres to Charles Jones of Mitchel Troy, joiner.

At a court held 25 November, 1743, William Jones of Mitchel Troy, yeoman (one of the sons and customary heirs of Richard Jones, late of the same parish, yeoman, deceased), surrendered the same to Thomas Watkins of St. Dial's in the parish of Monmouth, husbandman, and Mary his wife. At a court held 20 April, 1753, Richard Jones of the parish of All Saints, Bristol, yeoman (one of the sons and customary heirs of Richard Jones of Mitchel Troy, yeoman, deceased), surrendered a moiety of Ffoes-y-bwla to the said Thomas Watkins. Ffoes-y-bwla was afterwards purchased by Lewis Richards, and on 14 October, 1815, James Richards was admitted as son and heir of Lewis Richards. At a court held 26 September, 1843, James Richards, nephew of the said Lewis Richards, was admitted.

The farm called the Old Mill was conveyed by indentures dated 23 December, 1761, to William Tanner of Monmouth, esq., by Stephen Comyn, esq., and John Smith, gent., both of Lincoln's Inn, for 472*l.* 10*s.* Indentures are recited dated 2 January, 1759, between John Jones of Llanarth Court, esq., surviving trustee of the will of John Jones, late of Dingestow, esq., deceased ; Richard Jones of Dingestow, esq. (eldest son and heir of the said John Jones) ; and Edmund Rumsey Bradbury of Pilston in Llandogo, gent., an infant (only son and heir of Edmund Bradbury, late of Pen-y-clawdd, esq., who was the surviving trustee of the settlement made 13 January, 1732, upon the marriage of the said Richard Jones and Mary his wife, John Duncombe of [*blank*], esq., and Margaret his wife, one of the daughters of the said John Jones, deceased), of the first part, and others.

The Old Mill was sold by Charles Phillips of Monmouth, esq., grandson of William Tanner, to Lewis Richards in 1800.

Two meadows called the Mill Meadows were conveyed by the above Stephen Comyn by indenture dated 14 November, 1761, to Thomas Rosser of the Gockett, gent., for 110*l.*, described as two pieces of meadow, pasture and arable lands called Ynys[1] and Gworlod uwch y berllan.[2]

The farm called the Gocket[3] was at a court baron of viscount Windsor, lord of the manor of Trelech, held 17 February 1748, surrendered by William Fortune of Monmouth, gent., and John Rowland of Penallt, yeoman, to the use of Thomas Rosser. The property is described as—

All that mansion house called the Gockett with closes called Cae-hendre, Prisg-bach, Maes-mawr, Drain, Cae-Jack, Gworlod-cae-bach, Grove-cae-bach, Tir penty-bach, and a messuage called Brith-dy with gardens, orchards, etc., and a piece of land called Cae'r-gollen, all in the manor of Trelech, by the lands of Mrs Kemeys, of Thomas Gwyn, John Probyn, Thomas Griffiths, the lane from the Gockett house to

Cwmcarvan church and the lord's waste called the Gockett hill, in the possession of Thomas Rosser ; and three-eights part of a piece called Trawstor.

On 21 June, 1826, William Rosser and others, mortgagees and trustees, surrendered the same to James Richards.

On 5 September, 1829, George Ballard surrendered to James Richards Cae'r-ywen, 4 acres, and Bwlch-y-gwynt, situate near the road from Monmouth to Trelech and Graig-y-dorth.

The farm called Graig-y-dorth was at a court of the manor of Trelech on 26 November, 1762, surrendered by Stephen Comyn of Lincoln's Inn, esq., John Jones, late of Llanarth Court but now of Clytha, esq., Richard Jones of Dingestow, esq., and Edmond Rumsey Bradbury of Pilston in Llandogo, gent., then in the tenure of Robert Hitchens, to John Young of Mitchel Troy, yeoman, and Anne his wife. In 1782 John Young and Ann his wife surrendered to Francis Young of Cwmcarvan, butcher, and Anne his wife, and in 1813 these last surrendered to Francis Young their son. In 1818 Francis Young, sen. and jun., surrendered to Jonathan Powell of Monmouth, corndealer ; and in 1825 James Powell of Bristol, tanner (only son and customary heir of the said Jonathan Powell, deceased, a mortgagee of the premises), was admitted and surrendered the same to Benjamin Green of Monmouth, victualler, who sold to George Morgan, who in 1831 sold to James Richards.

The executors of the family of Richards have recently sold Cwmcarvan Court, with much of the land, to captain Walters, R.N., of Cae'r-llan.

Cwm-bychan.

Cwm-bychan (*the little cwm* or *dingle*), of which I have no account till 1761, is said to have been a mansion of importance.

By indenture dated 23 October, 1761, Stephen Comyn of Lincoln's Inn, esq., conveyed to George Catchmayd of Monmouth, gent., in consideration of 400*l.*, all that messuage, etc., called Cwm-bychan, then in the possession of Richard Jones of Dingestow, esq. In 1773 John Rollings of Monmouth, timber merchant, and Susanna his wife, George Catchmayd, esq., and others conveyed the same to William Lane of Gloucester, gent., for 1232*l.* 10*s.* By indentures dated 25 March, 1774, between the rt. hon. Henry, lord Chedworth, baron of Chedworth, co. Gloucester, and William Lenthall of Burford, co. Oxford, esq., of the 1st part ; John Grayhurst of the Grange in Llanfihangel Ystern Llewern, esq., and Margaret his wife of the 2nd part ; and John Gwynn of Cwmcarvan, yeoman, and William Mathews of Tre-Worgan in Llangarren, co. Hereford, yeoman, of the 3rd part ; reciting a release dated 3 April, 1773, between William Lane of Gloucester, gent., the said John Grayhurst (therein described as of Farmington, co. Gloucester, esq.), of the 1st part, the said Margaret his wife by the name of Margaret Strachan of Haymes Place, co. Gloucester, spinster, of the 2nd

---

1 *The island.* 2 *The meadow above the orchard.*
3 As to the word Gocket, *vide* p. 129.

part; and sir William Strachan of Haymes Place, bart. (brother of the said Margaret), and William Baghot de la Bere of Southam, co. Gloucester, esq., of the 3rd part, being a marriage settlement between the said John Grayhurst and Margaret of lands in Farmington and Little Barrington, co. Gloucester, and of Cwm-bychan (the latter purchased of William Lane with the marriage trust moneys), the latter property is conveyed to John Gwynn and William Matthews in trust for John Gwynn in fee.

In 1782 Cwm-bychan was mortgaged by John Gwynn and Elizabeth his wife to John Partridge of the Forge in the parish of Monmouth, ironmaster, and in 1835 Cwm-bychan was sold to John Ralph Norton Norton of Monmouth, attorney, for 2036l. In 1841 Norton sold the same to James Richards of Cwmcarvan, esq., for 1976l.

According to the story prevalent in the parish Cwm-bychan was the most important house within it, but of this I know nothing, except that around the shed which occupies the site there are considerable remains of foundations.

At the Middle Cwm are some large stone pillars supporting a shed; these were brought from the old mansion of Cwm-bychan.

A house and lands called Cae'r-bont, Gworlod-fach, Cae'r-ysgubor, Cae'r-quarrel and Cae'r-odyn, comprising 20 acres bounded by the lands of Francis Mills, gent., the glebe of Cwmcarvan, lands of Charles Phillips, of James Richards and the road from Ffosydd to Cwmcarvan church, were surrendered at a court held 6 October, 1787, by Thomas Evans of Llangattock Vibon Avel, esq., to Isaac Pask of Cwmcarvan, yeoman, for life, with remainder to Isaac Pask, jun., of Melin Griffith, co. Glamorgan, yeoman, for life, remainder to James Pask of London, carpenter (son of the said Isaac Pask, sen.), for life, remainder to Elizabeth, wife of Lewis Richards of Mitcheltroy, yeoman, remainder to Lewis Richards, jun., of Mitcheltroy, remainder to Elizabeth, daughter of the said Lewis and Elizabeth.

Copyhold lands called Gworlod-yr-odyn (*the lime kiln meadow*), to which James Richards of Cwmcarvan, esq., had been admitted in 1826, were on 5 September, 1829, surrendered to George Ballard of Shirehampton, co. Gloucester, esq. In 1835, on the bankruptcy of the said George Ballard, one of a company of Calcutta merchants, John Ralph Norton Norton purchased the same, which in 1841 were sold to the said James Richards. In 1843 James Richards, cousin of the above James Richards, was admitted to the same copyholds and also to Cae'r-ywen (*the yew tree field*), and also to a strip of land called Cae-bwlch-y-gwynt[1] (*the field of the gap of the wind*), also to Cae-gwyn and Cae-cromp.

A farm called Rosser's Farm is thus referred to in the assignment of release dated 4 November, 1763: John Rumsey of Trelech, esq. (only son and heir and executor of John Rumsey, late of Trelech, gent., deceased), of the 1st part; John Gwynne of Cwmcarvan, yeoman, of the 2nd part; and Morgan

Bullock of Monmouth, clk., and Pleasant his wife, and Sybil Penry of the same, spr. (executors in trust of Thomas Bullock, late of Chepstow, gent., deceased), of the 3rd part. Reciting that by release dated 24 June, 1757, between William Jones then late of Tre-Owen, but then of Tintern, yeoman, and Thomas Rosser of the Gockett, yeoman, of the 1st part, the said John Gwynne (eldest son and heir of Thomas Gwynne, late of the same, yeoman, deceased), of the 2nd part, and John Rumsey, deceased, of the 3rd part. Reciting that the said Thomas Gwynne being seized of the reversion of the freehold and copyhold hereditaments therein mentioned did by will dated 13 November, 1745, devise unto his wife Dorothy all his free and copyholds in Cwmcarvan, Mitchel Troy, Trelech and Penallt for her life, and then to his brother-in-law the said William Jones and his nephew the said Thomas Rosser upon trust to raise portions for his daughters Mary, Patience, Elizabeth, Ann and Sarah, and the residue to his son the said John Gwynne, and reciting agreement for mortgage by which the following lands, etc., have been surrendered: All that customary or copyhold messuage found in the tenure of the said Thomas Gwynne, but then of the said John Gwynne, called John Rosser's Farm with appurtenances, and ten closes containing 50 acres called Gworlod-dan-y-ty (*the meadow under the house*), Gworlod-y-gwyn-ress [?], Gworlod y lloysee, Yr-erw (*the acre*), Cae'r-odyn (*the kiln field*), Cae'r-bont (*the bridge field*), Coed ven, Cae-bwlch-y-gwynt (*the field of the gap of the wind*), Cae'r-felyn-sidr (*the cider mill field*), and Cae'r-ty-defaid (*the field of the sheep cot*) in Cwmcarvan; and also Gworlod-rhyd-gwern (*the meadow of the ford of the alders*), Rhyd-wern-fach and Rhyd-wern-fawr (*the ford of the great and little alders*) in Mitchel Troy; and also Cae'r-mynydd-mawr, Cae'r-mynydd-bach (*the great and little mountain field*), Gwaen-cae'r-mynydd (*the meadow of the mountain field*), Tir-Hoskin (*Hoskin's land*), and Tir-noon in Penallt; and also Gworlod-y-canol-y-tre (*the meadow of the middle of the town*), the Pleck, and the Stanks containing 29 covers; and also the Stanks, Cae-Jack-Tyler (*Jack Tyler's field*) and Erw-yr-delyn (*the harp meadow*), containing 24 acres in Trelech. In 1774 Pleasant Bullock, widow, and Sybil Penry sold to John Gwyn, who mortgaged to John Ballard of Portbury, co. Somerset, surgeon, who was succeeded by his only brother and heir George Ballard, on whose bankruptcy in 1835 John Ralph Norton Norton of Monmouth, attorney, became the owner, who sold in 1841 to James Richards for 1150l.

The *Perwg*[1] in 1763 belonged to Gwenllian, widow of John Evans, late of Cwmcarvan, yeoman, deceased, who sold it to John Young of Mitchel Troy, yeoman, described as being in the tenure of Walter Williams, butcher, between the way from Cwmcarvan church to Llanthomas, lands of Thomas Williams of Llanthomas, gent., and lands of Henry Edmonds of Gwaelod-yr-wlad, esq. In 1791 William Edwards of Bristol, cooper, conveyed the same to Lewis Richards of Troy, gent.

---

[1] This is elsewhere called *Windy hole*.

[1] *Parwg* means an enclosed field or park.

Little Cwmcarvan.

This place first appears in a suit in 1589 between Roger ap John of Chepstow and John ap John of Cwmcarvan. In 1614 William Rosser John conveys the property to John Thomas Turner, the surrender at the court dated 7 October, 12 Jac. (1614), being as follows :—

> Trellecke } Ad curiam, coram Georgio Catchmey, Dominium } Anthonio Williams, armigeris, et Willielmo Perkins, generoso, locum tenentibus Rowlandi Morgan, militis, capitalis seneschalli ibidem, venit Willielmus Rosser John de Cwmcarvan, yeoman, et Gwenlliana uxor ejus, Walter Stephen de eâdem, et Thomas Hoyskin de eâdem, yeomen, feoffatores terrarum custumarium prædicti Willielmi et Gwenllianæ, et sursum reddiderunt in manus domini quatuor clausuras vocatas[1] Gworlod-wlyb,[2] Hendre-Inon,[3] Cae-isaf,[4] and Gworlod-fach,[5] in parochiâ de Cwmcarvan, inter terras Jenkini Thomas, viam ducentem de Craig-coed-garth[6] versus ecclesiam parochialem de Cwmcarvan, terras Rogeri Edmonds, terras Margaretae William, viduæ, et alias terras prædicti Rogeri John, ad opus et usum Johannis Thomas Tyrnor de Mychelltroye.

On 13 November, 1622, William Rosser ap John conveys to Roger ap John of Cwmcarvan, yeoman, for 230l. a freehold estate called Cae ton y lleyn[7] containing 35 acres, Dis y cae ton,[8] Y darn isaf[9] or Cae dis'r-ysgubor,[10] Gworlod y lloi,[11] and Cae-newydd.[12]

In 1623 John Thomas Turner settles his estate on trustees John Davies of Llangoven and Robert Smith (who afterwards appears as Robert Shepard) of Usk.

> Uske } Ad portam castri praenobilis Willielmi, Castrum } Comitis Penbroocke, domini ibidem, xiiij° die Octobris, anno regni Domini nostri Jacobi, Dei gratiâ Angliæ, etc., 21°, coram Edmundo Morgan, generoso, locum tenente Rowlandi Morgan, militis, capitalis seneschalli domini ibidem, venit Johannes Thomas Turnor de Cwmcarvan, yeoman, per Davidem Lewis de parochiâ de Trellecke, yeoman, attornatum suum, et sursum reddidit messuagia, duo horrea, etc., in Cwmcarvan vocata Cae feglin, Gworlod-fawr, Hendre-Inon, Cae pwll Sais, Cae-tu-hwnt-r'ysgubor, Y croft, Cae-canol, Cae dwch law'r berllan, etc., juxta commune domini vocatum Craig coed garth, viam abinde versus Llanthomas, terras Hugonis Jones, terras Johannis Thomas de le Gader, terras Willielmi Thomas, terras heredum Richardi William Thomas, terras Willielmi Jankin, torrentem vocatum Pencam, terras Willielmi Rosser, etc., ad opus et usum Johannis Davis de Llangoven, yeoman, et Roberti Smith de Uske.

This settlement led to a lawsuit by John Thomas Turner against Philip Nicholas of Lanpill, who is alleged to have persuaded the former to part with his estate. John Thomas Turner had a son Rosser who died in his father's life time ; Rosser left an illegitimate son Walter, who is variously called Walter Rosser and Walter Rogers.[1] Philip Nicholas is in the plaint accused of keeping the lands which are said to have been purchased by Rosser ap John Thomas Turner (and by him given to his father) from Jenkin Thomas, William Jenkin, Walter Steven, John William, Thomas John, Hopkin Howell, and Thomas Jenkin. Walter Rosser pleads—

> To have a triall shortly, for I am but a poor man for because that hee doe keep my mense [means] wrongfully, for I have but leetell menes too mentain myselfe, my wife and children, and hee being a gret and mighty man with all the gentell sort.

The witnesses to be called are :—

Andrew Nicolas of Lansoy, the brother of defendant.
Rosser William.
David Lewis et uxor de Trellecke.
John David et uxor de Langoven.
Ann Watkin de Trellecke.
Elnor Harry, Thomas Jon Edmund, Jon Rosser, Moris David et uxor, Catring James, Maud Steuin.
Elizabeth John de Cumcaruan.
John Thomas de Lan Thomas.
William John Howell, a good witnes for mee.
John Warner, Thomas Rosser, William Rosser, Thomas Evan Howell de Cumcaruan.
Edward Watkin of Lansoy.
Ann Gwin, Doret Gwin de Michill Troy.
Catring Jon, Lanniangell.
James Tyler de Pen clauthe.
Alce Jenkin de Chepstow, David Gilbert.
William John Watkin, Sibill Riched, William Rice et uxor.
William Perkines, Griffith Morgan, William Griffith, William Wangout, gentlemen.
Trellecke : Water Euanes, Thomas Watkin et uxor.
Meredith Thomas of Woluesnewton.
William Lame et filij.
Cumcaruan : Walter Williams, Lewis Williams.
Mary, the wife of John David, did depose and declare that hee will swere soundly against Water Rosser at the com'icion.

A commission was issued out of the court of Star Chamber for taking the answer of Philip Nicholas, John David and Robert Shepard alias Smith the defendants, and sat 19 September, 1638, at the house of Charles Jones alias High in Trelech. The result of the trial does not appear, but a certificate of sir Ralph Whitfield, serjeant-at-law, dated 12 February, 1639, in camerâ stellatâ (Star Chamber), states that the defendants had not sufficiently answered certain of the interrogatories. But that the plaintiff was successful may be gathered, as a deed of poll exists dated 22 April, 1639, by which Philip Nicholas of Lanpill, gent., releases Walter Rosser of Cwmcarvan, yeoman, from all actions, suits and demands.

On 18 June, 1667, Walter Rogers and Tacy his wife surrender the estate to the use of Moses Rogers[2] their son and heir apparent. In 1693 Moses Rogers settles the estate on himself and his

---

1 I have given the correct spelling of these names.
2 *The wet meadow.* 3 *Inon's homestead.*
4 *The lower field.* 5 *The little meadow.*
6 *The rock of the wood of the enclosure.*
7 *The field of the glade of the low land.*
8 *Below the field of the glade.*
9 *The lower piece.* 10 *The field below the barn.*
11 *The meadow of the calves.* 12 *The new field.*

---

1 Rosser is the Welsh form of Roger.
2 In 1683 Moses Rogers had a lease from Philip, earl of Pembroke, of all that parcel of waste ground called Craig coed garth, 28 acres, with liberty to enclose the same, for 99 years on the life of himself and Catherine his wife, and Moses and John his sons, at the rent of 14s., an heriot of 7s., suit of court and mill.

wife Catherine (daughter of Christopher Dowle of Coxbery in Newland, co. Glouc.) to uses. In 1694 there is a suit by John Edmonds, gent., against Moses Rogers, in which the surrender of John Thomas Turner to Philip Nicholas is quoted, who settled the property on his daughter Ann, wife of John Jones of Trevildu, gent. The said Ann died about 1664 leaving an only son and heir, Philip Jones, who died about 1674, leaving two sons, John and William. On 26 March, 1692, John and William sold their interest to the plaintiff John Edmonds.

It may be imagined that the family of Turner or Rogers had had enough of lawsuits, for Moses Rogers answers that he is willing to pay rent and arrears.

In 1713 Moses Rogers, now described as of Streat[1] in the county of Gloucester, gent., appears at the court and surrenders the estate to the use of his sons John and Moses. In 1745 John Rogers, called of Tidenham, yeoman, surrenders the estate to Henry Harding of Chepstow, esq., and in 1761 the trustees of the late Henry Harding, Thomas Harding of Droynton, co. Stafford, gent., and his brother Brian Harding of Eton, co. Bucks, baker, surrender to James Richards.

Even after James Richards had purchased the estate the lawsuits would hardly seem to be at an end, for among the deeds is a letter to mrs. Richards from a mr. Bainton at Bristol, dated 19 September, 1810, saying that he is employed by mr. Churchman Rogers, brother and heir of the late Moses Rogers of Beachley, to apply for possession of an estate in the parish of *Comptcarvan*, her interest in which ceased on the death of the said Moses Rogers, who was only tenant for life. He adds that unless possession be immediately given he will deliver ejectment to recover the same.

Pedigree of the family of Richards of Cwmcarvan.

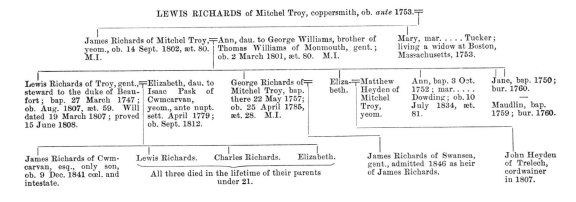

Cwm-collier and Croes-Robert wood belonged to the Proberts of the Argoed, and with that estate came to colonel Morgan-Clifford, who sold to doctor George Willis of Monmouth. His son, the late rev. William Armstrong Willis, rector of Llanvaches, succeeded his father as owner.

Cae'r-llan.

Cae'r-llan belonged also to the Proberts, and was sold with the Argoed by colonel Morgan-Clifford to mr. Richard Potter. The house now known as Cae'r-llan was built by doctor William Francis Price of Monmouth, in 1866, as a summer residence. His widow sold it in 1890 to captain Henry Edward Walters, R.N., who has very much enlarged it, laying out gardens and grounds.

1 Stroat, a hamlet in the parish of Tidendam.

Gwaelod-yr-wlad and Trealy.

Gwaelod-yr-wlad (*the bottom of the country*) is a name descriptive of the situation, the house being in the dingle through which flows the Carvan brook. This place, with Trealy and the Church-farm, were long the property of a family who settled down to the surname of Edmonds, part of it in 1611 belonging to Thomas John Edmond. By indentures dated 14 February, 8 Jac. (1611), John William Baker[1] of Cwmcarvan, gent., grants to Francis Watkins of Lydney, yeoman, all that mansion house, etc., wherein the said John William Baker doth inhabit, and one water mill adjoining between the way leading from the church of Cwmcarvan towards the town of Monmouth, a certain brook called Pencam,[2]

1 *Vide* Vol. I., p. 47, where John Baker of Cwmcarvan marries Jane, dau. to Ievan ap Thomas Herbert.

2 Pen-cam (*the crooked head*). This brook has lost its name, but it is that one which falls into the Carvan at Gwaelod-yr-wlad.

the lands of Thomas John Edmond, the river called Carvan, lands of the earl of Pembroke, a curtilage of Rowland Williams, gent., and lands of John Edmonds.

By indenture dated 4 March, 1657, Thomas Edmonds of Cwmcarvan, yeoman, Richard Vidler of the same, yeoman, and Blanch his wife (one of the daughters of the said Thomas Edmonds) grant, by way of settlement, to Nicholas Nicholas of Llansoy, gent., all that messuage wherein Thomas Edmonds dwelleth; and by indentures dated 18 July, 13 Car. II., 1661, Nicholas Nicholas and Bridget his wife and Richard Vidler grant in mortgage for 200*l.* to William Jones of Llanarth, esq. —

All that messuage or tenement wherein Thomas John Edmond did lately inhabit and wherein Thomas William doth now inhabit, containing three score acres called Cay keven,[1] Cay yr lloyd,[2] Ton dee,[3] Cay pant,[4] Cay isha,[5] Cay Rees[6] and Cay pwll[7] lying in Gwailod y wlade, between the lands of Alse Blower, widow, the lands of David Edmonds, the brook called Pencam, the lands of Thomas Pheellipp, the lands of the earl of Pembroke now or late in the occupation of Adam Jones, and the way leading from the stony bridge towards the church of Cwmcarvan; and also all that water mill now in the occupation of the said Nicholas Nicholas.

By indentures dated 25 June, 19 Car. II., 1667, William Jones of Llanarth conveys his interest in Gwaelod-yr-wlad to John Aylworth of Trecastle, gent., and in 1753 the trustees of John Aylworth convey the same to Henry Edmonds.

This Henry Edmonds was the last of his name at Gwaelod-yr-wlad. He made his will in 1772 (P.C.C., Taverner, 401), by which his successors were to take his name. This they did not do.

To my brother Francis 1*s.*—to Francis Mills, son of my late sister Sarah, 300*l.*, and to her other children 100*l.* each—to my nephew John Stock, son of my late sister Mary Stock, 300*l.*—to Jane, dau. of my late sister Elizabeth and now wife of Walter Pritchard of Monmouth, currier, 200*l.*—all my real estate to my friend Mr Wm Blower of Cwmcarvan in trust, to the use of my nephew John Mills, and in default to the family of Stock—all legatees to take the name of Edmonds—eight labouring men to carry me to the grave and have 2*s.* 6*d.* each—to Mary Blower, dau. of Wm Blower, 50*l.*—to my servant Elizabeth Lewis for her care of me in my long sickness and old age the best cow and best bedstead and 100*l.*, 10*l.* for mourning to her and Mary Blower—my nephew John Mills ex'or.

Codicil—legacy to Elizabeth Lewis revoked, she to have 3*s.* per week for life instead—Philip Meakings Hardwick trustee for her.

CAE'R LLAN.

The Gentleman's Magazine,[8] thus refers to the death of Henry Edmonds :—

Mr Edmunds of Monmouth, 29 Oct. 1772. He has bequeathed 10,000*l.* to one Mills, a poor relation, whom he never would speak to while he lived.

Henry Edmonds was succeeded in his estates by his nephew John Mills, who, however, did not comply with his uncle's will by taking his name. John Mills resided at Trealy, and made his will 12 April, 1774, proved 2 July, 1776 :—

My wife Hannah an annuity of 40*l.* out of my personal estate—my sister Sarah, wife of Jeremiah Morris of Clyrow, 100*l.*—Sarah, wife of Richard

Maisey of Painswick, 100*l.*—Mariam, wife of David Morgan of Monmouth, corvisor, 100*l.*—Jane, wife of Walter Prichard of Monmouth, currier, 100*l.*—my sister Clare Stephens of Painswick, widow, 100*l.*—my nephew Wm Stephens of Painswick 100*l.*—children of my sister Sarah 150*l.* between them—Wm Stephens the younger of Painswick, son of my said nephew Wm Stephens, 200*l.*—children of my nephew Wm Stephens 20*l.* a piece—my brother Francis Mills the use of my plate, linen, implements of husbandry, etc., and after him to my cousin John Stock, gent., if he will live at Treily—Elizabeth Blower, spr., dau. of Wm Blower of Cwmcarvan, 50*l.*—residue to Mariam, wife of the said David Morgan.

The three farms after this devolved on the family of Stock, and were sold in 1865 by John Shapland Edmonds Stock, of No. 7 Upper Brook Street, Grosvenor Square, London, esq., to Samuel Richard Bosanquet of Dingestow, esq.

---

1 Cae-cefn (*the ridge field*). 2 Cae-llwyd (*the grey field*).
3 Ton-du (*the black glade*). 4 Cae-pant (*the hollow field*).
5 Cae-isaf (*the lower field*). 6 Cae-Rhys (*Rees' field*).
7 Cae-pwll (*the pit field*). 8 Vol. xlii., p. 543.

𝔓𝔢𝔡𝔦𝔤𝔯𝔢𝔢 𝔬𝔣 𝔱𝔥𝔢 𝔣𝔞𝔪𝔦𝔩𝔶 𝔬𝔣 𝔈𝔡𝔪𝔬𝔫𝔡𝔰 𝔬𝔣 𝔊𝔴𝔞𝔢𝔩𝔬𝔡=𝔶𝔯=𝔴𝔩𝔞𝔡.[1]

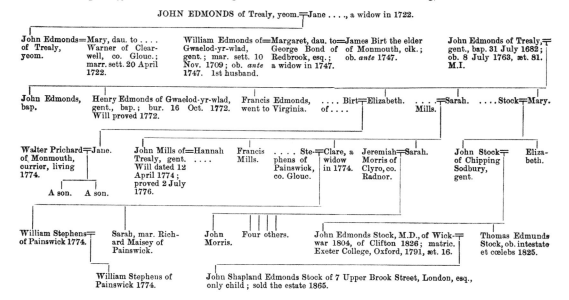

Llanthomas.

Llanthomas was a hamlet, the boundaries of which are lost, taking its name from an ancient church or chapel. The chapel is mentioned in the survey of the manor of Trelech.

At the beginning of the seventeenth century Edmund Thomas Philip, who was probably a brother of John Thomas Philip of Tal-y-van, was of Llanthomas. His will is dated 9 December, 1622, proved at Llandaff 16 December, 1622:—

> Cathedral church of landaff ijs.—reparation of the church of Comcarvan ijs.—to my dau. Ales Edmond one annuity of 10l. out of all my messuages and lands freehold or leasehold situate in langoven for 3 years after my decease—to Mauld my wife all my messuages, lands and woods in my possession called lanthomas howse, Cae Cary and Cae Yoroth, Gworlod newyth containing xxvi acres situate in lanthomas between the way leading from Usk towards Monmouth to the farm lands of Water Steven and the way leading from Trelleck towards Penyclawth for her life, and after to the use of my son William Edmond and his heirs —to my 2ᵈ son David Edmonds my messuages, lands, etc., in Comcarvan which I lately purchased of John Will'm Baker and Bridget his wife—to my son William all my lands called Tir llanne and Worlod newidd unqueathed lying in lanthomas between the way leading from Usk towards Monmouth, the lands of Jenett vᵌ Rosser, widow, and lands of Hugh Steven on all parts—to my son William Edmonds all my messuages, lands, etc., which I hold by demise and grant of Henry Lewis, esquior, lying in langoven—to Maud verch John Edmunds 2 heifers—the tithes of lanthomas which I hold of Sir Rowland Morgan, knt.
>
> Witnesses: John Thomas Phillip, John Thomas ap John, Hugh Johnes, Walter Will'ms of Dingestow.1

The will of Maud, the widow of Edmund Thomas Philip, daughter of Richard ap John Harry of Pen-y-clawdd, is dated 1 November, 1638, proved at Llandaff 15 July, 1641, by Isaac William her grandson. She leaves everything to her son William Edmonds, and makes her grandson Isaac William her executor.

Isaac Williams, grandson of Edmund Thomas Philip and Maud, was afterwards of Llanthomas. He made his will 8 September, 1711, proved at Llandaff 2 October, 1711:—

> 300l. to be raised for my young children, that is to say Henry and my dau. Elizabeth, my son Henry to have 100l. when of age, my dau. Elizabeth to have 200l. within two years' time—to my kinsmen and friends Henry Lewis of Treleck,2 gent., Edward Hoskins of Newchurch,3 gent., Isaac Williams of Llanihangel Tor y mynydd, gent., all my lands, etc., purchased by me of John David and also parcels of land called Gwyrlod y perbren, Cae mawr and Cae y pound, and two pieces called Gwyrlod y garn and Cae Cradock purchased by me of John Williams of Mitchel Troy, all which are in Llangoven and Llangwm, on trust that if Henry die before being of age his property is to be divided between my three children Thomas, Elizabeth and Isaac—my wife Elizabeth.

Of the subsequent ownership of this estate I am uncertain. The parish registers of Pen-y-clawdd record the burials of Hannah, daughter of Thomas Williams of Llanthomas, gent., 27 April, 1728; Elizabeth, wife of Thomas Williams of Llanthomas, gent., 23 January, 1735; mrs. Elizabeth Williams of Dursley 11 July, 1794; Isaac Williams of Llanthomas, esq., 18 October, 1806.

---

1 This last signature is in a very good hand.

1 The parish registers are full of the name, which are difficult to find a place for in the pedigree. The title-deeds shew—Thomas John Edmond, 1611; John Edmonds, 1611; Thomas Edmonds, 1657, whose daughter Blanch married Richard Vidler, yeoman.

2 Of Higga.　　　3 Of the Pantau.

Pedigree of the family of Williams of Llanthomas.

[For the descent from Llansantffraid *vide* Vol. I., p. 318.]

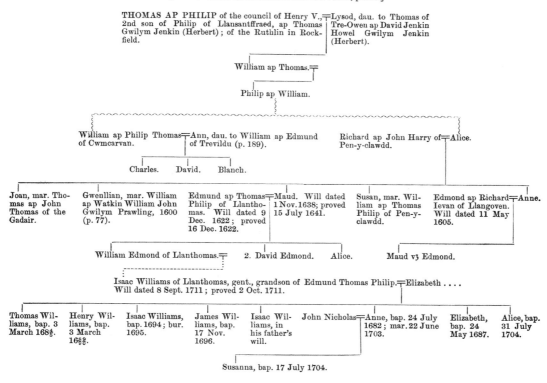

THOMAS AP PHILIP of the council of Henry V., 2nd son of Philip of Llansantffraed, ap Thomas Gwilym Jenkin (Herbert); of the Ruthlin in Rockfield. = Lysod, dau. to Thomas of Tre-Owen ap David Jenkin Howel Gwilym Jenkin (Herbert).

William ap Thomas. =

Philip ap William.

William ap Philip Thomas of Cwmcarvan. = Ann, dau. to William ap Edmund of Trevildu (p. 189).

Richard ap John Harry of Pen-y-clawdd. = Alice.

Charles. David. Blanch.

Joan, mar. Thomas ap John Thomas of the Gadair.

Gwenllian, mar. William ap Watkin William John Gwilym Prawling, 1600 (p. 77).

Edmund ap Thomas Philip of Llanthomas. Will dated 9 Dec. 1622; proved 16 Dec. 1622. = Maud. Will dated 1 Nov. 1638; proved 15 July 1641.

Susan, mar. William ap Thomas Philip of Pen-y-clawdd.

Edmond ap Richard Ievan of Llangoven. Will dated 11 May 1605. = Anne.

William Edmond of Llanthomas. = 2. David Edmond. Alice.

Maud vᴈ Edmond.

Isaac Williams of Llanthomas, gent., grandson of Edmund Thomas Philip. Will dated 8 Sept. 1711; proved 2 Oct. 1711. = Elizabeth ....

Thomas Williams, bap. 3 March 168⅘.

Henry Williams, bap. 3 March 16⁹⁰⁄₉₀.

Isaac Williams, bap. 1694; bur. 1695.

James Williams, bap. 17 Nov. 1696.

Isaac Williams, in his father's will.

John Nicholas = Anne, bap. 24 July 1682; mar. 22 June 1703.

Elizabeth, bap. 24 May 1687.

Alice, bap. 31 July 1704.

Susanna, bap. 17 July 1704.

In 1841 Llanthomas belonged to Thomas Bennett of Mitcheldean. In 1884 the property was put up for sale, comprising then Llanthomas 313 acres, Pentre-wylan 42 acres, and the New House 44 acres, and was purchased by the rev. .... Williams, whose executors are the present owners.

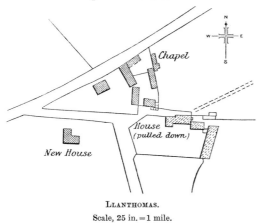

LLANTHOMAS.
Scale, 25 in. = 1 mile.

The house is an ancient building dating back in parts to the fifteenth century.[1] A room upstairs is called *sir John's room*, though who sir John was

there is no record. The chapel is now a calves' cot, and the only thing that marks it as having been used for a purpose different to the present one is that the plaster still remains on the walls.

A reference to the chapel will be found in the survey of the manor of Trelech, where the boundary is given as coming by Pen-y-lan and the Gader down the brook called Llymon to Llanthomas chapel.

Pentre-wylan (*the seagull's village*) belonged to Llanthomas till in recent years it was sold from the estate. It was built or rebuilt in 1683, as appears by a stone over the door:—

I
T M
1683

Trevildu.

Trevildu, properly Tre-fil-du, is the site of what was for about three centuries the seat of an important family. It is said to take its name from a sir Mil Ddu (*sir Miles the Black*), Tre Mil ddu (*the home of Miles Ddu*)[1] becoming, when formed into one word, Trefildu. In the fifteenth century

---

[1] Since this was written the old house has been pulled down and a new one erected on a fresh site, as will be seen by the plan.

[1] A *Mil du* occurs in the legend of Kilhwch and Olwen.

Hopkin ap Adam was resident here, who in the Cawdor MSS. in the Record Office is thus described :—

> This Hopkin was son to Adam, son to Sir Miles ddu of Trevildu, knt., son to Adam Avenal,[1] son to sir Morris Avenal, knt., that erected a park at Llangoven by Raglan called Park Morris.

The eldest son of Hopkin was Gwilym, whose brother Iorwerth had a son Thomas possessed of considerable wealth, as appears by his will, dated 7 August, 1525, proved (P.C.C., Bodfield, 40) 11 December, 1525 :—

> In the name of God Amen the 7th day of the month of August A.D. 1525. I Thomas ap Iouarthe ap Hopk' give my soul to God almighty and my body to be buried in the holy sepulchre of the church of the blessed virgin Mary of Monmouth.
>
> Item—I give and bequeath to the fabric of the cathedral church of Hereford xijd.
>
> To Master John Straensam, vicar of Monmouth, xijd. to pray for my soul.
>
> To the rector of the parish church of Monmouth for tithes forgotten xijd.
>
> To Sir John Lewys, parish priest there, xijd. that he may pray for me.
>
> To the high altar of Cumkarvan for tithes forgotten iijs. ivd.
>
> To the church of Troye for tithes forgotten xs.
>
> For repairing the said church of Troye vis. viijd.
>
> To the repair of the parish church of Penclouth ijs.
>
> To the structure or building of the new tower or belfry of the church of Cumkarvan x marks to be paid in four years after the beginning of the said tower.
>
> I bequeath to provide a fit priest to celebrate for my soul and the soul of Joan verз Hoysk' my pretended wife and for the souls of my parents and benefactors and of all the faithful deceased for one entire year in the church of St. Clement of Cumkarvan vli.
>
> For the repairing of a certain bridge called Walters Brigge placed upon the stream of Troye xs.
>
> To John ap Youarth my brother and John ap Watkin Baker all my term of and in all my farms which I lately purchased of Sir William Herbert, knight (two meadows, to wit, Nettais Mede and Harthans Mede, with four crofts of land arable called Terr' y tewe mawr and Terr' y tewe bagch, and also Ykteven coygh[2] and Kaye i'r parke yssa[3] excepted therefrom, and in the hands of the aforesaid John ap Youarthe, reserved as formerly he held them) and therefrom I ordain that of the increment of the aforesaid farms the said John ap Youarthe and John ap Watkin pay yearly during my term aforesaid to Joan Mason my wife xls.
>
> I give all my household goods now being in my house in Cumkarvan to be divided into two equal parts between Isabella verз Thomas my daughter one half part, and Joan and Katherine, daughters of John Brylle, together the other half part.
>
> I ordain Thomas Catchmay and Thomas ap Hopk' feoffees of all my lands within the parish of Cumkarvan, and also the other feoffees of all my lands within the parish of Troy shall hold and keep all the aforesaid lands and tenements to the use and behoof of Isabella verз Thomas my daughter and her heirs, and therefrom I will that the aforesaid Isabella verз

> Thomas my daughter pay yearly to the aforesaid Joan Mason my wife during the term of her life xiijs. ivd.
>
> I will that my ex'ors pay to Joan and Katherine, daughters of John Byrrell, xli., viz., to each of them vli., with this condition, that they release and surrender to the aforesaid Isabella my daughter, when she shall come to lawful age, their whole right of and in my lands within the parish of Cumkarvan.
>
> I bequeath to the aforesaid Isabella verз Thomas my daughter six oxen and ten cows which are at Cumkarvan, also all my grain and crops now coming and pertaining to me of the culture of Howell ap John ap Ievan there.
>
> I give to William Hopk' of Monmouth viijd.
>
> To Gwladys Youarthe my sister iijs. ivd.
>
> Richard Walkle owes me xxjli.
>
> Thomas Tonner owes me xviijs. for a horse.
>
> The relict of Howell ap Jankyn Watk' owes me xxs. which I paid for Thomas Ho' her son.
>
> I owe to Walter Baker of Monmouth iv marks.
>
> The residue of all my goods I give and bequeath in the disposition of William ap Youarthe my brother and Joan Mason my wife, whom I make my ex'ors.
>
> These being witnesses—Master John Straensam, vicar there; Sir John Lewys, parish priest there; James ap John, and many others.
>
> Proved 11 December A.D. 1525 by the oaths of the executors named in the said will in the person of Master John Falkern, public notary.

The will of Thomas Williams, described as Thomas William Edmond of Treveldee, is dated 15 April, 39 Eliz. (1597), proved at Llandaff 21 May, 1597, by James Arnald and William Nicholas :—

> To be buried in my parish church of Cwmcarvan within my chapel there—the cathedral of Landaf xijd.—reparation of the churches of Cwmcarvan, Llangoven, and Penclauth xijd. a piece—a moiety of the sheep of all my messuages, etc., in the parishes of Cwmcarvan, Mycheltroy, Penclauthe, and llanthomas to Blanshe Will'ms and Anne Will'ms my two daughters for 21 years for their preferment in marriage, the other moiety to Jane Will'ms my wife for life—if Arnald Will'ms my son and heir pay to my said daughters Blanche & Anne 240l. he to have the moiety—my son Rowland Will'ms land I of late purchased of Thomas ap Richard Jeyne and Richard John Hopkyn in the parish of llangoven now in the tenure of John Jenkyn and Thomas R'c Ievan, and also to him lands in Newchurch—to my dau. Barbara, wife of James Arnald, 2 oxen—Mary dau. of James Arnald—to Mary fortenne, wife of John fortenne, a heifer two years old —to Elizabeth Powell my niece a heifer—my brother George xxs.—my sister Anne xxs.—Will'm Nicholas of llansoy my cozen to be overseer.
>
> In the pr' of Wm Saunders, James Arnald, Edmond Dauid, Will'm Bowen, George Will'ms, Will'm Nicholas.

Jane, the widow of the above Thomas Williams, made her will 31 October, 1607, proved (P.C.C., 42, Windebank) 7 May, 1608, by her son-in-law Thomas Powell.

> Reparation of cathedral church of llandaff 12d.—towards forgotten tithes 12d.—to my son Rowland 20l. due to me by a bond from Mr William Hale, also a feather bed, bedstead, etc., which I have now in the parlour, with the carpet belonging thereunto, my silver salt, three silver spoons and my best crock—to my son Water one couple or yoke of my best oxen—

---

1 Robert Avenel held a knight's fee in Pen-y-clawdd in 1314.
2 Cefn-coch (the red ridge).
3 Cae'r parc isaf (the field of the lower park).

to my dau. Anne one yoke of oxen, half a dozen silver spoons, my best pan and my next best pan, three kine, etc.—to Marie Arnold, dau. to my dau. Barbara, four heifers, and one feather bed in the chamber above the parlour—to my brother Thomas Welshe 40s.—to Maulde Lewys 10s.—to my dau. Anne my best gown —to Mary Arnold my cloth gown—provided that if my son Rowland or any other persons molest my ex'ors any goods left them to be detained by my ex'ors & distributed amongst themselves—Thomas Powell and my son Water ex'ors.

Witnesses: Richard Lace, clerk, vicar of Rockfield, Maude Lewys, Bridgett Morgan, Elinor John, Hughe Watkins.

[Signed] JANE WILLIAMS.

Some time after this John Jones, second son of William Jones of Tre-Owen, was of Trevil-du, and by Anne his wife, daughter of Philip Nicholas of Lanpill, left an only son Philip, who died about 1674. Philip left issue two sons, John and William, who on 26 March, 1692, sold lands in Cwmcarvan to John Edmonds, gent.

In 1684 John Edmonds of Pen-y-clawdd, gent., was the owner of Trevil-du, then occupied by one Charles Gwyllim. By indentures dated 11 and 12 December, 1684, he and Thomas Holmes of Raglan, gent., mortgaged the estate for 500l. to Blanch, the widow of John Phillips of Tal-y-van, which mortgage was conveyed to their eldest daughter and coheir Elizabeth, who married William Feilding of Little Tintern. The issue of this marriage was an only child Elizabeth, who, by a fine levied in Easter term 1707 against Richard Edmonds, son and heir of the above John Edmonds, became possessed of Trevildu.

This lady married in 1727 John Curre, jun. (eldest son of John Curre of Rogerston Grange), to whom she took Tal-y-van and Trevildu. These two estates henceforth continued together, as shewn on page 62.

DOORWAY OF TREVILDU.

The existing farm-house of Trevildu is not on the site of the original dwelling. The ancient mansion, situated close to a brook half a mile north of the farm-house, and known as Lower Trevildu, is now but a cottage. It is, however, entered by the arched door-way of what was doubtless a castellated mansion erected in the fourteenth century. Around the cottage are signs of foundations of many buildings, and adjoining are remains of a water-mill.

Pedigree of the family of Williams of Trevildu.

ARMS.—Arg., on a bend sa. three pheons of the field.

HOPKIN ap Adam ap sir Miles Ddu, knt., ap Adam Avenal ap sir Morris Avenal, knt.

Gwilym ap Hopkin of Trevildu.=Mawd, dau. to Howel ap Thomas ap Gwilym of Perth-hir.

Henry ap Hopkin of Pen-y-clawdd, ob. s.p., when his property went to his brother Gwilym.

Iorwerth ap Hopkin.

Edmund ap Gwilym of Trevildu.=Margaret, dau. and co-heir to John Tomlyn of Llanllowel and widow of David ap Jenkin (Herbert). (Vol. I., p. 303.)

Reginald ap Gwilym.

Thomas ap Iorwerth ap Hopkin of Monmouth. Will dated 7 Aug., proved 11 Dec. 1525.=Joan Mason [Joan vᵥ Hoskin my pretended wife].

John ap Iorwerth.

William ap Iorwerth.

Gwladys vᵥ Iorwerth.

Isabella vᵥ Thomas.

William ap Edmund of Trevildu.=Margaret, dau. to Thomas Morgan of Machen, esq.

Thomas ap Edmund.=Mary, dau. to Philip Catchmay.

Thomas Lewis Hopkin.=Anne.

Bridget, mar. John Kes of Middlesex.

Margaret, mar. Thomas Philip Gwilym of Rhyd-y-maen.

Catherine, mar. John Prichard of Severney.

Thomas ap Reginald.

Margaret, mar. William Howel Rawling.

James ap Thomas ap Reginald.

Thomas Williams of Trevildu, esq., called in his will Thomas William Edmund. Will dated 15 April 1597; proved 21 May 1597.=Jane, dau. to Anthony Welsh of Llanwern, esq., by .... dau. to Christopher Baynham of Clearwell, esq. Will dated 31 Oct. 1607; proved 7 May 1608.

George Williams.=Ursula, dau. to John ap David ap William (Seymour) of Trelech.

Anne, mar. William Philip of Cwmcarvan. p. 187.

Richard Edmonds.=Gwenllian, dau. to Matthew Jones by Blanch, dau. to William Gwillim, esq.

Arnold Williams, eldest son, bur. at Mitchel Troy 27 May 1612.=Anne, dau. to sir Hugh Smith, knt.

Walter Williams.

Rowland Williams of Trevildu, esq.=Jane, dau. to Roger Mynors of Tre-Iago, co. Heref., esq.; bur. at Mitchel Troy 14 Aug. 1614.

Barbara, mar. James Arnold of Berthlwyd. Vol. I., p. 219.

Anne, mar. Thomas Powell of Campston.

Blanch, mar. John William of Campston.

Charles Edmonds.

Roger Williams of Trevildu. Mary. Blanch. Elizabeth. Catherine.

The Bourne.

An English or Saxon name is unusual in this neighbourhood, and how long this place has been called the Bourne I am uncertain. It possibly is so called from a person of that name. In the survey of the lordship of Trelech in 1677 (p. 134) it appears as *Bornes lands*, held by the heirs of Philip Jones, esq. This farm or estate belonged in 1759 to Richard Gorges[1] of Eye in Herefordshire, esq., who by indentures made 3 September, 33 Geo. II., 1759, conveyed it to his mother Elizabeth Gorges of the city of Hereford, widow, described as all that messuage called the Bourne, and all that close called Upper Cae-pant containing 4 acres, a close called Lower Cae-pant 4 acres, a close called Cae dish y berllan (*the field below the orchard*) 14 acres, a close called Cae-gwyn (*the white field*) 6 acres, an arable field called Cae-quarry 9 acres, another arable field called Little Cae'r-groes (*the field of the cross*) 3½ acres, two pieces of meadow called the Pinkett meadows, having the Pinkett brook on the east, a pasture called the Green pasture 6 acres, a pasture called Cae Shokey 8 acres, a pasture called Cae'r-groes 5 acres, a piece of coppice wood 9 acres, all in the parish of Cwmcarvan; and an orchard near the above dwelling house in the parish of St. Michael Troy, 4 acres.

Mrs. Elizabeth Gorges by her will, dated 18 October, 1759, proved 10 June, 1760, left the Bourn back to her son Richard, who, by his will dated 5 June, 1759, left all his manors, messuages, etc., to his wife Frances. This lady, then a widow living at Eye, joined with her eldest son Richard Gorges of Eye, esq., in conveying the Bourne to her second son Thomas by indenture made 5 March, 21 Geo. III., 1781. This Thomas Gorges, described as a captain in his Majesty's 10th regiment of foot, conveyed the Bourne by indentures dated 15 March, 1782, to James Duberley of St. Paul's, Covent Garden, esq. It has since descended with the estate of Dingestow.

The Glanau.

Glanau means the banks of a river, and refers to the Carvan brook, at whose source it is situated. In the early part of the seventeenth century Watkin Morris resided here, and by the reference to it in his will appears to have held a lease of it. The will, in which he is called Watkin Moris, yeoman, is dated 30 April, 1627, proved at Llandaff 8 January, 16 28/30 :—

> To be buried in the church of Cwmcarvan—reparation of the cathedral church of Landaffe six pence—my lands, messuages, etc., in a place now wherein I dwell called the Glanney in the lordship of Trellecke in the parish of Cwmcarvan to Nest my wife for her life, if my term in the said lands be then unexpired,

and after to my dau. Mary Watkin—lands called fforsydd ycha, fforsydd isa and Toneygwyne which my son Thomas Watkin hath in lease from me for the term of nine and twenty years—to my son William Watkin one house, being a mansion house, where I do now dwell with garden, etc., with the term unexpired, also lands called Y gerddinen containing 3 acres—Mary Watkin my dau.—Anne William my grandchild, being the dau. of William ap William—my grandchild Anne John, dau. of John Watkin late of the town of Monmouth—Blance William, dau. of William Watkin—my grandchild Thomas John, son of John Watkin—my grandchildren John ap John and James ap John, two sons of John Watkin late of the town of Monmouth—my grandchild John William, son of William Watkin—Anne Watkin, dau. of Wm Watkin—Dacie William, dau. of David William, clerke, curate of the parish of Cumcarvan—Alce Thomas my grandchild, being dau. of Thomas Watkin—my three grandchildren Margaret Thomas, Marie Thomas, and Thomas ap Thomas, son and dau'rs of Thomas Watkin—Anne William my grandchild, being the dau. of William ap William—the said Marie Watkin my said dau. sole ex'trix, to her for her labour all my household stuff. In the pr. of Thomas Edmonds, William Rosser, Charles Paske.

The Glanau, and much other property in Mitchel Troy and Trelech, belonged to William Morgan of Pencrug, esq., who by his will, dated 10 May, 1662, left to his daughter Dorothy, afterwards wife of William Kemeys of Kemeys, all his customary lands in Trelech and Cwmcarvan in the possession of William Thomas, and a mill in the possession of Howel Thomas, and lands in Trelech in the possession of Thomas Evans. William Kemeys died suddenly in 1681, leaving no provision for his younger children, and a chancery suit took place in 1690, in which the lands of Dorothy Kemeys are as follows[1] :—

> All her capital messuage called Whitehouse with appurtenances and all other her lands both free and customary in the parish of Trelleg and Cumcarvan and her mill then in the possession of one Lewis Richards .... rough ground called the Veadow Vaure in the parish of Trelleg formerly in the possession of one Thomas Evans, and other lands in Cumcarvan, Mitchel Troy, and Penalt in the lordship of Trelleg in the possession of George Probert, knight, excepting one tenement in Mitchel Troy called Rydwerne and two cottages in Penalt .... all which she had from her father William Morgan, esq., deceased.

This property descended in the family of Evans, and eventually became the property of the rev. Henry Bolton Power, who owns the Glanau with the woods called Ffos-y-bwla and the Fedw Fawr, in all about 270 acres, in this parish.

For many years a respectable family named Blower have been freeholders in this and the adjoining parishes. The name is not such as one would expect to find in a Welsh district, and may be of English origin. It first appears in the form of *Llowre*. At the court of the lordship of Usk, held in 1570, the heirs of Gwilym ap Howel Llowre are returned as paying 11s. 11d. for lands in Pen-y-

1 Richard Gorges was M.P. for Leominster 1754-61. He married Frances, daughter and coheir of Thomas Fettiplace, esq., by Frances, daughter and coheir of Edmund Bray of Llantarnam, esq. *Vide* pedigree, Vol. I., p. 467.

1 *Vide* p. 169.

clawdd and Llanthomas, late sir Walter Herbert, knt., and William ap Howell.

The will of William ap James Blower of Llangoven, dated 7 July, 1609, proved at Llandaff 7 January, 1610, is as follows :—

to the cathedral church of Llandaff xij*d*.—forgotten tithes xij*d*.—Katherine Moore my now wedded wife the moiety of all my messuages, etc., in Langoven, Pennyclawth, Comcarvan, Mycheltroie for her life—the other moiety and tenements in Langoven to William Blower my eldest son begotten on the body of the said Catherin; in default to James Blower my 2nd son; in default to Dorothie and Elizabeth, two of my daughters by the said Catherin; in default to Robert son of Robert Lace; in default to the issue male of Edmond Perkins lawfully begotten on the body of Gwenllian his now wife and my natural sister.

Another of the name was John ap Jenkin Blower. Of this one I have no note beyond his *Inquisitio post mortem.*

Inquisition taken at Ragland 26 Sept., 15 Car. I. [1639], before John Dove, gent., escheator, after the death of John Jenkin Blower, gent., who was seised of 1 mess. & 102 acres of land, arable, meadow, and pasture thereto belonging in Llangoven; 37 acres in Ragland; 20 acres in Llandenny; 8 acres in Llanissen. John Jenkin Blower died 3 July, 1 Car. I. [1625], John Blower is his son and heir and was 14 years and more when his father died.

Bridget Blower, relict of the said John, has taken the profits of the premises up to this time.[1]

Christopher Blower of Cwmcarvan, yeoman, in his will dated 20 September, 1695, proved at Llandaff 28 April, 1696, leaves his mansion and lands in Cwmcarvan to his wife Elizabeth, and then to his sons James and William.

The present representative is the rev. James Blower, rector of Gwernesney and Llangeview, whose father, the late rev. James Blower, held the same livings. The latter was son of James Blower of Gwehelog, gent., who was buried in the chancel of Llangeview in 1837.

---

[1] Inq. p. m. 17 Car. I., p. 3, No. 42.

CWMCARVAN CHURCH.

The Church.

The church consists of chancel and nave, with a handsome tower at the west end. There is a large porch on the south side of the nave, and another on the north side, the reason for this being said to be that the squires of Cwmbychan and Trevildu were on bad terms and could not enter by the same door. There would seem once to have been a chapel belonging to the owners of Trevildu, as Thomas William Edmund of that place desires in his will, 1597, to be buried " in my parish church of Cwmcarvan within " my chapel there."

The tower is an exceedingly handsome specimen of masons' work, built of smooth ashlar work, each stone dressed and cut square, and many of them of immense size. Though the style would suggest an earlier period, the tower was built after the year 1525, as appears by the will of Thomas ap Iorwerth ap Hopkin, who leaves in his will ten marks " to the " structure or building of the new tower or belfry of " the church of Cumkarvan to be paid in four years " after the beginning of the said tower."

In 1877 the church suffered considerably in the course of *restoration*, when many memorials to the dead perished, and the walls were denuded of plaster and left in their present bare condition. The barrel roof of the nave was allowed to remain, and the old font still does duty.

The oak pulpit was replaced by one of free stone, but on the other hand, the communion table was permitted to remain. This is of oak, and around the edge has a border of roses and the date 1637.

On the south of the chancel arch the door which led to the rood-loft remains.

By the church being dedicated to St. Clement it

may be inferred that this is not an ancient Welsh foundation, but that it was first built by the Clares, the lords of Usk, the parish church, Mitchel Troy, being so far off as to be of little service to this district.

The most ancient objects in the church are two incised stone coffin-lids. These are on the floor of the chancel, and are probably of the thirteenth century.

Scale, 1 in. = 1 foot.

It has always been considered a chapelry to Mitchel Troy, and attached to that living, but in 1526 Alexander Jones, clerk, was presented to the churches of Llangovan and Cwmcarvan *alias* Old Troy, *vice* Nicholas Horseman,[1] clerk, last rector.[2]

A feature of the wills of our ancestors was a bequest to the cathedral and the parish church. The will of John Lewis of Cwmcarvan is dated 28 December, 1623, proved at Llandaff 1 September, 1624.

To the cathedral church of Landaffe vj*d*.—towards buying new bell ropes for the bells of Comcarvan vij*d*. —to Lewis Watkin one *kowe* [cow] called Chery—to Wenthian Watkin another kowe called Rethy—to Elizabeth Watkin and William Watkin all household stuff after the death of Margarett my wife—Roger my godson.

1 The names of John and Anne Horseman appear as witnesses to a deed relating to Llantilio Crossenny, dated 2 August, 1600, preserved in the National Library of Wales. In the copy of the parish registers of Llantilio, preserved in the Bodleian Library, occurs the burial of Gladys, wife of David Horseman, 22 February, 1614.
2 King's Book of Payments.

There are two old books of registers both in a fair condition, one from 1662 to 1705, the other from 1728 to 1774. From the date of the appointment of William Morris as rector in 1672 there are several entries of interest, a fine taste in Latin being often displayed :—

1681, Mar. 28, buried John Evans of Bayly-Glasse, and was the first that was buried in wollen since the additional Act came in force.

Scale, 1 in. = 1 foot.

By 1686 an Irishman had entered the parish with evil result :—

168⅚, Jan. 30, Elizabetha, filia notha genita a Philippo Morphy, Hibernico, et a Rachell Thomas, viduâ, baptizata in Lanthomas.

[*Elizabeth, the bastard daughter born of Philip Murphy, an Irishman, and Rachel Thomas, widow, was baptized at Llanthomas.*]

The child is, however, buried in the April following, being called the daughter of Philip Morphy and Rachel *John*.

There were chosen for Churchwardens or Guardians at the Communion Table upon Palme Sunday according to the Antient Custome used in this Parish for to serve that office for the year 1697 these two persons followinge.

Wm Morris, Rector }
John Jones   } 1697.

169¾, Jan. 24, Tacy Rogers, senilis et longaeva vidua, sepulta fuit in Cœmiterio nostro juxta horologium solarium.

[*Tacy Rogers, an aged and long-lived widow, was buried near the sun-dial in our church-yard.*]

169⁴⁄, Jan. 28, Johannes George, antiquissimus mortalium in hâc viciniâ, sepultus fuit.

[*John George, the oldest mortal in this neighbourhood, was buried.*]

1695, Jun. 16, Blanchia, uxor Georgij William, sepulta in hâc ecclesiâ Comcaruanensi.

[*Blanch, the wife of George William, was buried in this church of Cwmcarvan.*]

This woman was brought from Langouen to be buried here, and Charles Pask hath promised for to pay the foure shillinges due for buriall as soon as it is demanded.

It was agreed upon by the consent of the Parishioners present upon the 21st day of July 1695 that the churchwardens shall disburse the summe of five shillinges for the reliefe of the sufferers at Warwicke by fire, for a great part of Warwicke was burnt with fire.

Attested by me Wm Morris.

1695, Oct. 8, Johannes Jones et uxor ejus Anna grauida et pregnans in vinculo matrimonij fuerunt juncti.

[*John Jones and his wife Anne heavy with child were joined in the bonds of matrimony.*]

Puella, filia senior Johannis Jones p'dicti, nata fuit et baptizata fuit per Johannem Llawlis in eodem mense, post matrimonium contractum sine meâ veniâ.

[*A girl, the eldest daughter of the aforesaid John Jones, was born, and baptized by John Llawlis in the same month, after a marriage contracted without my licence.*]

169⁵⁄, Jan. 8, Johannes, filius Johannis Tyler, operarij, natus in perbrevi temporis spatio post clandestinum matrimonium contractum, et baptizatus fuit in Combychan privatim.

[*John, son of John Tyler, labourer, born in a very short space of time after a clandestine marriage had been contracted, was privately baptized at Cwmbychan.*]

1695, Puella, filia Johannis Jones, baptizata fuit in meâ absentiâ, Johanne Lawlis vicino vicario domi privatim, mense Octobris, nescio diem.

[*A girl, the daughter of John Jones, was baptized in my absence at home, privately, by John Lawlis a neighbouring vicar, in the month of October, I know not the day.*]

1696, Maria Griffithes, femina pia, justa, et religiosa, sepulta fuit in nostrâ parochiali ecclesiâ tertio die mensis Aprilis.

[*Mary Griffiths, a woman pious, just and religious, was buried in our parish church the third day of April.*]

1696, Gulielmus Evans et Dorothea Davies de Llanthomas nupti illegaliter et privatim in mense Augusti, nescio quo die.

[*William Evans and Dorothy Davies of Llanthomas were illegally and privately married in the month of August, I know not which day.*]

1690, Johannes Rosserus, vir valde et mirifice pius, probus, et religiosus, hujus parochiæ fulcrum et columna, et, fere dixissem, unicus homo in quo primus Adamus non peccavit, e vivis emigravit. Et pia anima ejus immortalis in Coelum Empiricum verum et reale Elysium, beatorum sedem advolavit, cum in illâ supremâ regione Animabus Cœlicolis et Angelis Seraphicis societate conjunxit. Reliquiae ejus

mortales in nostrâ ecclesiâ Cumcarvanensi jacent sepultae, Ac in quiete hic jaceant usque ad supremum tubae clangorem, ad purpuream resurrectionis auroram, ad gloriosum Domini adventum. Heu, heu, heu! Vale, vale, vale, carissime amice! Oh beatissima anima! Et, vir mortalium justissime, vale iterum usque ad diem ultimi judicij horrisonum. Corpus ejus in sepulchro reconditum secundo die mensis Decembris, anno Domini 1690.

[*John Rosser, a man exceedingly and wonderfully pious, honest and religious, the support and pillar of this parish, and, I had almost said, the only man in whom the first Adam had not sinned, passed from among the living. And his pious soul immortal flew to the highest heaven, the true and real Elysium, the seat of the blessed, and joined in that highest region in company with souls the inhabitants of heaven, and angel seraphs. His mortal remains lie buried in our church of Cwmcarvan, and in quiet may they lie here till the last sound of the trumpet, till the purple aurora of the resurrection, till the glorious coming of our Lord. Alas, alas, alas! Farewell, farewell, farewell my dearest friend! Oh, most blessed soul! And, Oh man, most just among mortals, farewell again till the terrible-sounding day of the last judgment. His body was covered in the grave the 2nd day of the month of December in the year of our Lord 1690.*]

16—, Rosserus Williams, textor, vir honestus sed verecundus separatista a ritibus et cultu publico in parochiali nostrâ ecclesiâ, inhumatus.

[*Rosser Williams, weaver, was buried, an honest man, but a shame-faced abstainer from the rites and public worship in our parish church.*]

1697, Oct. 18, Margaretta Edmonds alias Browne, uxor Johannis Edmonds olim villiciani servi ejus, post longam corporis infirmitatem aut aegritudinem, sepulta fuit in nostro cœmiterio juxta prioris ejus mariti tumulum.

[*Margaret Edmonds otherwise Browne, the wife of John Edmonds formerly her farm servant, after a long frailty or sickness of body, was buried in our churchyard near the tomb of her former husband.*]

169⁷⁄, Feb. 20, David Stepheens, sutor pannosus, vir bonus et amicus Ecclesiae, in senectute suâ migrante vitâ.

[*David Stephens, a ragged cobbler, a good man and friend of the Church, his life passing away in his old age.*]

Thomas Evans of Pennalt was a croping of an Oke in madam Kemeys her lands in the Glanney farme, and the bough or limme of the tree that he was cuttinge fell upon the bough where he stood upon, and with the weight thereof kill'd him, on the 20th day of April, and was buried the 21st of April in the churchyard at Comcarvan 1700.

1700, Aug. 25, Judith, filia Danielis Phillips, Anabaptista, baptizata fuit Anabaptice a patre suo aut nominata fuit domi privatim.

[*Judith, daughter of Daniel Phillips, an Anabaptist, was baptized in the Anabaptist way by her father, or was named at home privately.*]

1701, William, son of Daniel Philip, an Anabaptist, who refuses to have his child baptized, was borne on Easter day the 5th of Aprill 1701.

It may be presumed that Daniel Phillips got over his objection to baptism, for on 8 May, 1704, he has a daughter Elizabeth baptized.

Monumental Inscriptions.

ON NORTH WALL OF CHANCEL.

Erected to the Memory
of John Edmonds
of Graige y dorth in this Parish
who died the 10th day of Aug. 1819,
aged 71 years.
Also to the Memory of
Sarah wife of the abovenamed
who died January 11th, 1848
Aged 87 years.

Underneath lie the Remains
of FRANCES BIGHAM wife of
WILLIAM BIGHAM
of the Parish of Langoven
who died 25th of Septr 1788
Aged 41 years.
Also the above Willm Bigham
who died 13th of June 1812
Aged 63 years.
Likewise Elizabeth Bigham
daughter of the above
who died 28th of May 1813
Aged 35 years.

Sacred to the Memory
of William Blower
of this Parish
who died November ye 23, 1823
Aged 53 years.

ON SOUTH WALL OF CHANCEL.

In Memory of
Elizabeth the wife of
Thomas Warner Gent
who departed this life April the 12, 1739
She was daughter of John Belfon &
sister to Maurice Belson Efq. late of
Brill in Buckinghamshire
Granddaughter by the mother's side
of Colonel Gage a Gentleman well
known for his Loyalty to King Charles
the first & keeping a troop of Horse
at his own Expense in his service.
Also in memory of
Sarah relict of the Reverend
Richd Horstone a Noted Divine
in Somersetshire who departed
this life Decbr the 28th, 1739.

ON SOUTH WALL OF NAVE.

In memory of the children
of Walter & Elizth Blower
Ann, Jane, & James, they all
Died in their Infancy.
Also the above named Walter
Blower who Died the 12th of
March 1787 Aged 55 yrs.

Here
lieth the Body
of John Blower spinster (sic)
who died 27 August 1660
Also here lieth the Body of
William Blower, Gent
Son of William & Ann Blower

of ye towne of Monmouth
who died December the 8
1766 aged 30 years.
Also here lieth Ye Body
of Elizabeth wife of
the late William Blower of
this Parish who died the . .
of April 1781 Aged 53 Years.

FLAT STONES IN NAVE.

Here
lieth the Body of
Lewis Charles of
this Parish who
departed this life
the 24th of June 1804
Aged 87 Years.

In Memory of Elizabeth
the wife of Charles Paske
who died 19 of February
1768 Aged 43 Years.
Also in memory of the above
Charles Paske who departed
this life the 3rd Novr 1806 Aged 8 . . . (?)

FLAT STONES IN THE CHANCEL.

Under the communion table :
John Edmonds.

HEARE VNDER LIETH
THE BODY OF ROWLA
ND BLOWER WHO DI
ED A BAHLER[1] AND WAS
BVRED THE 18 DAY
AVGVST AN'O DOM
1660.

Here
lieth the Body
of WILLIAM BLOWER of ye
town of Monmouth, Gent.,
who departed this life
28 of Septr 1741 aged 53.
Alfo here lieth the Body of
ANN, Reclict of the above
named William Blower, who
Departed this life ye 9 day
of June 1754 Aged 51 years.
In Memory of
ELIZABETH BIGHAM
daughter of
WILLM & FRANCES BIGHAM
of the Parifh of Langoven
who died May the 28th 1813
Aged 35 years.

IN THE CHURCHYARD.

An altar-tomb.   On the south side :
In Memory of
SUSANA wife of WILLM DAVIS
who died the 9 of July 1787
AGED 40 YEARS.
Alfo the above WILLM DAVIS
died the 17 of May 1810
AGED 76 YEARS.

1 Bachelor.

On the top, south slope:

Also MARY, wife of the under-named WILLIAM DAVIS, she died March 7th, 1876, aged 88 years.

On the north side:

In memory of Susanna, daughter of William and Mary Davis of the parish of Mitchel Troy, who died April 14, 1823, aged 9 years. Also Dina, daughter of the above-named, died April 27, 1823, aged 5 years. Also Diana, daughter of the above-named, died April 29, 1823, aged 7 years. Also Eliza, daughter of the above-named, died May 9, 1823, aged 2 years. Also William, son of the above-named, died May [blank] 1823, aged 9 months.

Also in memory of William Davis, father of the above & son of W. & S. Davis, died June 1831, aged 51 yrs.

At the east end:

Also Elizabeth Morgan, daughter of Wm and Susanna Davis, who died 5 Dec. 1821, aged 15 years.

Also William Davis, son of the before-named W. & Mary Davis, who died Sep. 8, 1829, aged 3 yrs.

At the west end:

In Memory of John, son of Willm & Susana Davis, who died Novr 16, 1803, aged 18 years.

An altar-tomb within rails. On the south side:

Sacred to the Memory of JAMES RICHARDS of this Parish, who died the 9th day of December 1841, Aged 63 years.

Within the same rails an altar-tomb. On the south side:

In Memory of LEWIS RICHARDS of Troy House, who died the — day of August 1807, aged 59 years.

On the north side:

Also in Memory of ELIZABETH, the wife of the aforesaid LEWIS RICHARDS, who died the — of September 18—, aged 55 (?) years.

An altar-tomb. On the south side:

In Memory of ANNE, wife of EDMUND BLOWER of the Parish of Wonastow, who departed this Life July 15, 1817, Aged 39 years.

Also SARAH, Daughter of the above-named, who departed this Life April 11, 1813, Aged 5 months and 3 weeks.

On the north side:

Sacred to the Memory of EDMUND BLOWER of the Parish of Dingestow, who departed this Life the 19th day of May 1836, Aged 52.

A pedestal. On the east side:

Sacred to the Memory of ELIZABETH, wife of WALTER BLOWER of the Parish of Wonastow, who died June 20, 1867, Aged 61 years.

On the north side:

In memory of SARAH JANE, daughter of Wm & ANNE BLOWER of the parish of Wonastow, who departed this life June 13th, 1872, aged 4 months and one week.

On the west side:

In loving memory of WILLIAM BLOWER, who died Feb. 19, 1897, aged 59 years.

On the south side:

Sacred to the memory of WALTER BLOWER, late of the parish of Wonastow, who died February 1st, 1863, aged 54.

An altar-tomb. On the south side:

In
MEMORY of JOHN
EDMONDS, GENT, late of
TREELY in this Parifh who
died ye 8 of July 1763
Aged 81 years.

On the north side:

In
MEMORY of HENRY
EDMONDS Efqr late of
GWAYLODYLADE in this
Parifh who died ye 12th of
October 1772 aged 80.
From respect to the memory of
his Great Uncle, JOHN EDMONDS
STOCK of BRISTOL, M.D.,
repaired this tomb
1809.

An altar-tomb. On the north side:

In memory of WILLIAM NICHOLAS of this Parifh, who died Novr 22nd, 1798, Aged 48 years.

On the south side:

In memory of WALTER NICHOLAS of this Parish, who departed this Life Decber 22nd, 1854, Aged 71 years.

Also ANN, relict of the above-named, who departed this life March 3rd, 1857, Aged 76 years.

An altar-tomb. On the south side:

In memory of WILLIAM NICHOLAS, late of Trostrey Lodge in this county, who died January 16th, 1847, aged 75 years.

An altar-tomb. On the south side:

In memory of WILLIAM NICHOLAS WIGGINTON, who died June —, 1827, aged 14 years.

Pen-y-clawdd.

 EN-Y-CLAWDD means the *top* or *end of the dyke*. It takes its name from the earth-work on which the church stands, one of the many mounds which the early Welsh raised for purposes of defence. On three sides of the churchyard is a road, so that all remains of the dry moat have disappeared, though the mound can clearly be traced.

It is a small parish containing 796 acres. The rateable value in 1815 was 340*l.*, and in 1912 was 517*l.*

The population has been as follows:—

Year	1801	1811	1821	1831	1861	1871	1881	1891	1901
No. of inhab.	38	43	41	46	53	70	75	66	65

There has been a slight increase in the number of houses, the number being, 1861, 11; 1871, 13; 1881, 14; 1891, 17; 1901, 17.

The Manor.

Among the knights' fees belonging to Gilbert de Clare, earl of Gloucester and Hertford, who was killed at Bannockburn in 1314, is one knight's fee in Pen-y-clawdd, held by Robert Avenel,[1] worth yearly 6*l.* 13*s.* 4*d.*, and a half knight's fee in Pen-y-clawdd, held by **Madog ap Walter**, of the yearly value of 100*s.*

Robert Avenel was one of the family from whom descended the Williams of Trevildu. Of this family was Ralph Avenal, who in 1190 held the manor and castle of St. Briavels, whose son William left a daughter Dulcia, married to John de Muscegros.[2]

Lower Pen-y-clawdd.

The chief house and estate in the parish was Lower Pen-y-clawdd. Of its early history I have no knowledge, but at the beginning of the eighteenth century it was the seat of Edmund Bradbury, esq., who in 1732 served the office of sheriff. This gentleman, who also had an estate at Crick, married Temperance, daughter of Charles Williams of Bristol, by Temperance, daughter of Henry Rumsey of Usk. This last Temperance married for her second husband sir John Williams of Llangibby, 4th baronet. Edmund Bradbury was followed by his son, Edmund

Rumsey Bradbury,[1] who is said to have dissipated his property by extravagant living. By his executors the estate was purchased by . . . . Williams, whose son John Williams died about 1850, aged about 92. This John Williams had a son William, and a daughter Catharine married to Robert Thomas, whose son is mr. John Thomas of the Court in Llanfihangel Ystern Llewern. By William Williams, who died in 1886, Lower Pen-y-clawdd was devised to his wife's relatives, Messrs. James and Charles Prichard of Penallt, who now own it.

The house is the usual type of seventeenth century small squire's residence. A room in which justice was administered by mr. Bradbury is called the *swearing-room.*

Upper Pen-y-clawdd, of which I have no account, was an ordinary farm-house until enlarged by John Hodges Winslow of Trelech,[2] who for a time resided here. He built a brick archway by which the premises are approached, on one pillar being the month MAY, and on the other 1861.

Ty-Harry.

Ty-Harry (*Harry's house*) probably takes its name from Harry, the grandfather of Richard ap John ap Harry, described as of Pen-y-clawdd in the sixteenth century. Richard married Alice, daughter of Philip ap William, descended from that branch of the Herbert family seated at Llansantffraid.[3]

In 1735 Ty-Harry belonged to Edward Proger of Wern-ddu, who, by indentures dated 5 November, 9 Geo. II., 1735, in conjunction with Elizabeth his wife, mortgaged it for 120*l.* to Thomas Gibbins of Clowerwall [Clearwell], co. Gloucester, wheelwright. It is described as that messuage called Tir-Harry and another messuage called the Pant, with closes called Cae-glan-y-nant (*the field on the bank of the brook*), Cae-canol (*the middle field*), Cae-dan-y-ty (*the field below the house*), Pen-y-lan (*the top of the bank*), Cae kill haith, Cae'r-pren (*the tree field*), Y-ffos-fach (*the little dyke*), Cae'r-pren-ywen (*the yew-tree field*), Cae-cefn-yr-onnen (*the field on the ridge of the ash*), in two parcels, and Coed-tir Harry (*the wood of Harry's land*), in the parishes of Pen-y-clawdd and Llangoven, lately in the occupation of

---

1 *Vide* p. 189.
2 Bristol and Gloucestershire Archæological Society, iv., 318.

---

1 Edmund Rumsey Bradbury was born 4 February, 17$\frac{18}{19}$, and baptized at Pen-y-clawdd 7 February, 17$\frac{18}{19}$. *Vide* pedigree, p. 139. A mistake is made there in saying that he died in 1739.
2 *Vide* p. 40.
3 *Vide* pedigree, Vol. I., p. 318, and II., p. 187.

Edward Steward, as tenant by lease from Jeronyma Proger, mother of the said Edward Proger, and now in the occupation of Walter Steward,[1] son of the said Edward Steward, as tenant to the said Edward Proger, at the annual rent of 32l. 10s., and also that tenement of lands in the occupation of William Laurence in Llangoven.

Further indentures of mortgage were made 9 February, 22 Geo. II., 1748, between Edward Proger of Wern-ddu, esq., and William Proger of Wern-ddu, gent., only son and heir-apparent of the said Edward Proger, of the 1st part; John ffoyle Small of Uley, co. Gloucester, gent., and Mary his wife, formerly Mary Phelps, of the 2nd part; and William Phelps, late of Raingworthy, but now of Cote, co. Gloucester, esq., and John Purnell of Dursley, mercer, of the 3rd part. Reciting indentures dated 16 and 17 October, 1745, between the said Edward Proger and Elizabeth his wife, and the said William Proger of the one part, and the said Mary Small, by her then name of Mary Phelps, spinster, of the other part, whereby it was witnessed that in consideration of 500l. the said Edward Proger granted the premises; and whereas the said Edward Proger having occasion for a further sum of 50l., has applied to Mary Small.

PEN-Y-CLAWDD CHURCH.

The result of these mortgages was that William Proger had to sell the estate, James Duberly of Dingestow being the purchaser at the price of 1400l., the deed of sale being by indentures quadripartite dated 30 September, 1771, between John Purnell of Dursley, esq., of the 1st part; John Small of Uley, only son and heir of John ffoyle Small, late of the same place, gent., by Mary his wife, formerly Mary Phelps, spinster, and also administrator of the said Mary Small, his late mother, of the 2nd part; William Proger, formerly of Wern-ddu, but now of Llanfoist, esq., only son and heir of Edward Proger, late of Wern-ddu aforesaid, gent., by Elizabeth his wife, both deceased, of the 3rd part; and James Duberly of Dingestow, esq., of the 4th part.

Ty-Harry since this has continued as one of the farms on the Dingestow estate, now belonging to mr. Samuel Courthope Bosanquet.

The Church.

The church consists of chancel and nave, with a bell turret at the west end. The edifice underwent considerable alterations about the year 1860, when the chancel arch of the Norman period was replaced by a gothic shaped one of Bath stone; the bell turret was at the same time raised in height. In 1885 further alterations were carried out, the walls being denuded of the original plaster and imitation pointing substituted. At this date the ancient porch

[1] In the list of non-jurors to king George I., 1715, is Edward Bowyer (see p. 74), with an estate at Pen-y-clawdd and Llanishen, occupied by Edward Steward. Edward Steward must have been a stranger and a settler in the district, and, as he testifies on p. 198, knew little or no Welsh. He married the daughter of one Walter George, as appears by the baptism of his daughter Anne in the registers of Cwmcarvan:—

169⅘, Jan. 9, Anna, filia Eduardi Stewart, coriarij, generi Walteri George, baptizata domi privatim.

[*Anne, dau. of Edward Stewart, currier, son-in-law of Walter George, baptized at home privately.*]

The will of Walter *Stuart* of Llangoven, farmer, is dated 8 December, 1762, proved at Llandaff 7 January, 1763:—

To my brother Charles Stuart of the said parish 1s.—my sister Ann Prichard of Penyclawdd—to my sister Sarah Stuart of Chepstow 1s.—to my nephew Wm. Robert, now of Cwmcarvan, 1s.—to my niece Ann Robert of Llangoven, spr., 1s.—my wife Rachell Stuart.

was replaced by the present one. The oldest register book commences with the year 1727. No Welsh services have been held for many years, but in an inventory of 1849 a Welsh Bible is mentioned. There is a fine silver chalice with lid used for paten, on which is the date 1576.

The church is said to be dedicated to St. Martin. The living has always been held with Llangoven, both having been perpetual curacies until recently, when by an order in council they were formed into a vicarage. Of the incumbents John Lawlis was a Carmarthenshire man, and his name occasionally is found in the register books of the neighbouring parishes as doing duty. Charles Evans was a son of Theophilus Evans, vicar of Llangammarch, the well known author of *Drych y Prif Oesoedd*. The vicarage house was built by mr. Homfray.

The following depositions[1] are of interest, by which it appears that at that time, 1725, most of the parishioners had come to understand the English language.

Depositions of witnesses taken at the dwelling-house of Thomas Pye in the town of Monmouth, innholder, 1 Oct., 1725, in a cause between Walter Churchey,[2] esq., complainant, and the archdeacon and chapter of Llandaff, defendants. Edward Stewart[3] of the parish of Penclawdd, gent., aged 53, hath known Penclawdd and Llangoven for above 30 years, and hath been inhabitant within the said parishes, or either of them, for above 30 years. John Jones of Dingestow, esq., was owner and occupier of the tithes of the said parishes when this deponent first knew the same, and continued so until about 6 years since, when plaintiff came to own them by lease from defendants.

One John Lawless did officiate and read divine service in the said parish churches when this deponent first remembers them. Upon his decease, about 12 or 13 years since, John Watkins officiated until last August three years, when he was arrested and imprisoned in Monmouth gaol, where he continued for above 12 months. When he came out of prison he did not officiate. He was excommunicated by the then bishop, and is now a prisoner for debt in Brecon county gaol. After his arrest there was no service for a month, till mr. James came from Llangwm. Afterwards one Hugh Pugh was appointed to the cure, and has ever since read divine service on Sundays and holidays, and preached every Sunday in the two churches alternately to the satisfaction of the parishioners. He (the deponent) is an Englishman, and understands little or no Welsh, but all or most of the inhabitants of both parishes do understand English, and there is a Welsh bible now in the said churches, and there was a Welsh com'on prayer book formerly there brought by Watkins, but the com'on prayer book and bible are only used there.

Hugh Pugh of Llangoven, clk., aged 43. He is paid by the complainants 20*l*. a year for serving the cure.

William Walter of Llangoven, gent., aged 70.

Thomas Davies of Landaffe, gent., aged 44. The archdeacon and chapter do and ought to pay the curates of the said parishes their stipends. John Watkins was appointed curate of the said parishes 30 June, 1710.

INCUMBENTS OF PEN-Y-CLAWD AND LLANGOVEN.

PATRON.	DATE OF INSTITUTION.	INCUMBENT.
. . . . .	. . . .	Nicholas Barton, resigned 1394 on presentation to Wonastow, in exchange with Philip Bost.[4]
. . . . .	4 Feb. 1394.	Philip Bost, previously vicar of Wonastow.
. . . . .	. . . .	John Lawlis in 1691 and to 1709,[5] a native of Llandysilio, co. Cardigan, admitted to priest's orders 2 Aug. 1696, with the title of curate of Llangoven and Llanishen; died about 1710.
. . . . .	30 June 1710.	John Watkins; in 1725 was in prison for debt in Brecon gaol.
. . . . .	. . . .	Hugh Pugh, officiating in 1725.
. . . . .	19 Nov. 1723.	John Watkins,[6] buried at Wolvesnewton 26 Nov., 1755.
. . . . .	. . . .	Charles Evans, son of Theophilus Evans, vicar of Llangammarch, officiated in 1752-3-4; also vicar of Dingestow.
Archdeacon & chapter of Llandaff.	3 March 1756.	Rice Davies.
Do.	. . . . 1774.	Thomas Davies, buried at Pen-y-clawdd 16 Dec. 1784.
Do.	. . . . 1789.	John Saunders, *vice* Davies, deceased;[7] was head master of the grammar school at Usk.
Archdeacon & chapter	3 March 1790.	William Williams; in 1796 appointed vicar of Magor and Redwick; died 1821, buried at Pen-y-clawdd.
. . . . .	9 Aug. 1822.	Hugh Lewis.[8]
. . . . .	. . . . 1836.	Thomas Kemp Phillips, died 2 March, 1838, aged 39; buried at Llangoven.
. . . . .	28 Nov. 1838.	James Farquhar, M.A. Jesus College, Oxford, son of Robert Farquhar of Trevethin, gent.; he resided at Court St. Lawrence; resigned 1852, on appointment to Llanddewi Scyrrid.
Dean & chapter .	26 Oct. 1852.	Kenyon Homfray, M.A. Worcester College, Oxford, son of Francis Homfray, clk., vicar of Llanarth and rector of Llanfair Cilgedin.
Do.	. . . . 1873.	Evan James Davies, B.A. Clare College, Cambridge, formerly curate of Monmouth, and afterwards curate of Machen.
Do.	. . . . 1878.	John Powys David, son of the Welsh bard Dewi Wyn o Essyllt; died 1888.
Do.	. . . . 1888.	William Rees, resigned 1909.
Do.	. . . . 1909.	Daniel James Sproule, B.A. Lampeter College, previously curate of St. Mark's, Newport.

1 Exchequer Depositions, 12 Geo. I. (1725), Mich., 3 Monm.
2 Walter Churchey was of a family long settled in Abergavenny. The name seems at one time to have been Shershaw, *vide* Vol. I., p. 288. His interest in this parish was that he had recently purchased Court St. Lawrence, p. 200.
3 Edward Stewart was the occupier of Ty-Harry farm, *vide* p. 197.   4 *Cal. Rot. Pat.*, Ric. II., 1391-6, p. 549.
5 Children of John Lawlis, clk., are baptized at Llangoven between these dates.
6 This may be the same John Watkins as the one above.   7 *New Annual Register*, vol. lix., p. 217.
8 Buried at Bryngwyn, 1835. *Vide* p. 109.

The only ancient monument is one that was found buried under the floor when the church was restored in 1885. This was then placed on the floor of the chancel, and has recently been fixed upright against the wall. It is the figure of a priest of the fourteenth century. The head is broken away, but the robe is decorated with a cross having fleur-de-lys terminals.

Scale, 1 inch = 1 foot.

Monumental Inscriptions.

There are no memorials in the church, with the exception of a flat stone inside the tower:—

HEARE VNDER LYETH THE
BODY OF RICHARD EDWARDS
OF PENYCLAWDD, AND WAS
BVRIED THE 12 DAY OF
MARCH IN THE YEARE OF
OVR LORD GOD 1673.

FLAT STONE IN THE PORCH.
HERE LYETH THE BODY
OF WALTER EDMONDS
INTERRED THE 25
DAY OF MARCH 1676.

A FLAT STONE OUTSIDE THE PORCH.
Here lieth ye body of
Francis Hall of Tetbury
in Glofterfhire, who
died February ye 18, 1766
Aged 72 years.

IN THE CHURCHYARD.

An altar-tomb. On the south side:
Erected
in Memory of SUSANNAH
wife of WILLIAM WILLIAMS,
Minister of this parish,
who died the 14th day of January, 1808,
Aged 58.

On the west side:
Erected
in Memory of
WILLIAM WILLIAMS, CLERK,
Vicar of Magor and Redwick
in this County,
Who died 30th Nov., 1821,
Aet. 73.

On the east side:
In Memory of James Williams of the parish of Cwm-carvan, son of the Rev. William & Susannah Williams, late incumbent of this parish, who departed this life the 2 day of Sep., in the year of our Lord 1825, aged 42 years.

On the west side:
Also to the memory of Howell Williams, late of Ponty-pool in this County, son of the before-named William & Susannah Williams, who died Jany the 20th, 1860, aged 70.

An upright stone:
MARY, wife of ARNOLD BARNOLD *of the parish of Din-gestow*, who died Jan. 13th, 1846, aged 55 years.
Also Thomas, son of the above, died in his infancy.
Also of the above named ARNOLD BARNOLD,[1] who died April 15th, 1848, aged 74 years.

An altar-tomb:
Sacred to the memory of JAMES, son of JOHN and ANN WILLIAMS of this parish, who died Dec. 7th, 1804, aged 9 weeks.
RACHEL, their daughter, died April 7th, 1808, aged 9 weeks.
Also ANN, wife of JOHN WILLIAMS, died July . . . 18 . . . .
In memory of ELIZABETH, the daughter of JOHN and ANN WILLIAMS, who died July . . . 18 . . . . aged . . . .

An altar-tomb:
In affectionate remembrance of MARY, wife of WILLIAM WILLIAMS of this parish, who died Feb. 18th, 1880, aged 75.
Also of WILLIAM WILLIAMS of Lower Pen-y-clawdd, died July 28th, 1886.

A tablet fixed on the west wall of the church records the only charity:—

Charity to be received from the Poors' land of Lanishen, the above is taken from an abstract of the Will & Testament of William Jones of Tregyrog, in the Parish of Lanishen in the County of Monmouth, Gentleman, towards the Relief of the poor & impotent people of the parish of Pen-y-clawdd in manner & form following, that is to say, to the Poor of Pen-y-clawdd aforesaid Forty shillings a year for evermore.

---

1 This is almost an unique instance of ap Arnold becoming Barnold, as ap Owen becomes Bowen. For this man's pedigree, *vide* Vol. I., p. 259, where he is described as Arnold Arnold, in 1799 of Triley mill. By his wife Mary he had issue John, James, Ann, Mary.

Llangoven.

LANGOVEN takes its name from St. Cofen, the founder of the church, though more is not known of him except that he is said to have lived in the seventh century and to have founded St. Cofen's church in Pembrokeshire. His festival is on 3 June.[1]

In the list of benefices belonging to the see in the time of Henry, bishop of Llandaff 1193-1218, this place appears as *ecclesia de lanchouian,* and worth yearly 4*l.* 10*s.* (iiii libræ et x solidi).[2]

The parish contains 1898 acres, and the rateable value in 1815 was 1009*l.,* in 1891, 1139*l.,* and in 1912 1103*l.*

The population has been as follows :—

Year .	1801	1811	1821	1831	1841	1861	1871	1881	1891	1901
No. of inhab.	141	133	137	136	136	137	89	120	113	115

The number of houses has continued much the same :—

Year.	Inhabited Houses.	Uninhabited Houses.	Building.
1861 . . .	24	0	0
1871 . . .	21	2	0
1881 . . .	23	6	0
1891 . . .	23	4	2
1901 . . .	25	0	0

Court St. Lawrence.

In Welsh this place is called *Llanlawrence,* by which it may be inferred there was once a church here dedicated to St. Lawrence. In 1622 the manor of Llanlawrence was held of the earl of Pembroke under the castle of Caerlleon by sir Charles Jones of Dingestow, knt. (lately Arnold Williams, esq.), by knight's service and suit of court. Sir Charles, by his will proved in 1637, left this manor with other property to his eldest son John, on condition of payment of 300*l.* to his daughter Jane.

In 1677 Thomas Jones, grandson of sir Charles, held the manor, whose son John Jones of Dingestow, esq., by indenture dated 6 October, 1702, conveyed to Thomas Webb of Gloucester, gent., by way of mortgage for 800*l.*

All that messuage in Llangoven in the possession of David Lewis called Wern Obrey, with lands, etc., and the messuage called St. Lawrence, and a messuage called the ffower Ashes, in the possession of John James.

1 Iolo MSS., p. 558.
2 Book of Llan Dâv, appendix, p. 284.

By indenture dated 19 August, 1714, between the said Thomas Webb of the 1st part, sir William Compton of Hartpury, co. Gloucester, bart., of the 2nd part, the said John Jones of the third part, and Josiah Larkin of Bristol, merchant, of the 4th part, a further charge is made, in which the premises are described as :—

All that messuage or tenement and farm called Wern Ober in Llangoven, and lands called Cae pedair onnen, Cae'r-berllan, Cae'r velin syder, Cae nant y berttaine, Y palsie bach, Gworlod y velin cyder, Gworlod y symon, Cae'r ffwrndu, all mearing with the lane from Four Ashes to Pont Erfill, and with lands of George Thomas and the Pant lands, and in possession of Charles Morris; and messuages called Saint Lawrence and Four Ashes farms with the lands called Cae'r-park, Cae'r-pwll coch, Cae'r pell frening, Cae'r tir march, Cae'r park issa, Cae'r odyn, Gworlod y park, Gworlod yr hendre, Cae'r bont, Cae'r bont faith, Cae dan y ty, Cae'r velin, Cae main, Cae'r fald, Cae cefn y vorland vawr, Cae'r pistyll, Cae'r quarrel, Cae'r gelli, Gworlod ucha, Gworlod issa, all in Llangoven, and in the possession of John Williams, containing 350 acres.

By indenture dated 30 December, 1719, the said John Jones and Catherine his wife convey to Walter Churchey of Usk, esq., in consideration of 2421*l.,* the manor of St. Lawrence and the farms of St. Lawrence and the Four Ashes called Pedair Onnen containing 87 acres and 90 acres, Wern obrey 90 acres, the Pant 34 acres and Gorsmonth 70 acres, in Llangoven; the Kelldy farm and Burgess wood in the parish of Usk.

Walter Churchey sold the same 6 March, 1733, for 4000*l.* to Roger Coningsbye, esq. After this Charles de Lack owned the manor and estate, who on 11 April, 1776, sold the same for 6000*l.* to Henry Morgan of Caerlleon, esq. (as trustee for Richard Lee of Clytha, esq.), and on 16 January, 1789, the said Henry Morgan as trustee mortgaged the estate to William Jones of Clytha, esq.

By indenture dated 25 August, 1802, between the said William Jones of the 1st part; Mary Morgan and Elizabeth Morgan, both of Caerlleon, spinsters, of the 2nd part; the said Richard Lee of the 3rd part; and Edward Berry of Monmouth, esq., of the 4th part, reciting that the said Henry Morgan had lately died, leaving the said Mary and Elizabeth his only children, co-heirs at law . . . the said parties conveyed the estate to Edward Berry for 4000*l.*

Mr. Edward Berry, who thus became the purchaser of Court St. Lawrence, was a Yorkshireman, and in conjunction with Robert Vaux, also from Yorkshire, founded silk mills at Spitalfields, where they made a fortune. Settling at Court St. Lawrence, which till then had not been more than a farm house, he rebuilt the house and made numerous plantations of trees, which are now in full maturity. Some time before his death, which occurred in 1818, mr. Berry purchased Lower Llancayo, near Usk, to which he removed and built there a new house. He is buried in Usk churchyard. Court St. Lawrence was then occupied by mr. Robert Vaux. In 1819 Berry's estates were put up for sale, and Vaux purchased Court St. Lawrence. The next purchaser was the rev. Robert Williams of Rhyd-y-croesau, near Oswestry, the well-known scholar and author of a Welsh grammar. He sold in 1870 to John Henry Skyrme of Ross, solicitor, who in 1873 sold to Hugh Grainger Earnshaw, who made many improvements both to the house and the surroundings, and resided here till his death.

Certain lands were sold in 1819 by the trustees of Edward Berry to James Richards of Cwmcarvan, viz., the Red pear tree meadow, bounded on the north-west by the road from the Kingcoed to Pen-y-clawdd; Cae'r-groes-las, bounded on the east by the road from Usk to Pen-y-clawdd; the Yewtree field; the Longfield; and another close, parcel of Gorsmoth farm in Llangoven.

Trecastle.

Trecastle, properly Tre'r-castell (*castle town*), is an ancient dwelling standing on early earthworks. By the plan it will be seen that the earthworks are of considerable extent, and appear to consist of two separate mounds, each of which has been entirely surrounded by wet moats, and in a large degree are still so surrounded. The mound on the north of the house is circular and about 20 ft. in height, while the one on the eastern side of the house is lower, and apparently was also circular. The house itself stands on what has been an out-work, and in its present form seems to have been built or rebuilt in the seventeenth century. There is a panelled hall, from which is entered a parlour with a decorated ceiling. It has long been occupied by farmers. The place was in the seventeenth century the residence of a family named Aylworth, presumably of Gloucestershire origin.[1] They mostly remained catholic, and William Harcourt, the notorious jesuit concerned in the plots of Titus Oates, is said to have been in reality William Aylworth, and to have been born in Monmouthshire in 1625.[2]

The first of whom I have any note is John Aylworth, who died in 1660. His wife was a sister of Matthew Nelson of Penrhos, also a catholic.[3] John, the last to reside here, appears among those who refused the oaths to George I., his estate at

Llangoven being returned as worth 64*l*. 7*s*. 6*d*. per annum.

Described as of Trecastle, gent., he made his will 8 January, 1725, proved at Llandaff 5 April, 1726, by Elizabeth, the widow :—

> All my messuage wherein James Stockings[1] did lately inhabit called the Gader farm in the hamlet of Llanthomas to Thomas Lewis of Monmouth, mercer —messuage called the Pant in Lanvair Cilgedin to Thomas Lewis, mercer, and after to my nephew John Gosling of Chepstow, cooper, and all my mefs's in Cwmcarvan and Mitchel Troy, the hamlet of St. Brides, Landevenny, Wilgrig, Langoven, Lanishen and Comyoy to Thomas Lewis—Hannah, wife of Robert Jacob of Chepstow, yeom.—Ann, Elizabeth, Winifred and Hannah, four dau's of John Prichard of Skenfreth, yeom., by Anne his wife, my niece—Wm Gosling of Bristol, ship's carpenter—my wife Elizabeth—my nephew Henry Cadogan of Kemeys Commander—all that my leasehold messuage and farm called Trecastle to the said Thomas Lewis for the use of my wife for life, and after to my nephew John Gosling—my nephew Roger Cadogan of Landenny—Roger, son of Roger Cadogan of Bristol—Jane, wife of Wm Humphreys of Tidenham—Winifred, wife of Mr Herbert and dau' of Henry Scudamore of Pembridge castle—Elizabeth Rowles of St. Maughans 20*s*.

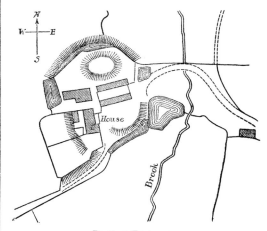

PLAN OF TRECASTLE.
Scale, 25 in. = 1 mile.

John Gosling of Chepstow, cooper, to whom the estate of Trecastle was left by his uncle John Aylworth, made his will 5 January, 1741, proved at Llandaff 9 January, 174½ :—

> To my brother William Gosling of the city of Bristol, carpenter, 6*l*. yearly out of my lands at Trecastle—to my niece Mary Prichard, youngest dau. of John Prichard of Skenfrith, carpenter, 100*l*.—when the lands, mess's, etc., bequeathed to me by my uncle John Ailworth, late of Trecastle, shall come into my ex'or's hands, lands and mess's in Chepstow, Cwmcarvan, Mitchel Troy, St. Brides, Llandevenny, Wilerick, Llangoven, Llanishen, Cwmyoy and Llanvair Cilgedin to my friend Wm Evans of Chepstow, bellfounder, in trust that, in 4 years after the death of my aunt Elizabeth Ailworth, he pay William

---

1 There are pedigrees of Aylworth in the parish of Naunton in the Visitation of 1623 (Harl. Soc., xxi., 7), and of 1683 (Fenwick and Metcalfe, 1884).

2 *Records of the English Province of the Society of Jesus*, by Foley, v., 480.

3 *Vide* p. 98.

VOL. II.

Gosling aforesaid 6*l.* yearly—Anne Prichard, eldest dau. of John Prichard of Skenfrith—my niece Hannah Jacob—40*s.* to be distributed among the poor present at my funeral at Llangoven church.

Elizabeth, the widow of John Aylworth, made her will 26 March, 1745, proved at Llandaff 18 November, 1747, in which she mentions her niece Catherine Wood of Redmark, co. Worcester, Daniel, Anne, Mary, Sarah and Catherine, children of the said Catherine; her niece Elizabeth, wife of John Holder of Redmark, yeoman; and John, Elizabeth, Cathe-rine and Mary, children of the said John and Elizabeth Holder.

I give the pedigree, but am unable to continue it to the present day.

In later times the estate belonged to the 5th duke of Beaufort, and it is possible that it was never the freehold estate of the Aylworths, but was held by leases under the Somerset family. The farm has recently been sold by the 9th duke of Beaufort to the County Council, who intend to cut it up into small farms under the Small Holdings Act.

Pedigree of the family of Aylworth of Trecastle.

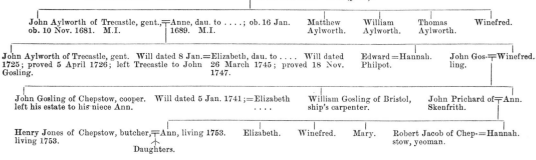

Somewhere in Llangoven, probably at Court St. Lawrence, lived in the sixteenth century Saunder John, who married Jane, daughter of David ap Philip (Herbert) of Llansantffraid.[1] There is an elegy by Dafydd Benwyn, the Glamorgan poet, on the death of Sawnder Sion.

> Bar'nod Sawnder Sion o Went
> Hiraeth am wr hir waith mwy
> Y sy ymwes is Mynwy.
> Dydd y fu fal dydd y farn.
> Dreio hil Drahaearn,
> Hil hau Ieuan fraylan frig,
> Y mae hiraeth ym heirig.
>
> Sawndwr, milwr y moliant,
> Sion od gwin Dafydd Gam dant
> Yn iach bod yn wybodus.

[*I have a longing in my bosom for one I shall never see*
Again in lower Monmouth.
The day he died was as the judgment day.
The stock of Trahaiarn were on their trial,
The stock of Ievan, the alert offspring,
Are in sorrow for one from Meurig.

Saunder, the soldier worthy of praise,
John, whose wine was like that of David Gam,
Being strong and clever.]

The references to his descent imply that he was descended from Trahaiarn,[2] who was lord of Penrhos Fwrdios and steward of the lordship of Caerlleon in 1454. Trahaiarn was the son of Ievan, lord of Penrhos in 1433, who was the son of Meurig, son of Howel Fychan, son of Howel Gam ap David, the latter living at Penrhos in 1326, and so descended from Rhys Goch.

The following lines shew that he was buried in Llantarnam church, that he was a poet and a supporter of the monastery there, and that he was skilled in falconry and coursing. He is also spoken of as a player on the harp—telynwr o'n iaith :—

> Yn nghôr Mihangel inghaf
> Y mae wely mi wylaf.
> Yno y mae ywenydd
> A dysg wych a dewis gwydd.
>
> A llew'r fonachlog oll aeth
> Ddeuma'n hwyr ddoe mewn hiraeth.
>
> Na cheisynt roeddynt ba rhaid
> Heibio ogylch hebogiaid,
> Na moliant na mwy o berch.
> Wylwm na milgwn na meirch.

[*In the choir of St. Michael*
Is a bed, I shall weep.
There is poetry there
And great learning and choice knowledge.

And there went the lion of the monastery
Of Deuma yesterday to our regret.

They will not have what was needful
By the flying of falcons around,
No more praise or reverence,
We weep that there are no greyhounds or steeds.]

---

1 *Vide* pedigree, Vol. I., p. 319.
2 From Trahaiarn descended sir Roger Williams who died in 1595, author of *Actions in the Low Countries.*

Of this family was William ap Edmond Saunders of Llangoven, probably grandson of Saunder John, who made his will 2 April, 1625, proved at Llandaff 24 April, 1625 :—

The vicar of Langoven for tithes xij*d.*—the cathedral church of Landaph xij*d.*—Blanche Tho. of Lansoye x*li.*—Roger W^m of Lanyssen xx*li.*—George ap John of Dignestowe v*li.*—Doritie Tho. of Langoven v*li.* xs.—William Richard of Langoven vij*li.*—Walter Thomas of Langoven iiij*li.*—Maude Harry my wife, 2 parcels of land called Tyre pelley egha and Tyre pelley yssa in the parish of Langoven—William Edmond my brother—Johan Edmond of Cumcarvan my sister—Anne W^m my supposed dau.

In the pr' of Andrew Nicholas ; John Harry George ; William Edmond, iunior ; Maude John, the wife of William Richard of Langoven.

Another will of the same family is that of William Saunders of Llangoven, gent., dated 13 March, 1612, proved (P.C.C., 3, Cope) 24 January, 1615, by Philip Saunders, the son :—

To be buried in the church of Langoven—cathedral church of Landaff 12*d.*—for forgotten tithes 6*d.*—to Phillip, son of Margaret Watkin, being the supposed son of me, three score pounds, two great candlesticks, one dozen of my best pewter dishes or platters, two great brazen crocks, two of my best pans, two of my best feather beds with appurt's, one great table in the hall, one chair, one long cleaning board in the chamber over the hall, one trunk, two of my best coffers, two great andirins, one great cupboard, one great spit and furniture, three of my best barrels—Philip, the son of Margaret Watkin, being the supposed son of me the said William Saunders, ex'or.

Witnesses : Morgan Amorgan de Lanvappley, William Howell of Lanbaddogge, Thomas Gwillim of Monmouth, William Watkins, Alice Morris.

Debts due to me :—

Sir Charles Jones, knight, xli*li.*, received thereof ix*li.* Item—due from the said knight for specialty lxxxx*li.*

The Church.

The church consists of chancel and nave with a bell turret at the west end supported on arches. The door and steps to the rood loft from the chancel are intact, though nothing remains of the loft except a beam above the arch. The appearance of the edifice is early English, though the chancel arch would seem to be Norman. The porch on the south side is not so old as the nave, as it partly conceals a pointed window of early English design. At the west end is a handsome Tudor doorway with a holy-water stoup in a niche.

LLANGOVEN CHURCH.

In the churchyard are the base and four steps of an ancient cross, to which were added in 1903 by Mrs. Earnshaw of Court St. Lawrence a new shaft with carvings displaying on the west the rood, and on the east a figure representing the patron saint crowned, and holding the model of a church.

The living is a vicarage united to Pen-y-clawdd, the two having always been held together.

The porch referred to above as not being so old as the church would seem to have been erected some time after 1625. John Jenkin of Llangoven leaves in his will a sum for this purpose, dated 19 June, 1625, proved at Landaff 4 August, 1625 :—

To the cathedral church of llandaffe xij*d.*—reparation of the church of llangoven towards the erecting of a new porch there 5*l.*—to the curate of llangoven for forgotten tithes iij*s.*—to my son John my best brass pan, etc.—to my dau. Susan half the household stuff—my sister Gwenllian—Bridget my wife, the other moiety of household stuff—my sister Katherine.

Monumental Inscriptions.

ON WALL OF THE BELL-TURRET.

Near this place lie the Remains of Mary the wife of William Williams of the parish of Lansoy, who died Jany the 8th, 1795, Aged 72 years.

The following has been removed from the chancel :—

In the centre of this chancel within the Communion rails lie the remains of the Revd Thomas Kemp Phillips, for about two years perpetual curate of Llangoven and Pen-y-clawdd. He died universally regretted on the 2nd day of March, 1838, Aged 39 years.

FLAT STONES IN THE CHANCEL.

HERE LIETH THE
BODY OF MARY,
THE WIFE OF
LYSON THOMAS,
WAS BVRIED THE
24 OF AVGVST
1684
Here lyeth alſo the body of
CHARLES Howell who
departed this life January
the 6 Day and was buread the
8 Day Anno Dom' 1705.

HEAVN'S IN MY EYE, ITS
BEAVTIES ARE
MY PRIZE, HEAVEN'S A REWARD
For him that EARTH
DENIES.

Here lyeth the Body of William Lawrence who departed this life ye 7th day of May Anno Dom' 1740, aged 73 years.

HEREVNDER LIETH THE BODY OF
JENKIN GEORGE WHO DEPARTED
THIS LIFE AND WAS BVRIED
THE 6 DAY OF APRIL IN
THE YEAR OF OVR LORD
GOD 1681.

HERE LYETH INTERRED THE BODY
OF JOHN AYLEWORTH, GENT
WHO DECEASED THE TENTH DAY
OF NOUEMBER ANNO DOM' 1681
MORIOR VT VIVAM.

Then follows some fanciful carving, a circle with IHS, and W. M., CARVER.

HERE ALSO LYETH THE BODY OF JOHN
AYLEWORTH, GENT., FATHER TO THE
ABOVE SAID JOHN AYLEWORTH, WHO
DIED THE 22TH OF JANVARY 1660.
AND HERE ALLSO LYETH MARTHA AYL' HIS
WIFE WOH DIED THE 20 OF OCTOBER 1669.

HERE VNDER LYETH
THE BODY OF ANE AYLEWORTH
WIFE TO JHON AYLEWORTH,
GENT., WHO DIED ON THE
16 DAY OF JANVARY
AN'O DOM' 1689.

Followed by carving and IHS.

VNDER THIS STONE
INTERRED HERE DOTH LY
THE MIRROR OF ALL PARTS
FOR HER CHARITIE.
RELIGION WAS HER RVLE,
CHRIST WAS HER GVIDE,
A VERTVOVS LIFE SHEE LEDD,
AND SO SHEE DIED.

FLAT STONES IN THE PORCH.

Here lyeth ye Body of Henry Williames who departed this Life y^e . . . day of May, 1734, Aged 43 years.

Here lyeth ye Body of Anne Williams of this parish, who departed this life the 25 day of October, Anno Dom. 1736, Aged 36 years.

ON THE WALL.

To the Glory of God and in loving memory of Harry Popplewell Earnshaw, who was born 12th Oct., 1870, and fell during the attack on Gatyis Kraal, Marandellas, South Africa, 20th Oct. 1896.

Grant him, O Lord, eternal rest, and may light perpetual shine upon him.

IN THE CHURCHYARD.

An altar-tomb. On the north side :

Here Interred doth lye ye Body of Elizabeth Lewis ye wife and Relict of David Lewis of Llanishen, Gent. She departed this life ye 1st Day of September 1718, Aetatis suae 56.

On the top :

Here . . . Thomas Lewis of Llanishen in this County, Gent., who departed this life December the 10th, 1728, aged 36.

On the south side :

Mary, wife of James Davies of Lanerthill, Gent., died 27 Sept. 1739.

Mary, wife of David Lewis of Usk, Gent., died 10 May 1754, aged 31.

On the west end :

[In raised letters] 1718.[1]

A flat stone :

Here lyeth the Body
of Margareat ye daugh
ter of John Tudor of
this Pariſh who died
the 29 day of April
Anno Domini 1751.

Her Parents Speaks ye 26th
Year of Her Age God
Call Her From This
Mortal Stage And Said
Here In A Bed Of
Clay Short Was Her
Life Much Was Her Pain
Great Was Our Love
Much Was Her Gain.

An altar-tomb. On the north side :

In Memory of GWELTHIAN
WALTER of the Pariſh of Lanishen
She die Dec. 28th, 1729, aged 84 years.
Also
GEORGE WILLIAMS of the pariſh of
Lanishangel he die April 25th, 1739
Aged 68 years.

---

[1] The people memorialized here appear in the pedigree of Lewis on p. 46.

On the south side :

In Memory of PETER WILLIAMS
of the parifh of Lanishangel tormynydd
he die Feby 6th, 1782, aged 62 years.
ALSO
FRANCES, relict of the above named
She die January 23rd, 1799
Aged 82 years.

An altar-tomb. On the south side :

To the memory of Mary, wife of Charles Herbert of the Church Farm in this parish, departed this life May 18th, A.D. 1824, aged 41 years.

Also Thomas, son of the above-named, who departed this life April 9th, 1818, aged 11 months.

On the north side :

Also to the memory of Charles Herbert, who departed this life October 6th, A.D. 1839, aged 70 years.

An upright pedestal. On the north side :

In memory of Robert Vaux, Esq., of Court St. Lawrence in this parish, and of West Green, Tottenham, Middlesex, who departed this life the 7th of June, 1838, aged 70 years.

On the west side :

Also Georgiana Louisa his daughter, and wife of the Rev. James Farquhar, born June 4th, 1812, died April 26th, 1897. Interred at Llanthewy Skirrid.

On the east side :

Also his three other daughters, Emma Vaux died 23rd Sept. 1876, Hannah Matilda Botcherly died 3rd August, 1865, Lavinia Soper died 12th Feby 1874. Interred in Highgate Cemetery, London.

In memory of Robt Chas Vaux, Esq., son of Robt Vaux, Esq., of Court St. Lawrence in this parish, who departed this life 29th Augt 1837, aged 38.

Arms : *A bend chequy.* Crest : *An eagle's head erased, ducally gorged.*

An upright pedestal. On the south side :

In memory of Georgiana Louisa, daughter of the Rev. James Farquhar, M.A. (minister of this parish), and Georgiana Louisa his wife. She died January 13, 1846, aged 14 months and 8 days.

On the north side :

Also Matilda Louisa his daughter, born July 17th, 1851, died July 4th, 1864. Interred at Llanthewy Skirrid.

On the west side :

Also of the Rev. J. Farquhar, M.A., J.P., Rector of Llanthewy Skirrid, born Nov. 15th, 1812, died Nov. 16th, 1879.

Also Robert Vaux his son, born April 12th, 1841, died July 10th, 1890.

Interred at Llanthewy Skirrid.

Llandogo.

LANDOGO is so named from the founder of the church Docheu, in Latin Oudoceus, the 3rd bishop of Llandaff, who lived in the sixth century. This bishop is usually spoken of by the Latinised form of his name, which in the *Liber Landavensis* appears in the compound form of Lann Oudocui. The name would in modern Welsh be written Euddogwy, or shorter Docheu, and in old Welsh is found as Eudoce in the *Life of St. Cattwg.*[1] Oudoceus was the son of Buddig, a native of Cornouailles in Brittany, by Anawfedd, a sister of Teilo. In the *Life of St. Oudoceus*[2] it is related that Einion, king of Glewyssig, was hunting a stag among the rocks and woods of the river Wye, when the stag reaching the cloak of Oudoceus lay down on it, the hounds being then unable to touch it. Oudoceus, who was full of age, served God on the brook Caletan (now Cleddon), of whom king Einion and the hunters asked pardon as if they had committed a crime. The king gave the stag to Oudoceus, and gave to the see of Llandaff the territory round which he had gone during the day following the track of the stag. The situation abounding in fish and honey, Oudoceus built a house and an oratory, and there resided after he had resigned the see. Further on is the grant of the church to the see of Llandaff by Morgan, king of Glewyssig. The boundaries are:—

> From the Cyfylchi to the stone of Oudoceus, to the ridge of the cliff along the upper side to the ford as far as the Caletan. Along the ridge as far as the bottom of the Weun to the middle of the mountain, to the red pool as far as the Olwy. Thence from the Gwenffrwd to Trylec Bechan.

Among the witnesses are Oudoceus and king Morgan.

The boundaries as given above represent a larger piece of ground than the parish at present occupies, extending into Trelech parish, but with the same frontage to the river Wye as now. The stone of Oudoceus is that locally called the *Money stone.*

The meadow (weun) still exists, now known as Waun-y-parc.[3] The red pool near the Olwy is the Virtuous well at Trelech. Whitebrook (Gwenffrwd) is still so called.

Buddig, the father of Oudoceus, has his name preserved in the wood called Coed-Buddig,[1] and also in Bigsweir, while Coed-Ithel, a house and small estate in the parish, records the existence of king Ithel, the son of Arthrwys, a contemporary of Oudoceus.

The Manors.

The estate of Pilston in the northern part of the parish is held as of the lordship of Trelech. The rest of the parish is a manor belonging to the see of Llandaff.

The parish contains 1821 acres of land and 44 acres of water. The rateable value in 1815 was 1011*l.*, in 1891, 2078*l.*, and in 1912, 2020*l.*

The population has been as follows:—

Year	1801	1811	1821	1831	1841	1861	1871	1881	1891	1901
No. of Inhab.	589	612	612	646	660	648	679	583	552	487

While the population has decreased, there has been a similar decrease in the number of houses:—

Year.	Inhabited houses.	Uninhabited houses.	Building.
1861	148	7	0
1871	154	6	0
1881	134	15	0
1891	137	17	0
1901	130	13	0

The main road from Monmouth through Llandogo and Tintern to Chepstow was made between the years 1826 and 1830, and at the same time the bridge over the river Wye at Bigsweir was built.

The parish comprises a long strip of land with narrow meadows along the river Wye, backed on the west by a steep hill covered with woods. The village is picturesquely situated in the dingle which runs up to Cleddon. Here is one of the few water-falls in the county, the Cleddon brook falling precipitously down the ravine, and known as Cleddon Shoots. There was at one time a considerable traffic carried by ships locally called sloops, which carried timber and other products to Bristol. This trade has almost disappeared, but a few sloops are still employed.

The chief residence in the village is that known as the Falls or the Priory. This was built by lady Gough about 1846, and about the year 1870 was

---

1 *Cambro-British Saints*, p. 92.

2 *Liber Landavensis*, pp. 123 and 370; *Book of Llan Dâv,* p. 130.

3 This appears in the revised edition of the ordnance map as Wern-y-parc.

---

1 This figures in the ordnance map as Coed-Beddick.

purchased by Antonio Gallenga, who much improved it. Mr. Gallenga was a writer of some repute, and engaged on the *Times* as a writer of articles. He was by birth an Italian who left his country owing to political differences with the authorities. It has since been purchased by mr. Henry de la Pasture.

Pilston.

The natural meaning of Pilston might be the town on the pil, the latter word being in common use for a brook entering the sea or a river. There is, however, no such pil here. It is probable, therefore, that Pil is a man's name, the place being so called as the town or home of Pil. In the *Lives of the Cambro-British Saints*, p. 89, Pill lector (*Pill the reader*) is a witness to a grant.

The manor of Pilston, *alias* Tal-y-van, was held of the lords of Usk and Trelech by a quarter of a knight's fee. William ap John ap Perkin, descended from Sitsyllt, prince of Meirionydd, came from North Wales in the sixteenth century and married Jane, the daughter and heir of Madog ap Robert of Pilston, and his descendants, known as Perkins, continued to own the estate till the close of the eighteenth century. In a rent-roll of the manor of Usk in 1570 George ap Robert, esq. [of Pant-glas], holds freely lands in Llandogo, late of Walter ap Robert, in the occupation of Christopher Perkin, at the rent of a red rose.

By a deed[1] dated 14 July, 1571, Richard Catchmay of Llandogo, gent. (afterwards sir Richard Catchmay of Bigsweir, knt.), conveys to the same Christopher Perkins a meadow called Russell's Meadow, situated in a field called Broadfield:—

> . . . . totum jus meum etc. in uno prato vocato Russells Medowe in quodam campo ibidem vocato Brodefyld, in longitudine et latitudine inter terras Thome Som'sett, armigeri,[2] terras Johannis Bozley seu terras Thome Cachemay, generosi, et terras Georgij Catchemay, ex omnibus partibus etc.

PILSTON.

Russell's Meadow or Mead again appears in a deed[1] of 1633 by which, with another meadow called Black Thorns, it is granted by William Perkins (son of the above Christopher) and his son and heir Edward to sir Richard Catchmay.

> Sciant presentes quod nos Gulielmus Perkins et Edwardus Perkins, filius et heres mei predicti Gulielmi Perkins de Pilston in parochia de landoggoe, generosi, dedimus etc. Richardo Catchmay, militi, duas parcellas terrarum vocatas Black Thornes et Russells Meade continentes septem et dimidium acras etc. 23 Sept., 1633.

The above William Perkins is described as of Pilston, gent. His will was proved (P.C.C., 68, Essex) 10 May, 1648, by Edward Perkins the son.

> My body to be buried in the parish church of Landogo—to Moore Perkins my natural son[2] 5*l*.—to my grandchildren Elizabeth P. and Edmond P., dau. and son unto the said Moore P. my son, 5*l*. a piece at 21—to my dau's Mary Edmonds, Elizabeth Phillips, and Anne Herbert xx*s*. a piece—to my grandchildren Elizabeth P., Margaret P., Jane P., and X'topher P., son and dau. to my son Edward P., 5*l*. a piece—to my grandchild Martha P. 30*l*. on day of marriage—to Richard P. xx*s*. to be laid out in apparel for him after my decease—to my servants John Younge and Thomas Rosser xx*s*. a piece—to my servants Sara Brumage, Mary Mathew, and Jone Williams 5*s*. a piece—to the parish church of Landogo a sufficient pulpit cushion and pulpit cloth—to the poor of Landogo 5*l*.—to John Kearney, minister of Landogo, in regard to his frequent visiting of me during my sickness and his labour in dictating this my will, for that I nominate him to preach my funeral

---

1 In the National Library of Wales.
2 I do not think that *natural* here means illegitimate.

1 Carta penes auctorem.
2 Thomas Somerset, esq., was second son of Henry, second earl of Worcester. He was M.P. for co. Monmouth in 1553, and died in the Tower of London in 1586.

sermon, 3*l.* to be paid the day of my burial—I appoint Edward Perkins my son sole ex'or, and I give him Pilson with all my lands and all houses, cattle, plate, etc.

Witnesses: Mary Perkin, John Kerny, Jo. Tilden.

A certain portion of the estate, if not all, seems to have been leasehold under the lords of Trelech, as the following lease to Mary, widow of Edward Perkins (son of the above William), shews:—

This ind're made 12 March, 20 Car. II., 1667, between the rt. hon. Philip, earl of Pembroke and Montgomerie, lord Herbert of Cardiff, baron of Shurland, lord Parr and Ros of Kendall, lord Marmion and St. Quintin, and lord ffitz Hugh, of the one part, and Mary Perkins of Pilstone, widow, of the other part, witnesseth that the said earl, in cons'on of the surrender of an estate for the lives of John Williams and Mathew Perkins as also for the sum of 10*l.* fine, doth demise and to ffarm let to the said Mary P. all that dwelling house with appurt's together with three parcels of arable, woodland and pasture, called the Grove, the Hillclose, and the Cutts Hay; the two former situate in the parish of Landogoe and lordship of Trelegg situate between the lands called the Heall and Pwll Blethin, the lands called the Millclose and the place where a water mill heretofore stood and the lands late of Edmund Perkins; the Cutts Hay lying between the lands of Zacharie Cadell, the lands in the holding of William John Will'm, and the lands in the holding of John Robert on all sides, all which were in the possession of X'pofer Perkins, gent., and now in the possession of the said Mary, to have and to hold for fourscore and nineteen years, if the said Edward Perkins, son of the said X'pfer Perkins late of Pilstone, esq., dec'd, Edward White of Hewersfield, gent., grandson of the said Mary Perkins, Mathew Perkins, son of Moore P. of Sully, co. Glamorgan, esq., or either of them so long live, paying the yearly rent of 3*l.* 10*s.*, and also doing suit of court and suit of mill by grinding his and their grist at some mill or mills of his lordship's inheritance, etc.

[Signed]   PEMB. AND MONTGOMERY.

In the presence of :
Henry Rumsey, John Aldey, Christopher . . . .

The above Mary Perkins made her will 30 November, 1675, proved at Llandaff 17 October, 1683.

To be buried in the church of Landogo—to the four children of my son and dau. Reynalds, both deceased—my dau. Jane and her children—my grandchild Mary Bond—my dau. Jane Jones—to my grandson Edward Perkins my leases of messuages, woods, etc., held under the noble lord of Pembroke in the parish of Landogo appertaining to his estate of Pilstone — my servant and kinswoman Elizabeth Edwards—the rest to my dau. Margaret de la Hay, she sole ex'trix.

The will is signed with a ✕. The seal has on it a rose slipped and leaved.

The last of the name to reside here was Edward Perkins, who on 4 October, 1747, met with a melancholy fatality. Driving down the steep lane by Pen-y-van from a visit to his friend mr. Rumsey at Trelech, the horses ran away, and mr. Perkins got entangled in the harness and was killed. His wife, to whom he had been married less than two years, was with him at the time, but was uninjured. She was a miss Smith of Isleworth, sometimes called Thistleworth, and had a fortune of 20,000*l.*,[1] and it is presumed she went back to her own home, as Pilston was allowed to get into disrepair, and the furniture, pictures, etc., were ruined by the rain which came in through the roof. Edward Perkins, nephew of the above Edward, was the heir, and he died without issue in 1770, when the estate devolved on Thomas Eagles of Bristol, whose father William had married Cecilia, sister of Edward Perkins. It does not appear that Thomas Eagles ever lived here, he being described as of Bristol, and about 1830 the estate was sold for 20,000*l.* to captain George Rooke of Bigswear, son of colonel James Rooke, who was wounded at Waterloo.

In 1801 Pilston was in ruins, and in the ordnance map of 1830 it is marked *ruins*, and was in this condition when captain Rooke purchased it. He pulled down the remains of the old mansion, much of which had previously been carried off by the small proprietors in the neighbourhood to repair their cottages, and with the materials built the present house a few yards north of the old site. He, however, never occupied the house, preferring to live in the Florence on the opposite side of the river, which he had built after the model of a cottage he had brought with him from Switzerland.

Dying without issue he left Pilston to his kinsman major-general sir Willoughby Rooke, K.C.H., whose great-grandson, mr. George Douglas Willoughby Rooke, now owns the estate.

Of the old house there are no remains left standing, though the site is pointed out in the shrubberies. In the wall of the new house is a stone evidently taken from the old building—

. . . .

THE 16
1686.

Around the house are plantations of trees, some being valuable specimens of Wellingtonias and other kinds of fir made by sir Willoughby Rooke, and on the bank behind the house is a terraced kitchen garden, which appears to have belonged to the old house.

---

[1] *Gent. Mag.*

Pedigree of the family of Perkins of Pilston.

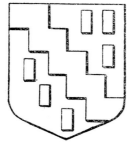

PERKINS OF PILSTON.

SITSYLLT, PRINCE OF MEIRIONYDD.

The early part of this pedigree is from an illuminated roll, dated 1647, belonging to major Leonard John Graham-Clarke, D.S.O. The atchievement of arms on this roll is—*Quarterly : 1, Arg., a lion pass. sa. between 3 fleur-de-lys gu. ; 2, Gu., a lion ramp. reguard. or* (ELYSTAN GLORYDD); *3, Arg., 3 boars' heads couped sa.* (RHYN AP EDNOWEN); *4, Per bend sinister erm. and ermines, a lion ramp. or* (TEWDWR, PRINCE OF FFERLIS). Crest: *A lion pass. sa., holding in his dexter foot a fleur-de-lys gu.*

In 1634 the following coat and crest were granted by Richard St. George, Clarenceux king of arms, to William Perkins of Pilston, gent., son of Christopher Perkins of the same place : *Or, a bend dancettée between 6 billets sa.* Crest: *A hand issuing out of a cloud sa. to the sinister, holding a pomegranate slipped and erect, both ppr.* Notwithstanding this grant the roll referred to above takes no notice of it, and throughout assigns to Perkins the ancient coat.

A bookplate exists in which the granted coat is erroneously drawn—*Arg., a bend dancettée erm. between 6 billets vert.* The crest is similar to that granted, except that there is no cloud. Motto : UTILE DULCI. Subscription :—

Edw*d* Perkins, ESQ :
PILSTON, MONMOUTHSHIRE,
1744. BATH Skinr. Sculp.

SITSYLLT, prince of Merionydd. (*Arg., a lion passant sa., armed and langued gu., between 3 fleur-de-lys of the 3rd.*)

Einion ap Sitsyllt.

Goronwy ap Einion＝Metherys, dau. to Owen Cyfeiliog, prince of Powys. (*Arg., a lion ramp. sa., armed and langued gu.*)

Sir Tewdwr, knt. of the sepulchre.＝

Gruffydd ap Sir Tewdwr.＝

Perkin Gruffydd＝Jane, dau. to John ap Iorwerth. (*Per bend sinister erm. and ermines, a lion ramp. or.*)

John Perkin＝Jonet, dau. and heir to David ap Llewelyn of Builth. (*Quarterly : 1 and 4, Gu., a lion ramp. reguard. or ; 2 and 3, Arg., 3 boars' heads couped sa.*

William Perkin＝Jane, dau. to Madog ap Robert of Pilston. (*Arg., on a bend sa. 3 mullets of the field.*)

John Perkin＝Maud, dau. to David ap Goronwy ap Ieuan. (*Arg., semée of trefoils vert, a lion ramp. or.*)

William Perkin, left his country＝Joyce, dau. to John Llewelyn. (*Arg., a chevron between for slaughter. 3 boars heads couped sa.*)

John Perkin of Tintern＝Maud, dau. to John Llywarch. (*Arg., a chevron between 3 ravens sa., in the beak of each an ermine spot.*)

William Perkin of Pilston. The first in the pedigree at the＝. . . . dau. to . . . . of Trefildu. (*Arg., a fesse heralds' visitation, 1683. between 3 annulets gu.*)

Richard Perkin of Pilston＝Marian, dau. to Thomas Catchmay of Mitchel Troy. (*Arg., on a chevron gu. between 3 demi-lions ramp. az., as many bugle-horns or.*)

Christopher Perkins of Pilston,＝Jane, dau. to Christopher Hall of＝Moore Gwillim of Monmouth, esq., M.P. Monmouth 1584-5 and 1586-7 ; gent., living 1571. Highmeadow, esq. bur. at Monmouth 17 June 1611. 2nd husband.

William Perkins of Pilston, gent., living 1647.＝Eleanor, dau. to George Edmund Perkins. William Jones of＝Jane, only child Had a grant of arms 1634, *Arg., a bend* Catchmay of Bigswear, Llanarth, esq. and heir. *dancettée between 6 billets sa.* esq. (Arms as above.)

Vol. I., p. 306.

1. Edward Per-＝Mary, dau. to Roger Mor- | 2. George | 3. Moor Per-＝Elizabeth, dau. | 1. Ann, mar. | 2. Elizabeth, mar. | 3. Mary, mar*d* kins of Pilston, | gan of Llanfrechfa, gent. | Perkins of | kins of Sully, | to William | Richard Her- | Thomas Phillips of | David Ed- esq., ob. circa | Will dated 30 Nov. 1675 ; | London. | co. Glamor- | Mathew of | bert of Calde- | Tal-y-van in Cwm- | munds of 1650, æt. circa | probate 17 Oct. 1683. | | gan, esq. | St. Y Nil, co. | cot, gent. | carvan, gent. | Cwmcarvan. 66. | (*Or, a gryphon segreant* | | | Glamorgan. | | | *sa.*)

A ... B ... p. 62.

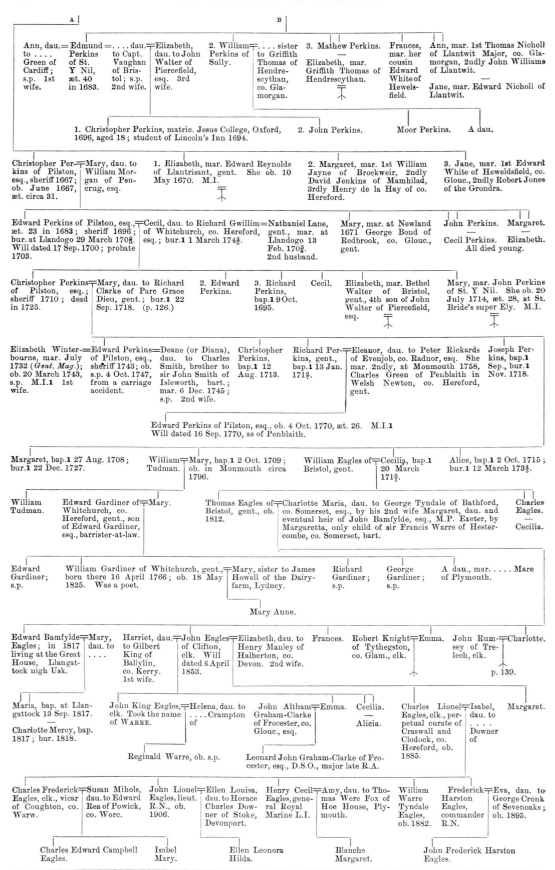

A | B |

Ann, dau. = Edmund = ... dau. = Elizabeth, | 2. William = ... sister | 3. Mathew Perkins. | Frances, | Ann, mar. 1st Thomas Nicholl
to .... | Perkins | to Capt. | dau. to John | Perkins of | to Griffith | — | mar. her | of Llantwit Major, co. Gla-
Green of | of St. | Vaughan | Walter of | Sully. | Thomas of | Elizabeth, mar. | cousin | morgan, 2ndly John Williams
Cardiff; | Y Nil, | of Bris- | Piercefield, | | Hendre- | Griffith Thomas of | Edward | of Llantwit.
s.p. 1st | æt. 40 | tol; s.p. | esq. 3rd | | scythan, | Hendrescythan. | White of | —
wife. | in 1683. | 2nd wife. | wife. | | co. Gla- | | Hewels- | Jane, mar. Edward Nicholl of
| | | | | morgan. | | field. | Llantwit.

1. Christopher Perkins, matric. Jesus College, Oxford, | 2. John Perkins. | Moor Perkins. | A dau.
1696, aged 18; student of Lincoln's Inn 1694.

Christopher Per- = Mary, dau. to | 1. Elizabeth, mar. Edward Reynolds | 2. Margaret, mar. 1st William | 3. Jane, mar. 1st Edward
kins of Pilston, | William Mor- | of Llantrisant, gent. She ob. 10 | Jayne of Brockweir, 2ndly | White of Heweldsfield, co.
esq., sheriff 1667; | gan of Pen- | May 1670. M.I. | David Jenkins of Mamhilad, | Glouc., 2ndly Robert Jones
ob. June 1667, | crug, esq. | | 3rdly Henry de la Hay of co. | of the Grondra.
æt. circa 31. | | | Hereford.

Edward Perkins of Pilston, esq., = Cecil, dau. to Richard Gwillim = Nathaniel Lane, | Mary, mar. at Newland | John Perkins. | Margaret.
æt. 23 in 1683; sheriff 1696; | of Whitchurch, co. Hereford, | gent., mar. at | 1671 George Bond of | — | —
bur. at Llandogo 29 March 170⅔. | esq.; bur. 1 March 1744. | Llandogo 13 | Redbrook, co. Glouc., | Cecil Perkins. | Elizabeth.
Will dated 17 Sep. 1700; probate | | Feb. 170¾. | gent. | All died young.
1703. | | 2nd husband.

Christopher Perkins = Mary, dau. to Richard | 2. Edward | 3. Richard | Cecil. | Elizabeth, mar. Bethel | Mary, mar. John Perkins
of Pilston, esq.; | Clarke of Parc Grace | Perkins. | Perkins, | | Walter of Bristol, | of St. Y Nil. She ob. 20
sheriff 1710; dead | Dieu, gent.; bur. 1 22 | | bap. 1 9 Oct. | | gent., 4th son of John | July 1714, æt. 28, at St.
in 1725. | Sep. 1718. (p. 126.) | | 1695. | | Walter of Piercefield, | Bride's super Ely. M.I.
| | | | | esq.

Elizabeth Winter- = Edward Perkins = Deane (or Diana), | Christopher | Richard Per- = Eleanor, dau. to Peter Rickards | Joseph Per-
bourne, mar. July | of Pilston, esq., | dau. to Charles | Perkins, | kins, gent., | of Evenjob, co. Radnor, esq. She | kins, bap. 1
1732 (Gent. Mag.); | sheriff 1743; ob. | Smith, brother to | bap. 1 12 | bap. 1 13 Jan. | mar. 2ndly, at Monmouth 1758, | Sep., bur. 1
ob. 20 March 1743, | s.p. 4 Oct. 1747, | sir John Smith of | Aug. 1713. | 171⁹⁄. | Charles Green of Penblaith in | Nov. 1718.
s.p. M.I. 1 1st | from a carriage | Isleworth, bart.; | | | Welsh Newton, co. Hereford,
wife. | accident. | mar. 6 Dec. 1745; | | | gent.
| | s.p. 2nd wife.

Edward Perkins of Pilston, esq., ob. 4 Oct. 1770, æt. 26. M.I. 1
Will dated 16 Sep. 1770, as of Penblaith.

Margaret, bap. 1 27 Aug. 1708; | William = Mary, bap. 1 2 Oct. 1709; | William Eagles of = Cecilia, bap. 1 | Alice, bap. 1 2 Oct. 1715;
bur. 1 22 Dec. 1727. | Tudman. | ob. in Monmouth circa | Bristol, gent. | 20 March | bur. 1 12 March 173⅘.
| | 1796. | | 171⁹⁄.

William | Edward Gardiner of = Mary. | Thomas Eagles of = Charlotte Maria, dau. to George Tyndale of Bathford, | Charles
Tudman. | Whitchurch, co. | | Bristol, gent., ob. | co. Somerset, esq., by his 2nd wife Margaret, dau. and | Eagles.
| Hereford, gent., son | | 1812. | eventual heir of John Bamfylde, esq., M.P. Exeter, by | —
| of Edward Gardiner, | | | Margaretta, only child of sir Francis Warre of Hester- | Cecilia.
| esq., barrister-at-law. | | | combe, co. Somerset, bart.

Edward | William Gardiner of Whitchurch, gent., = Mary, sister to James | Richard | George | A dau., mar. .... Mare
Gardiner; | born there 16 April 1766; ob. 18 May | Howell of the Dairy- | Gardiner; | Gardiner; | of Plymouth.
s.p. | 1825. Was a poet. | farm, Lydney. | s.p. | s.p.

Mary Anne.

Edward Bamfylde = Mary, | Harriet, dau. = John Eagles = Elizabeth, dau. to | Frances. | Robert Knight = Emma. | John Rum- = Charlotte.
Eagles; in 1817 | dau. to | to Gilbert | of Clifton, | Henry Manley of | | of Tythegston, | | sey of Tre- |
living at the Great | .... | King of | clk. Will | Halberton, co. | | co. Glam., clk. | | lech, clk. |
House, Llangat- | | Ballylin, | dated 6 April | Devon. 2nd wife. | | | | p. 139.
tock nigh Usk. | | co. Kerry. | 1853. |
| | 1st wife. |

Maria, bap. at Llan- | John King Eagles, = Helena, dau. to | John Altham = Emma. | Cecilia. | Charles Lionel = Isabel, | Margaret.
gattock 13 Sep. 1817. | clk. Took the name | .... Crampton | Graham-Clarke | | — | Eagles, clk., per- | dau. to |
| of WARRE. | of | of Frocester, co. | | Alicia. | petual curate of | .... |
Charlotte Mercy, bap. | | | Glouc., esq. | | | Craswall and | Downer |
1817; bur. 1818. | | | | | | Clodock, co. | of |
					Hereford, ob.
Reginald Warre, ob. s.p.	Leonard John Graham-Clarke of Fro-		1885.
	cester, esq., D.S.O., major late R.A.

Charles Frederick = Susan Mihols, | John Lionel = Ellen Louisa, | Henry Cecil = Amy, dau. to Tho- | William | Frederick = Eva, dau. to
Eagles, clk., vicar | dau. to Edward | Eagles, lieut. | dau. to Horace | Eagles, gene- | mas Were Fox of | Warre | Harston | George Cronk
of Coughton, co. | Rea of Powick, | R.N., ob. | Charles Dow- | ral Royal | Hoe House, Ply- | Tyndale | Eagles, | of Sevenoaks;
Warw. | co. Worc. | 1906. | ner of Stoke, | Marine L.I. | mouth. | Eagles, | commander | ob. 1895.
| | | Devonport. | | | ob. 1882. | R.N.

Charles Edward Campbell | Isabel | Ellen Leonora | Blanche | John Frederick Harston
Eagles. | Mary. | Hilda. | Margaret. | Eagles.

1 At Llandogo.

Pedigree of the family of Rooke of Bigsweir and Pilston.

ARMS.—*Arg., on a chevron engrailed between 3 rooks sa. as many chess-rooks of the field.*

[I am indebted for most of this pedigree to *The Genealogist*, vol. iv., p. 195 *et seq.*]

HEYMAN ROOKE of Isleworth, co. Middlesex (son of Lawrence Rooke of=Disney, Monkhorton, Kent, by Barbara, dau. to Sir Peter Heyman, knt., descended from | dau. to Thomas Rooke of Mersham, Kent, whose will was proved in 1538), major-general | .... in the army; bur. at Isleworth 16 Jan. 172⅘.

The lady Mary Tudor, base dau. of king=James Rooke, *jure uxoris*=Jane, dau. to Tracy Catchmay | Brudenel Rice=Anne, dau. to Tho-
Charles II. by mrs. Mary Davis. Her | of Bigsweir, esq., an officer | of Bigsweir, esq., and sister | Rooke, esq., | mas Millington of
1st husband was Edward, earl of Der- | in the army; bur. at St. | and sole heir of William Catch- | captain in the | St. Margaret's,
wentwater; her 2nd husband was Henry | Briavels 18 June 1773. | may of Bigsweir, esq.; mar. at | army. | Westminster, esq.
Grahame of Levens, co. Westmorland, | | St. Briavels 3 July 1735. 2nd
esq. 1st wife. | | wife.

James Rooke of Bigsweir, esq.,=Elizabeth | Barbara, mar. Martin | Jane, mar. Thomas Birt, | Eleanor, mar. Charles Wyndham of
general in the army, M.P. co. | Brown, | Barry, clk., vicar of | clk., vicar of Newland, | Clearwell, co. Glouc., esq.
Monmouth; bur. at St. Briavels | mar. 1777. | Down Hatherley, co. | co. Glouc.; s.p.
11 Oct. 1805. | | Glouc.; s.p. (p. 65.) | | *A quo* Lord DUNRAVEN.

James Rooke of Bigsweir, esq., lieut.-colonel=Mary, dau. and coheir | Jane Sophia, | Eleanor, mar. 1st colonel Patterson; 2ndly, at
in the army, aide-de-camp to the prince of | to Thomas Rigge of | ob. unmar. | Newland 7 Sep. 1802, lieut.-colonel Thomas
Orange at Waterloo; died in 1819 of a wound | Clifton, co. Glouc., | | Probyn, 18th Foot, son of Edmund Probyn of
received in action while a colonel in the | M.D.; mar. 1798. | | Newland, esq.; 3rdly, captain Charles Fallon,
Venezuelan army. | | | 11th Dragoons.

George Rooke of Bigsweir, esq., ob. cœl. 1839. Left Bigsweir and Pilston, which he purchased, to his kinsman sir Henry Willoughby Rooke.

Hayman Rooke, major in | Robert Rooke, | Henry Rooke, an officer=.... | Charles Rooke,=Elizabeth, dau. to Am- | Elizabeth, mar. John
the army, ob. cœl. 1806. | an officer in the | in the army, born 1742; | colonel in the | brose Dawson of Lang- | Douglas, clk., bishop
— | army; killed at | ob. June 1821; bur. in | army, died at | cliffe Hall, co. York, | of Salisbury.
Brudenel Rooke, ob. 1776. | the Senegal; | St. George's Chapel, | Windsor Castle | esq., by Mary, sister of
| s.p. | Windsor. | 1827. | sir Willoughby Aston,
| | | | bart.

Selina Mary, ob. 3 Feb.=Sir Henry Willoughby Rooke, K.C.H., C.B., | John Charles Rooke, lieut.- | Elizabeth Dinah.   Hannah Maria.
1859; bur. at Llan- | succeeded to Bigsweir and Pilston from his | colonel 3rd Guards; died of | ‿_____‿
dogo. | kinsman George Rooke in 1839; ob. 1869, | wounds in the Peninsular | Both unmar.
| æt. 87. | war.

George Charles=Eliza, | Caroline, dau.=Willoughby John Edward=The hon. Cathe- | William Fre- | Jane, born 1807; | Selina Elizabeth,
Rooke of Bigs- | dau. to | to Henry An- | Rooke, clk., vicar of Tun- | rine, dau. to | derick Hill | ob. unmar. 1836. | mar. William
weir and Pil- | .... | thony Little- | stall and Little Wymond- | Thomas Lister, | Rooke, born | — | Douglas, esq.
ston, esq., capt. | Neave. | dale, esq. 1st | ley, Herts, Dom. Chaplain | 1st lord Ribbles- | 1813; ob. | Caroline, unmar.
3rd Guards, | | wife. | to the duke of Cambridge. | dale. 2nd wife. | 1845.
born 1805; ob. | |
1840. | |

Willoughby Sandilands Rooke of Bigsweir and of Pilston, esq.,=Constance Lawson, dau. to Henry
lieut.-colonel Scots Fusileer Guards, born 1837. | Adams of London.

George Douglas Willoughby Rooke of Bigsweir=Aileen Isabel, dau. to | Dr. Alexander Graham Speirs=Constance Mary
and Pilston, esq., born 12 Aug., bap. 19 Sep. | Arthur Bosanquet of | Logie of Raglan. | Willoughby.
1867 at St. Briavels. | Cleddon Hall, esq.

Charles Douglas Willoughby Rooke, born 1894.   Aileen Disney Willoughby, born 1899.

Bigsweir.

On the eastern or English side of the river Wye, in the parish of St. Briavels, stands the mansion of Bigsweir, taking its name from the weir which was formerly in the river. Bigsweir is so called from Buddig, the father of Oudoceus, and, as will be noticed further on, appears as Bikeswere, Brithekeswere, and Blikeswere.

This was the chief seat and estate of the family of Catchmay or Catchmayd, and though once of great importance and influence, the family in the male line is now extinct. The name is said to have a legal origin, and to be connected with *attachment*, formerly pronounced *catchment*. Of the same origin is *catchpole*, a bailiff.

The first mention of the name is that of sir Alexander Catchmay, who figures in the Welsh pedigrees as being lord of Troy and *Brixwere* soon after the conquest. He is said to have had a daughter and heir Jane, married to sir Alan Scudamore, from whom is descended the family of Scudamore of Kentchurch. Bigsweir (*i.e.*, the weir in the river) appears in 1315, as will be seen further on. Rudder mentions Bigsweir as belonging to the bishop of Llandaff in 13 Edw. II. [1319-20], and to the abbey of Tintern in 19 Edw. II. [1325-6],[1] but it is obvious that in each case it is the weir and not the mansion that is intended.

The following deed[2] shews a John Catchmay living in the parish of St. Briavels in 1325, doubtless at Bigsweir itself, though that place is not mentioned. The curious names of Cout[3] and Foxtail, the latter apparently being the modern equivalent of *ffuketayle*, are now unknown, and it is probable that they were mere nicknames which did not descend as permanent surnames.

Sciant presentes et futuri quod ego, Rogerus le Carpenter de Sancto Briavello, dedi, conceſſi, et hac preſenti carta mea confirmavi Johanni Cout[3] de eadem unam dietam[4] terre jacentem in loco vocato Stancrofte, videlicet dicta dieta terre extendit se in longitudine a terra Johannis Cout uſque ad terram Johannis Cachemayde, et in latitudine a terra dicti Rogeri le Carpenter uſque ad viam regalem ducentem de Sancto Briavello verſus Trilleck, habendam et tenendam dictam dietam terre cum ſuis pertinentijs de capitali domino feodi illius per ſervitia annuatim inde debita et de jure conſueta, videlicet, unum denarium argenti ad feſtum Sancti Michaelis, praenominato Johanni Cout et heredibus ſuis, ſeu aſſignatis, libere, quiete, bene, et in pace, in feodo et hereditate imperpetuum. Et ego, praedictus Rogerus le Carpenter, et heredes mei, dictam dietam terre cum ſuis pertinentijs praenominatis Johanni Cout et heredibus ſuis ſeu aſſignatis contra omnes mortales warantizabimus et imperpetuum defendemus. In cujus rei teſtimonium huic preſenti carte ſigillum meum [apposui], hijs teſtibus

Waltero Daungeuile, Willielmo Mescher, Johanne Cachemayde, Rogero Muriel, Johanne ffuketayle et multis alijs. Datum apud Sanctum Briavellum die dominica in feſto pasce, anno regni regis Edwardi, filij regis Edwardi, decimo octavo [1325].

[*Know all men, present and to come, that I, Roger le Carpenter of St. Briavels, have given, granted and by this my present deed have confirmed to John Cout of the same one* dieta *of land lying in a place called Stancrofte, to wit, the said* dieta *of land extends itself in length from the land of John Cout to the land of John Cachemayde, and in breadth from the land of the said Roger le Carpenter to the king's highway leading from St. Briavels towards Trelech, to have and to hold the said* dieta *of land with its appurtenances from the capital lord of that fee by services yearly therefor due and by law accustomed, to wit, one penny of silver at the feast of St. Michael, to the aforesaid John Cout and his heirs or assigns, freely, quietly, well and in peace, in fee and inheritance for ever. And I, the aforesaid Roger le Carpenter and my heirs, will warrant the said* dieta *of land with its appurtenances to John Cout and his heirs or assigns, and will defend it for ever. In witness whereof [I have set] my seal to this present deed. These being witnesses—Walter Daungeuile, William Mescher, John Cachemayde, Roger Muriel, John ffuketayle, and many others. Dated at St. Briavels on Sunday at the feast of Easter in the 18th year of the reign of Edward, the son of Edward (1325).*]

The following deed shews that the family were settled at Bigsweir in the fifteenth century :[1]—

Sciant presentes et futuri quod ego, Johannes Cachmayde de Bykeswere, filius et heres Thome Cachmayde, dedi, conceſsi, et hâc preſenti cartâ meâ confirmavi Elizabethe Cachmayde, vidue, uxori nuper predicti Thome Cachmayde, tria meſsuagia cum pertinentijs in villâ de Monemouth insimul in vico vocato Mareystrete, in latitudine inter meſsuagia Thome Cachmayde de Troy in tenurâ Walteri Baker ex unâ parte, et burgagium Juliane Mareys ex alterâ parte, et extendentia se in longitudine a dicto vico ex uno capite usque ad foſsatum[2] de Chippyngham ex altero capite, habenda et tenenda predicta tria meſsuagia cum pertinentijs prefate Elizabethe heredibus et aſsignatis suis imperpetuum de capitalibus dominis feodi illius per servitia inde debita et de jure conſueta. Et ego vero, predictus Johannes Cachmayde, et heredes mei predicta meſsuagia cum pertinetijs prefate Elizabethe, heredibus et aſsignatis suis, contra omnes gentes warantizabimus imperpetuum. In cujus rei testimonium huic preſenti carte mee sigillum apposui. Datum apud Monemouth nono die Maij, anno regni regis Henrici Septimi viceſsimo primo [1506].

[*Know all men, present and to come, that I, John Cachmayde of Bykeswere, son and heir of Thomas Cachmayde, have given, granted, and by this my present deed have confirmed unto Elizabeth Cachmayde, widow, late wife of the aforesaid Thomas Cachmayde, three messuages with their appurtenances in the town of Monmouth together in the street called Mary street, in breadth between the messuages of Thomas Cachmayde of Troy, in the tenure of Walter Baker, on the one part, and the burgage of Julian Mareys on the other part, and extending in length from the said street on the one head as far as the ditch of Chippenham on the other head, to have and to hold the aforesaid messuages with*

---

1 *History of Gloucestershire*, p. 309.

2 This deed belongs to the late mr. John Harvey Hooper of Tunstal, near Worcester, a representative in the female line of a branch of Catchmay. It measures 10⅜ in. by 3⅜ in., and is in excellent preservation.

3 This word may be *Cont*.

4 *Dieta* means a day's work, hence the amount of land would be what a man could plough in a day.

---

1 Penes auctorem.

2 The ditch outside the town wall. This is now Glendower-street.

*their appurtenances to the aforesaid Elizabeth, her
heirs and assigns, for ever, from the chief lords of that
fee by the services therefor due and by law accustomed.
And I, indeed, the aforesaid John Cachmayde and my
heirs will warrant the aforesaid messuages with
their appurtenances to the aforesaid Elizabeth, her
heirs and assigns, against all persons for ever. In
testimony whereof I have affixed a seal to this my
present deed. Dated at Monmouth the 9th day of May
in the twenty-first year of the reign of king Henry VII.
(1506).]*

Coed-Ithel.

Coed-Ithel (*Ithel's wood*) is a house and small
estate on the bank of the Wye, taking its name from
Ithel, son of Arthrwys, king of Glamorgan in the
sixth century.

Some of this property was purchased by Thomas
Catchmay of Bigsweir from William Powell Gwyn
in 1549, as appears by the following deed :1—

Sciant prefentes et futuri quod ego Will'mus ap
powell Gwyne alias Sare2 de llanlaughour in comitatu
Glamorgan, hop^r, in confideratione cujufdam pecunie
fumme per Thomam Catchemayd, generofum, michi
pre manibus folute et contente, vendidi, dedi, donaui,
conceffi et hac prefenti carta mea confirmavi eidem
Thome omnia meffuagia mea, terras, et tenementa,
pafcua, prata, et pafturas, redditus, reverciones, et
fervitia fituata et jacentia infra parochiam de llandogo
in comitatu Monemouth, habenda et tenenda omnia
predicta meffuagia, terras, et tenementa ac cetera
premiffa cum omnibus et fingulis pertinentijs fuis
prefato Thome Catchemayd, heredibus et affignatis
fuis, ad opus et ufum ejufdem Thome, heredum et
affignatorum fuorum imperpetuum de capitali domino
feodi illius, per fervitia prius debita et de jure confueta. Et ego, vero, predictus Will'us ap powell
Gwyn et heredes mei omnia predicta meffuagia, terras,
et tenementa, cum omnibus et fingulis pertinentijs
fuis prefato Thome Catchemayd, heredibus et affignatis fuis, ad opus et ufum ejufdem Thome, heredum
et affignatorum fuorum contra omnes gentes warrantizabimus et imperpetuum defendemus per prefentes.
In cujus rei teftimonium huic prefenti carte mee
figillum meum appofui. Datum apud llandogo pre-
dictam decimo fexto die menfis Junij, anno regni
Edwardi Sexti, dei gratia, Anglie, ffrauncie et Hibernie
regis, fidei defenforis, ac in terra ecclefie Anglicane
et Hibernice fupremi capitis, tertio [1549].

Endorsed :
    Wytnes to thys
    Will'm p'kyn.
    Ryc' p'kyn.
    John vele.
    d'd John.
    Thom's ap Hopkyn.
    Will'm Johns.

George Catchmay of Bigsweir, son of the above
Thomas, in 1596 purchased more land at or near
Coed-Ithel from William Davies of Tintern Abbey,
as by the following deed :1—

Sciant presentes et futuri quod ego Georgius
Davyes de Abba de Tynterne in comitatu Monmoth,
yoman (pro summa octo librarum legalis monete
Anglie michi per Georgium Cachemayd de Byggef-

were, generofum, in manibus foluta), dedi, conceffi, et
hac prefenti carta mea confirmavi eidem Georgio
Cachemayd, heredibus et affignatis fuis imperpetuum,
unum meffuagium et duo gardina cum pertinentijs
infimul jacentia et exiftentia in llandogo, inter terras
Ricardi Cachemayd et viam ibidem ducentem verfus
ecclefiam de llandogo predicta ex omnibus partibus,
Ac etiam unum pomarium cum pertinentijs jacens et
exiftens in llandogo predicta inter terras comitis
Wigornie, terras predicti Georgij Cachemayd, terras
Thome Perkyn, et regiam viam ducentem verfus
ecclefiam de llandogo predicta ex omnibus partibus,
habendum et tenendum predictum meffuagium,
gardina et cetera premiffa cum omnibus fuis pertinentijs prefato Georgio Cachemayd, heredibus et
affignatis fuis, ad proprium opus et ufum ipfius
Georgij Cachemayd, heredum et affignatorum fuorum
imperpetuum de capitalibus dominis feodi illius, per
redditus et fervitia inde prius debita et de jure confueta. Et ego vero, predictus Georgius Davyes et
heredes mei predictum meffuagium, gardina, et cetera
premiffa cum omnibus fuis pertinentijs prefato
Georgio Cachemayd, heredibus, et affignatis fuis, ad
opus et ufum predictum contra omnes gentes warrantizabimus et imperpetuum defendemus. In cuius rei
teftimonium huic prefenti carte mee figillum meum
appofui. Datum quinto decimo die Maij, anno regni
domine noftre Elizabethe, dei gratia, Anglie, ffrancie,
et Hibernie regine, fidei defenforis, etc., tricefimo
octavo [1596].

Endorsed :
    Witneffes to the fealinge and deliu'y herof and to
the liu'ye and feafon givinge
        Brian Laurence.
        Will'm Parrye, cler'.
        Thomas Cutts.
        John Cutt.

In 1618 sir Richard Catchmay, son of the above
George, settled Upper Coed-Ithel on his wife in
jointure, the trustees being William and Edward
Bell. This property is stated to have been purchased
by sir Richard from Charles and Edmond Williams
of Monmouth priory, and it looks, therefore, as
though Upper Coed-Ithel had previously been part
of the possessions of the priory :—

Omnibus Chrifti fidelibus ad quos hoc presens
fcriptum meum indentatum pervenerit, Richardus
Catchmay de Bixweare in comitatu Gloucestrenfi,
miles, Salutem in domino fempiternam. Sciatis me
prefatum Richardum Catchmay, militem, tam pro
magna amore et affectione quod habeo et gero ad et
erga dominam ffrancifcam Catchmay uxorem meam ac
pro meliori junctura ipfius domine ffrancifce Catchmay,
quam pro diverfis alijs bonis caufis et rationabilibus con-
fiderationibus me fpecialiter moventibus, dediffe, con-
ceffiffe, affuraffe, feoffaffe, et confirmaffe, ac per presentes dare, concedere, affurare, feoffare, et confirmare
Will'mo Bell et Edwardo Bell, generofis, omnia illa
mefuagia mea, domos, horrea, edificia, tofta, cottagia,
gardina, pomaria, terras, tenementa, prata, pafcua,
pafturas, bofcos, fubbofcos, communias, pifcarias,
redditus, reverfiones, libertates, privilegia, com-
oditates, ac alia hereditamenta mea libera quecunque
cum omnibus et fingulis fuis juribus, membris et
pertinentijs quibuscunque communiter cognita et
vocata per nomen de *Upper Cordythel* feu per aliquod
aliud nomen vel aliqua alia nomina nuper terras, tenementa, et hereditamenta quorundam Charoli Williams,
generofi, et Edmundi Williams de nuper prioratu de
Monmoth, generofi, modo defuncti, vel eorum unius,

---

1 Carta penes auctorem.   2 Saer, carpenter.

modo in tenura, poffeffione five occupatione Phillippi Catchmay de llandogo vel affignatorum fuorum, fituata, jacentia, et exiftentia infra parochiam de llandogo predicta, per metas, limites, et bundas ibidem ab antiquo ufitata et cognita, Que omnia et fingula premiffa cum pertinentijs fuis univerfis Ego predictus Richardus Catchmay, miles, nuper habui et perquifivi michi et heredibus meis imperpetuum ex dono et conceffione predictorum Charoli et Edmondi Williams vel eorum unius, habenda et tenenda predicta meffuagia [*etc., ut supra*], prefatis Will'mo Bell et Edwardo Bell, heredibus et affignatis fuis imperpetuum, ad feparalia opus, ufum, et profita fubfequentia, videlicet, ad folum opus et ufum proprium mei predicti Richardi Catchmay, militis, pro et durante termino vite mee naturalis, abfque impetitione vafti, Et poft deceffum mei predicti Richardi Catchmay, militis, habendam et tenendam unam medietatem five dimidium omnium et fingulorum premifforum predictorum cum pertinentijs fuis univerfis Will'mo Bell et Edwardo Bell ac heredibus fuis, ad opus et ufum proprium predicte domine ffrancifce Catchmay uxoris mee pro et durante termino vite fue naturalis tantum. Et poft deceffum fuum habenda et tenenda omnia et fingula predicta meffuagia [*etc., ut supra*] ad opus et ufum mei predicti Richardi Catchmay, militis, heredum et affignatorum meorum imperpetuum et ad nullum alium ufum feu propofitum, tenenda de capitalibus dominis feodi illius per redditus et fervitia inde prius debita et de jure confueta. Et ego vero Richardus Catchmay, miles, et heredes mei predicta meffuagia [*etc., ut supra*]

prefatis Will'mo Bell et Edwardo Bell heredibus et affignatis fuis ad feparalia opus et ufum fuperius expreffa, recitata, et limitata ac modo et forma predictis contra omnes gentes warrantizabimus et imperpetuum defendemus per prefentes. In cujus rei teftimonium uni parti hujus prefentis fcripti mei indentati penes prefatum Will'm Bell et Edwardum Bell remanenti Ego predictus Richardus Catchmay, miles, figillum meum appofui, alteri vero parti ejufdem fcripti mei indentati penes me Richardum Catchmay, militem, remanenti predicti Will'mus Bell et Edwardus Bell figilla fua appofuerunt. Datum apud Landogo predicta duodecimo die Octobris, anno regni domini noftri Jacobi, dei gratia, Anglie, ffrauncie, et Hibernie regis, fidei defenforis, etc., fexto decimo et Scotie quinquagefimo fecundo, 1618.

[Signed] Ri. Catchmay.

Sealed and delivered in the presence of Edward Lewes, John madock.

A seal appendant has a plain shield of Catchmay, *Barry of 6, on a canton 5 billets.*

Coed-Ithel afterwards passed out of the hands of the Catchmays, and in 1830 captain Richard Howell Fleming, R.N., owned it and resided there. This gentleman, who had seen much naval service during the Peninsular war, died in 1856, aged 77, having married Eliza, daughter of Philip George, an alderman of Bristol.

𝔓𝔢𝔡𝔦𝔤𝔯𝔢𝔢 𝔬𝔣 𝔱𝔥𝔢 𝔣𝔞𝔪𝔦𝔩𝔶 𝔬𝔣 𝔠𝔞𝔱𝔠𝔥𝔪𝔞𝔶 𝔬𝔣 𝔅𝔦𝔤𝔰𝔴𝔢𝔦𝔯.

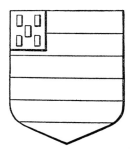

Arms.—*Arg., on a chevron between 3 demi-lions ramp. az. as many bugle-horns stringed or* (or *crescents arg.*). The family also bore: *Or, a fesse between 3 demi-lions pass. az.* But the coat generally used was, *Barry of 6 . . . . and . . . ., a canton erm.* This appears in the hall at Bigsweir and on the monument to William Catchmayd in Mitchel Troy church, and is impaled by Robert Jones on his bookplate. The Visitation of Monmouthshire, 1683, gives *Barry of 6, on a canton 5 billets,* but disallows it for want of proof. The last coat seems to be that of Inglosse.

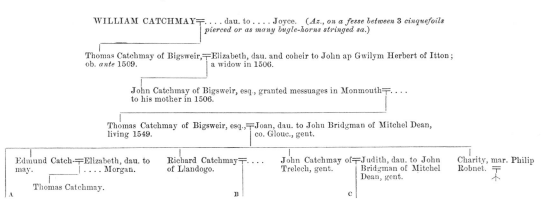

WILLIAM CATCHMAY ⊤ . . . . dau. to . . . . Joyce. (*Az., on a fesse between 3 cinquefoils pierced or as many bugle-horns stringed sa.*)

Thomas Catchmay of Bigsweir, ⊤ Elizabeth, dau. and coheir to John ap Gwilym Herbert of Itton; ob. *ante* 1509.   a widow in 1506.

John Catchmay of Bigsweir, esq., granted messuages in Monmouth ⊤ . . . . to his mother in 1506.

Thomas Catchmay of Bigsweir, esq., ⊤ Joan, dau. to John Bridgman of Mitchel Dean, living 1549.   co. Glouc., gent.

Edmund Catchmay. ⊤ Elizabeth, dau. to . . . . Morgan. | Richard Catchmay ⊤ . . . . of Llandogo. | John Catchmay of ⊤ Judith, dau. to John Trelech, gent.   Bridgman of Mitchel Dean, gent. | Charity, mar. Philip Robnet. ⊤

Thomas Catchmay.

A   B   C

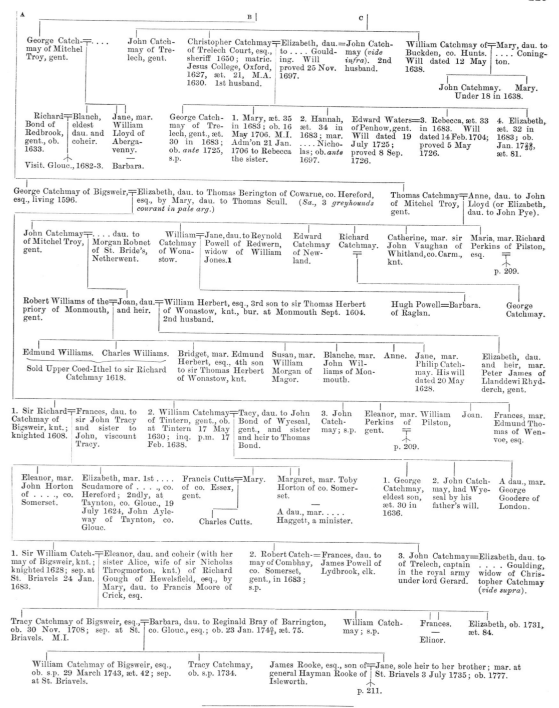

A

George Catchmay of Mitchel Troy, gent. = ...

John Catchmay of Trelech, gent.

Christopher Catchmay of Trelech Court, esq., sheriff 1650; matric. Jesus College, Oxford, 1627, æt. 21, M.A. 1630. 1st husband. = Elizabeth, dau. to .... Goulding. Will proved 25 Nov. 1697. = John Catchmay (vide infra). 2nd husband.

William Catchmay of Buckden, co. Hunts. Will dated 12 May 1638. = Mary, dau. to .... Conington.

John Catchmay. Mary. Under 18 in 1638.

Richard Bond of Redbrook, gent., ob. 1633. = Blanch, eldest dau. and coheir. Visit. Glouc., 1682-3.

Jane, mar. William Lloyd of Abergavenny. — Barbara.

George Catchmay of Trelech, gent., æt. 30 in 1683; ob. ante 1725, s.p.

1. Mary, æt. 35 in 1683; ob. 16 May 1706. M.I. Adm'on 21 Jan. 1706 to Rebecca the sister.

2. Hannah, æt. 34 in 1683; mar. .... Nicholas; ob. ante 1697.

Edward Waters of Penhow, gent. = 3. Rebecca, æt. 33 in 1683. Will dated 19 July 1725; proved 8 Sep. 1726.

Will dated 14 Feb. 1704; proved 5 May 1726.

4. Elizabeth, æt. 32 in 1683; ob. Jan. 17 38/39, æt. 81.

George Catchmay of Bigsweir, esq., living 1596. = Elizabeth, dau. to Thomas Berington of Cowarne, co. Hereford, esq., by Mary, dau. to Thomas Scull. (Sa., 3 greyhounds courant in pale arg.)

Thomas Catchmay of Mitchel Troy, gent. = Anne, dau. to John Lloyd (or Elizabeth, dau. to John Pye).

John Catchmay of Mitchel Troy, gent. = ... dau. to Morgan Robnet of St. Bride's, Netherwent.

William Catchmay of Wonastow. = Jane, dau. to Reynold Powell of Redwern, widow of William Jones.1

Edward Catchmay of Newland.

Richard Catchmay. =

Catherine, mar. sir John Vaughan of Whitland, co. Carm., knt.

Maria, mar. Richard Perkins of Pilston, esq. = p. 209.

Robert Williams of the priory of Monmouth, gent. = Joan, dau. and heir. = William Herbert, esq., 3rd son to sir Thomas Herbert of Wonastow, knt., bur. at Monmouth Sept. 1604. 2nd husband.

Hugh Powell = Barbara. of Raglan.

George Catchmay.

Edmund Williams. Charles Williams. Sold Upper Coed-Ithel to sir Richard Catchmay 1618.

Bridget, mar. Edmund Herbert, esq., 4th son to sir Thomas Herbert of Wonastow, knt.

Susan, mar. William Morgan of Magor.

Blanche, mar. John Williams of Monmouth.

Anne.

Jane, mar. Philip Catchmay. His will dated 20 May 1628.

Elizabeth, dau. and heir, mar. Peter James of Llanddewi Rhydderch, gent.

1. Sir Richard Catchmay of Bigsweir, knt.; knighted 1608. = Frances, dau. to sir John Tracy and sister to John, viscount Tracy.

2. William Catchmay of Tintern, gent., ob. at Tintern 17 May 1630; inq. p.m. 17 Feb. 1638. = Tacy, dau. to John Bond of Wyeseal, gent., and sister and heir to Thomas Bond.

3. John Catchmay; s.p.

Eleanor, mar. William Perkins of Pilston, gent. = p. 209.

Joan.

Frances, mar. Edmund Thomas of Wenvoe, esq.

Eleanor, mar. John Horton of ...., co. Somerset.

Elizabeth, mar. 1st .... Scudamore of ...., co. Hereford; 2ndly, at Taynton, co. Glouc., 19 July 1624, John Ayleway of Taynton, co. Glouc.

Francis Cutts of co. Essex, gent. = Mary. Charles Cutts.

Margaret, mar. Toby Horton of co. Somerset. A dau., mar. .... Haggett, a minister.

1. George Catchmay, eldest son, æt. 30 in 1636.

2. John Catchmay, may, had Wyeseal by his father's will.

A dau., mar. George Goodere of London.

1. Sir William Catchmay of Bigsweir, knt.; knighted 1628; sep. at St. Briavels 24 Jan. 1683. = Eleanor, dau. and coheir (with her sister Alice, wife of sir Nicholas Throgmorton, knt.) of Richard Gough of Hewelsfield, esq., by Mary, dau. to Francis Moore of Crick, esq.

2. Robert Catchmay of Combhay, co. Somerset, gent., in 1683; s.p. = Frances, dau. to James Powell of Lydbrook, clk.

3. John Catchmay of Trelech, captain in the royal army under lord Gerard. = Elizabeth, dau. to .... Goulding, widow of Christopher Catchmay (vide supra).

Tracy Catchmay of Bigsweir, esq., ob. 30 Nov. 1708; sep. at St. Briavels. M.I. = Barbara, dau. to Reginald Bray of Barrington, co. Glouc., esq.; ob. 23 Jan. 174 8/9, æt. 75.

William Catchmay; s.p.

Frances. — Elinor.

Elizabeth, ob. 1731, æt. 84.

William Catchmay of Bigsweir, esq., ob. s.p. 29 March 1743, æt. 42; sep. at St. Briavels.

Tracy Catchmay, ob. s.p. 1734.

James Rooke, esq., son of general Hayman Rooke of Isleworth. = Jane, sole heir to her brother; mar. at St. Briavels 3 July 1735; ob. 1777. p. 211.

Catchmayd of Monmouth.

A branch of the family whom I am unable to connect with the parent stem was long settled in Monmouth. They were attorneys residing in the house called Oak-house, which contains some good panelled rooms, and their names constantly appear in legal documents of the eighteenth century as trustees, mortgagees, etc.

William Catchmayd of Monmouth in his will, dated 11 September, 1635, proved (P.C.C., 20, Pile)

13 February, 163 5/6, mentions his father Christopher, his wife Cecil, and his son Christopher. Cecil the widow married secondly Charles Watkins, and she made her will, described as of Caerlleon, 14 August, 1664, proved 1 February, 1670.

To be buried in the church of St. Mary at Monmouth as near as may be to my late husband

1 William Jones was the son of Thomas ap John of Wonastow and brother of John Jones, who was the father of William Jones. The last, by his will, dated 20 December, 1614, founded the grammar school at Monmouth, endowing it with valuable property.

Wm Catchmay, deceased—to Edward Watkins, nephew to my late husband Charles Watkins, 20*l.*—to my sister Bridget Jones, widow, 10*l.*—to my sister Elizabeth Howell, clothes—to Wm Watkins, baker, kinsman to my late husband, 5*l.*—all my freehold whatsoever that descended to me and came by my father Thomas Scudamore, deceased, in the parishes of Little Salisbury, Magor, St. Bride's and Wilcrick, unto Samuel Jones the younger, son and heir apparent unto Samuel Jones the elder, late of Little Salisbury, my nephew and sister's son—to my niece Rebecca, the wife of Charles Beale of Monmouth, one silver beer bowl—to my niece Sarah, wife of John Pierson of Monmouth, furniture—to the wife of my nephew Samuel Jones the elder, one wrought waistcoat—to the five younger children of my nephew Samuel Jones the elder, five silver spoons called apostle spoons, and 20*l.* between them—my nephew Samuel Jones the elder overseer—my nieces Sarah Pierson and Rebecca Beale joint ex'ors.

William Catchmayd of Monmouth assumed in 1782 by royal licence the surname of Gwinnett on inheriting the estate of Shurdington in Gloucestershire left him by Mary, widow of George Gwinnett of that place. On his death without issue Shurdington went to his brother George, who also assumed the name of Gwinnett. This George (Catchmayd) Gwinnett deserted his family and went off with his wife's waiting-maid, leaving his daughters to be brought up by a farmer in the neighbourhood. Maria the eldest married a farmer from Herefordshire named James Biggs, whose descendants are given in the pedigree.

Another family descended from the Catchmayds whose pedigree is worthy of record is that of Woollett, who until quite recently have for more than a century been notable medical men in the county. John Spencer Woollett, surgeon, came to Monmouth in consequence of his marriage with the daughter of Robert Jones, surgeon and apothecary. He adopted the religion of his wife, who was a catholic, to which form of religion the Woolletts have since adhered. It is interesting to note that Robert Jones had his religion from his mother Alice, daughter of William Prichard of Plâs Ifor, who had it from her mother Mary, daughter of Richard Croft.

In Volume I., p. 65, is given an account of the estate and ancient mansion of the Waen. This, as appears by the will of Rice Jones, was first of all mortgaged to him by Morgan, and subsequently purchased. The will of Rice Jones, in which he is described as of St. Paul's, Covent Garden, merchant taylor, is dated 10 June, 1699, proved (P.C.C., 67, Dyer) 19 May, 1701, by Ann Jones and Matthew Jones.

To my wife Ann Jones 15*l.* per ann.—to Henry Jones my eldest son 15*l.* per ann.—the messuages, lands, etc., called the Wayne in or near the parish of Skenfrith to me formerly mortgaged by one m^r Morgan and his wife and their eldest son, and since by me absolutely purchased, and also those mess's in Llanvair ar y brin and Mothvey, co. Carmarthen, by me pur-

chased of George Gwynne of Llwyn Howell, to my s^d wife Ann for her life—to Ann my sister 4*l.* per ann.—after the death of my wife the s^d lands to my second son Matthew Jones with rem^r to my two dau's, Mary, now the wife of m^r Edward Rouse, and Ann, now the wife of m^r Richard Fitzgurard, equally—to my s^d son Matthew all the sums owing to me from sir Rice Rudd, bart., by mortgage or otherwise—to my 3^d son John Jones 10*l.* per ann. for life—to my wife the interest on all the moneys owing to me from Thomas Cornwallis, esq., and from Roger Mainwaring, esq., by mortgage or otherwise, and after to my son Matthew—to my two grand-children Ann and Mary Rouse, dau's of Edward Rouse by Mary my dau., 200*l.* each at 21—to the poor of Talley, co. Carmarthen, 5*l.* to be divided by my brother William Jones, living in that parish—to my godson Rice Jones, son of my nephew John Jones, 20*l.*—to my honoured good friend sir William Morgan 40*s.* to buy him a ring—residue to Ann my wife, then to Matthew Jones my 2^d son, they joint ex'ors.

In presence of Wm Davies, Evan Evans, Rich. Harris.

Matthew Jones, son of the above Rice, resided at the Waen, and after his death about 1721 his widow married John Halfpenny, probably an attorney, who came to the Waen to live. The following deed shews the relationship, being the mortgage of a small farm called Rhyd-Iago (*James' ford*) and Wern-y-felin (*the alder trees of the mill*). Rhyd-Iago is situated on the brook Llymon, and adjoins the Waen.

Ind're made 1 July, 14 Geo. II. [1740], between John Halfpenny of the Wayne, gent., and Alice his wife, late widow and relict of Matthew Jones heretofore of the Wayne, gent., and William Jones of the Wayne, gent., eldest son and heir of the s^d Matthew, and Penelope his wife of the one part; and Wm Watkins, late of Hendre in the parish of Llangattock Vibon Avel, but now of the town of Monmouth, gent., of the other part. The said John Halfpenny and Alice, Wm Jones and Penelope demise to the s^d Wm Watkins the dwelling-house called Rhyddyago with 18 acres, also lands called Wern y vellyn cont^g 6 acres, all in Skenfrith, between the Wayne, lands late of Thomas Prosser, gent., and the highway leading from Skenfrith towards Bergevenny, etc.

Of the children of Matthew Jones, Robert became a surgeon in Monmouth, residing in the house near the back entrance to the *Beaufort Arms* hotel; over the front door are letters and date—

B

H . I

1678.

This house has, since the death of Robert Jones in 1791, continued to be the residence of the Woolletts.

Another family descended from the Catchmayds, though not resident in this county, Hooper of Worcester, is worthy of notice here, for Thomas Hooper, M.D., was seated at Pant-y-goitre and served the office of sheriff in 1780, as did also his father-in-law William Winsmore, the latter gentleman being sheriff in 1766.[1]

---

[1] *Vide* Vol. I., p. 407.

Pedigree of the family of Catchmayd of Monmouth.

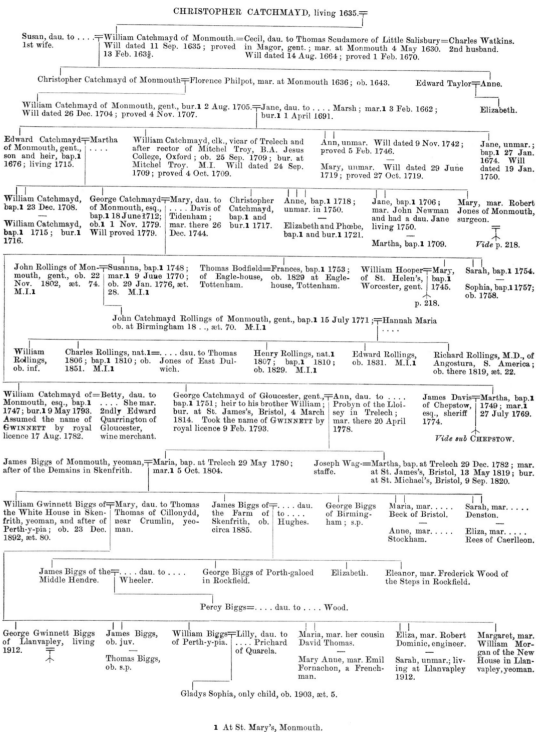

CHRISTOPHER CATCHMAYD, living 1635.

Susan, dau. to .... = William Catchmayd of Monmouth. = Cecil, dau. to Thomas Scudamore of Little Salisbury = Charles Watkins.
1st wife. | Will dated 11 Sep. 1635 ; proved in Magor, gent. ; mar. at Monmouth 4 May 1630. | 2nd husband.
13 Feb. 163⅝. | Will dated 14 Aug. 1664 ; proved 1 Feb. 1670.

Christopher Catchmayd of Monmouth = Florence Philpot, mar. at Monmouth 1636 ; ob. 1643. | Edward Taylor = Anne.

William Catchmayd of Monmouth, gent., bur.**1** 2 Aug. 1705. = Jane, dau. to .... Marsh ; mar.**1** 3 Feb. 1662 ; | Elizabeth.
Will dated 26 Dec. 1704 ; proved 4 Nov. 1707. | bur.**1** 1 April 1691.

Edward Catchmayd = Martha | William Catchmayd, clk., vicar of Trelech and | Ann, unmar. Will dated 9 Nov. 1742 ; | Jane, unmar. ;
of Monmouth, gent., | .... | after rector of Mitchel Troy, B.A. Jesus | proved 5 Feb. 1746. | bap.**1** 27 Jan.
son and heir, bap.**1** | | College, Oxford ; ob. 25 Sep. 1709 ; bur. at | — | 1674. Will
1676 ; living 1715. | | Mitchel Troy. M.I. Will dated 24 Sep. | Mary, unmar. Will dated 29 June | dated 19 Jan.
| | 1709 ; proved 4 Oct. 1709. | 1719 ; proved 27 Oct. 1719. | 1750.

William Catchmayd, | George Catchmayd = Mary, dau. to | Christopher | Anne, bap.**1** 1718 ; | Jane, bap.**1** 1706 ; | Mary, mar. Robert
bap.**1** 23 Dec. 1708. | of Monmouth, esq., | .... Davis of | Catchmayd, | unmar. in 1750. | mar. John Newman | Jones of Monmouth,
— | bap.**1** 18 June 1712; | Tidenham ; | bap.**1** and | | and had a dau. Jane | surgeon.
William Catchmayd, | ob.**1** 1 Nov. 1779. | mar. there 26 | bur.**1** 1717. | Elizabeth and Phœbe, | living 1750. |
bap.**1** 1715 ; bur.**1** | Will proved 1779. | Dec. 1744. | | bap.**1** and bur.**1** 1721. | — | Vide p. 218.
1716. | | | | | Martha, bap.**1** 1709.

John Rollings of Mon- = Susanna, bap.**1** 1748 ; | Thomas Bodfield = Frances, bap.**1** 1753 ; | William Hooper = Mary, | Sarah, bap.**1** 1754.
mouth, gent., ob. 22 | mar.**1** 9 June 1770 ; | of Eagle-house, | ob. 1829 at Eagle- | of St. Helen's, | bap.**1** |
Nov. 1802, æt. 74. | ob. 29 Jan. 1776, æt. | Tottenham. | house, Tottenham. | Worcester, gent. | 1745. | Sophia, bap.**1** 1757;
M.I.**1** | 28. M.I.**1** | | | | | ob. 1758.
| | | | p. 218.

John Catchmayd Rollings of Monmouth, gent., bap.**1** 15 July 1771 ; = Hannah Maria
ob. at Birmingham 18 .., æt. 70. M.I.**1** | ....

William | Charles Rollings, nat.**1** = ... dau. to Thomas | Henry Rollings, nat.**1** | Edward Rollings, | Richard Rollings, M.D., of
Rollings, | 1806 ; bap.**1** 1810 ; ob. Jones of East Dul- | 1807 ; bap.**1** 1810 ; | ob. 1831. M.I.**1** | Angostura, S. America ;
ob. inf. | 1851. M.I.**1** wich. | ob. 1829. M.I.**1** | | ob. there 1819, æt. 22.

William Catchmayd of = Betty, dau. to | George Catchmayd of Gloucester, gent., = Ann, dau. to .... | James Davis = Martha, bap.**1**
Monmouth, esq., bap.**1** | .... She mar. | bap.**1** 1751 ; heir to his brother William ; | Probyn of the Lloi- | of Chepstow, | 1749 ; mar.**1**
1747 ; bur.**1** 9 May 1793. | 2ndly Edward | bur. at St. James's, Bristol, 4 March | sey in Trelech ; | esq., sheriff | 27 July 1769.
Assumed the name of | Quarrington of | 1814. Took the name of GWINNETT by | mar. there 20 April | 1774. |
GWINNETT by royal | Gloucester, | royal licence 9 Feb. 1793. | 1778. | | Vide sub CHEPSTOW.
licence 17 Aug. 1782. | wine merchant.

James Biggs of Monmouth, yeoman, = Maria, bap. at Trelech 29 May 1780 ; | Joseph Wag- = Martha, bap. at Trelech 29 Dec. 1782 ; mar.
after of the Demains in Skenfrith. | mar.**1** 5 Oct. 1804. | staffe. at St. James's, Bristol, 13 May 1819 ; bur.
| | at St. Michael's, Bristol, 9 Sep. 1820.

William Gwinnett Biggs of = Mary, dau. to Thomas | James Biggs of = ... dau. | George Biggs | Maria, mar. .... | Sarah, mar. ....
the White House in Sken- | Thomas of Cillonydd, | the Farm of | to .... | of Birming- | Beck of Bristol. | Denston.
frith, yeoman, and after of | near Crumlin, yeo- | Skenfrith, ob. | Hughes. | ham ; s.p. | — | —
Perth-y-pia ; ob. 23 Dec. | man. | circa 1885. | | | Anne, mar. .... | Eliza, mar. ....
1892, æt. 80. | | | | | Stockham. | Rees of Caerlleon.

James Biggs of the = ... dau. to .... | George Biggs of Porth-galoed | Elizabeth. | Eleanor, mar. Frederick Wood of
Middle Hendre. | Wheeler. | in Rockfield. | | the Steps in Rockfield.

Percy Biggs = ... dau. to .... Wood.

George Gwinnett Biggs | James Biggs, | William Biggs = Lilly, dau. to | Maria, mar. her cousin | Eliza, mar. Robert | Margaret, mar.
of Llanvapley, living | ob. juv. | of Perth-y-pia. | .... Prichard | David Thomas. | Dominic, engineer. | William Mor-
1912. | — | | of Quarela. | — | — | gan of the New
| Thomas Biggs, | | | Mary Anne, mar. Emil | Sarah, unmar.; liv- | House in Llan-
| ob. s.p. | | | Fornachon, a French- | ing at Llanvapley | vapley, yeoman.
| | | | man. | 1912.

Gladys Sophia, only child, ob. 1903, æt. 5.

1 At St. Mary's, Monmouth.

Pedigree of the families of Jones of the Waen and Woollett of Monmouth.

Robert Jones has a bookplate inscribed *Robt Jones SURGEON.*

The arms are : *A lion ramp., a crescent for difference* ; impaling *Barry of 6, a canton erm.*
Crest : *A fox* (or *wolf*) *pass.*
Motto : HONOR SOLUS DEI EST.

.... JONES.

Rice Jones of St. Paul's, Covent Garden, merchant tailor,=Ann, dau. to .... ;
ob. 7 March 1700, æt. 67 ; bur. in Skenfrith Church.   ob. 4 Aug. 1703,
Will dated 10 June 1699 ; proved 19 May 1701.   æt. 60.

William Jones of Talley,
co. Carmarthen.

1. Henry Jones.

2. Matthew Jones of=Alice, dau. to William=John Halfpenny,
the Waen, gent. Will Prichard of Plâs-Ifor, gent. 2nd hus-
proved 1722. 1st hus- gent. ; mar. 25 Jan. band.
band.   170¼.

3. John Jones.

Edward Rouse=Mary.

Ann, mar. Richard fitz Gerard.

Ann.   Mary.

Eliza-=Thomas Wool-=Hannah
beth lett of Rye, ...
....   Sussex.   2nd wife.
1st
wife.

William Jones=Penelope, dau. to John
of the Waen, James Prichard Jones.
gent. ; living of Plâs-Ifor,
there 1760. gent.

Robert Jones=Mary, dau.
of Monmouth, to Edward
surgeon ; bur. Catchmayd
there 2 Aug. of Mon-
1791.   mouth, gent.
   (p. 217).

Walter Jones, bap.
at Skenfrith 1 July
1717.
—
Richard Jones,
bur. 1705.

Anne.
—
Mary,
bur.
1704.

John Spencer Woollett of Monmouth, surgeon,=Dorothy.
bap. at Rye 1758 ; ob. 30 Nov. 1825.

Edward Catchmayd Jones,
bur. 1748.

Thomas Woollett=Maria Charlotte, dau. to Herbert
of Monmouth, Abrahall Lloyd of Carthage in
surgeon, nat. Foy, co. Hereford, esq., son of
1788 ; ob. 1839. Percival Lloyd by Ann, dau. to
  Herbert Aubrey of Clehonger,
  esq.

Robert Francis=Elizabeth,
Woollett of dau. to ....
Usk, surgeon. Prosser of
  Usk.

William Woollett,
surgeon, Hon. E.I.
Co.'s Service, 28th
Foot ; ob. circa
1835.

John Wool-=.... dau.
lett.   to ....
  Williams.

Mary,
ob. unm.
1856.

Maria Char-
lotte, nat.
1810 ; ob.
1884.

Mary Anne, nat. 1821 ;
mar. Charles Grafton ;
ob. 1868.

Winefred,
nat. 1824 ;
ob. 1887.

Helen Arabella, nat. 1828 ; mar.
1853 Joseph Anthony Spencer.

Thomas Wool-
lett, nat. 1816 ;
ob. at sea 1840.

Robert Francis
Woollett of
Newport, sur-
geon, nat. 1817 ;
ob. 1887.

Ann, mar
Thomas
Williams.

Thomas Woollett=Mary Elizabeth, dau. to
of Newport, soli- George Forster Harri-
citor and town son, captain 5th regt.
clerk, nat. 1807 ; royal veteran batt. ; ob.
ob. 1882. 1867, s.p.

John Spencer
Woollett, ob.
juv.

William Llewellyn Wool-
lett, catholic priest and
naval chaplain, nat. 1812 ;
ob. 1874.

John Moore=Emma,
Woollett of dau. to
Monmouth, Charles
surgeon, Crosby.
ob. 1879.

Herbert Aubrey Wool-
lett, catholic priest and
naval chaplain, nat.
1817 ; ob. 1888.

Charles Jerome Woollett of=Dolly, dau. to
Monmouth, surgeon, after- .... Mackay.
wards of London, nat. 1853.

George Nicholas Wool-
lett, nat. 1855.

Bernard Casimir Wool-
lett, nat. 1860.

Basil Joseph
Woollett, ob.
s.p. 1906.

Frances Theresa.
—
Emma Scholastica.

John Charles Woollett, nat. 1891.   Winifred Theresa.   Emma Mary.

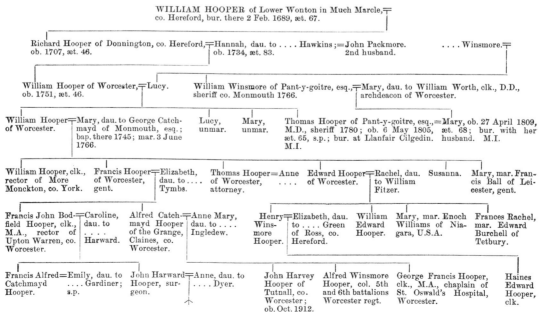

Pedigree of the family of Hooper of Worcester, descendants of Catchmayd.

WILLIAM HOOPER of Lower Wonton in Much Marcle,=
co. Hereford, bur. there 2 Feb. 1689, æt. 67.

Richard Hooper of Donnington, co. Hereford,=Hannah, dau. to .... Hawkins ;=John Packmore.
ob. 1707, æt. 46.   ob. 1734, æt. 83.   2nd husband.

.... Winsmore.

William Hooper of Worcester,=Lucy.
ob. 1751, æt. 46.

William Winsmore of Pant-y-goitre, esq.,=Mary, dau. to William Worth, clk., D.D.,
sheriff co. Monmouth 1766.   archdeacon of Worcester.

William Hooper=Mary, dau. to George Catch-
of Worcester. mayd of Monmouth, esq. ;
  bap. there 1745 ; mar. 3 June
  1766.

Lucy,
unmar.

Mary,
unmar.

Thomas Hooper of Pant-y-goitre, esq.,=Mary, ob. 27 April 1809,
M.D., sheriff 1780 ; ob. 6 May 1805, æt. 65 ; bur. with her
æt. 68, s.p. ; bur. at Llanfair Cilgedin. husband. M.I.
M.I.

William Hooper, clk.,
rector of More
Monckton, co. York.

Francis Hooper=Elizabeth,
of Worcester, dau. to ....
gent.   Tymbs.

Thomas Hooper=Anne
of Worcester, ...
attorney.

Edward Hooper=Rachel, dau.
of Worcester. to William
  Fitzer.

Susanna.

Mary, mar. Fran-
cis Ball of Lei-
cester, gent.

Francis John Bod-=Caroline,
field Hooper, clk., dau. to
M.A., rector of ....
Upton Warren, co. Harward.
Worcester.

Alfred Catch-=Anne Mary,
mayd Hooper dau. to ....
of the Grange, Ingledew.
Claines, co.
Worcester.

Henry=Elizabeth, dau.
Wins- to .... Green
more of Ross, co.
Hooper. Hereford.

William
Edward
Hooper.

Mary, mar. Enoch
Williams of Nia-
gara, U.S.A.

Frances Rachel,
mar. Edward
Burchell of
Tetbury.

Francis Alfred=Emily, dau. to
Catchmayd .... Gardiner ;
Hooper.   s.p.

John Harward=Anne, dau. to
Hooper, sur- .... Dyer.
geon.

John Harvey
Hooper of
Tutnall, co.
Worcester ;
ob. Oct. 1912.

Alfred Winsmore
Hooper, col. 5th
and 6th battalions
Worcester regt.

George Francis Hooper,
clk., M.A., chaplain of
St. Oswald's Hospital,
Worcester.

Haines
Edward
Hooper,
clk.

A family named Bacheler were settled in Llandogo in the fifteenth century, as the following deed shews:—

> Omnibus [*etc.*] Nicholaus Bacheler, filius et heres Roberti Bacheler nuper de llandethogo in Marchijs Wallie, falutem. Sciatis me prefatum Nicholaum remififfe [*etc.*] Will'mo Bacheler, filio et heredi Thome Bacheler nuper de llandethogo predicta [*etc.*] totum jus meum [*etc.*] in omnibus illis terris [*etc.*] infra parochiam de llandethogo predicta poft deceffum predicti Roberti Bacheler patris mei [*etc.*]. Hijs teftibus, Johanne Cachemay, Will'mo Hopkyn, Johanne Robert, Nicholao Hopkyn, Thome Robert juniore, et multis alijs. Datum apud llandethogo predicta fecundo die Novembris, anno regni regis Henrici Septimi poft conqueftum Anglie vicefimo tertio [1507].

The seal bears the letters W ๖.

The River Wye and the Weirs.

Until recent years, when roads were made through this district and coaches were able to travel, which was not till about 1815, most of the carrying of merchandise to and from Monmouth was by means of barges. At the same time the passage of the river was much blocked by weirs which had been erected for the purpose of catching the salmon, and these weirs, which belonged to various people, were a source of litigation owing to their owners raising the height of them to an excessive extent.

The earliest reference to the weirs is in the grant by king Morgan in the sixth century, when Llandogo *cum coretibus* (with its fishing weirs) was granted to the see of Llandaff.

In the grant of William Marshall, earl of Pembroke, to Tintern Abbey in 1223 several weirs are named.

In 1315 a dispute arose as to whether a moiety of Bigs-weir belonged to the bishop of Llandaff or to the king.

On the 3rd of March, 1315, a commission was issued to Thomas de Berkelegh [Berkley], master John Walewayn [Walwyn] and Richard de Rodeney, upon petition by John,[1] bishop of Llandaff, who alleges that a moiety of a weir in the Wye by the king's castle of St. Briavels, which weir is called *Bikeswere*, belongs to him and his bishoprick, and that such moiety upon the death of his predecessor, together with other lands and tenements of his predecessor, was taken into the hands of king Edward I., and are now in king Edward II.—to certify whether the moiety belongs to the bishop or not—inquisition to be made by oath by good men of the county of Gloucester, in the presence of the constable of the castle of St. Briavels or his lieutenant.[2]

The result of the above enquiry does not appear, but ten years later king Edward II. grants, 16 October, 1326, in frank almoin to the abbot and convent of Tintern, a moiety of the weir of *Brithekeswere* [Bigsweir] with the fishery there, but he is not to claim, by reason of this grant, timber in the forest of Dean for repairs of the said moiety.[1]

The abbot of Tintern exceeded his rights by raising the weirs higher than they had been, in consequence of which a commission was issued 2 March, 1334, to Robert de Sapy, William de Bradewell and Robert Dapetot, reciting that a commission had been lately directed to Henry de Pembrugge, Robert de Aston, and Adam Lucas to make inquisition in the counties of Gloucester and Hereford touching a complaint by Henry, earl of Lancaster, that the abbot of Tintern had raised divers weirs in the river Wye, to wit *Blickeswere* [Bigsweir], *Ithelswere*, *Assheweir*, *Walwere*, *Plumpwere* [Plumweir], *Stawere*, *Battingswere* and *Brocwere*, higher than they used to be, so that ships could no longer pass to his town of Monmouth and the adjacent parts, and that the commissioners had, in the exercise of their powers therein, caused the weirs of Ithelswere to be thrown down and intend to do the same with the remainder, reciting further that the abbot had since presented a petition before the king and council, praying that the execution of the said commission may be stayed, on the ground that all these weirs, except a moiety of *Blickeswere*, are within the liberty of Striguil in Wales belonging to the king's uncle Thomas, earl of Norfolk, the marshall, and are without the body of the county of Gloucester, and of every other English county; to make inquisition by men of the county of Gloucester and the said liberty, and certify the king whether the weirs are in England or Wales.[2]

An interesting account of the weirs on the river Wye is given by Rowland Vaughan of Newcourt in Herefordshire in his book on waterworks, printed in 1610.[3] He petitions his kinsman the earl of Pembroke to " take pitty on a whole country groning " vnder the burthen of intollerable Weares." He does not name the weirs, but refers to the earl of Pembroke, the earl of Worcester, sir Roger Bodenham of Rotherwas, and sir John Scudamore of Holm Lacy as owners of weirs, and speaks of the complaints of the inhabitants on both sides of the river from Tintern to Cwmdauddwr in Radnorshire. These weirs had been raised in the time of the wars of the Roses—" the riuer of *Wie* (their free & Mother- " Riuer) was (in the troublesome times between the " houses of *York* & *Lancaster*) so *Weared* & fortified " as if the Salmons therein (on paine of imprison- " ment) had beene forbidden their vsuall walkes, and " on paine of death (as in case of high treason) not " to trade with any of the Earle of *Marches* men." Rowland Vaughan was one of the commissioners of *Shewres* [sewers], and at a meeting of that body at Chepstow he saw when riding over the bridge " the " water swolne with a *sea* of Salmon." And again,

---

1 John de Monmouth, bishop from 1296 to 1323.
2 *Cal. Rot. Pat.*, Edw. II., 1313—17, p. 310.

1 *Cal. Rot. Pat.*, Edw. II., 1324—27, p. 382.
2 *Ibid.*, Edw. III., 1330—34, p. 572.
3 MOST APPROVED | And | Long experienced VVATER- | VVORKES | . . . . By ROWLAND VAVGHAN, Esquire | 1610. A most scarce book, of which the writer has a copy.

referring to the quantity of salmon, he says "that "the Riuer of *Wye* did yeeld *Salmon* so plentifully "as *Sturgeon* in some partes of *Germany* : and that "a *Hereford-shire* seruant would surfet on fresh "*Salmon* as oft as a *North-Hampton-shire*-man on "fatt Venison," as many as thirty salmon being taken in a morning at a draught. The weirs had been heightened in the time of king Edward VI., and had such been done in the reign of king Henry VIII. "he would haue taken the like order with them as "hee didde with *Abbeyes* and *Monasteries*. As an "Heresie is bred and hatched amongst those that "vnderstands no true Religion soonest, so, in the "tender time of that sweete and gracious King "*Edward* the sixt, these Weares had their *breeding* "and *increase*."

The weir at Monmouth was the subject of a cause which in the 19 Jac. I. was heard in the court of the duchy of Lancaster at Westminster between Benedict Hall, esq., plaintiff, and John Mason, George Warrel and Thomas Powell, defendants, by which it appeared that queen Mary was seised of the manor of Monmouth with the appurtenances, and of a free fishing in the river Wye and of a weir and fish-yard there, which were erected in her time in the place where an old foundation of an ancient weir had stood. This weir had been let by the said queen and by queen Elizabeth, and previously by the earls and dukes of Lancaster by yearly rents, and had been let by king James in the tenth year of his reign to John Abrahall, esq., for 31 years at the rent of 6*l*. 13*s*. 4*d*. Abrahall in the same year assigned the same to William Hall, esq., at whose death in the 12 Jac. the complainant became possessed. In the 19 Jac. the commissioners of sewers caused a jury to be empanelled who delivered this verdict[1] :—

> That Benedict Hall, the complainant, was possessed of the said Were called Monmouth Were upon the river of Wye, which was excessive high and hurtfull, and was an impediment to the common passage of boats, barks and ballangers up and down the said river, and by means thereof they could not pass but in great danger, which, if the said Were were not, boats of two or three tuns might pass the river ; and that the said Were had been the death and drowning of one of the king's subjects, and is the cause of the scarcity, dearnefs and want of salmons and other fish within the said river, by reason many of them were taken in gins of the said Were when they were out of season, and that the same was a great abuse, wrong, enormity and annoiance to the whole country.

The commissioners accordingly ordered :—

> That the said Were should be overthrown, and that the timber and stone thereof should be removed, whereby the channel should be cleared for passage of boats.

The defendants were therefore directed to over-throw the weir, which they did. Against this the plaintiff appealed, and the cause was heard in the duchy court before sir Humphrey May, chancellor of

the duchy, sir John Denham, baron of the exchequer, sir Thomas Chamberlain, one of the king's justices of the bench, and sir Edward Mosley, attorney of the said court, who decided :—

> That the said Were being an ancient Were by prescription and custome, it ought not to have been overthrown by the decree of the commissioners of sewers, and that the said verdict of the jurors was defective, because, though they presented the said Were to be over high and inhaunced, yet in regard they did not present in *quanto* nor in *qua parte*, the said Were was inhaunced above the ancient assize, therefore they esteemed the said verdict of no validity.

In 14 Car. II. [1662] an act was passed impowering sir William Sandys of Ombersley in the county of Worcester, knt., Windsor Sandys and Henry Sandys to make the rivers Wye and Lugg navigable. They were thereby impowered to set up locks, weirs, turnpikes, pens for water-cranes, wharves, foot rails, to make a path on either side of the river for the towing of boats, provided that they finish the work by the 29th day of September, 1665, between the cities of Hereford and Bristol ; *provided always* that they shall in every weir leave open near the bottom of the lock a passage 16 inches high and 12 inches wide for the passage of salmon up the said river ; *provided also* that this act shall not be prejudicial to the right honourable the marquis of Worcester and the lord Herbert, his son and heir apparent, in the county of Monmouth, or to the weirs called Monmouth weir and Tintern weir, but that the said marquis and lord Herbert shall enjoy such fishing in the river and maintain these said two weirs, as the same were used, etc., at the time of the making of this act and for these forty years last past ; *provided* also that it shall be lawful for any persons to use any boat for conveying goods, etc., and that neither sir Wm. Sandys, Windsor Sandys, nor Henry Sandys shall erect kiddles, wears, snares, nets, etc., in any lock whereby to catch any manner of fish. A body of commissioners, twenty in number, were to be appointed for executing the powers of this act, of whom ten were to be of the county of Hereford, five of the county of Gloucester, and five of the county of Monmouth.

Not much followed from this act, and in 7 Gul. III. [1695] another act was passed. The people of Herefordshire favoured it, and at the assizes at Hereford on the 30th of March, 1691, the grand jury made a presentment in favour of the bill. The people of Monmouthshire being interested in their fishings and mills raised an agitation against the bill. Among the objections raised to the bill, it was said—

> If this bill passes 'twill undo the town of Monmouth by ruining its market and of the markets adjoining and all the inhabitants of that county who depend thereupon, and will also undo all those persons in the counties of Monmouth, Gloucester and Hereford (which are numerous) that subsist and maintain their families by land-carriage, and consequently will sink the rents in those counties. The multitude of

---

1 *The Reading of the Famous and Learned Robert Callis, Esq., upon the Statute of* 23 *Hen.* 8, *cap.* 5, *of Sewers, as it was delivered by him at Gray's Inn in August* 1622. *London,* 1885, p. 262 *et seq.*

men and horses now made use of will then be idle, sent away, or take and be used to such courses of living as do harm to the public.

In another paper of objections, dated 1695, it is stated :—

> Many of the wears have iron mills or forges and other mills, dwelling houses, etc., which by taking down the wears will become of no value. Several of the mills, forges and wears are not let at improved values, but are in the owners' or occupiers' own occupations and are of great value, and particularly the earl of Kent's [the new wear at Whitchurch] is worth 300l. per annum. If this bill passes into an act it will destroy above fifty mills. Upon the earl of Kent's wear stands one of the best iron mills or forges of England which lately being rebuilt on an old foundation, the same and the dwelling houses, etc., cost above 3000l.

The earl of Kent's case presented that, among other things, at his forge at the new weir he had two hammers and three chaferies or refineries, that he had several royalties of fishing in the river Wye and one in particular of six miles on both sides the said weir, and that ever since the rebuilding of the weir he had had ten puncheons or engines for catching salmon at the said wear, that he had been offered 6000l. for his interest in the said weir.

The earl therefore proposed that, if his weir and forge might be permitted to stand—

> To alter a lock already built at the proposal of some of the gentlemen of Herefordshire or to build a new one; to build a dwelling house for a servant to attend the lock whose salary the earl will pay.
>
> To keep open at the bottom of the weir a stream of 16 inches high by 14 inches wide to allow the salmon to pass up the river.
>
> To take away 8 of his puncheons and to keep only two.

It is added that the new weir was once tumultuously pulled down, and he who headed the rioters was sued for it and forced to compensate the owner.

In this act it is recited that whereas by the act of the 14 Car. II. sir William Sandys, knt., Windsor Sandys, esq., and Henry Sandys were empowered to make the rivers Wye and Lugg navigable, but that they did nothing towards making the Lugg navigable, and what they did towards the work on the Wye was done so slightly that most of the locks made by them did in a few years fall utterly to decay, etc.

At this time there were the following mills and wears on the river Wye :—

> At Monington, 2.
>   Bridge Solars, 2.
>   Sugwas, Mr Symonds', 3.
>   Hereford, 6 fulling mills, 3 corn mills.
>   Fownhope, 1.
>   Hancox (?), 1.
>   Carey (?), 2.
>   Foy, 3.
>   Wilton, 2.
>
>   25 mills.

New weir forge and building [at Whitchurch].

Fishing Wears on the Wye.

Lin wear ⎫
Ash wear ⎬ wears in the tideway, near Tintern.
Wall wear ⎭

Wears on the Wye out of repair.

Lidbrook weir ⎫
Park weir   ⎪
Chit weir   ⎪
Old weir   ⎬ between Ross and Monmouth.
Bishop's weir ⎪
Marten's weir ⎪
Hadnock weir ⎭
New weir.
Ithel's weir.
Bigs weir.
Coed-Ithel weir.
Brock weir.
Plum weir.

The promoters of the navigation set to work immediately they secured their bill, and a paper undated, but soon after the passing of the act, gives a list of the wears pulled down :—

> Monington.
> Bridge Solars.
> Sugwas.
> Hereford.
> Fownhope.
> Hancocks.
> Carey.
> Ingston.
> Wilton.
> Monmouth ⎫
> Lin wear   ⎪ all four fishing wears, no mill at
> Ash wear ⎬   either of them.
> Wall wear ⎭

Another paper gives the prices paid to some of the owners for the purchase of their wears :—

> Henry Probert of Penallt [the Argoed], esq., for the purchase of Lin weir 450l.
> Henry, duke of Beaufort, for Ash weir, Wall weir and Tintern or Abbey weir 1580l.
> Charles, marquis of Worcester, for Monmouth wear 1120l.
> James, lord Chandos, for Wilton weir 400l.
> Sandys Lechmere of Fownhope, esq., for Fownhope weir 500l.

Beyond the purchase and demolition of the weirs nothing seems to have been done, and certainly no locks were ever made. A tow path was, however, formed, and a considerable trade was done in the conveyance of merchandise up and down from Hereford to Chepstow. The demolition of the weirs would seem to have been only partially carried out, for in 1800 the foundations still remained, and Heath describes the exertions of the men to get their barges over the rapids caused by the hidden masonry. The new weir at Whitchurch was the last to remain, as this was retained by mr. White for the benefit of his iron-works.

Navigation on the river continued till shortly after 1873, when the railway, made in that year from Ross to Monmouth, absorbed all the carrying formerly done by the barges, and it is now some years since a barge was seen on the river. The tow-path has also disappeared, though it has in many places become a public foot-path.

The weirs, of which remains still exist, are as follows :—

New weir, just above the Florence.
Bigs weir, opposite the mansion.
Ridingstream weir, below the *Ship* inn at Llandogo.
Coed-Ithel weir, ¼ mile above Coed-Ithel.

Brock weir, above the new bridge.
Lyn weir, close below the railway bridge.
Ash weir, above the tramway bridge.
Plum weir, below Tintern abbey.
Stow weir, opposite Linen-well road.
Wall weir, above the Livox farm.
Hook weir or Battings weir, below the Livox.
Troughs weir, under the Windcliff.
Walter's weir, under Piercefield.
Chit weir, opposite Pen-moel.

LLANDOGO CHURCH.

Whitebrook is said to have been the site of the first manufactory of wire, which was here established in the early part of the seventeenth century by John Hanbury of Pontypool, who brought Germans[1] or Swedes to practise their art here.[2] This was afterwards removed to Tintern. On the ruins of the ironworks were afterwards erected three large paper mills. In 1810 the owner of these mills was Kingsmill Grove of Thornbury in Gloucestershire, messrs. Brown and Morris being the proprietors of the works which then (1810) were in a flourishing condition. The paper was conveyed in barges to Bristol, from whence it was distributed. By 1850 the manufacture of paper was entirely given up, and the mills in a state of ruin. Since then some of the ponds have been purchased by mr. Markham David, who has established a farm for rearing trout.

The Church.

The church contains no architectural features, having been entirely rebuilt in 1860, when the monuments disappeared.

At Whitebrook a chapel of ease was built in 1860.

The living was until the year 1818 annexed to the prebend of Caerau in Llandaff cathedral, curates doing the work of the prebendary. From being a perpetual curacy it became a vicarage in 1820, and is now a rectory.

1 *Account of Tintern Abbey*, by Charles Heath, 1810.
2 *Memoirs of Monmouthshire*, by Nathan Rogers, 1708, p. 34.

PATRON.	DATE OF INSTITUTION.	INCUMBENT.
. . . . .	. . . .	John Kerny in 1648.
. . . . .	. . . . 1696.	John Quick, M.A., New Inn Hall, Oxford, ordained deacon with the title of this curacy 20 September 1696; also in 1697 rector of Tintern Parva.
. . . . .	24 Mar. 1717.	Thomas Rodd, licensed to officiate as curate here, and at Chepstow.
John Cookson, clk., prebendary of Caerau.	13 June 1798.	Thomas Edmunds, died 1804-5.
Wm. Birkin Meackham, clk., prebendary of Caerau.	22 Mar. 1805.	Samuel Clarke Caswall, LL.B., resigned 1810.
. . . . .	23 Mar. 1810.	Henry Birkin, M.A., resigned 1818.
. . . . .	7 Oct. 1818.	David Jones, died 1833.
. . . . .	16 Feb. 1834.	Thomas Langley, B.A.
. . . . .	. . . . 1852.	Richard Wm. Ferguson, son of Joseph Ferguson of Carlisle, resigned 1875 on appointment to the vicarage of Llandaff.
. . . . .	. . . . 1875.	Benjamin Lloyd, B.D. Lampeter, resigned 1884 on appointment to Mountain Ash.
. . . . .	. . . . 1884.	John Rees Jenkins, died 1887.
. . . . .	. . . . 1887.	Llewellyn Arnott Rees, M.A. Queen's College, Cambridge.

Monumental Inscriptions.

No monuments are left except the two following, which have been placed in the porch :—

In hopes of awaking to a glorious Resurrection here sleep the Remains of Edward Perkins of Pilston in this County, Esqre, who after a very long and tedious illnefs which he bore with becoming Patience and Resignation departed this Life the 4th Day of October, 1770, aged 26 years.

In memory of Edward Perkins of Pilstone in this County, Esqre, who departed this Life without Issue October 4, 1747, aged 32.

Whose amiable Qualities rendered him an Ornament and Blessing to his Country, and made his death Universally lamented as a sensible Loss to the Publick.

He had to his first wife Elizabeth Winterbourn, who died March 20, 1743.

On ye 6th of December, 1745, he married his second wife Deen Smith, one of ye Coheirefes of Charles Smith, Esqre, Brother of John Smith of Thistleworth in the County of Middlesex, who out of Great Regret to the best of Husbands erected this monument.

IN THE CHURCHYARD.

March 20, 1695
Here lyeth the Body of Mary
the wife of Christopher Bromage,
who deceased.

Here lyeth the body of William
Byde who deceased the 4 day of
June in the yeare of our Lord God 1663.

Llansoy.

LANSOY takes its name from Tissoi, the saint to whom the church is dedicated, of whom nothing seems to be known, except that he was a pupil of St. Dyfrig, the first bishop of Llandaff in the fifth century.

The boundaries given in the *Liber Landavensis* appear to be similar to the present boundaries, the parish lying between the brooks Olwy and Pill.[1]

The parish contains 1415 acres of land and 4 acres of water. The rateable value in 1815 was 1583*l*., and in 1912, 978*l*.

The population has been as follows :—

Year .	1801	1811	1821	1831	1841	1861	1871	1881	1891	1901
No. of inhab.	143	143	139	148	158	168	175	147	130	111

The number of houses is shewn thus :—

Year.	Inhabited Houses.	Uninhabited Houses.	Building.
1861 . . .	30	2	1
1871 . . .	30	3	0
1881 . . .	28	4	0
1891 . . .	28	3	0
1901 . . .	26	0	4

The most ancient feature in this parish is the large camp or earthwork situated one mile north-west of the church, 300 feet above sea level, commanding the broad meadows through which the river Olwy runs, and which are but 100 feet above sea level.

In this parish and Llanfihangel Tor-y-mynydd, the chief landowners in the sixteenth and seventeenth centuries were descendants of Brychan Brycheiniog, though when they first came here is not clear. Perhaps the house known as Cwrt-Brychan was their first settlement. In Llansoy the family descended from Brychan, who in the seventeenth century adopted the surname of Nicholas, was the principal one. I am uncertain which house, until they inherited Lanpill by marriage, was their residence. In wills and deeds they appear only as *of Llansoy*, and therefore it is probable that Ty-mawr (*the great house*) was their abode.

The first to assume a surname was William Nicholas, the son of Nicholas ap William Gruffydd, who made his will 5 May, 1622, proved at Llandaff 16 June, 1624 :—

> To be buried in the church of Lansoy—the parson of llansoy for forgotten tithes iij*s*. iiij*d*.—cathedral church of Landaff ij*s*.—to Catherine my wife, one moiety of all my linen, pewter and brass for her life, with household stuff and one silver boule and one

silver sault and viij silver sponnes, and after her decease the said moiety to Andrewe Nicholas my son—whereas I hold by several leases and grants one grist mill called Radyr's mill[1] and the moiety of one other grist mill called Magor's mill of the r*t* hon. Edward, earl of Worcester, and one tenement of land of the r*t* hon. Henry, lord Herbart, being part of the old park in the co. of Mon., these I give to the s*d* Andrew Nicholas my son—to Phe' Nicholas my son the lease of the tithes of Newchurch—to Ann Nicholas, dau. of my son Phe', xx*s*.—my son Phe' Nicholas out of the profits of the s*d* tithes to make yearly payment unto Gilles Nicholas, son of the s*d* Andrew Nicholas, 5*l*.—to my men servants and maid servants 5*s*. a piece—to Elizabeth, dau. of my dau. Bridgett, vi*l*. xiij*s*. iiij*d*., and if the s*d* Elizabeth die before she is 16 the s*d* sum to the children of my son Andrew and my dau. Dorothy equally—to W*m* Nicholas, my grandchild, one black colt—the rest to Catherine my wife.

Nicholas Nicholas (son of Andrew, son of the above William Nicholas) appears in a deed as follows :—

> Ind'res made 18 July, 13 Car. II., 1661, between Nicholas Nicholas of Llansoy, gent., and Bridget his wife and Richard Vidler, late of Cwmcarvan, yeom., and Blanch his wife of the one part ; and William Jones of Lanarth, esq., of the other part. In cons'on of 200*l*. the said Nicholas Nicholas and Richard Vidler grant to William Jones all that messuage wherein Thomas John Edmund did lately inhabit, and wherein Thomas William doth now inhabit cont*g* three score acres called Cay keven, Cae yr lloyd, Ton dee, Cay pant, Cae isha, Cae Rees, Cay pwll, lying in Gwailod y wlade in the parish of Cwmcarvan between the lands of Alse Blower, widow, the lands of David Edmonds, the brook called Pencam, the lands of Thomas Pheellipp, the lands of the earl of Pembroke, now or late in the occupation of Adam Jones, and the way leading from the stony bridge towards the church of Cwmcarvan, and also all that water mill now in the occupation of the s*d* Nicholas Nicholas.

Giles Nicholas,[2] the brother of the above Nicholas Nicholas, became a clergyman, and was rector of Llangynidr in Breconshire, a living that continued in the hands of his descendants, as will be seen by the pedigree, for many years.

Philip Nicholas, the eldest brother, continued the family at Llansoy, and was father of Andrew, a barrister, who was drowned in 1671, leaving an only child Frances, who died unmarried.

Philip Nicholas, the second son of William Nicholas, whose will is given above, was also of

---

[1] p. 178 Latin ; p. 437 English.

[1] In the parish of Llanbadog.

[2] So uncertain was the use of surnames at this date, that Giles is baptized as the son of Andrew Williams, *i.e.*, as the son of Andrew the son of William—1606, *September* 21, *Ghiles, son of Andrewe Williams, bapt. on sunddaie beinge St. Mathewe daie* (par. reg.).

Llansoy, and was father of Edward, who served the office of sheriff in 1682, and entered his pedigree in the Heralds' visitation of that year. His second wife Judith was widow of Thomas Evans, who, with Robert Jones, and Thomas Jones of Trevethin, was appointed in 1650 one of the commissioners for sequestration of estates under the commonwealth. In March, 1654, he was appointed sole sub-commissioner to manage estates and receive rents, receiving an allowance of 12d. in the pound on all he paid in. In November, 1654, he died, and his widow was required to pay up the sum of 1806l. 2s. of arrears.[1] Judith soon after married Edward Nicholas, and in 1658 sold land in Llantilio Crossenny to Charles Powell of Bristol, son of Thomas Powell, the son of Walter Powell of Llantilio.

This ind're made 15 April, 1658, between Edward Nicholas of Trelleck Grange, gent., and Judith his wife of the one part, and Charles Powell of Bristol, apothecary, of the other part. Whereas Robert Knight of Tallycoed, gent., by ind're of feoffment duly executed with livery of seizin dated 21 Nov., 1656, in cons'on of 100l. paid him by Judith Evans of Trelleck, widow, sold to the sd Judith all those two parcels of meadow called Lantrothy ycha and Gworlod y gwaire contg 16 acres in Lantilio Crossenny, between the lands of Charles Powell, gent., other lands of the sd Robert Knight, the late lands of Walter Powell, gent., decd, the highway leading from Monmouth to Bergevenny, and the river Trothy, on all or some parts. And whereas the said Judith intermarried before the sd day of payment (20 Nov. last past) with the said Edward Nicholas, and in cons'on of 106l. the sd Edward & Judith grant to the sd Charles Powell, etc.

Andrew Nicholas owned Llangunnock, and is buried in the chapel there.

Andrew Nicholas (the son of Philip, son of Andrew, son of William ap Nicholas) was a barrister, who being drowned in 1671, left an only child Frances, who died unmarried. Philip Nicholas, brother of the above Andrew, then succeeded, and left a son Philip, who seems to have been the last of the race to have any connection with the parish. He made his will 8 December, 1711, proved at Llandaff 10 January, 171½, described as of the town of Usk, gent.

Whereas I am entitled to the reversion, after the death of Ann Curr of Monmouth, widow, of a messuage, etc., in Gwernesney, heretofore purchased by Philip Nicholas, gent. [testator's grandfather], of John Charles, now or late in the possession of Joan Thomas, widow, tenements and woods in Llangwm Isha, three tenements in the town of Usk in the street called Twyn y daley du, I leave the said premises to my wife Hannah Nicholas for her life, and after her decease to John Ambrose, second son of William Ambrose my brother-in-law, provided the sd John Ambrose shall change his name to Nicholas, and also that he pay 100l. to Philippa, an infant now living with me, whom I make my adopted daughter, and in case the sd John Ambrose do not perform these conditions, I leave the same to William Ambrose, gent., son of my said brother-in-law William Ambrose, on the same conditions.

The Church.

The church was founded in the time of bishop Berthgwyn in the latter part of the sixth century by one Cynhageu[1] or Conhae,[2] when he gave the mansion of St. Tysoi, the pupil of Dyfrig (Dubritius) which formerly belonged to Dyfrig, to God and the holy apostle St. Peter. The boundaries are described as

Between the wood and the field, and between the rivulet Ilgui [Olwy] and Pill; and in the other part from Ilgui to Pill towards the east, from the influx of Ceninuc into Ilgui, along Ceninuc upwards to the influx of the Ffinnant, along the Ffinnant to its source, from the source along to the hollow downwards to Pill, along Pill to the brook Murn, along Murn to its source to Carn Enuin, from the side of Caer Tollcoit to the head of the Cinahi, following downwards by the stone of Cinahi to the Ilgui, along Ilgui to the influx of Ceninuc, where it began.

The church consists of chancel and nave with a tower at the west end and porch on the north side. The stairs to the rood-loft on the south side of the chancel remain. A notable object in the church box is the silver chalice with initials and date, W. P. 1577, on the lid.

The advowson has until recently been in the hands of the lords of Usk and Trelech. In 1322 Llansoy with other churches was conveyed by Hugh le Despencer (whose wife Eleanor was daughter and coheir of Gilbert de Clare, earl of Gloucester and Hertford) to Elizabeth (another daughter of Gilbert), widow of John de Burgh. Since then the advowson has descended as the lordship of Usk and Trelech. By an order in council dated 13 January, 1902, the patronage was transferred by Henry, ninth duke of Beaufort, to the bishop of Llandaff.[3]

The old parish register book begins in 1599, and is complete to 1812. Among the entries is one relating to the belfry and the casting of a bell.

Churchwardens— . . . . Christopher Williams 1688 & for ye yeare 1689, who first built the bellfree with stones, And cast the Greate bell which cost besides the raising and carrying of the stones 60l.

The building of the tower had been initiated by the rector Geoffrey Prise, who died in August, 1620, and is noticed thus :—

Whereas Geffrey Price, late rectr of the p'sonadge of llansoy by his last will and testamt did geve and bequeth towards the errectinge and newe buyldinge of a steeple w'thin lansoy the some of five pounds, and in the meane tyme of the buyldinge thereof that the interest should remayne towards the releef of the poore of the same p'ishe w'ch said vli. was paid in the hands of George Harrie xxo January 1620, and the interest thereof paid to the use aforesaid, and the said

---

1 *Old Wales*, II., 77 et seq.

1 *Liber Landavensis*, p. 437.
2 *Book of Llan Dâv*, p. 187.
3 *Vide* p. 131.

Pedigree of the family of Nicholas (Brychan) of Llansoy.

The arms entered at the Visitation of 1683 were: *A chevron between 3 choughs, on a canton a chaplet* (no colours). CREST.—*On a chaplet a chough.* To this the herald has added, *no proof*. The paternal arms which this family ought to have borne were BRYCHAN and EINION AP SELIF quarterly, as shewn on p. 231.

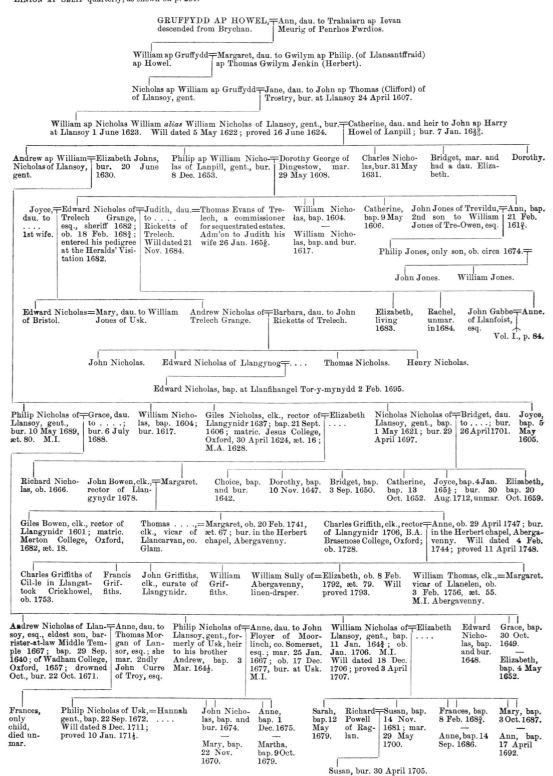

GRUFFYDD AP HOWEL, descended from Brychan. = Ann, dau. to Trahaiarn ap Ievan Meurig of Penrhos Fwrdios.

William ap Gruffydd ap Howel. = Margaret, dau. to Gwilym ap Philip. (of Llansantffraid) ap Thomas Gwilym Jenkin (Herbert).

Nicholas ap William ap Gruffydd of Llansoy, gent. = Jane, dau. to John ap Thomas (Clifford) of Trostry, bur. at Llansoy 24 April 1607.

William ap Nicholas William *alias* William Nicholas of Llansoy, gent., bur. at Llansoy 1 June 1623. Will dated 5 May 1622; proved 16 June 1624. = Catherine, dau. and heir to John ap Harry Howel of Lanpill; bur. 7 Jan. 16$\frac{38}{39}$.

Andrew ap William Nicholas of Llansoy, gent. = Elizabeth Johns, bur. 20 June 1630.

Philip ap William Nicholas of Lanpill, gent., bur. 8 Dec. 1653. = Dorothy George of Dingestow, mar. 29 May 1608.

Charles Nicholas, bur. 31 May 1631.

Bridget, mar. and had a dau. Elizabeth.

Dorothy.

Joyce, dau. to . . . . 1st wife. = Edward Nicholas of Trelech Grange, esq., sheriff 1682; ob. 18 Feb. 168$\frac{3}{4}$; entered his pedigree at the Heralds' Visitation 1682. = Judith, dau. to . . . . Ricketts of Trelech. Will dated 21 Nov. 1684. = Thomas Evans of Trelech, a commissioner for sequestrated estates. Adm'on to Judith his wife 26 Jan. 165$\frac{5}{6}$.

William Nicholas, bap. 1604.

—

William Nicholas, bap. and bur. 1617.

Catherine, bap. 9 May 1606.

John Jones of Trevildu, 2nd son to William Jones of Tre-Owen, esq. = Ann, bap. 21 Feb. 161$\frac{0}{1}$.

Philip Jones, only son, ob. circa 1674. =

John Jones. William Jones.

Edward Nicholas of Bristol. = Mary, dau. to William Jones of Usk.

Andrew Nicholas of Trelech Grange. = Barbara, dau. to John Ricketts of Trelech.

Elizabeth, living 1683.

Rachel, unmar. in 1684.

John Gabbe of Llanfoist, esq. = Anne. Vol. I., p. 84.

John Nicholas. Edward Nicholas of Llangynog = ... Thomas Nicholas. Henry Nicholas.

Edward Nicholas, bap. at Llanfihangel Tor-y-mynydd 2 Feb. 1695.

Philip Nicholas of Llansoy, gent., bur. 10 May 1689, æt. 80. M.I. = Grace, dau. to . . . .; bur. 6 July 1688.

William Nicholas, bap. 1604; bur. 1617.

Giles Nicholas, clk., rector of Llangynidr 1637; bap. 21 Sept. 1606; matric. Jesus College, Oxford, 30 April 1624, æt. 16; M.A. 1628. = Elizabeth . . . .

Nicholas Nicholas of Llansoy, gent., bap. 1 May 1621; bur. 29 April 1697. = Bridget, dau. to . . . .; bur. 26 April 1701.

Joyce, bap. 5 May 1605.

Richard Nicholas, ob. 1666.

John Bowen, clk., rector of Llangynydr 1678. = Margaret.

Choice, bap. and bur. 1642.

Dorothy, bap. 10 Nov. 1647.

Bridget, bap. 3 Sep. 1650.

Catherine, bap. 13 Oct. 1652.

Joyce, bap. 4 Jan. 165$\frac{4}{5}$; bur. 30 Aug. 1712, unmar.

Elizabeth, bap. 20 Oct. 1659.

Giles Bowen, clk., rector of Llangynidr 1601; matric. Merton College, Oxford, 1682, æt. 18.

Thomas . . . ., clk., vicar of Llancarvan, co. Glam. = Margaret, ob. 20 Feb. 1741, æt. 67; bur. in the Herbert chapel, Abergavenny.

Charles Griffith, clk., rector of Llangynidr 1706, B.A. Brasenose College, Oxford; ob. 1728. = Anne, ob. 29 April 1747; bur. in the Herbert chapel, Abergavenny. Will dated 4 Feb. 1744; proved 11 April 1748.

Charles Griffiths of Cil-le in Llangattock Crickhowel, ob. 1753.

Francis Griffiths.

John Griffiths, clk., curate of Llangynidr.

William Griffiths.

William Sully of Abergavenny, linen-draper. = Elizabeth, ob. 8 Feb. 1792, æt. 79. Will proved 1793.

William Thomas, clk., vicar of Llanelen, ob. 3 Feb. 1756, æt. 55. M.I. Abergavenny. = Margaret.

Andrew Nicholas of Llansoy, esq., eldest son, barrister-at-law Middle Temple 1667; bap. 29 Sep. 1640; of Wadham College, Oxford, 1657; drowned Oct., bur. 22 Oct. 1671. = Anne, dau. to Thomas Morgan of Lansor, esq.; she mar. 2ndly John Curre of Troy, esq.

Philip Nicholas of Llansoy, gent., formerly of Usk, heir to his brother Andrew, bap. 3 Mar. 164$\frac{1}{2}$. = Anne, dau. to John Floyer of Moorlinch, co. Somerset, esq.; mar. 25 Jan. 1667; ob. 17 Dec. 1677, bur. at Usk. M.I.

William Nicholas of Llansoy, gent., bap. 11 Jan. 164$\frac{3}{4}$; ob. Jan. 1706. M.I. Will dated 18 Dec. 1706; proved 3 April 1707. = Elizabeth . . . .

Edward Nicholas, bap. and bur. 1648.

Grace, bap. 30 Oct. 1649.

—

Elizabeth, bap. 4 May 1652.

Frances, only child, died unmar.

Philip Nicholas of Usk, gent., bap. 22 Sep. 1672. Will dated 8 Dec. 1711; proved 10 Jan. 171$\frac{1}{2}$. = Hannah . . . .

John Nicholas, bap. and bur. 1674.

—

Mary, bap. 22 Nov. 1670.

Anne, bap. 1 Dec. 1675.

—

Martha, bap. 9 Oct. 1679.

Sarah, bap. 12 May 1679.

Richard Powell of Raglan. = Susan, bap. 14 Nov. 1681; mar. 29 May 1700.

Susan, bur. 30 April 1705.

Frances, bap. 8 Feb. 168$\frac{3}{4}$.

—

Anne, bap. 14 Sep. 1686.

Mary, bap. 3 Oct. 1687.

—

Ann, bap. 17 April 1692.

v*li.* xx° January 1621 was deliu'd into the hands of Harrie d'd and the interest thereof paid to the use af'rsaid and the said some of v*li.* xx° January 1622 was deliu'd unto Walter Cipry & was paid alsoe xx° January 1623 into the hands of Andrew Nicholas and the interest thereof to the poore as aforesaid, w'che said some of v*li.* is to remain from one p'ishn' to another, the interest thereof to be paid yearly towards the poor until suche tyme that the steepill of llansoy be newelie erected according to the true meaning of the testator Jeoffrey Price.

by me ANDREW NICHOLAS.

Another note dated 21 November, 1650, says that Roger William [who was buried in 1630] left 5*l.* for the same purpose, the interest of which was, until the steeple should be built, to be given to the poor ; and Walter Cipery [who was buried 20 July, 1640] left a similar sum.

The will of Roger William referred to above,

described as of Lansoy, yeoman, dated 16 November, 6 Car. [1630], proved at Llandaff 2 December, 1630, is as follows :—

Church of Landaff 2*s.*—my parish church of Lansoye 6*s.*—towards the bilding of Lansoye stipell five pownd, the use of this five pownd untill the stipell be bilded to be destrebuted among the poor—to Evan Thomas, son to my brother Thomas William, eight pound, to William Thomas his brother two pound—to Walter William, son to William Lewis, five pound —to Rice John my nevo [nephew] ten pound to put to use for his two sons—to John Evan my brother-in law three pound—to Jaine John, dau. of John Evan, fower pound—to Elizabeth John, the other dau. of John Evan, ten pound—to Jaene, wife of Edward Will'm, and his three dau's ten pound equally—to the seven children of David John Howell ten shillings a piece—Elinor, wife of William Lewis, five pound [other legacies].

[Signed]   ROGER WILL'.

LLANSOY CHURCH.

A note dated 2 June, 1659, referring to the money in hand, proceeds—

Nowe findinge that the belfree is readie to fall downe & the tymber altogeither rotten & not to be rep'ed, therefore the p'ishon's of Lansoy unanimously consent and agree to build up a new belfree (with the Lord's assistaunce) as soone as possible may be, and doe agree that the s'd ffiue pounds in the hands of the s'd John Watkin shall be paid into the hands of the churchwardens of Lansoy to be imployed to bring materrialls and to paie workmen for the digging up of stonns towards the said worke.

By this it may be concluded that the tower as it

is seen now was built about 1688, and took the place of one which was of timber.

In 1613 the plague appeared in the parish, noted thus in the parish register :—

1613, August—In the Beginninge of this monthe two housses were Infected, the Tavarne house and m^r W^m nicholas. In the tavarne there died a maid, Batman & his wife, Robart and Joan fortune—In m^r W^m nicholas house there died Briget and the maid-servant. 1613, Aug. 31, Margaret Bowen died of the plague & was Buried the last daie of August.

JENKIN MORGAN & THOMAS EDWARD p'curatores.[1]

---

[1] Procuratores, *overseers.*

Patron.	Date of Institution.	Rectors.
. . . . .	. . . .	Nicholas de Bagethorp, licentiate of civil law and bachelor of canon law, resigned Llansoy, value nine marks, on being appointed to a living in the gift of the bishop, prior, and chapter of Ely, August 1347.[1]
. . . . .	1 July 1388.	John Usk.[2]
	. . . .	David ap Howel, resigned 1388.[3]
The king, by reason of the custody of the lands and heir of Edmund Mortimer, earl of March.	18 Nov. 1388.	Howel ap David,[3] chaplain.
. . . . .	24 March 1389.	John Usk.[4]
. . . . .	. . . .	David Howell, resigned 1390 on appointment to Shulton in the diocese of Lincoln, in exchange with John Glasyer.[5]
The king, by reason of his custody of the lands and heir of Edmund Mortimer, earl of March.	10 Oct. 1390.	John Glasyer, vicar of Shulton, in exchange with David Howell;[5] resigned 1398 on appointment to Trelech, in exchange with Gregory ap David.
The king, by reason of the wardship of the land and heir of Roger, earl of March.	15 Feb. 1398.	Gregory ap David, previously vicar of Trelech, on exchange with John ap William Glasyer;[6] ratification of his estate 20 Feb. 1399.[7]
. . . . .	. . . .	Roger William in 1535.[8]
. . . . .	. . . .	John Howel in 1560.
. . . . .	. . . .	Morgan Thomas in 1592, in which year he commenced the register book. (Hugh Powell, curate in 1594 and to 1601.)
. . . . .	. . . . 1603.	Geoffrey Prise, M.A., in 1604 and to 1620; previously vicar of Caerwent; buried 12 Aug. 1620.
William, 3rd earl of Pembroke, K.G.	22 Aug. 1620.	William Arney, M.A. St. Edmund Hall, Oxford; also vicar of Nash, where he probably resided. (John Waters, curate in 1623.)
William, 3rd earl of Pembroke, K.G.	23 March 16$\frac{29}{30}$.	John Clegge, M.A. St. Alban Hall, Oxford, archdeacon of Llandaff in 1646 for five months only; also rector of Llangibby, where he resided; deprived by the puritans for being unable to preach in Welsh, etc.; resigned Llansoy 1666; ob. circ. 1668. (William Thomas, curate in 1631 and to 1634.) (Francis Price, curate in 1636 and to 1639; his wife Cecil buried 20 Dec. 1637.) (Hugh Walter, curate in 1643.) (Morgan Jones, curate in 1647.) (Thomas Davies, curate in 1664.)
Philip, 5th earl of Pembroke.	4 May 1666.	John Powell, M.A., resigned 1668.
Philip, 5th earl of Pembroke.	7 May 1668.	Thomas Watkins, also vicar of Llanarth, where he resided; left a charity to both parishes; died 1723. (Thomas Davies, curate in 1707.) (Elias Thomas, curate in 1730.) (Evan Thomas, licensed to the curacies of Raglan, Llandenny and Llansoy, 30 March 1745.)
. . . . .	. . . .	William Robinson, M.A. St. John's Coll., Camb., also rector of Mitchel Troy; died 1740; buried there. (John Harris, B.A., appointed curate in 1732.)
Herbert, 2nd viscount Windsor.	31 Dec. 1745.	James Davies, B.A.
. . . . .	4 May 1781.	Thomas Leach; also in 1781 vicar of Raglan.
Henry, 5th duke of Beaufort.	10 March 1796.	John Powell, M.A. Wadham Coll., Oxford, also head master of the Monmouth Grammar School; son of John Powell, vicar of Llangattock Vibon Avel; died 1836.[9] (Henry Williams, curate in 1795 and to 1804. His wife was Rachel, and six of their children are baptized here.)
Henry, 7th duke of Beaufort, K.G.	. . . . 1849.	Richard Macdonnell Evanson, B.A. Oriel Coll., Oxford, son of William Alleyne Evanson of Cork, Ireland, clk.; died 1891.
Henry Charles, 8th duke of Beaufort, K.G.	. . . . 1891.	William Jones; also from Dec. 1912 rector of Llanfihangel Tor-y-mynydd.

1 *Cal. of Papal Registers*, vol. iii., p. 261.
2 *Cal. Rot. Pat.*, Ric. II., 1385—89, p. 478.
3 *Ibid.*, p. 512.
4 *Ibid.*, Ric. II., 1388—92, p. 22.
5 *Ibid.*, p. 306.

6 *Ibid.*, Ric. II., 1396—99, p. 412.
7 *Ibid.*, Hen. IV., 1399—1401, p. 157.
8 *Valor Ecclesiasticus.*
9 For his pedigree *vide* Vol. I., p. 206.

Monumental Inscriptions.

There are no mural monuments left, only flat stones.

Within the communion rails :

HERE LIETH THE
BODY OF IOYES[1]
HARYS WHO
DEPARTED THIS
LIFE THE 6TH
DAY OF OCTOBER
AND WAS IN
TERED THE 8TH.
[the rest is cut away.]

HERE LYETH THE
BODY OF WILLIAM NI
CHOLAS DEPARTED THIS
LIFE THE . . DAY OF
JANVARY 1706.[2]

HERE LYETH THE BO
DY OF SVSAN THOMAS
WIFE OF THOMAS IO
NES OF LANTRISHEN
WHO DEPARTED THIS
LIFE THE 29 DAY OF
JANVARY IN THE YE
ARE OF OVR LORD
1698.[3]
LET YOVTH AND AGE
IN TIME THINKE ON
THE GLAS THAT RV
NS FOR MAN WHI
CH TIME HE CAN
NOT PAS.

There is also cut on the same stone :

In Memory
of Jane Highings Daugh.
of Robert and Elizabeth
Kemp who died the 4th
. . . . 1770 aged 54.[4]

. . . .
. 1671
HERE LYETH YE BODY OF
PHILLIP NICHOLAS GENT
BVRIED YE X DAY OF MAY
1689 AGED 80 YEARS.[5]

Corpus Georgij Thomas in hoc tum.
. . . . ad mortem fuccubuit
Vicefimo quinto Die Mensis Martij
Anno Dom. 1713
Also Here Lye Ye Body
of Elizabeth the Wife of
Robert Kemp Gent. of
The Parish of Woolves
newton who Died the
28th day of December 1736.

1 Joyce.
2 170⁴⁄₅, Jan. 24, sep., Gulielmus Nicholas p'ochiâ de Lanfoy. (Par. reg.)
3 169⁷⁄₈, Jan. 31, sep., Susanna Jones de Lantriffen. (Par. reg.)
4 1770, Jan. 17, bur., Jane Hitchins of Llandenny. (Par. reg.)
5 1689, May 10, bur., Phillip Nicholas, gent. (Par. reg.)

Outside the communion rails :

. . . . . .
. . . . . ye 26th of March
Anno Dom. 1733
HERE
Also lyeth the Body of
George Howell who
Departed this life
March the 1st, 1742 Aged
52 years.
Likewise the Body of
Mary wife of
George Howell who
Departed this life
November ye 12th, 1753
Aged 66 years.[1]
In love they lieved in faith.

In the nave :

HERE
Lieth the Body
of Frances Jones
Daughter of Susannah Cadogan of this Parish who
departed this life the 15th Day
of June in the year of our Lord
1761 aged 2 months and 3 days.

Here lyeth ye Body of
William Drack of ys Parish
Who Died ye 28th Day of
November 1741 Aged 73 years.

In memory of John Harris Who Departed this Life April 28th, 1769, aged 2 years, son of John and Rachel Harris of the Parish of Lanvihangell. Allso of Temperance their Daughter, Died December 1791, aged 26 years.

In Memory of John Harris of the Parish of Lanvihangell who died October the . . . . 1805, aged 98 years. Also in memory of Ann Lewis, who departed this life April 9th, 1834, aged 78 years.

IN THE CHURCHYARD.

An altar-tomb.   On the south side :

In memory of James and Cornelius, sons of the Rev. Henry & Rachel Williams—James died 6 June, 1798, aged 14 years and 10 months.   Cornelius died 14 Sept., 1803, aged 10 months.

Alfo in memory of Ann, daughter of Thomas and Mary Williams, who died 25 Auguft, 1817, aged 19 days.

On the north side :

Here rests in humble hope of a joyful resurrection the body of the Rev. Henry Williams, late of the parish of Llanishen, who departed this life 15 Sept., 1816, aged 74 years.

Alfo of Rachel, wife of the above named, who departed this life 9 Dec., 1809, aged 48 years.

Alfo of Ann, daughter of the above nam'd, who died 20 May, 1810, aged 6 years.

On the west end :

Also lie the remains of the Rev. John Williams, son of the aforesaid Rev. Henry Williams and Rachel his wife, who died March 7th, 1821, aged 29 years.

1 1753, Nov. 13, bur. Mary Howel. (Par. reg.)

Llanfihangel=tor=y=mynydd.

THIS means *the church of St. Michael on the breast of the mountain,* descriptive of the situation about 500 feet above sea level.

The parish contains 1186 acres. The rateable value in 1815 was 1182*l.*, and in 1913, 978*l.*

The population has been as follows :—

Year .	1801	1811	1821	1831	1841	1861	1871	1881	1891	1901
No. of Inhab.	178	179	213	204	197	197	175	163	136	127

The houses shew a decrease in numbers:—

Year.	Inhabited houses.	Uninhabited houses.	Building.
1861 . . .	45	2	0
1871 . . .	42	4	0
1881 . . .	40	7	0
1891 . . .	38	6	0
1901 . . .	35	6	0

This parish, with which the hamlet of Llangunnock (Llangynog) is now joined, was in the sixteenth and seventeenth centuries mostly the property of descendants of Brychan Brycheiniog, as was Llansoy. The dukes of Beaufort more recently were the chief landowners, in whose manor of Usk this parish was.

Lanpill.¹

Lanpill¹ would be more fully Glanpill, and takes its name from its situation on the Pill¹ brook. It is an ancient house, and was once the seat of a family of considerable distinction descended paternally from Brychan Brycheiniog. To Dafydd Philip o Went is a *marwnad* or funeral elegy by Dafydd Benwyn the poet, who wrote about the year 1590.

rrylew phylipp rri oloedd
[*Rhylew Phylip ! rhi oloedd*]
rhywl wych ag wyl hywel oedd
[*Rhiwl wych, ag wyr Hywel oedd*]
. . . .
ymddifaid ỹnn am ddavydd
[*Ymddifaid ym am Ddafydd*]
llif noe yn llansoe y sydd
[*Llif Noe yn Llansoe y sydd*]
kat derwen aeth kaid draw n wych
[*Câd derwen aeth caed draw'n wych*]
karw mynwy benn kawr mwyn wych
[*Carw Mynwy ben cawr mwynwych*]
. . . .
llan soe a phob y sydd
[*Llansoe a phob [llan] y sydd*]
llin went heb fawr llywenydd
[*Llin Went heb fawr llawenydd.*]

Exceedingly valiant Philip ! chief of after-times [?]:
He was a fine ruler, and the grandson of Howel.

. . . .
We are destitute for David ;
The flood of Noah is in Llansoy ;
The war-oak is gone ! yonder was found doughty
The stag of Monmouth, the head giant gentle and noble.

. . . .
Llansoy and every other llan,
[*And] the line of Gwent, are without joy.*

His wife *Maestres Mawd* is mentioned, and he is said to be *Penn teir Gwent* and *pwrcaswr pob parc* (head of the three Gwents and purchaser of every park). He was buried at Llangynog.

The son of Dafydd Philip was sir William Powell, who was knighted by king James I. 7 January, 160⅘. To him is also a poem by Dafydd Benwyn.

Pwy sy o went pass ai wyr
[*Pwy sy o Went passa'i wyr ?*]
pwy wrth o val pai arthyr
[*Pwy wrtho falpai Arthyr ?*]
y maestr powel a welir
[*Y Maestr Powel a welir*]
o lann soe haela ny sir
[*O Lansoe haela'n y sir*]
maestr wiliam yn meistroli
[*Maestr Wiliam yn meistroli*]
mwyn wr braü mewn aür a bri
[*Mwyn wr brau mewn aur a bri*]
hydd o ddavydd oedd ddifalch
[*Hydd o Ddafydd oedd ddifalch*]
ny ffaela byth ffylib walch
[*Ni ffaela byth Phylib walch*]
Bryttwnn dad y dad ydoedd
[*Brytwn dad i dad ydoedd*]
yn iaith brytanniaid yn oedd
[*Yn iaith Brytaniaid in' oedd.*]

. . . .

Who in Gwent surpasses his men ?
Who, compared with him, is as if he were Arthur ?
Mr. Powel of Llansoy
Is seen the most liberal in the county—
Mr. William commanding
(Fragile gentleman !) in gold and dignity.
A hart from David he was without pride,
Philip the hawk will never fail [or *become extinct*].
A Briton from father to father he was
In the language of the Britons to us.

Lady Powell was the daughter of sir Thomas Morgan of Pen-coed, and sister of sir William Morgan of the same. Sir Thomas, who married Cecil, daughter of sir George Herbert of Swansea, was the son of sir William Morgan and grandson of sir Thomas Morgan, so that the lady is accurately

---

¹ Pill is pronounced in the Welsh way, the *ll* having an approximate sound to *lth.*

described below as the grandchild of two knights, the great-grandchild of another knight, and sister of yet another knight.

gwawr lan o vorgan vawrgost
[*Gwawr lân o Forgan fawrgost,*]
ai bryd ar rhoi brwd a rhost
[*A'i bryd ar roi brwd a rhost.*]
o wraig weddaidd wraigaidd wych
[*O ! wraig weddaidd, wreigeiddwych !*]
vn sad maestres fflywrens wych
[*Un sad, Maistres Fflywrens wych.*]

ag wyr daü varchog yw gall
[*Ag wyr dau farchog yw, gall ;*]
ag orwyr marchog arall
[*Ag orwyr marchog arall ;*]
a chwaer marchog rhywiog rhwydd
[*A chwaer marchog rhywiog, rhwydd*]
avr glod mwy nog vn arglwydd
[*Eurglod mwy nog un arglwydd.*]

A fair dawn from wealthy Morgan,
Intent upon giving boiled and roast [*meat*].
Oh ! becoming, elegant and wifely wife !
A discreet one, Mistress Florence fine.

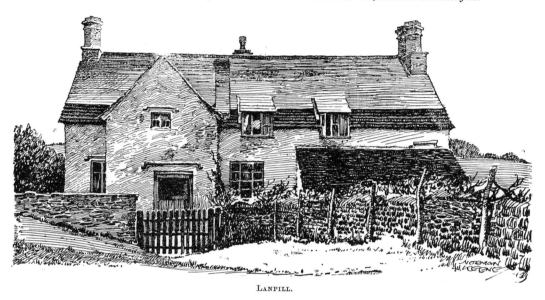

LANPILL.

Pedigree of the Family of Powell (Brychan) of Lanpill.

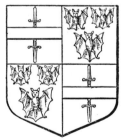

ARMS.—*Quarterly : 1 and 4, Sa., a fesse or between two swords arg., hilts and pomels of the second, that in chief pointing upwards, the other downwards* (BRYCHAN BRYCHEINIOG) ; *2 and 3, Or, 3 vespertilios az.* (EINION AP SELIF, LORD OF CWMWD).

The intervening descents from Brychan Brycheiniog will be found in *The History of Breconshire*, by Theophilus Jones, vol. i., app., p. 8.

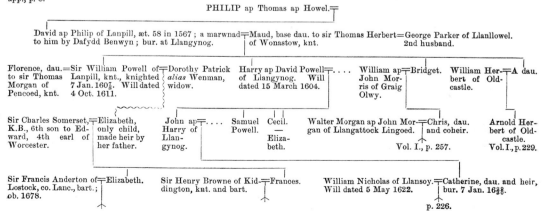

And the grandchild of two knights she is, wise ;
And the great-grandchild of another knight,
And the sister of a knight genial, free,
Of a golden fame, more than any lord.[1]

Sir William Powell's will, dated 4 October, 1611, is at Llandaff, but with no probate :—

My body to be buried in the church in Xtian burial—Dorothie Patrick *al's* Waynman, widow, all my plate, jewells, goods and chattels, moveables, howsthold stuff and implements of howsthold, etc., for her life, and afterwards all the same to sir Charles Som's't, knight, and Dame Elizabeth his wife, my reputed and well beloved daughter—my lands, tenements, manors in co. Mon. to the said Dorothie Patrick and her afsigns for her life, and after to sir Charles Som's't, knight, and Dame Elizabeth his wife, in default of issue to the right heirs of me the said

[1] For the above lines, taken from the MS. of Dafydd Benwyn's poems written in his own hand, which are deposited in the Central Library of Cardiff, I am indebted to Mr. Ifano Jones, the learned Welsh librarian, who has been kind enough to give not only the actual words as written, but also, in square brackets, the same as they would be in modern Welsh. He has also given the exact translation.

William Powell—sir Charles Som's't and Elizabeth his wife ex'ors.

Witnesses : Daniel Arundell. James Hughes.
Tho. Hughes. Thomas Will'ms.
Henry Rumsye. William Herbert.
John Rumsye.

Sir William Powell had no issue by his wife, and, as seen by his will, he left his personalty to his illegitimate daughter Elizabeth, the wife of sir Charles Somerset, K.B., sixth son of Edward, fourth earl of Worcester, K.G. The issue of this marriage was two daughters, Elizabeth, wife of sir Francis Anderton of Lostock in Lancashire, baronet, and Frances, wife of sir Henry Brown of Kiddington in Oxfordshire, baronet, from whom many families are descended.

Lanpill, which was doubtless entailed, seems to have gone to his nephew John ap Harry Howel or Powell, whose daughter and heir Catherine took it to her husband William ap Nicholas William. Their son Philip Nicholas, called of Lanpill in the parish register, was buried in 1653.

After this I have no information of Lanpill, except that it belonged to the dukes of Beaufort, and was sold by the ninth duke in 1901.

LLANFIHANGEL TOR-Y-MYNYDD CHURCH.

The Church.

The church is a small one, with nave and chancel. The west doorway has a handsome arch, as has also the porch on the south side, which has bold mouldings. The steps of the cross remain, but no base or shaft.

The parish register commences with the year 1602. It contains the usual entries, few of which are worthy of noting here.

1602, Sept. 12, bap., Jevanus morice, filius Mawricij William Edmund.

Richardus Thomas et
Will'mus Thomas edmund } gard. ib'm.

Maurice William Edmund, whose son Evan is baptized above, made his will as *Maurice Will'm* of *Lanvihangle Tourmoneth* 26 November, 1625, proved at Llandaff 24 October, 1633 :—

Cathedral ch. of Landaffe twelve pence—parson of Lanvihangle aforesaid for tithes twelve pence—to the

preacher of my funeral sermon at my burial six shillings, eightpence—whereas by my ind're between me of the one part and Edmund Maurice of Lanvihangle aforesaid my second son of the other part, I gave to Walter John James of Lanvihangle aforesaid, yeom., all that close called Gworlod yssa containing 6 acres in Lanvihangle between the lands of sir Edward Lewis, knt., the lands of Will'm Thomas Edmond, other lands of me the said Maurice, and a lane called Hewl errough on all parts—to Joane my dau. 20*li*.—my sons Evan and . . . . ex'ors—my son George—my son Edmond.

In pr. of Edw. Aleston

Abr' Drewe, viccar of Chepstow.

[Signed] Maurice W^m.

1603, May 30, chr., Margaret p'fonnes the doughter of one m^r p'fonnes of the p'ifhe of Wilchcome in the com' of Wiltfheere, gent., was borne in the houfe of David James the xxix^th day of maye and chriftened the xxx day of maye An'o D'ni 1603, An'oq. Regni Regis Jacobi Primo, p' me Georg'm Griffithe, rectorem ibidem.

160⅔, Mar. 10, chr., George morice son of Morice Will'm Edmund.

1607, Oct. 4, chr., Juan, dau. of Morice Wm. edmund.

1603, Jul. 27, sep., Margaret P'sonnes, p' me Georgium Griffith, clericum, rectorem ibidem.

1604, July 5, bur., Elizabeth Harbert, wife of Morice William Edmund.

166⅔, Feb. 18, bur., Florence Thomas, wife of William Thomas, daughter to Thomas David, vicar of Colwinston & Penlline in Glamorgan shire & mother-in-law to Robert Jones, rector of Lanvihangle Tor y mynydd.

1699, Aug. 31, nupti, Williel' Drake de Penalt et Alicia Griffith de Lanvihangell Tor y mynyth.

Patron.	Date of Institution.	Rectors.
. . . . .	. . . .	Philip, rector in 1307.[1]
. . . . .	. . . .	John Vaughan, in 1535.[2]
. . . . .	. . . .	John Jenkin, in 1560.[3]
. . . . .	. . . .	Morgan Thomas, in 1594 and to 1599; also rector of Llansoy.
. . . . .	. . . .	George Griffith, rector in 1603 and until his death 18 March, 1647. He made his will 19 May, 1646, as George Griffin:—

To be buried in the chancel of llanvihangell tor mynith's church—cathedral church of Landaffe twelve pence—church of llanvihangell iijs. iiijd.—to Joane Jone (*sic*) my beloved wife, two young bullocks, etc., lease of mortgage of lands in Gwernesney made by John Phillipp Harry of Gwernesney, late dec^d, and Elizabeth his wife with a band of 240*l*., also a band on William Edwards of Michael troy dated 13 Oct., 1643—to Walter Jones my wife's grandchild, and to his sisters 40*s*. a piece, to his wife 40*s*., to his mother 40*s*.—my wife ex'trix. In pr. of John Jones, John Howells, John Jenkin, Hugh Jenkins, Cadwalader Jenkins.

The inventory amounts to 17*l*. 15*s*., the *prizors* (appraisers) being Jenkin Taunte, Will'm Phellipp thelder and Juhen Jones [his wife]. The will is at Llandaff, but has no probate. His widow's will, as Johan John, is dated 14 April, 23 Car. [1647], proved at Llandaff 8 Oct., 1647. In this she leaves to her grandchild Walter Jones, the cottage, stable, drying kiln and lands in Gwernesney called Kae ywch lawr twy, Kae wrth y twy, Kae pella,[4] containing 26 acres.

(Henry Thomas, curate in 1640.)

Patron.	Date of Institution.	Rectors.
Archdeacon of Llandaff	1 May 1661.	Robert Jones, resigned 1665.
Do. . . .	29 Nov. 1665.	John Thomas; also 27 Nov., 1665, vicar of Llangwm.
Do. . . .	20 May 1674.	Philip Thomas; died 1695.
Do. . . .	8 Aug. 1695.	Walter Watkins, B.A. Jesus College, Oxford, son of Walter Watkins of Usk; died 1719.
		(Thomas James, curate in 1695.)
Do. . . .	13 Jan. 17$\frac{19}{20}$.	Thomas Jones; resigned 1722.
Do. . . .	13 June 1722.	Samuel Price, B.A.; died 1735.
		(Charles William, curate in 1725.)
. . . .	1 Jan. 173¾.	Elias Thomas.
		(Rees Davies of Llanishen, licensed to the curacy 5 July, 1747.)
. . . .	16 March 1775.	Lewis Thomas.
. . . .	30 June 1781.	William Prosser, died 1809.
John Probyn, archdeacon of Llandaff.	28 Sept. 1809.	Henry Prowse Jones, B.A.
. . . .	26 Dec. 1837.	Arthur Henry Price, M.A. Wadham College, Oxford, son of Thomas Price of Kingsbury, co. Warwick, clk.; resigned 1847, afterwards vicar of Lugwardine, co. Hereford.
. . . .	13 Oct. 1847.	John Price; also perpetual curate of Cilgwrwg.
. . . .	. . . . 1884.	Thomas Phillips Rogers, B.A. Lampeter; resigned 1898.
. . . .	. . . . 1901.	Charles Carne Williams, also rector of Wolvesnewton; died 22 Nov., 1912.
Archdeacon of Llandaff	Dec. 1912.	William Jones, also from 1891 rector of Llansoy.

---

1 Charter Rolls, Vol. III., 1300—26, p. 103. 2 *Valor Eccl.* 3 Browne Willis.
4 Cae uwch law'r ty (*the field above the house*); Cae wrth y ty (*the field by the house*); Cae pella (*the furthermost field*).

Monumental Inscriptions.

The only mural tablet is one on the west wall :

Sacred to the memory of Edmund Jones of Ty bach in this Parish, whose mortal remains are deposited beneath. He died the 19th day of January 1839 in the 68th year of his age. He was a member of the Established Church and an Exemplary Christian.

FLAT STONES.

Inside the communion rails :

Here lyeth ye body of Lysand Williams of this Parish of Lanvihangell, who departed this Life ye 7th day of june Año Dom 1708.

In the chancel :

Here lyeth The Body of John Morris of this parish, Deceased ye 14th Day of September 1727.

.. LIETH THE BODY OF [WALT]ER MORRIS DECESED THE 25 OF APRIL 1660. HEAR LIETH THE BODY OF WATER MORRIS DECESED THE 20 OF AVGVST 1691 (? 1695).

.. THE BODY OF CATHERINE IONES THE WIFF OF GEORGE IONES WHO DEPARTED THIS LIFE . . . .

Also here lieth ye body of Edmd. Iones, who departed ys life ye 14th day of december 1736, aged 38 years.

THE RUINED CHURCH OF LLANGUNNOCK, THE CHANCEL ARCH.

The top of this stone is hidden by a pew :

Mary Jenkins of this Parish.

Here also lieth the Body of Mary Williams of this Parish.

Here also lieth the Body of Elizabeth Williams of this Parish.

Here also lieth the Body of Henry Williams of this Parish, who departed this Life the . . . . day of November 1739, Aged 13 years.

Here also lieth the Body of Jane, the wife of William Hall of the Parish of Lansoy, who departed this Life the 9th day of January 1768, aged 38 years.

Here also lieth the Body of William Hall of the Parish of Langonnogg Tormynydd, who Departed this Life the 22nd day of August 1791, Aged 65 years.

HERE LYETH THE BODY OF KATHERINE Yᴱ DAVGHTER OF GIORGE IONES WHO DEPARTED THIS LIFE Yᴱ 16ᵀᴴ DAY OF IVLY ANN. DOM. 1708.

Also here lieth ye body of Katharine ye daughter of Edmund and Esther Iones who departed ys life ye 14th day of December 1736, aged 15 years.

Here lyeth the Body of Bridget Morris of This parish, who Deceased this life the 8th of August 1728.

Draw nere My friend and . . . . and eye
Then Go Thy wayes prepared to die.

Here also lyeth the body of Edmund Morris of this Parish, who departed this life the . . . . of november in the year 1739, aged 79 years.

In the nave :

. . . . . .

Also here lieth ye Body of Ane ye wife of Iohn Harry of ys Parish, who departed ys life Octr ye 18th, 1732, aged 69 years.

G. J. 1818.

Underneath Lieth the Body of John (?) Jones of this Parish, who departed this Life the . . . . Day of August 1779, aged 78 years.

In Memory of JOHN JONES of Cevengolo in the Parish of Wolvesnewton, who Departed this Life the 28 of August 1830, Aged 61 years.

Here lieth ye Body of . . . . mas Lewis of this Parish, who departed this Life ye . . . .

Llangunnock.

Llangunnock is properly Llangynog, the church of St. Cynog, who was one of the sons of Brychan Brycheiniog, lord of the country now known as Brecknockshire in the fifth century.

This seems without doubt to be the place mentioned in the *Liber Landavensis*[1] as *Henlennic Cinauc ar Pill, i.e.,* Henllan Cynog ar Pill (*the old church of Cynog on the river Pill*), where the boundaries are—

The influx of the Gunnic to the Pill, following Gunnic upwards to the clay pit (*prid pull*), from the clay pit to the ridge of the hill, the boundary of the land of llanngunnhoill, following the ridge of the hill towards the west, along to the Pill, following the Pill downwards to the Gunnic where it began.

Llangynog church has long been in ruins; at the present time the chancel arch and the west wall remain, and also part of the south wall with the coigns on one side of the doorway.

On the floor of the chancel is a flat stone still legible:—

HERE LIETH THE BODY OF EDWARD
NICHOLAS LATE OF TRELLICKS
GRAINGE IN THE COUNTY OF MON
MOUTH ESQ. WHO ENDED THIS LIFE
THE 18 DAY OF FEBRUARY
ANNO DOM.
1683.
Also in Memory
of HENRY NICHOLAS late
of Crumbland who
died the . . . .
1818 Aged . . . .

Arms.—*A chevron between 3 . . . .; a crescent for difference.*

Llangunnock was a manor within the great lordship of Usk. In the *inquisitio post mortem* of Gilbert de Clare, earl of Hertford and Gloucester, 1296, the manor of Llangunnock, written *Lancanok,* appears as held by half a knight's fee by John Martel,[1] and in 1314 in the inquisition of Gilbert (son of the above Gilbert), *Lucannouk* and *Bravelston* are held by John Martel by half a knight's fee.[2]

Llangunnock belonged in the sixteenth century to David ap Philip Powell of Lanpill (the father of sir William Powell), who was buried in the chapel. His son Harry was of Llangunnock, and made his will as *Harry David Powell of Langenocke* 15 March, 1604:—

To Cissill my dau. four oxen in the custody of George Waters of llanissen—Elizabeth Harry my dau.—to Cissill my dau. one cottage and five parcels of lands adjoining the churchyard of llangume Echa, and parcels in llangum Echa, late lands of Thomas Skidmor, dec^d—John Harry my son—Samuel Powell my son—Cecil Harry my dau., sole ex'trix.

It will be observed that the testator calls only one son Samuel by the surname of Powell, while to the rest he, after the Welsh fashion, gives his own christian name Harry as a surname. But his son John, called John Harry by the testator, is called John ap Howel in the pedigree, and was father of Catherine, who married William Nicholas, and took the estate of Llangunnock and also Lanpill, which came to her or her father from sir William Powell. Llangunnock descended to Edward Nicholas, son of Philip, son of the above William and Catherine, who was sheriff in 1682 and died the next year, being buried in the chapel. Edward Nicholas sold Llangunnock to David Lewis of Llanerddil, who by his will, proved in 1708, left it to his second son Thomas Lewis.[3]

1 *Liber Landavensis,* Latin, p. 241; Eng., p. 517.

1 Inq. p.m., vol. iii., no. 371.   2 *Ibid.,* no. 538.
3 *Vide* p. 46 for pedigree of Lewis.

Wolvesnewton.

IT is often supposed that this parish takes its name from its once having been the abode of numerous wolves, but it is so called from the family of Wolf, who for many centuries were lords of this place. In Welsh it is called *Tre-newydd-dan-y-gaer* (New town under the fort), referring to the ancient earthworks a quarter of a mile from the church, which was the residence of the Wolfs.

The parish contains 2656 acres. The rateable value in 1815 was 1524*l.*, and in 1912, 1337*l.*

The population has been as follows :—

Year	1801	1811	1821	1831	1841	1861	1871	1881	1891	1901
No. of Inhab.	207	244	222	248	224	193	199	168	158	159

The number of houses has decreased :—

Year.	Inhabited houses.	Uninhabited houses.	Building.
1861 . . .	41	0	0
1871 . . .	40	0	1
1881 . . .	31	6	0
1891 . . .	32	4	0
1901 . . .	32	3	0

The family of Wolf, from whom the parish takes its name, were said to have been resident here from the first to the sixteenth century. The first to come was, according to Lewis Dwnn,[1] Bardwlff or Rodolphus, son of the earl of Thuringia, who came into Britain with Getulius Serealis the Roman in A.D. 79 to fight against the Silures and Scots, and received in return for his services the fortress and lordship of Caer-fawr, which was afterwards called after his name, Wolf's Newton, the Latin name Rodolphus becoming in Welsh Rodwlff or Wllph. Sir Fwniel, lord of Wolf's Newton, is said to have received christianity in A.D. 188, and to have built the church at his own expense.[2]

Were there any records to refer to, it would be of interest to trace the history and doings of this ancient family during the fifteen centuries they lived here. They came with the Romans in the first century ; they saw the Romans, after being settled in Britain for nearly three centuries, depart ; they saw christianity come into Wales in the first century ; they heard of Augustine bringing it to the pagan Saxons in England in the fifth century, and perhaps they took part in the ecclesiastical disputes which raged in those days ; they saw king Arthur holding his brilliant courts at Caerlleon ; they heard of the conflicts going on in England, and witnessed the retreat of numbers of their countrymen into Wales, and the establishment of Saxon government in England ; they saw the conquest of England by the Normans, and probably helped to resist the raids made into Gwent by fitz-Hamon and his followers, and the gradual submission of the men of Gwent to Norman rule ; and they saw the final subjugation of Wales.

After the conquest by the Normans this parish was included within the great lordship of Newport and Usk belonging to the Clares. In the *inquisitio post mortem* of Gilbert de Clare, earl of Gloucester and Hertford, who died in 1295, Wolvesnewton is returned as being held by Simon le Botiler and de la Garston by half a knight's fee.[1] In the inquisition of Gilbert, earl of Gloucester and Hertford (son of the former Gilbert), who was killed at Bannockburn in 1314, Wolvesnewton was held, as to one moiety, by Simon le Botiler and Joan his wife, and Sarah and Wenllian her sisters, of the yearly value of 60*s.*, and as to the other moiety by Ralph le Wolf of the same value.[2] This Ralph le Wolf does not figure in the pedigree as printed in Lewis Dwnn's works ; but about this time sir William Wolf married Gwladys, daughter and heir of Gwaryn Goch, lord of Werngochen in Llantilio Pertholey,[3] to which place his grandson moved. Sir William is said to have made away with most part of his lands. By the eighteenth century the name of Wolf had disappeared, what male representatives there were having adopted the name of Morgan.

The residence of the Wolfs was on the earthwork where is now an ordinary farm-house called Cwrt-y-gaer. The mound occupies about an acre and a half of ground, and is nearly circular. On the south and west is a moat with a constant supply of water.

In the eighteenth century the chief house and estate was Ty-mawr, or the Great-house. This was purchased from Rowland Morgan, gent., in 1663 by John Rumsey of Rhyd-y-maen (*the stony ford*) in Llandenny. For two or three generations this branch of Rumsey made this their home till they removed to Trelech Court. It descended to the late colonel Edward Waugh Rumsey,[4] and has recently been sold

---

[1] *Visitations,* by Lewis Dwnn, vol. i., p. 11, where is a long pedigree.

[2] *Ibid.* Hwn a dderbynodd ffydd Grist anno 188, ag ef a wnaeth eglwys ar ei gost i hun.

[1] Inq. p.m., vol. iii., no. 871.

[2] *Ibid.,* no. 538 ; Close Rolls, Edw. II., 1313—18, p. 137.

[3] *Vide* Vol. I., p. 200.

[4] For pedigree of Rumsey *vide* p. 138.

to colonel Edward Curre. There is nothing of particular interest about the house, which is that of the usual type occupied by the smaller gentry of the seventeenth century.

A considerable portion of the eastern part of the parish belonged in the nineteenth century to the duke of Beaufort, and was put up for sale in the year 1900, when all his grace's property in this parish was purchased by Henry Simpson. This

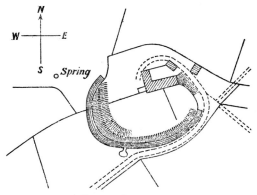

PLAN OF CWRT-Y-GAER.
Scale, 25 inches = 1 mile.

gentleman built a residence at Tre-deon, which was subsequently sold to mr. William Walker Hood. The greater part of mr. Simpson's estate was purchased by colonel Curre. The manor of *Treyrdeon* belonged in 1453-4 to Morgan ap Llewelyn ap Ievan ap Jenkin, and in that year was conveyed to John ap Gwilym of Itton (Edeton).[1] Tredeon-isha was the residence of a major Eaton, who is said to have fallen at Waterloo ; he made great additions to the house, which were never completed.

Porth-Vaenor.

Porth-Vaenor would be more correctly Porth y faenor (*the gate of the manor*), probably so called from being the place where the lord's rents for this district were paid.

William Morgan of Porth-Vaenor, yeoman, made his will 27 November, 1646, proved at Llandaff 20 March, 1647 :—

Cathedral church of Landaffe, xij*d*.—my messuages, lands, etc., in Woolsnewton and Langowm ycha, the one moiety to Elizabeth my wife for life, and after to my son Walter Morgan, the other moiety to her, she to pay 40*l*. to my creditors and 20*l*. a piece to my four dau's Jane, Alice, Tassie and Margaret equally—my brother-in-law Walter William of Alta Villa, and my cozen Thomas James to be seised to the use of house, etc.—Ann, wife of my son Walter—my friend Edmond Jones of Lansoy, esq., and Walter Williams of Alta Villa, gent., overseers.

In pr. of Walter Harries, clke.
   Edward Nicholas.
   Thomas James.
   Walter Williams.
   James Phillipps.
   Ann Will'm.
Inventory of goods—71*l*. 0*s*. 0*d*.

Cwm-Vagor belonged to Thomas Wakeman the antiquary, who left it to the family of Herbert of the Mardy. Cwrt-Valkin was long the residence of a family named Davies, four of whom in succession had the christian name of Francis. In the early part of the nineteenth century Francis Davies was the master of a pack of hounds which were trencher fed.

The Pantau (*the hollows*), the house being just within the boundary of Newchurch parish, was the estate for several generations of the family of Hoskins, commemorated by a memorial stone in the church. There is also a memorial to the family in Cam church in Gloucestershire. In 1800 the Pantau belonged to Nathaniel Wells of Piercefield, from whom it passed by purchase to . . . . Smedley, and was recently owned by Walter Smedley of St. Arvans. On the death of the latter it was purchased by mr. Charles Montagu Crompton Roberts.

In this parish, as in other similar ones, there were many freeholders whose pedigrees and descents I am unable to trace, but the following wills will throw light on them for future investigators.

Henry Prosser of Wolvesnewton made his will 26 December, 1623, proved at Llandaff 22 January, 162¾ :—

Cathedral church of Landaff, vj*d*.—parson of Wolvesnewton for tithes forgotten, vij*d*.—to my wife Grace during her life half of my lands in Wolvesnewton except one parcel called Maise minocke, this to my brother Rowland.

Walter Prosser of *Woolphes Newtone* made his will 31 January, 1648, proved at Llandaff 26 January 1649 :—

Church of Woolphesnewtone, 2 shillings—cathedral church of Landaff, 1*s*.—poor of Woolphesnewtone, 2*s*.—my two dau's Cathering Prosser and Ann Prosser 40*l*. between them at 21, one close called Maese Mynoge towards raising the 40*l*.—the mansion house where I now live to my wife for life, and after to my son John Prosser, he to allow my son Harrie Prosser 20*l*.— to my nephew & godson Wm John, 2*s*.— my wife sole ex'trix.

In pr. of Row. Roger.
   Will' Morgan.
   Christopher Morgan.
   William Meredith.
An inventory is attached—72*l*. 10*s*. 00*d*.

The Church.

The church is dedicated to St. Thomas à Becket, and would, therefore, appear to be a Norman foundation. But if tradition and Lewis Dwnn are to be trusted, a church was built here in the year 188 by sir Fwniel, lord of this place, who then received christianity.[1] The church comprises chancel, nave, and a bell turret, but has no features of particular interest. The register book begins with the year 1680.

---

[1] *Ancient Deeds*, vol. iv., p. 107, A 6985.

[1] *Vide* p. 236.

A remarkably fine chalice is still in use, inscribed :—

> ANNO DOMINI 1586 27 OF IANVARY WOLS
> NEWTON IN THE COVNTI OF MONMOTH.
> PHILIP IHON ROSSER AND IHON VP[1] IHON
> HOWELL THEN PROCERS.[2]

On the lid is   WATER PROSER
                   PHILLYP POEL WILLIAM.

---

[1] AP (son of).
[2] Contracted for procuratores (*overseers* or *church-wardens*).

The living was early appropriated to the priory of Chepstow, afterwards in the king's gift, and about the year 1865 was ceded to the bishop of Llandaff. By an order in council dated 11 August, 1884, the rectory of Wolvesnewton and the perpetual curacy of Cilgwrwg, the patronage of which belonged to the archdeacon of Llandaff, were united, the gift of the united benefices to be for the future alternately exercised by the bishop and archdeacon.

WOLVESNEWTON CHURCH.

PATRON.	DATE OF INSTITUTION.	INCUMBENTS.
The king, by reason of the priory of Chepstow being in his hands on account of the war with France.	20 Feb. 1350.	Elias de Roudon.[1]
Ibid.	10 March 1351.	Thomas de Cantbrigge ;[2] resigned 1352 on presentation to Llanmartin in exchange with Roger de Mesyndon.[3]
Ibid.	27 June 1352.	Roger de Mesyndon, previously parson of Llanmartin.[3]
. . . . . .	. . . .	Lawrence ap Morgan, in 1535.[4]
. . . . . .	. . . .	John Howel, parson in 1650 ; also rector of Llansoy.
. . . . . .	. . . .	Andrew Vaughan or Vaen, B.C.L. All Souls' Coll., Oxf., prebendary of Sanctæ Crucis in Llandaff Cathedral ; also vicar of Christchurch ; died 1619 ; buried in the church.
. . . . . .	. . . .	John Mapp, in 1632.
. . . . . .	. . . . 1633.	Walter Harris ; deprived by the puritans for alleged drunkenness and assisting his majesty. His will is dated 1 Jan. 1651, proved (P.C.C., 240, Brent) 20 June, 1653, by William Harris, lawful brother of testator. To my niece Alice Lane a silver bowl and six spoons—to my nephews Francis Lane and Rowland Morgan books—my wife Tacie Harris ex'trix—my niece Jane Morgan—mr. Rowland Morgan overseer.
Charles II. . .	7 May 1661.	John Cragge, M.A., also vicar of Llantilio Pertholey ;[5] died about 1665.[6] (Henry Thomas admitted curate 20 Dec. 1663.)
Charles II. . .	15 March 166⅘.	John Ellis, M.A., chaplain to the earl of Oxford.
Charles II. . .	24 Sept. 1681.	Robert Vaughan, M.A. Jesus College, Oxford, son of Humphrey Vaughan of Harlech, co. Merioneth ; died about 1708 ; buried in the church.
Anne . . .	27 June 1708.	Andrew Cuthbert, M.A., afterwards head master of Monmouth grammar school and rector of Llanfair Cilgedin ; died 1749.[7]

---

[1] *Cal. Rot. Pat.*, Edw. III., 1348—50, p. 477.   [2] *Ibid.*, Edw. III., 1350—4, p. 50.
[3] *Ibid.*, p. 303.   [4] *Valor Eccl.*   [5] *Vide* Vol. I., pp. 163, 209.
[6] As Cragge is presented on the death of the last incumbent, there is a name missing before him.   [7] *Vide* his pedigree, Vol. I., p. 266.

PATRON.	DATE OF INSTITUTION.	INCUMBENTS.
. . . . .	. . . .	John Watkins. His will is dated 28 May 1752, proved at Llandaff 14 Oct. 1756 by Walter Watkins, son and heir of testator— My natural son Walter Watkins the dwelling house called Treduon Isha in Wolvesnewton and Llanvihangel Tor-y-mynydd— my son Walter Watkins—my dau. Anne Wensley—my grandson John Wensley—Elizabeth Wensley when 14—my dau. Mary Mercer—my grandchildren Joan Mercer, Anne Mercer, Thomas Mercer—my said natural son Walter Watkins ex'or.
. . . .	18 Oct. 1772.	Abednego Prichard.
. . . .	2 Nov. 1780.	Theophilus Prosser, died 1793-4.
George II. .	5 Mar. 1794.	Robert George, M.A. Jesus Coll., Oxf., son of James George of Usk ; died 1815.
. . . .	27 Nov. 1816.	James Barnard Davies, M.A. Jesus Coll., Oxf., son of Thomas Davies of Usk, and grandson of James Davies of Llanerddil; also rector of Kemeys Inferior ; J.P. co. Mon.; resigned 1833 ; died 1846.[1]
William IV. .	9 Nov. 1833.	David Jones.
. . . .	25 May 1858.	George Henry Moller, B.A.
. . . .	11 Mar. 1863.	George Platt Dew, B.A. Jesus Coll., Cambridge ; resigned 1891 on appointment to Shirenewton.
Bishop of Llandaff .	4 Dec. 1891.	Charles Carne Williams, M.A. Jesus Coll., Oxford, son of John Williams, clk., rector of Marcross, co. Glamorgan ; previously rector of Llanfihangel Ystern Llewern, also from 1901 rector of Llanfihangel Tor-y-mynydd; died 22 Nov. 1912, aged 67, buried at Wolvesnewton.
Archdeacon of Llandaff.	2 Apr. 1913.	John Jones, previously rector of Llangynwyd, co. Glamorgan.

[1] For his pedigree *vide* Vol. I., p. 225.

Monumental Inscriptions.

ON NORTH WALL OF CHANCEL.

In this chancel lies interred the remains of Edmund Hoskins of the Pantee in the Parish of Newchurch, Gent., who died Nov[r] 29th, 1680.

Also of John Hoskins (son of the said Edmund) and Mary his wife, one of the Daughters of Andrew Lewis of Higha in the Parish of Trelleck, Gent.

He } died { August 16th, 1716.
She } { May 8th, 1707.

Also of Edmund and Elizabeth, Son and Daughter of the said John and Mary Hoskins.

He } died { March 10th, 1701.
She } { Sept[r] 14th, 1702.

Also of Edward, son of the aforesaid John and Mary Hoskins and Elizabeth his wife, eldest daughter of Edward Hill, late of Alveston, in the county of Gloucester, Esq.

He } died { August 22nd, 1742.
She } { Sept[r] 5th, 1766.

Aged { 54 } years.
{ 67 }

Also of John, Edward, Martha and William, sons and daughter of the said Edward and Elizabeth Hoskins.

John } died { March 24th, 1753.
Edward } { Dec[r] 18, 1768.

Martha } died { May 15th, 1728.
William } { Feb[y] 22nd, 1728.

At the top of the monument is the coat wrongly coloured, but which ought to be : *Per pale gu. and az., a chevron engrailed or, between three lions ramp. arg.*

Chancel. Flat stones :

Here lieth the Body of Walter Spencer of this Parish, who departed this life the 29th day of March 1739, aged 39 years.

Here lieth y[e] Body of Robert Vaughan, Rector of this Church, deceased the 27th of May 17—, aged 61.

Here also lyeth y[e] Body of Anne, Relict to the above Robert Vaughan, Rector of Llanllowell, died 22 May 1743 (?), aged 71 years.

Here also lieth Charles, son of Robert Vaughan.

Nave. Flat stones :

Here lieth the Body of Ann, the daughter of Thomas and Elizabeth Parry of this Parish, who died the .... February 1776, aged 24 years.

Here lieth the Body of Thomas Parry of this Parish, who departed this life the 21st day of October 1759, aged 52 years.

Here lieth the Body of Elizabeth, Daughter of the said Thomas Parry, who Died the 16th Day of .... 1759, aged 12 years.

Underneath this Stone lieth the Body of Ann, y[e] wife of Richard Reece of the Parish of Cumcarvan, who departed this life the 4th day of February in the year of our Lord 1774, Aged ....

Underneath this stone lieth the Body of Richard Reece of the parish of Cumcarvan, who departed this life the 23rd day of March in the year of our Lord 1780, Aged 85 years.

Cilgwrwg.

IL-GWRWG would mean the retreat of Cwrwg. This is probably the *Villa Cerruc* of the *Liber Landavensis,* where king Ithael, son of Morgan, gives three *unciæ* of land in Cwm Cerruc to the see of Llandaff. This was in the time of bishop Berthgwyn in the sixth century.[1]

The parish contains 666 acres of land. The rateable value in 1815 was 222*l.*, and in 1912, 291*l.*

The population has been as follows :—

Year .	1801	1811	1821	1831	1841	1861	1871	1881	1891	1901
No. of inhab.	56	81	113	129	133	121	103	103	92	90

The number of houses is thus shewn :—

Year.	Inhabited houses.	Uninhabited houses.	Building.
1861 . . .	25	0	0
1871 . . .	23	1	0
1881 . . .	22	4	0
1891 . . .	21	0	0
1901 . . .	19	2	0

For many years the whole parish, with the exception of a small farm called Little Cilgwrwg, belonged to the dukes of Beaufort. In 1900 mr. Simpson purchased the duke's estate here and also Little Cilgwrwg, which had belonged to the estate of Tintern Parva.

The manor, as appears by the *inquisitio post mortem* of Gilbert de Clare, who died in 1295, was held by Philip le Latimer by quarter of a knight's fee.[1]

The Church.

The church is a very small one, containing nothing of interest.

The living was a perpetual curacy; is now a rectory, and since 1884 has been annexed to Wolvesnewton.

Some few pages of the 1620 Welsh Bible still remain in the church.

The advowson in 1756 was in the hands of John Gratwicke of Bristol, but some time afterwards of the archdeacon of Llandaff. By an order in council dated 11 August, 1884, the livings of Cilgwrwg and Wolvesnewton were united, the patronage to be alternately exercised by the bishop and archdeacon.

[1] *Lib. Land.,* Latin, p. 170; English, p. 428.

[1] Inq. p.m., vol. iii., no. 371.

PATRON.	DATE OF INSTITUTION.	INCUMBENT.
. . . . .	16 Mar. 174½.	Samuel Redmond, to the curacy.
. . . . .	. . . .	Samuel Vaughan, died 1755-6.
John Gratwicke of Bristol, gent.	13 Apr. 1756.	Edward Hyett, to perform the office of curate of the church or chapel of Cilgwrwg.
. . . . .	. . . .	John Davies, died 1809-10.
John Probyn, clk., archdeacon of Llandaff.	23 Mar. 1810.	Henry Berkin, son of Wm Berkin of Bristol, esq.
Archdeacon of Llandaff.	. . . . 1847.	John Price, also rector of Llanfihangel Tor y Mynydd.
Do.	. . . . 1884.	George Platt Dew, also rector of Wolvesnewton.
Bishop of Llandaff .	4 Dec. 1891.	Charles Carne Williams, with the rectory of Wolvesnewton annexed; died 1912.
Archdeacon of Llandaff.	. . Dec. 1912.	John Jones, previously rector of Llangynwyd.

There are no memorials in the church. In the churchyard is an altar-tomb, at the west end of which is :—

Here lyeth ye Body of William Nicholas of this Parish, who departed this life Dec. 9 Anno Dom. 1729.

On the south side is :—

Here lys a man whose youthful time was spent
In warlike acts, in riper years was lent
His helping hand to ye diftrefsed Poor
& found his wealth thereby increased the more.
In his declining age he always ftood
Firm to his friends & for his Countries good,
But now he refteth in this sacred ground
Secured here till ye laft Trump shall found.
Grant Lord when I from Death shall wake
I may of endlefs Light partake,
My Soul when I shake off this Dust
Lord in thy arms I will intrust.
One Ray of all thy quickening Light
Difpels ye floth & clouds of night.

Llanishen.

LANISHEN takes its name from the saint Isan or Nissien, of whom more will be said further on.

The parish contains 1575 acres of land. The rateable value in 1815 was 927*l*., in 1891, 1040*l*., in 1913, 1133*l*.

The population has been as follows :—

Year .	1801	1811	1821	1831	1841	1861	1871	1881	1891	1901
No. of Inhab.	174	222	255	296	307	320	278	241	202	194

The number of houses is shewn as follows :—

Year.	Inhabited Houses.	Uninhabited Houses.	Building.
1861 . . .	72	2	0
1871 . . .	66	4	0
1881 . . .	59	3	0
1891 . . .	48	9	0
1901 . . .	45	3	0

The earliest mention of Llanishen is in the *Liber Landavensis*,[1] where it figures among the churches restored to the bishopric of Llandaff by Morgan Hen, king of Gwent and Morganwg in the tenth century, in the time of bishop Gwgan.

The boundaries are there given as :—

> From the top of the acclivity (rhiw) of the three acre island (Ynys Tair Erw) on the bank of the Olwy, along the Olwy upwards to the brook Cichmann, along the brook Cichmann to its source, from its source to the willow grove, to the source of the Anghidy Fawr, along it downwards as far as the meadow (weun) on the west side of the stone house (Maen-dy), direct to the source of the Little Anghidy (Aghiti Bechan), from its source upwards to the hill (Allt) of Hilguid, through the wood to the acclivity (rhiw), along the acclivity to the breast of the hill (allt) below the church of Nissien, along it down Ynys Tair Erw to the Olwy, where it began.

Nissien, above mentioned, is the same saint as that one called Isan by Rees,[2] whose festival was on 6 May, and said to have been a member of the college of Illtyd. In a bull of pope Honorius II. addressed to Urban, bishop of Llandaff, dated 9 April, 1128, Llanishen appears as the *village of Tanasan with its church*,[3] and in another bull of the same pope, dated 4 April, 1129, it is similarly called.[4]

In the *inquisitio post mortem* of Joan, widow of Gilbert de Clare, daughter of Edward I., 1307, it is called the *chapel* of Landenassan; in the grant to Tintern abbey it is *ecclesia* Sancti Dionisii Lan-

nissan.[1] In modern church books the patron saint is said to be St. Dennis.

In the inquisition of Gilbert de Clare who died in 1295, husband of the lady above mentioned, is a reference to the manor of Trelech, which included 102 burgages then lying vacant by fire in the wars; the earl had toll of the market and fair, a smithy, the mill of Gryll, pleas of the hundred, rents of free tenants and customary at Gryll, Penallt, Whitebrook, and Wyespool, the mill of Landinisien, pannage of the forest, a fishery of the Wye, of two pools, and preserve of Gryll.[2]

Tre-Geirog.

The chief residence and estate in this parish in the seventeenth and eighteenth centuries was Tre-Geirog (*the house of Ceirog* or *Ceiriog*), though who this person was is uncertain. *Tregeryauk* and *Lanveyr* appear in the *inquisitio post mortem* of Gilbert de Clare, earl of Gloucester and Hertford, who died in 1295, as being two parts of one fee held by Iorwerth ap Nicholas.

The court roll of the lordship of Usk in 1570 records the following free tenants in the manors of *Trergeiroc* and *llanvayr*, viz., George ap Robert, esq., late Gwilym ap Howel Meurig at the rent of 16*d*., and lands late of Jenkin Meurig; William Thomas Philip, late Llowarch ap Meurig, 7*d*.; David Philip Howel, lands called *llowargh*, 2*d*., and lands late Thomas ap Jeuan Grono, 21*d*.; Henry John ap Richard for land called *Tyre abellyer*, 3*s*.

George ap Robert also held *Glanolwye*, and lands late of Jenkin ap Howel ap Jeuan, 2*s*.; and lands called Pont Jenkin, 3*d*.

Howel Richard held land in Llanishen at 9½*d*.; and Walter John Ychan, 2*s*. Of Llanwinny[3] it says :—

> Homagium de llanwini. De tenentibus custumariis ibidem in grosso per annum quousque particulariter facere possunt declarationem quantum quilibet tenens solvere debet, 29*s*. 4*d*.

In 1619 the free tenants in Llanishen were Thomas Richard Weely, late Philip Howel, 15*d*.; Philip Williams of Rhyd-y-maen, gent., late his father, 7*d*.; William Probert of Pant-glas, gent., 16*d*.; Elizabeth, relict of Walter John Howel, 8*d*.; Charles Somersett, knt., formerly Thomas ap Evan Grono, and a meadow called *Gworlod lloarch Mirick*,

1 *Liber Landavensis*, pp. 231, 504; *Book of Llan Dâv*, pp. 242, 379.
2 *Welsh Saints*, 1836, p. 257.
3 *Lib. Land.*, pp. 31, 571.
4 *Ibid.*, pp. 42, 583.

1 *Monasticon*, vol. v., p. 267.
2 Inq. p.m., vol. iii., no. 371. There is no place now called Gryll that I can hear of.
3 Llanwinny sounds as though a church ought to be here. There is nothing of the sort, nor is there any tradition of one.

23*d*.; George William Harry and the heirs of Evan Thomas Harry, messuage and lands called *Kelly*, 3*s*.; William Probert of Pant-glas, gent., lands called *Tyr Pant Jenkyn*, 3*d*. The customary tenants at Llanwinny were Reginald John David Penry, lands late of his father called Pen-y-gare, 16*d*.; John Thomas Philip of Tal-y-van, lands called *Y coome*, 16*d*.; John Rynold, lands called *Caer Onnwyd* and *Tyr feglyn*, 9*d*.; John William Harry and George William Harry, a parcel of lands called *Croft yr odyn*, 4*d*.; Thomas Evan and Thomas Water, lands formerly of William John of Langwenthore, 4*s*. 10½*d*.; David Evan, late Watkin David Penry, lands called *Vanhaddlog*, 18*d*., and lands formerly of Philip Thomas Gwilym called *Trawstyr* and *Tyr-y-pant* and *Y gyderowe*, 2*d*.

In the same year Charles Somerset, knt., held the manor of *llanveyre* and *Tregyrok* at a quarter of a knight's fee, also two parts of the manor of Wolvesnewton called *Court Thomas ap David* and *Court Peerce* at half a knight's fee; also a third part of the manor of Wolvesnewton at one quarter of a knight's fee; also the manor of *Bryndyrok* and *Lanvihangell*, and a moiety of the manor of *Tredeon*; also the manor of *Treallon* at one eighth of a knight's fee.

Those who held by indenture were Walter Morgan Woolph, William Wolph and John Wolph his sons, by indentures made 14 December, 26 Eliz. [1583], lands called *Priscoed*, 60 acres, and *Tyr Cutta*, 12 acres. John William John of Llanishen, Walter John ap John of Llandenny, Richard William John of Llanishen, by indentures made 28 October, 36 Eliz. [1594], lands called *Tyr Lucas* in the manor of New Grange.

In the seventeenth century Tre-Geirog was the seat of a family who settled to the surname of Jones, descended from Rhiryd Flaidd (*Rhiryd the Wolf*), lord of Penllyn in Merioneth, in the eleventh century, who bore *Vert, a chevron between three wolves' heads erased or*. Of this family was Edmund Jones of Buckland, M.P., a personal friend of Oliver Cromwell, whose connection with his relatives at Tre-Geirog is not clear.[1]

John ap John of Tre-Geirog made a settlement of his lands dated 4 September, 40 Eliz., 1598, by which he settled his land on his second son William, having also sons David and William and a daughter Margaret, wife afterwards of David Prichard of Tre-Worgan. The descendants of these subsequently engaged in law-suits as to the division of the property.

William, the second son, who thus had Tre-Geirog, made his will 16 April, 1651; proved (P.C.C., 37, Bruce) 26 May, 1664.

To be buried in the church of Lanishen—lands in Penyclauthe to my nephew John Edmunds—lands purchased of my brother David Jones, Thomas Sternhold, John Sternhold, Henry Hall, John Anderson, gent., Philip Griffith, George Griffith and others, to my kinsman William Prichard, son of my nephew Walter Prichard—customary lands called Glangwenthur to the use of the said Wᵐ Prichard, freehold lands of Glangwenthur to the said Wᵐ Prichard—tenements and lands in Langoven in the tenure of Edmund Howell to my nephews Walter Prichard, John Edmunds, William Jones (son of my brother Walter Jones), and my cousin Thomas Bevan of Gwerneythig, being ex'ors of my will—to the sᵈ ex'ors tenements and lands in Lanishen in the tenure of Lewis Lawrence towards the relief of the poor in Lanishen and Penyclauth; ten'ts and lands in Langoven in the tenure of Maud Richard *alias* Maud of the Keven, with ten'ts in the tenure of Wᵐ Symon, to sᵈ ex'ors for relief of the poor; land in Lansoy called Tir y gwrgageth in the tenure of Elinor Lewis, widow, to sᵈ ex'ors for the poor of Lansoy—to my kinsman Wᵐ Harris, son of George Harris late of Lansoy, land—to my godson Wᵐ Jones, son of my nephew David Jones late of Uske—to my nephew Thomas Jones of Keven Coed lands in Landenny—to my nephew John Jones of Keven Coed ten't in Landenny—to my nephew Wᵐ Jones of Dingestow lands and ten'ts in Landenny in the tenure of John Thomas, Wᵐ Phillips the butcher, David Jones, and Evan David—to my niece Ann Edmonds—to my niece Cecil Fortune—to my niece Ann Jones of Monmouth—to Mary Williams wife of Evan Williams 5*l*. yearly out of lands I purchased of her father mʳ Philip Williams—to the two dau's of mʳ Edmund Williams of Rydymane 10*l*.—to my nephew David Charles—to Cecil Davies wife of David Evans 10*l*.—to Joan Jones, daū of my nephew Jones—to Elizabeth wife of Matthew Wolfe 20*l*.—to build a fair bridge in Landenny 20*l*.—to captain Jones of Bergavenny 40*s*.—to Mary, Elizabeth, and Catherine, dau's of George Harris of Lansoy—to Elizabeth wife of David Jones of Dingestow—to the bridge called Pont yr yarn (?) and wall about it 40*s*.—to the highway farm at Croft y lloy 4*l*.—towards lloydarth causeway[1] 40*s*.—to mrs. Jane Jones, dau. of sir Charles Jones, knt., 20*l*.—to my cousin Wᵐ Morgan of Barnard's Inn, London, 10*s*.—whereas my said nephews Thomas Jones and John Jones encroached upon the common called Kincoed and enclosed two acres, my will is they shall within one year after they receive any benefit from my will cause the sᵈ cottage and buildings to be pulled down and laid open as it was before—Thomas Jones, son of my nephew David Jones—my nephew Wᵐ Jones, son of my brother David Jones—Wᵐ Jones, son of my nephew David Jones—my nephews Walter Prichard, John Edmonds, Wᵐ Jones (son of my brother Walter Jones), and my said cousin Thomas Bevan of Gwerneythyg to be ex'ors—my loving friends Walter Cradock of llangwm, gent., Edmund Jones, esq., and Philip Nicholas of Lanpill, gent., to be overseers.

Witnesses: Edward James.
Edmund Jones.
William Jones.
James Phillips.

William Jones of Llanwinny (son of Walter Jones who was brother of William the above testator), on 15 May, 1667, filed a bill of complaint in chancery claiming that whereas William Jones died without issue possessed of 300 acres of land in Llangoven, etc., he is entitled to the estate

---

[1] Pp. 41, 42.

[1] Lydart Causeway is still so called. It is the old road between Lydart mansion and farm-house, and is to a great extent paved. *Vide* p. 170.

called Llanwinny, containing 150 acres, but that Walter Jones of the Parlour, gent., William Jones of Cefn-coed, gent., William Jones of Llansoy, gent., and Thomas Ayleworth of Llangoven, yeoman, had alleged themselves to be the heirs of the said testator.[1]

On 28 June, 1667, Walter Jones, great grandson of John ap John, being son of William, son of David, eldest son of John ap John, filed a bill against Walter Prichard of Tre-Worgan, esq., stating that he was heir to the lands, which in all were worth 200*l.* per annum, but that Walter Prichard had possessed himself of all the lands settled by John ap John.[2]

William Jones of Llanwinny, described as living then at Pen-y-lan in Llanishen, made his will 25 May, 1683, in which he mentions his daughter Joan Jones, his daughter Bridget Howell and her children, his daughter Maudlen Long, his step-

----

[1] Chancery Proceedings before 1714, Whittington, 490.
[2] *Ibid.*, 491. One of the grandsons of John ap John, whose place in the pedigree is not clear, was Thomas Jones, who had a daughter Bridget, wife of Charles Cust of Bristol, yeoman, in 1670.

daughter Elizabeth Jenkins, and his son William Jones.

William Jones named in the above will may be the William Jones of Llandenny who made his will 17 July, 1720; proved at Llandaff 19 July, 1721.

> I am executor to my kinswoman Cecil Williams who devised 10*s.* yearly to the poor of Llandenny—I also give 10*s.* yearly on land called Yr hafod—three parcels called Ynys kelling and Cae ynys kelling in Llandenny to my granddaughter Margaret Hitchins, in default to Mary Hitchins her mother—to my kinsman Walter Williams of Usk 10*l.*—to my kinsman John David of Llandenny 1*l.*—my dau. Mary Hitchins ex'trix, my kinsman Thomas Jones of Caye to assist her.

Among the wills at Llandaff is that of Gwenllian Walter of *Tregurog* in Llanishen, widow, dated 7 December, 1729; proved 24 January, 17$\frac{29}{30}$. She mentions her nephews Andrew Prichard, James Prichard, and William Prichard, her goddaughter Margaret wife of Evan William of Parc Grace Dieu, and her nephew John Prichard of Stavarney.

Mary, daughter of William Water of Tre-Geirog, is baptized 18 May, 1712.

Pedigree of the family of Jones of Tre-Geirog.

JOHN ap John of Tre-Geirog, gent., settled his estate, 4 Sept. 1598, worth 200*l.* per annum.

1. David Jones. . . .

2. William Jones of Tre-Geirog, esq.=Elinor Will dated 16 April 1651; proved . . . . 26 May 1664, s.p.

Walter Jones. . . .

David Prichard of Tre-Worgan, gent.=Margaret. p. 45.

William Jones=. . . .

John Jones of Cefn-coed in Llandenny.

David Jones=. . . . of Usk.

William Jones of Llanwinny, gent.=. . . . Will dated 25 May 1683.

Walter Jones of the Parlour in Dingestow, gent., plaintiff in 1667.

William Jones of Llansoy, gent., in 1670.

Thomas Jones.

William Jones.

Joan. . . . .=Bridget. Howell.

. . . .=Magdalen. Long.

After this William Tregose was the owner of Tre-Geirog, but who he was or how he came here I am not aware. He made his will in 1749 (P.C.C., 27, Lisle), in which he mentions his wife, his only son Daniel, his daughters Mary and Philippa, and his nephew Richard Baker of Tre-Geirog. The son Daniel Tregose lived here and served the office of sheriff in 1756 and died in 1800, leaving an only daughter who died without issue. The estate then descended to Daniel Tregose's niece mrs. Crause, and is possessed by her descendants.

The Mardy Mill.

The Mardy mill with lands comprising about sixty-three acres belonged to Charles Probert of the Argoed,[1] who died unmarried in 1725, leaving all his lands to his sister Eleanor, wife of Richard Morgan of Hurst in Lydney. Mrs. Morgan left her lands to her daughter Eleanor, wife of Andrew Lewis of Higga, whose son, the rev. Henry Lewis—the forged will of whom was the subject of a trial[2]—dying intestate, the Mardy mill went to the heir-at-law

----

[1] *Vide* pedigree, p. 143.   [2] *Vide* p. 146.

Thomas Morgan, eldest son of Richard Morgan of the Argoed. Thomas Morgan by indentures dated 3 January, 1797, conveyed the Mardy mill to Lewis Richards of Troy, the duke of Beaufort's agent. Three moieties of the same property appear to have gone to other heirs-at-law, who conveyed the same to Lewis Richards, as will be seen by the surrenders at the court of the manor of Usk :—

> Usk castle. To the castle gate of the most noble Henry, duke of Beaufort, lord of the manor of Usk, on Friday, 1 May, 1801, before James Davies, deputy steward, and Richard George, Thomas Davies and John Williams, homagers there, came Milbourne Williams of Bristol, surgeon, devisee under the will of Mary Williams, late of Bristol, spinster, deceased, and which said Mary Williams was only sister and customary heir of Grace Cornish, late of Bristol, widow, deceased, and which said Mary Williams and Grace Cornish were two of the customary heirs of Henry Lewis, late of Higga, deceased, as to one moiety of the premises, and surrendered by the rod a moiety of premises called the Mardymill, to the use of Lewis Richards of Troy House, gent. 22 April, 1802, Elizabeth Jones of Usk, widow, by direction of John Lewis of Bristol, brickmaker (trustee of the will of Susannah Harman of Bristol, widow of James Harman, late of Bristol, pawnbroker, deceased, and

which said Susannah Harman is one of the customary heirs of Henry Lewis, late of Higga, clk., deceased, as to a moiety of the premises), and also by the direction of Daniel Baynton of Bristol, gent., by virtue of a letter of attorney to him made by Thomas Hooker of Bristol, malster, the rev. John Bull of Bristol, clk., & the said John Lewis, surrendered a moiety of the Mardy mill to the said Lewis Richards.

On 28 July, 1801, similar surrender was made on behalf of Thomas Webber and Francis Webber of Newbern, North Carolina, U.S.A., two of the customary heirs of the said late rev. Henry Lewis of Higga, being sons of Thomas Webber, deceased, by his wife Ann (also deceased), daughter of Wm. Lewis of Bristol, by his wife Susannah, elder of the two sisters of Andrew Lewis, father of the said Henry. Lewis Richards died about 1817, and on 12 June,

1818, James Richards, his only son and customary heir, was admitted at a court at Usk castle to the Mardy mill.

Llanfair.

This must be, from the name, the site of an ancient church of which no remains are left. Tradition says that the church was on the opposite side of the road to the farm buildings. The farm of Llanfair belonged in 1738 to Roger Jones of Buckland, M.P. for Brecon, who in that year conveyed it to Elizabeth Cornish, spinster, and John Upton of Ingmire Hall in the parish of Sedbergh, co. York, esq., only son of John Upton, esq., and Elizabeth his wife. John Upton, esq. (grandson of the above John), sold the estate on

LLANISHEN CHURCH.

19 November, 1800, to Lewis Richards of Troy, gent., for 1660l., being described as:—

> The messuage, etc., called Llanvair with lands called Cae'r-groes, Cae Kenfyd, Maes Lanwyny, Caer yr odyn, Cae dan y derri, Court Ythyn, Gworlod Robert, Ynys Hunidd, Cae Cummed mane, Cae bach dan y glyn, Ynys Nichol, Y ynys, Perllan, Gworlod Meyrick, Hen berllan and Llanvair grove; also Gworlod fach, Cae maen, Cae Tippin, Erw Caradog, and the Little Mead in Llanishen. Also Gworlod y penarth in three parcels containing 8 acres, Cae'r-ysgubor, Cae-gwyn, Cae-bach, Cae'r-fallen, Cae'r-mynydd, Cae'r-lloi in the parish of Trelegg, all which were late in the possession of John Jones, and now of David Waters. And a parcel of a meadow in Llanishen purchased from Mary Kane of Monmouth, widow.

It afterwards passed into the possession of the

dukes of Beaufort, and was sold by the ninth duke in 1901. It comprises about 110 acres, and was for very many years occupied by the family of Walters, whose tombs are in the churchyard.

The Church.

The church has been entirely rebuilt, nothing of the original building remaining. Over the door is inscribed:—

This Church was Erected
Anno Domini
1854.
Rev. Henry Warrilow, Minister.
Stephen Prosser ⎫
Edward Arnold ⎭ Churchwardens.

The living is now a vicarage, but was a perpetual curacy, and seems always to have been held with Trelech Grange, and until 1802 with Chapel Hill also.

Of the incumbents, Elias Thomas made his will 28 October, 1765, proved at Llandaff 16 October, 1766:—

To Margaret my wife, with whom I have lived happily for almost 50 years, all my household stuff & cattle, &c.—to my son Thomas, my son Lewis, my dau. Mary, my dau. Anne 2s. 6d. each—to my son Lewis my collection of books.

Lewis the son is probably the Lewis Thomas who was appointed to the living in 1768.

In the churchyard is the old cross. The parish registers begin with 1591, but have been irregularly kept.

The 1620 Welsh Bible was in the church until about the year 1870, when the vicar, not knowing what to do with it, *buried* it in his garden.

PATRON.	DATE OF INSTITUTION.	INCUMBENTS.
. . . . .	. . . .	Hugh Powell, in 1601.[1]
. . . . .	. . . .	George Griffith, in 1602.[1]
. . . . .	. . . .	John Lawlis, in 1692.[2]
. . . . .	. . . .	Thomas James, in 1712.[3]
. . . . .	. . . .	Elias Thomas, died 1765-6.[4]
. . . . .	6 March 1766.	John Williams, also same date Trelech Grange and Chapel Hill.
. . . . .	19 Oct. 1768.	Lewis Thomas, also same date Trelech Grange and Chapel Hill; probably son of the above Elias Thomas.
. . . . .	25 June 1781.	Thomas Hughes, also same date Trelech Grange and Chapel Hill; died 1801-2.
Henry, 5th duke of Beaufort.	28 June 1802.	Henry Williams, also same date Trelech Grange.
. . . .	11 June 1821.	John Saunders, also same date Trelech Grange; master of Usk grammar school; died 1831, aged 71.
Henry Charles, 6th duke of Beaufort.	31 Dec. 1832.	Henry Warrilow, also same date Trelech Grange; died 1861.
Henry, 8th duke of Beaufort.	3 July 1861.	James Oakeley, also same date Trelech Grange; B.A. Jesus College, Oxford; resigned 1887.[5]
Henry, 8th duke of Beaufort.	. . . . 1887.	Richard Ebenezer Jones, M.A., also Trelech Grange; son of John Jones of Langston, co. Hereford, esq.; resigned 1896; appointed to Llanddewi Scyrrid 1901.
. . . . .	. . . . 1897.	Thomas Arthur Davies, also Trelech Grange; B.A. University of Wales.

[1] Par. reg. [2] *Vide* p. 198. [3] 1731, April 15, bur., Catherine, widow of Thomas James, late curate of Llanishen (par. reg.).
[4] 174½, March 20, died, Margaret, dau. of Elias Thomas, minister of this parish, and Margaret his wife, æt. 14 (par. reg.).
[5] For his pedigree *vide* p. 170.

Monumental Inscriptions.

ON THE SOUTH WALL OF THE CHANCEL.

In memory of Daniel Treagose of Tregirog in this parish of Llanishen in the county of Monmouth, who died 13th of May 1800, aged 69 years.

Also of Mary Treagose, sister to the above-named Daniel Treagose, who died 11th of July 1811, aged 87 years.

Also of James Bowen, who died March 13th, 1826, aged 66 years.

Also of Philippa Bowen, niece of the above-named Daniel Treagose, who died the 25th of August 1833, in the 83rd year of her age.

Sacred to the memory of Charles Harrison Powell, Esq., who died the 29th Septr 1848, in the 73rd year of his age.

He was deputy lieutenant & a magistrate for this County, and eldest son of the late William Powell, Esq., Surgeon, of the town of Monmouth. His remains lie buried in this churchyard.

Also of his wife Letitia Catherine Powell, who died the 9th of Septr 1859, aged 79 years.

ON NORTH SIDE OF NAVE.

William Jones, Esqr, of Tregirog-house in the parish of Lanishen & County of Monmouth, left by his last will dated the 16th day of April 1651 an estate consisting of three Fields, lying in the Parish of Lanishen containing 18 acres 2 roods called the poor's land; which Estate is to be let according to law & the Money to be given half-yearly for ever, One pound to the Parish of Penyclawth & the remainder to the old & infirm Parishioners of Lanishen (who are not paupers) at the disposal of the Minister, the Churchwardens, the Overseer and the Magistrate acting for the Division.

CHURCHYARD.

An altar-tomb within iron rails. On the north side:
In memory of William Treagoie
late of Tregirog. He departed this
life ye 25th of November, 1748,
Aged 65.
On the south side:
Alſo of PHILLIPA SLEAD his daughter who died
February 21, 1779, aged 51 years.
Alſo of ELIZA PHILLIPA BOWEN, granddaughter of
the above named PHILLIPA
SLEAD and greatgranddaughter of William
Treagoſe, who died an infant.

An upright stone :

Here lieth the Body
of Thomas Watters of
this parifh who departed
this life the 25ᵗʰ day of
May, 1765, aged 65 years.
Here alſo lieth the Body of
Mary the wife of William Davis
of this parifh who departed
this life the 27ᵗʰ day of
May 1802 aged 88 years.

An altar-tomb.   On the south side :

In memory of
David Walters of this parifh,
who died May 15ᵗʰ, 1812
Aged 63 years.

On the north side :

In memory of Ann,
wife of David Walters
late of this parifh,
who died June 3ʳᵈ, 1822
Aged 82 years.

A pedestal.   On the west side :

In memory of
David, son of John & Mary
Walters of Lanvair
in this parifh,
who died 4 Aug., 1810,
aged 2 years
and 4 months.

On the south side :

In memory of
Catherine fourth daughter
of the foresaid John Walters
who died Sept. 30, 1893, aged 68 years.

On the east side :

In Memory of
Mary the wife of
John Walters of the parish of
Llandenny who died
on the 31ˢᵗ of January
1867 aged 80 years.

Trelech Grange.

RELECH GRANGE is a sparsely populated parish situated on high ground from 400 to 500 feet above the sea.

The parish contains 1818 acres of land and 2 acres of water. The rateable value in 1815 was 1491*l.*, and in 1913, 1049*l.*

The population has been as follows :—

Year .	1801	1811	1821	1831	1841	1861	1871	1881	1891	1901
No. of Inhab.	141	134	91	170	126	137	120	126	123	116

Though the population has decreased, the number of houses has increased :—

Year.	Inhabited Houses.	Uninhabited Houses.	Building.
1861 . . .	22	2	0
1871 . . .	19	6	0
1881 . . .	22	4	0
1891 . . .	21	3	0
1901 . . .	24	2	0

The earliest mention of Trelech Grange is in the *Liber Landavensis,*[1] where king Ffernwael grants to the see of Llandaff Trylec Lann Mainuon. It is said to be like an island in the sea (*ut insulam in salo*) between the two rivers, the great and little Aghiti (*infra duo flumina, Aghiti mawr et Aghiti bichan*), accurately describing the position of the church and parish. These brooks are now called Angidy, and joining one another below Trelech Grange run into the river Wye at Tintern.

The district, afterwards called Trelech Grange from the neighbouring town and parish of Trelech, was granted to the monks of Tintern in the twelfth century by Richard de Clare, lord of Striguil or Chepstow, created earl of Pembroke in 1138. The monks with their usual industry cleared and cultivated it, making it the principal farm for the support of the abbey. The abbey and its possessions

---

[1] *Liber Landavensis,* p. 452. *Book of Llan Dâv,* pp. 199, 217. Both mr. Wakeman and dr. Gwenogvryn Evans who follows him attribute this place to Trelech, which cannot, by the boundaries, be possible.

were granted, 28 Hen. VIII., 1536-7, to Henry, second earl of Worcester, and so descended to the eighth duke of Beaufort, who about the year 1875 sold Trelech Grange to the late Charles Henry Crompton-Roberts. It now belongs to lieut.-colonel Charles Montague Crompton-Roberts.

At the time of the civil wars Henry Somerset of Trelech Grange compounded for his estate for 35*l.* He was probably the Henry Somerset, who was son of lord John Somerset, the second son of Henry, first marquis of Worcester, and was afterwards of Pauntley in Gloucestershire. It is likely that he was lessee of Trelech Grange under his uncle Edward, second marquis of Worcester.

The occupier of Trelech Grange after this was Edward Nicholas, who served the office of sheriff in 1682.

The Church.

The church is a small one, situated in the midst of farm buildings, and is peculiar in having no separate chancel. It was rebuilt on the old foundations in 1861. There are no monumental inscriptions inside except a brass to the memory of Charles Henry Crompton-Roberts of Drybridge, esq., the owner of this place, who was born in 1832 and died in 1891.

In the churchyard is a stone nearly obliterated, which may refer to a branch of the old Parkers of Llanllowel :—

Martha wife of Jacob Parker of this Parish died Jan. 23, 18 . . . Aged 72 years.

. . . Parker died Sept[r] 18th, 1837, Aged 81.

James Parker died Jan[y] 17th, 1838, Aged 45.

The living is a perpetual curacy held with Llanishen, under which parish will be found the incumbents.

The chalice was the gift of the duke of Beaufort, and is engraved :—

D.B.   T.G.   1746.

Tintern Parva.

INTERN PARVA or Little Tintern, so called to distinguish it from the adjoining parish of Chapel Hill or Abbey Tintern, is a small parish with a picturesque village on the bank of the river Wye.

The parish contains, according to the census of 1871, 827 acres; and, according to that of 1901, 795 acres with 16 acres of tidal water and 3 acres of foreshore.

The rateable value in 1801 was 584l., and in 1913, 1404l.

The population has been as follows:—

Year.	1801	1811	1821	1831	1861	1871	1891	1901	1911
No. of Inhab.	248	258	285	313	335	326	306	288	325

The number of houses is shewn thus:—

Year.	Inhabited houses.	Uninhabited houses.	Building.
1861	79	6	0
1871	66	5	0
1881	72	3	0
1891	69	6	0
1901	67	12	1

The greater part of the parish is covered with coppice woods on the slope of the steep hill which rises precipitously from the river. The woods formerly gave a considerable amount of employment to the inhabitants, who were skilled wood-cutters, hoop-shavers, hurdle-makers, etc. This branch of industry has greatly declined, but the village has become a popular resort for tourists, who come to see the famous abbey which is situated in the next parish.

The earliest mention of the place is in the *Liber Landavensis*, when Cynfelin, son of Cynog, bought of Rhodri, son of Ithel, the land of Louhai which he sacrificed to the see of Llandaff, Cadwared being then bishop. This was in the ninth century. The boundary is given as[1]

The influx of Catfrut into the Wye, along it upwards directly opposite to the ridge of Tintern, to the cliff, upwards to the ridge of Tintern, from the ridge of Tintern downwards to the Wye, along the Wye with its weirs to the influx of Catfrut where it began.

Catfrut is the brook now called Catbrook, more properly Cad-ffrwd (*the battle stream*), which descends from the high ground in the parish of Trelech and enters the Wye at Coed Ithel.

The Manor.

This was a mesne manor held under the Clares, earls of Gloucester and Hertford. In the survey of Wentwood, 1271, it is said that the father of Philip Champeney was first seized of Little Tintern, and the jury are ignorant whether he ought to have housebot and haybot or not.

Gilbert de Clare, who was slain at Bannockburn in 1314, died without issue, his heirs being his sisters. In the *Inquisitio post mortem*[1] of this nobleman, dated 28 September, 8 Edw. II. [1315], among much other property was:—

Little Tintern, 17 acres of land, etc., with the fisheries at Lynwere and Broxwere, and a rent called " kilgh."

The chief estate in Tintern Parva belonged in the seventeenth century to Richard Herbert (eldest son of the celebrated Edward, lord Herbert of Chirbury), afterwards the second lord Herbert of Chirbury. He inherited it from his mother's father, sir William Herbert of St. Julians, and, by indentures dated 9 February, 1640, sold it for a sum not mentioned to his kinsman Thomas, afterwards sir Thomas Herbert of Tintern, baronet.

This ind're made 9 Feb., 1640, 16 Car., between Richard Herbert of St. Julians, esquire, sonne and heir apparant of the right honble Edward, lord Herbert, baron of Chirbury and Castle Island, of the one pt., And Thomas Herbert of the citie of Westm', esquire, of the other pt. WITNESSETH that the sd Richard Herbert in cons'on of a competent sum of money grants, sells, enfeoffs, etc., to the sd Thomas Herbert, All that capital messuage and one water corn mill with appurt's in Tinterne Magna and Tinterne Parva, now in the tenure of Thomas Berrington, gent., and Tacy his wife, And also all that other mess' in the same late in the occupation of John Williams, decd, and now or late in the occupation of the sd Thomas Berrington and Tacy, And also all that other mess' in the occupation of the sd Thomas Berrington and Tacy, And also all that mess' in the occup' of Robert Smith, And also all that other mess' or cottage in the same in the occup of Elizabeth Jayne, And also all that wood called Kebedicke in the same contg 200 acres in the occup' of John Catchmay, gent., And also all those six acres of meadow and eight acres of pasture in the same in the tenure of Hester Geathen and Alice Geathen, And also all those several parcels of land in the same heretofore in the occup' of George Harris, and now also in the occup' of the said Thomas Berrington and Tacy, And also of one acre of meadow in the same, late in the occup' of [*blank*] Lymes, and now of the said Thomas Berrington and Tacy, with all lands, woods, free warren, heriots, rents, etc., in

1 *Liber Landavensis*, pp. 199 and 463, *Book of Llan Dâv*, p. 209.

1 *Cal. of Inq.*, vol. vii., no. 538.

the said parishes TO HAVE AND TO HOULD until a good and perfect estate in fee simple shall be made, etc., which said messuages are the right of the said Richard Herbert or the said Edward, lord Herbert, and dame Mary his wife, or sir Will'm Herbert, knt., dec^d, late grandfather of the said Richard Herbert, etc.

[Signed] RICHARD HERBERT.

Endorsed—Sealed and delivered in the presence of
Geo. ffletcher.
Richard Herbert.
Tho. Pierfon.
Will'm—W. B.—Blonck's mark.

Sir Thomas Herbert, who thus purchased the estate of Tintern Parva, was the son of Christopher Herbert of York, where his family had been settled as merchants, and was born there in 1606. Descended from Thomas, a base son of sir Richard Herbert of Coldbrook (the latter slain at Banbury in 1469), he in early life renewed his family connection with his kinsman William, third earl of Pembroke, who, recognising the relationship, obtained for him a post in the suite of the British ambassador in Persia. When the civil wars broke out he at first attached

VIEW OF OLD HOUSE (demolished).[1]

himself to the parliament, but afterwards became a staunch adherent of the king, whose sole companion he was during the last few months of his life, and whom he accompanied to the scaffold. King Charles immediately before his execution gave him his watch, and this and the king's cloak, and the 1632 edition of *Shakespeare*, on the flyleaf of which the king had written *Dum spiro spero*, were carefully preserved by him, and are still existing. He wrote *A Description of the Persian Monarchy*, 1634, and other books. His MSS. he gave to the Bodleian library.[2] On 3 July,

1660, he was created a baronet by king Charles II., and died 1 March, 168¼. Though he had purchased the house and estate of Tintern Parva, it is doubtful if he ever lived here. He had a house in London and another in York.

Sir Thomas Herbert died in his house at Petergate, near York Minster, and was buried near his ancestors in the church of St. Crux.[1] This church has since been pulled down, and the brass which was placed to his memory is now preserved in a room used for parochial purposes.

---

[1] Whether the above sketch represents the mansion of sir Thomas Herbert is doubtful. It is taken from a water-colour drawing made by the late mrs. Bagnall-Oakeley about the year 1860, and is described as the *abbot's house at Tintern Parva.* [2] *Dict. Nat. Biogr.*

[1] A very full and complete account of sir Thomas Herbert by the late Robert Davies, F.S.A., will be found in the *Yorkshire Archæological Journal*, 1870, vol. i., p. 182 *et seq.*, where is a reduced rubbing of the brass. A rubbing of the brass is also among the collections of rubbings in the rooms of the Society of Antiquaries.

POSTERITATI SACRUM
Heic sitæ sunt reliquiæ THOMÆ HERBERT,
e nobili et antiquâ HERBERTORVM *de* COLEBROOKE
in agro MONVMETHENSI *familiâ oriundi.*
Cui ineunte aetate tam intensus peregrinandi fuit ardor ;
ut itineris sui, in celebriores AFRICÆ, ASIÆQ. *majoris partes*
(*præcipue* PERSIÆ, *Orientalis* INDIÆ, *insularumq. adjacentium*)
(*Anno D'ni* MDCXXVI *suscepti*) *observationes selectissimas*
in lucem edidit, quas maturâ ætate consummate perpolivit.
Qui per totum vitæ dimensum, ob morum elegantiam, vitaeq. probitatem conspicuus
Historiarum et penitioris Antiquitatis indagator sedulus.
Queis in accuratâ gentis HERBERTIANÆ *historiâ*
(*Ex Archivis Regijs, Authenticis Chartis alijsq. indubitatae*
Antiquitatis monumentis, manu propriâ exaratis ;
et Armorum, Sigillorum et Tumulorum Ectypis,
Graphice delineatis) *specimen eximium perhibuit.*
Serenissimo Regi CAROLO, *martyri, per binos ac ultimos vitæ*
tristissimae annos, ab intimis cubiculis Servus extitit fidelis,
rerumq. dicti Regis, infestâ solitudine, gestarum, commentariola contexuit.
exindi per illustrissimum nunc Regem CAROLVM II^{um}
in gradum BARONETTI *merito evectus est.*
LVCIAM *filiam* GVALTERI ALEXANDER *Equitis Aurati*
in Vxorem primam duxit ;
quae fatis cessit A° D'ni MDCLXXI
ex hac
PHILIPPVM, HENRICVM (*Paterni honoris haeredem superstitem*)
MONTGOMERVM, THOMAM, GVLIELMVM *ap* THOMAM,
filiasq. quatuor suscepit ;
TERESIAM, ALEXANDRO BRAFIELD *de* HANSLAP *in Agro* BVCK. *nuptam ;*
ELIZABETHAM, ROBERTO PHAIRE *de* ROSTBLON *in* HIBERNIA ;
LVCIAM, *imprimis* IOHANNI FROST *de* CLAPHAM *in comitat.* SVRR.
deinde GVLIELMO HERBERT *de* CALDICOT *in agro* MONVMETHENSI ;
et ANNAM, *provectiori ætate defunctam.*
Postea cum ELIZABETHA *filiâ* GERVASII CVTLER *de* STAINBVRG
in Comitatu EBOR. EQVITIS AVRATI
modo superstite secundas inivit nuptias ;
e quâ
ELIZABETHAM *trimestrem Feb.* XXI *A° D'ni* MDCLXXIII *extinctam genuit.*
tam celebris et charissimi MARITI *maestissima* VIDVA
ut amoris sui, et virtutum tam insignis Viri
Longaevum praeberet Testimonium,
Hocce Monumentum L.L.M.**1** *posuit.*
ex hac luce pientissime emigravit
I° die MARTII *A° D'ni* MDCLXXXI *Ætatis suae* LXXVI.

Above the inscription is a shield with HERBERT in the centre. On the dexter : *Per pale arg. and sa., a chevron between two mullets in chief, and in base a crescent, all counterchanged* (ALEXANDER) ; on the sinister : *Az., three dragons' heads erased or* (CUTLER). CREST.—*A sheaf of arrows, banded.*

[*Sacred to posterity.*

Here are placed the remains of Thomas Herbert, descended from the noble and ancient family of the Herberts of Colebrooke in the county of Monmouth. To whom in his youth there was such a strong love of travelling that he edited a most valuable account of the journey he undertook in the year 1626 in the well-known parts of Africa and of Greater Asia (principally of Persia, the East Indies and the adjoining islands), which in later life he elaborately completed. Who, through the whole course of his life, conspicuous on account of the excellence of his manners and the uprightness of his life, was a diligent investigator of history and of deep antiquity, of which he produced an excellent example in the exact history of the race of Herbert (extracted with his own hand from the royal archives, authentic deeds and other monuments of undoubted antiquity, and graphically drew sketches of arms, of seals and of tombs).

He was a faithful servant of the bedchamber to the most

serene king Charles the martyr during the last two years of his most sad life, and compiled commentaries of the things done by the said king in his dread solitude. At length he was deservedly raised to the degree of baronet by the present most illustrious king Charles II. He married as his first wife Lucy, daughter of Walter Alexander, knt., who died in 1671. By her he had issue Philip, Henry (the surviving heir of his father's honour), Montgomery, Thomas, William ap Thomas ; and four daughters, Teresa married to Alexander Brafield of Hanslap in the county of Bucks ; Elizabeth married to Robert Phaire of Rostblon in Ireland ; Lucy married first to John Frost of Clapham in the county of Surrey, and afterwards to William Herbert of Caldicot in the county of Monmouth ; and Anna, who died in middle age.

Afterwards he married as his second wife Elizabeth, who still survives, daughter of Gervais Cutler of Stainburgh in the county of York, knt., by whom he had issue Elizabeth, who died aged three months, 21 February, 1673.

The most sad widow of a husband so famous and most dear, that she might afford an everlasting testimony of her love for him and of the virtues of such an illustrious man, placed this monument to him who so well deserved it. He most piously departed this life 1 March, 1681, aged 76.]

It will be observed that in the above memorial reference is made to the *History of the race of Herbert* (accurata gentis Herbertianae historia) which sir

---

1 Libentissime merito.

Thomas had compiled. This is preserved in the Free Library at Cardiff, and is a folio MS. book containing much valuable information, with beautifully executed water-colour drawings of tombs, and sketches of seals, etc.

Thomas Herbert, the ancestor of this family, with his son Richard first went to Yorkshire with the countess of Northumberland, Maud, daughter of William, first earl of Pembroke of the first creation, wife of Henry, earl of Northumberland, and there they continued until sir Thomas moved southwards and rose to fame.

The estate afterwards became the property of William Feilding, whose only child and heir Elizabeth married John Curre of Rogerston Grange in St. Arvans. This gentleman dying without issue in 1777 left Tintern Parva to the person who should be heir to his wife.[1] The estate in 1787 was owned by Nathaniel and John Osborne, the latter gentleman having married Elizabeth, daughter and heir of George White, brother of Richard White, who had the iron-works at Abbey Tintern.

1 *Vide* p. 62.

Pedigree of the family of Herbert of Tintern.

ARMS granted by Richard St. George, Norroy King of Arms, 29 April 1614, to Richard Herbert of York.—*Per pale gu. and az., 3 lions ramp. erminois.* CREST.—*A demi-lion ramp. erminois, supporting a broken tilting-spear ppr.* Sir Thomas Herbert, baronet, bore, however, the usual Herbert coat.

For previous descents *vide* Vol. I., p. 189.

THOMAS HERBERT, base son to sir Richard Herbert of Coldbrook, knt., by Jane=Elizabeth, dau. to sir Christopher
v3 Thomas John David, went into Yorkshire; bur. in Beverley Minster. Mathew of Llandaff, knt.

Richard Herbert of York, esq., bur. in Beverley=Margaret (or Barbara), dau. to sir John Pudsey of Church 1557, æt. 69. Richmond, co. York, knt.

Thomas ap John Poiskin=Nest. of co. Monmouth.

Christopher Herbert of York, esq.,=Elizabeth, dau. to John Hemsworth of Hemsworth, ob. 1589, æt. 57. co. York, esq., ob. 1618, æt. 93.

Evan Herbert.=

Walter Poiskin, coroner.

Mary, dau. to=Thomas Herbert of=Alice, dau. Thomas Har- York, esq., alderman to Peter rison of An- and lord mayor, ob. Newark. caster, esq. 14 Oct. 1614, æt. 60. 2nd wife.

Richard Herbert of York, had a grant of arms 1614. — Christopher Herbert.

Mary, mar. Thomas Lovell of Shelton, esq.

.... Hed-=Ann=Thomas worth of Groves Hedworth. of York. 1st hus- 2nd hus- band. band.

Richard=Herbert.

Henry, s.p.

Christopher=Jane, dau. to John Herbert of Acroyd of Fogga- York, esq. thorpe, co. York, gent.

William Herbert, s.p.

Richard Hed-=Elizabeth. worth of Hedworth, esq.

Sir John Con-=Frances. yers of Hor- den, bart.

....=Susan. Lamb- ton.

John Her- bert.

Lucy, dau. to sir=Sir Thomas Herbert of Tintern,=Elizabeth, dau. to sir Gervais Walter Alexan- bart., so created 3 July 1650; Cutler, knt.; she mar. 2ndly, der of St. James, born at York, and there died in 1672, Henry Edmonds, esq.; knt. 1st wife. 1 March 168½, æt. 76. ob. at York March 1672.

William Herbert, s.p. — Christopher Herbert, s.p.

Emanuel Herbert.

William Ed-=Alice. wards of Rhuallt, co. Flint, esq.

1. Philip Herbert, ob. juv.

Anne, dau. to sir=2. Sir Henry=Anne, dau. to Thomas Harrison Herbert of sir George of Allerthorpe, Tintern and Vane of Long co. York, knt., by of Middleton, Newton, co. Margaret, dau. co. York. Durham. to Conyers, lord 2nd bart. 2nd wife. Darcy. 1st wife.

3. Alexander Herbert, ob. juv. 4. Montgomery Herbert, ob. juv.

5. William ap Tho- mas, ob. juv. Theresa, mar. Fran- cis Bradfield of Hanslap, co. Bucks, esq.

Elizabeth, mar. at St. Werburgh's, Dublin, 16 Aug. 1658, colonel Ro- bert Phayre.

Lucy, mar. 1st John Frost of Clapham, co. Surrey; 2ndly, at St. Mary le Belfry, York, 18 Sept. 1669, William Herbert of Caldicot, co. Mon.

Thomas Herbert, ob. juv.

Henry Herbert.

Henry Herbert.

Lucy.

Mary.

Lionel Maddison of Salt-=Margaret. wellside, co. Durham.

Theresa.

Anne.

Thomas Place, recorder of York=Anne.

George Herbert, ob. 1687.

Sir Humphrey Herbert,=Mary Dewtris=Thomas Ward 3rd bart., bur. at St. Crux, of York. of York, gent. York, 28 June 1701. 2nd husband. 1st husband.

Sir Henry Herbert, 5th bart., bur. at Badsworth, co. York, 1732.

Rice Herbert, living 1701. Lionel Herbert, bur. 1693.

Richard Herbert, bur. 1681. Charles Herbert, living 1701.

Sir Thomas Herbert, 4th bart., born 1700; ob. cœl.; bur. at St. James's, Westminster, 13 March 172¾.

In 1838 Edward Davis, a timber merchant, was the owner, who in that year bequeathed it to two brothers named Gale. These gentlemen in 1856 sold the estate, including the manor with the residence called Nurtons and advowson of the living, to the rev. Robert Vaughan Hughes, who in 1889 sold the property to various persons.

It is probable that the owner of this estate before lord Herbert of Chirbury acquired it was Lewis Morris, who in 1635 is described as of Tintern Parva. Lewis Morris was an officer in the parliamentary army, on whose behalf he raised a regiment of foot, and was present at the siege of Chepstow castle. On the restoration of Charles II. he went to Barbadoes and afterwards to New York, where he became a prominent man. His brother Richard was a captain in the same regiment, and another brother William was great-grandfather of Valentine Morris, who purchased and settled at Piercefield in St. Arvans.

The house, which was, so far as can be judged from what is left, a large Tudor mansion, stood on the edge of the main road, of which one window is left looking out into the road, with a portion of a large fireplace adjoining. There are other ruined walls which indicate the size of the building. The site, with a small amount of land, was purchased by Arthur Pontifex Price, who resides in the modern dwelling-house close by, which still bears the name of the *manor-house*.

The residence called Nurtons, which is approached by an avenue of trees with about 20 acres of land,

TINTERN PARVA CHURCH. (From a drawing made shortly before the rebuilding in 1846.)

was purchased by Henry John Williams, the rector, who sold it to Clement Alfred William Cruttwell, vicar of Frankley, Cheshire.

Coed Beddick, the large wood which has its name from Buddig, father of Docheu (Oudoceus),[1] has been purchased by the Crown, which now owns about two-thirds of the parish.

The Church.

The church stands on the bank of the river Wye. It was practically rebuilt about the year 1846, the only ancient part left being the porch. The advowson was early appropriated to the priory of Chepstow. In the eighteenth century it was attached to the manor, and so continued till recently. It is now in the Crown. The patron saint is Michael.

[1] *Vide* p. 206.

Monumental Inscriptions.

ON THE SOUTH WALL.

A marble tablet on which is carved a death-bed scene, three persons standing weeping over the dying person.

Sacred to the memory of Julia, the wife of John Roberts of this parish, who died the 15th of August, 1838, aged 31 years.

Also of Fredk Saml their infant son, who died the 2d of August, aged 7 weeks.

Elvira, daughter of the above, died 12th July, 1840, aged 3 years.

John, son of the above, died 19th June, 1845, aged 13 years.

Also the above-named John Roberts, died May 19th, 1875, aged 70.

William Hughes died Jan. 30, 1848, aged 21; Charles Edwin died Sept. 8, 1877, aged 43; Nehemiah George died Nov. 9, 1890, aged 55; sons of the above John Roberts.

PATRON.	DATE OF INSTITUTION.	INCUMBENT.
The king, by reason of the priory of Chepstow being in his hands on account of the war with France.	22 Dec. 1348.	Adam de Couton.[1]
The king, for the same reasons.	26 Feb. 1350.	William Baker, chaplain.[2]
Do.	22 May 1389.	Hugh ap David,[3] resigned 1391 on appointment to Lee in the diocese of Rochester, in exchange with William Glastynbury.[4]
Do.	10 May 1391.	William Glastynbury, previously parson of Lee in the diocese of Rochester, in exchange with Hugh ap David; resigned 1395[4] on appointment to Thundurle.
Do.	8 July 1394.	John Golmonchestre, vicar of Thundurle in the diocese of London,[5] in exchange with Wm. Glastynbury.[5]
Do.	21 Sept. 1394.	David Carlion, chaplain of a charity in the collegiate church of Leicester, in exchange with Wm. Glastynbury.[6] (These two could not have taken effect.)
Do.	26 Jan. 1395.	Adam Payne, on the resignation of Wm. Glastynbury.[7]
Do.	14 June 1396.	John ap David,[8] resigned 1399 on appointment to the chantry of Marnhull in the diocese of Salisbury, in exchange with Adam Russheburye.
	26 July 1399.	Adam Russheburye, chaplain of the chantry of Marnhull, in exchange with John ap David.[8]
		Walter de Bury, resigned 1402 on presentation to the chantry at Lytlyngton in the diocese of London, in exchange with Peter Warde.[9]
The king	20 Nov. 1402.	Peter Warde, previously chaplain of the chantry at the altar of St. Mary in the church of Lytlyngton.[9]
		Walter Loring in 1412.[10]
	.... 1632.	William Prichard, M.A. Jesus College, Oxford, son of Francis Prichard of Abergavenny.
		Hugh Evans, died about 1697.
The bishop	19 July 1697.	John Quick, M.A. New Inn Hall, Oxford, son of John Quick of Burringham, co. Somerset; resigned 1702.
Wm. ffielding, esq.	15 Sept. 1702.	Amos Boyland.
John Curre, esq., guardian of Elizabeth ffielding, a minor.	9 Aug. 1713.	Anthony Barrow, B.A. Jesus College, Oxford, son of Edward Barrow of St. Briavels, gent.
George I.	31 July 1719.	Thomas Hill, M.A. Magdalen Hall, Oxford, son of Thomas Hill of Hereford; also in 1723 vicar of Llanarth.
		George Harris; resigned 1734.
John Curre, esq.	20 Sept. 1734.	Mallet Bateman, Pembroke and Jesus College, Oxford, son of Richard Bateman of Prendergast, co. Pembroke.
John Curre of Itton, esq.	18 Jan. 1752.	Edward Lewis.
Do.	8 Dec. 1756.	John Williams.
	.... 1768.	Thomas Edmunds; died 1804-5.
Thomas Fielding Manning and Sarah his wife; Wm. Shopp Osborne; Isaac Freeme; and Wm. Osborne.	24 June 1805.	Daniel Drape.
	25 Sept. 1827.	John Mais, B.D. Queen's College, Cambridge. (William Richard Ferguson, curate in 1851, afterwards rector of Llandogo.)
	.... 1871.	Henry John Williams; resigned 1878.
	.... 1878.	Joseph Frederick Jones.
	.... 1882.	Edward Richard Godley; resigned 1887; also held Chapel Hill; resigned 1886.
	.... 1887.	William Elitto Rosedale, M.A. New College, Oxford; resigned 1889.
	.... 1889.	Alfred Trask Pullin, B.A. Trinity College, Dublin.
	.... 1892.	Harold Barclay Hennell; also held Chapel Hill.
	.... 1901.	William Donald Istance Mackintosh; also held Chapel Hill.[11]
The crown	8 Oct. 1903.	Alfred Wm. Washington Palmer, son of Alfred Vaughan Palmer; also holds Chapel Hill.

---

1 *Cal. Rot. Pat.*, Edw. III., 1348—50, p. 216.   2 *Ibid.*, p. 471.   3 *Cal. Rot. Pat.*, Ric. II., 1388—92, p. 40.
4 *Ibid.*, p. 464.   5 *Ibid.*, p. 466.   6 *Ibid.*, p. 480.   7 *Ibid.*, p. 527.   8 *Ibid.*, p. 714.
9 *Cal. Rot. Pat.*, Hen. IV., 1401—5, p. 173.   10 *Ibid.*, 1408—13, p. 448.
11 I have been unable to obtain the names of the patrons who presented the above clergymen. The *Directories* give them—in 1851 (Lascelles') William Gale; in 1861 (Webster's) Robert Vaughan Hughes, clk.; in 1884 (Kelly's) Robert Hamilton Williams and Henry Edward Burney.

On the floor of the nave is a stone with a floreated cross and part of an inscription around it which is illegible, of the fourteenth century.

There is also a flat stone inscribed:

Here lyeth Elizabeth Feilding
late wife of William Feilding of
this parifh, gent., and Daughter
of John Phillips of Tallavan in this
county, gent., who dyed January
24, 170¾.

In the Churchyard.

In Memory of Gwenllyan, wife of D. Vaughan, who died in childbed Sepr 24th, 1776, aged 36 years.

David Vaughan, their son, died January 13th, 1841, aged 70 years.

Jane, wife of the above, died September 12th, 1843, aged 62 years.

Richard, their son, died April 12th, 1841, Aged 20 years.

Here lieth y^e Body of Charles Prichet of this Parish, who Died June y^e 6th, 1750, Aged 31 years.

Chapel Hill or Abbey Tintern.

CHAPEL HILL is the name by which this parish is generally known, but by the older people it is often called Abbey Tintern, after the ecclesiastical building for which the place is famous. In Welsh it is *Llanandras* from the dedication of the church to St. Andrew.

The parish contains 1307 acres of land and 4 acres of inland water, 40 acres of tidal water, and 27 acres of foreshore in the river Wye.

The population has been as follows :—

Year .	1801	1811	1821	1831	1841	1861	1871	1881	1891	1901
No. of inhab.	390	420	464	590	521	497	367	411	462	309

The number of houses has decreased :—

Year.	Inhabited houses.	Uninhabited houses.	Building.
1861 . . .	101	13	0
1871 . . .	86	22	0
1881 . . .	101	12	0
1891 . . .	98	8	0
1901 . . .	74	30	0

The earliest reference to Tintern is the story of Tewdrig ap Teithfallt, king of Gwent and Morganwg in the fifth century, the founder of (among other institutions) the cathedral of Llandaff. Giving up his kingdom to his son Meurig he retired to Tintern, where he lived the life of a hermit. While he resided here the Saxons, who were then pagans, began to invade the district, when an angel appeared to Tewdrig, telling him he was to shew himself in the battle and their enemies would be put to flight, though he himself would receive a mortal wound. This so happened ; the enemy fled, and Tewdrig, standing on the banks of the Wye near the ford of Tintern, received a wound from a lance. The next morning the wounded king was conveyed in a carriage drawn by two stags yoked till they came to a meadow near the Severn where fountains flowed, and there he died and was buried. His son Meurig built a church on the spot called Merthyr Tewdrig (*Tewdrig the martyr*), since shortened to Mathern.[1]

In the *Myfyrian Archæology* the place is called Dinteyrn Uchaf (*Upper Tintern*), as distinguished from Dinteyrn Isaf (*Lower Tintern*).

[1] *Lib. Land.*, p. 383 ; *Book of Llan Dâv*, p. 141 ; *Iolo MSS.*, p. 353.

Tintern Abbey.

So many books and pamphlets have been written about this noble ruin, dealing with it from the historical as well as from the sentimental point of view, that it is difficult to say anything that has not been already printed.

The abbey was founded for the Cistercian order in the year 1131 by Walter de Clare, younger son of Richard de Clare, or de Tonbridge, who came into England with William the Conqueror, for the good of his soul and the souls of his kinsmen, and dedicated to St. Mary.

It took many years to complete, the original church erected giving way to the present one, in which mass was first celebrated at the altar in 1288. Meanwhile, the Clares had become extinct in the male line, but the work was carried on faithfully by the Marshalls and Bigods, descendants in the female line and lords of Striguil or Chepstow ;[1] and it was in the time of Roger Bigod, the last marshall of that name, that the church was finished. This Roger died in 1306, having surrendered his estates in 1302 to Edward I.

The monastery was dissolved in 28 Hen. VIII. [1536-7], there being then thirteen monks, and was granted with much of its possessions to Henry Somerset, 2nd earl of Worcester. The revenues were then worth, according to Dugdale, 192*l.* 1*s.* 4½*d.*, and according to Speed, 256*l.* 11*s.* 6*d.*

From that time until about the year 1900 the site of the institution and most of the lands continued in the Somerset family, when the abbey with the woods and lands adjoining were purchased by the Crown from the 9th duke of Beaufort.

Of the church itself the walls still remain nearly to their original height, together with the windows, some of which retain the handsome tracery peculiar to the period in which they were designed. The west window is the most perfect, and is much to be admired on account of its just proportions, and as a specimen of what the other windows must have been like.

The church as seen now does not represent the size of the original church, which was smaller than the existing one. The first church that was built stood partly inside the present one, and the foundations of the south wall can be traced in the north

[1] A pedigree of the Clares will be given under Chepstow.

aisle, while the north wall can be seen in the cloisters. The east end of the original church was just outside the wall of the north transept. Roger Bigod built the existing church, commencing the work about the year 1269, on a scale much superior to the first one.[1] It comprises the presbytery and quire with a north and south transept, and the nave, with aisles on both sides running the whole length of the edifice. The total length is 228 feet, and the width across the transepts is 152 feet. To the north of the nave are the cloisters, and west of the cloisters, at the north end of the north transept, is the chapter-house. The domestic buildings are on the north side of the cloisters, and away to the west at a distance of about 30 yards was the infirmary, the foundations of which have been recently excavated. This was connected with the main buildings by two covered passages, one leading to the church and the other towards the domestic apartments. To the north of the infirmary are remains of other buildings, and on the south was a garden. On the western side of the premises are remains of other buildings with what appears to have been a pond, perhaps for a mill. The area enclosed within the precincts was about 27 acres, and the wall enclosing this can be traced in most places. The present main road is a comparatively modern one, and cuts through the enclosed ground from north-east to south-west. The ancient road is the rough lane going from the George inn at the north-east end, and continuing at the back of the Beaufort Arms hotel towards Penterry. Along this lane the wall is seen as it was originally built. The main entrance gate was where the lane from the parish church joins the above-mentioned lane. This has disappeared, but the chapel which adjoined it has been incorporated in the modern house known as *St. Anne's,* which is said to be on the site of the abbot's guest-house.

TINTERN ABBEY : NORTH-WEST VIEW.

The first charter[2] that has been quoted is that of William Marshall, earl of Pembroke, the second of his name in 1223. As this charter gives the boundaries of the abbey property and many names of places, I give so much of it as is of interest :—

Carta Willielmi, comitis Marescalli junioris, de confirmatione abbatiae de Tynterne.

Willielmus, mareschallus Angliae, comes Penbrochiae, universis hominibus suis Francis et Anglicis, Walensibus, Hibernicis, et omnibus amicis ballivis et fidelibus suis, salutem in domino. Noverit universitas vestra nos intuitu Dei et pro salute animae meae et pro animabus bonae memoriae Walteri filii Ricardi filii Gilberti Strongbowe avi mei et Willielmi Marescalli patris mei et Ysabellae matris meae et animarum antecessorum haeredum et successorum nostrorum concessisse et presenti carta mea confirmasse Deo et ecclesiae beatae Mariae de Tynterna, abbati et monachis et eorum successoribus ibidem Deo servientibus in liberam puram et perpetuam elemosynam omnes terras et possessiones et libertates et liberas consuetudines subscriptas quas habent ex donis antecessorum nostrorum et aliorum fundatorum seu donatorum sive ex dono nostro, videlicet, totam hayam de Porthcassek[1] et aquam quae vocatur Angidy[2] et de Angidy per Wayam[3] usque ad nemus de feodo Porthskywet[4] et ex altera parte co-opertum nemoris usque ad vallem quae descendit ad terram de Pentir[5] et sic de valle per montem usque ad fontem Achur et sic ad Angidy ;

1 For some of what follows I am indebted to a most useful guide to the abbey by Messrs. Harold Brakspear and Morton Evans, 1908.

2 Dugdale's *Monasticon,* v., 267.

1 The farm of Porth-caseg.

2 Angidy, the brook which enters the Wye at Tintern.

3 The river Wye.

4 The fee of Portskewet.

5 Pentir for Penterry.

Et piscariam de Walwere, Halfwere, Badingswere[1] cum omnibus pertinentijs suis, et totum dominium de Wlaveston[2] cum advocatione ecclesiae, etc., et quicquid habent in feodo de Tudeham[3] de piscariis, terris, boscis, aquis, tenentibus et redditibus in villa de Tudeham et libere piscari in toto dominio meo in Sabrina[4] et gurgites facere contra terram dictorum abbatis et monachorum de terra de Aberdeston[5] usque ad Waldingespull et omnes tenentes sui in chacia nostra pasturam animalium suorum et rusticorum ad ardendum de Ascaurewe usque ad Brawere sine aliquo impedimento, etc.; Et totam terram de Modesgat cum omnibus suis pertinentijs et pasturam omnium animalium suorum ubique in chacia nostra de Tudiham et de terra in dicta chacia quicquid eis necefsarium fuerit ad ardendum et ad haias claudendas et plantandas et alia necessaria grangiae perficienda; Et Kibeham cum una pulla de Londemere usque ad Lynwere; Et Brocwere .... et quicquid habent in Lanchaut et unam pullam quae vocatur Wayfhers cum prato ex una parte; Et piscariam de Badyngwere, Halfwere, Walwere, Astandwere,[6] Plumwere et medietatem de Aswere[7] .... Et grangiam de Assarto[8] cum villa de Porcassek; Et in mora de Magor totam terram sicut per fossas dividitur et per circuitum terrae fossare et in dicta fossa quicquid voluerint facere, et cursus aquae ubicunque interius vel exterius ordinare ad commodum suum sicut viderint melius expedire; Et omnes terras .... in Magor et Pulla, Wondy et Rodewey; Et omnia prata .... et plenarium pasturam quorumcunque animalium suorum in la Grenemore et alibi .... et Marthirgerin et quicquid ad Marthingerye pertinet in ecclesia in bosco plano ....; Et in Scimoc quaterviginti acras prati in mora et pratum quod Robertus de Sancta Brigida tenuit in mora de Magor; Et quicquid habent in Pentiry et duas areas in orto meo de Magor scilicet extremas versus occidentem; Et totam molturam meam et hominum meorum de Pentiry et Porcassek et Tinterna et Landirogods ad moledinum suum de Angidy; Et grangiam de Rogerston ....; Et quicquid habent in Landreston, Sancto Wormeto, Howyk, Sancto Arunno[9] cum Cophill, Bernardeswode, Bernatties; Et quicquid habent infra burgum Strugull Trillek et Usk ....; Pencreck et Hennefoth .... Item pro animabus bonae memoriae Willielmi Mareschalli patris mei et Ysabellae matris meae et Gilberti et Ricardi Strongbowe et pro salute animae nostrae animarum antecessorum et heredum nostrorum, dedimus .... Deo et ecclesiae de Tynterna .... totam landam et terram de Trillek quas dicti monachi habuerunt de donis dicti Gilberti Strongbowe et Ricardi avi mei per bundas subscriptas, videlicet, de via quae ducit de Monimutta per Spintam ex una parte et veterem capellam ex altera parte directe versus Strugull usque Nantrlinat sub denigro rivulo directe ascendendo ad summitatem montis et sic per summitatem montis et circuitum inter Wenhalt et Kilvechyn et sic per circuitum Kilwechyn directe descendendo usque ad

rivulum qui vocatur Angedy et sic per Angedy et vivarium ascendendo per terras hominum Wallensium ex una parte Angedy ad vallem quae vocatur Coverpantegoylin et de fonte usque ad summitatem montis et sic per summitatem montis usque ad viam quae ducit versus Uskam juxta ecclesiam Sancti Dionisii Lannissan[1] et sic descendendo per caput Sapant[2] usque ad fontem qui vocatur caput Angedy[3] et sic per Angedy usque ad rivulum qui vocatur Acanelth[4] sive Assees et sic per rivulum usque ad caput Frinunkayr[5] vernby sive Blaenaranelth et sic per terras hominum de Trellek usque ad viam quae ducit de Monimutta versus Strygull .... totam terram cum bosco de Pochlenny[6] cum omnibus pertinentijs suis infra bundas subscriptas videlicet per rivulum qui vocatur Aberwin[7] ex una parte et ita per circuitum usque ad Horston et sic directe usque ad Fovemhen et ita usque ad aquam de Usk et sic per aquam de Usk et in Usk usque ad terram hominum Walensium et sic ascendendo contra torrentem per nigrum fagum[8] directe per terras hominum Walensium usque ad aquam de Aberthin[7] et in tota aqua de Usk cum diversis instrumentis et retibus piscari et medietatem unius gurgitis ubicunque eligere voluerint aedificare et pullas facere .... Datum apud Strigull 22 die Martii anno regni regis Henrici, filii regis Johannis, septimo [1223].

These gifts were confirmed subsequently by charters. In 1302 an *inspeximus* is quoted whereby Roger le Bygod, earl of Norfolk and marshall of England, confirmed the same.[9] In 1307 an *inspeximus* recites charters, (1) whereby Richard [Marshall], earl of Pembroke, with the consent of Isabel his mother, confirms the grant of Porthcasseg and Penterry, (2) whereby Gilbert [Marshall], earl of Pembroke, with consent of the countess Isabel [his mother, only child of Richard de Clare, earl of Pembroke] for the soul of his ancestors, confirms all the gift of his uncle Walter,[10] to wit, the hay of Porthcasseg and Pentier [Penterry], (3) whereby the said Gilbert confirms the same.[11]

Among the valuable possessions of the abbey was the estate of Monkswood called in Welsh Capelcoed-y-mynach, which was probably part of the original endowment by Walter de Clare. At different times additions were made to the monastic property by grants of land by individuals, and the grant quoted below seems to be the farms in the parish of Llanvihangel Pont-y-moel, known as Mynachdy (*monastery*). In 1307 an *inspeximus*[12] of deeds relates that Maud Luvel of Trelech, with the

---

1 Badingswere, *i.e.*, Baitings weir, also called Hook weir.
2 This is a misreading. What is intended is Woolastone, co. Gloucester.
3 Tidenham.
4 Free fishing in the Severn.
5 Alveston.
6 Astandwere, probably for Stanwere, *i.e.*, Stone weir, which may be that on p. 219 as Stawere, and on p. 222 Stow weir.
7 Ash weir.
8 The assarted or cleared land. This is probably that called Rogerston's Grange in St. Arvans.
9 St. Arvans.

1 Llanishen church.
2 Sychpant, the dingle in which the Olwy brook runs. Pant-glas, an ancient mansion, is situated here.
3 The well at Higga.
4 This is the brook now called Nant-y-gaer.
5 *Recte Ffynnon-y-gaer* (the spring of the fortress).
6 Pelleny, *vide* Vol. I., p. 415. The boundary following is that of Monkswood, near Usk.
7 Now called the Berthin brook.
8 *The black beech.* This is probably the spot occupied by a clump of beech trees in the Glasgoed, considered to be the centre of the county.
9 *Cal. Charter Rolls*, III., 1300—26, p. 31.
10 Walter de Clare, the founder, would have been great-great-great-uncle to Gilbert Marshall.
11 *Cal. Charter Rolls*, III., 1300—26, p. 97.
12 *Cal. of Charter Rolls*, Vol. III., p. 103, 1300—1326.

assent of sir Richard de Clare, earl of Gloucester and Hertford [who died in 1262], gave to the church of St. Mary at Tintern 60 acres of arable land between the lands of the monks [*i.e.*, Monkswood] on the one side and land of Philip, rector of Llanvihangel, on the other side, in free almoin, saving to the earl at Whitsunday 6*d.*, for which gift the abbot and convent gave 13 marks. The witnesses are: Reginald ap Adam, Mahel de Usk, Roger son of Nicholas, Griffin ap Meyrick, Hugh the forester, Philip de Lannvihangel, Nicholas ap Adam, Ralph the tailor.

Of the proceedings of the monks but little can be gleaned except from occasional references in the *Calendars of Patent Rolls*.

On 20 November, 1407, pardon for all money in arrear was granted to the abbot and convent of Tintern, in consideration of the greater part of the abbey and country of the diocese of Llandaff being wasted by the recent rebellion of the Welsh.[1] In 1411 John, abbot of Tintern, received licence, in return for two marks paid by Robert Martham and William Frysseby, clerk, to receive in mortmain six acres of pasture in Acle (?) to the said John, the abbot.[2] On 14 May [1 Id. Ma.], 1413, John Limeburgh, cistercian monk of Tintern, was appointed papal chaplain.[3]

On 28 June, 1462, Stephen, abbot of St. Mary at Llantarnam, Thomas, abbot of St. Mary at Tintern, Lewis ap Howel of Llantarnam, chaplain, and Thomas Phillips, a monk there, were summoned by Maurice Denys, esq., sheriff of Gloucester. They did not appear, but the king granted a pardon to the abbot of Tintern, and restored to him his lands.[4]

TINTERN ABBEY: INTERIOR, LOOKING EAST.

It has often been wondered how money was raised for the building of the magnificent churches such as Tintern and others. One way was for the pope to grant indulgences in return for alms. On 3 March (5 Non. Mar.), 1414, Relaxation was granted during ten years to penitents who on the feast of our Lord and certain other feast days visit the west door of the church of the cistercian monastery of St. Mary the Virgin at Tintern, and give alms for the repair and decoration of its buildings and ornaments, in which chapel a picture (imago) of St. Mary the Virgin has been fairly and honestly and devoutly placed (collocata), and, although the attempt has been more than once made, has been unable to be placed elsewhere, on account of which miracle, and because mass is said daily by the monks at the altar of the said chapel, a very great multitude resort to the chapel.[5]

William Marshall, earl of Pembroke, who died in 1219, was a great benefactor to this abbey. He also founded the abbey called after this one, Tintern de Voto in Ireland, in consequence of a vow he made when at sea in danger of shipwreck.

William Botoner or de Worcester the traveller, who visited Tintern in 1453, gives details of the

1 *Cal. Rot. Pat.*, Hen. IV., 1405—8, p. 378.
2 *Ibid.*, 1408—13, p. 284.
3 *Papal Registers*, VI., 174.
4 *Cal. Rot. Pat.*, Edw. IV., 1461—7, p. 229.
5 *Cal. of Papal Registers*, Vol. VI.

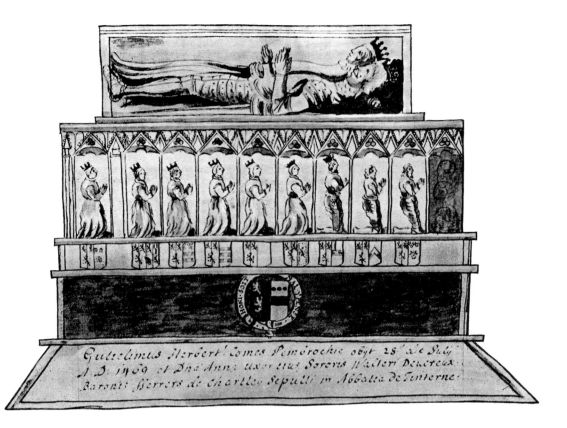

Gulielmus Herbert Comes Pembrochie obijt 28 die July A.D. 1469 et Dna Anna uxor eius Sororis Walteri Deuereux Baronis Ferrers de Chartley Sepulti in Abbatia de Tinterne.

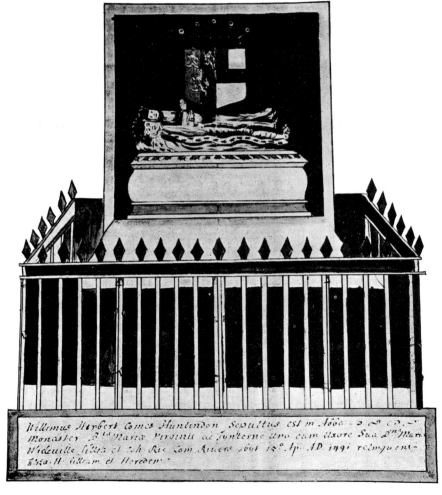

Willimus Herbert Comes Huntendon Sepultus est in Abba... Monaster Bta Maria Virginis de Tynterne una cum uxore Sua Dna Maria Wideuille filia et ioh Ric Com Riuers obijt 16° Ap. A.D. 1491 relinquens filia et Heredem.

Tombs of
WILLIAM HERBERT, EARL OF PEMBROKE, K.G., AND THE COUNTESS OF PEMBROKE,
AND
WILLIAM HERBERT (SON OF THE FORMER), EARL OF HUNTINGDON, AND THE COUNTESS OF HUNTINGDON,
Formerly in Tintern Abbey.

(From *Prosapia Herbertorum*, by sir Thomas Herbert, bart.)

dimensions of the building, and says that it was built by Roger Bigod, earl marshal, for whom, among other distinguished people, masses were sung.[1]

Many persons of eminence have been buried in the abbey church—Walter de Clare, the founder. Gilbert de Clare, earl of Pembroke, nephew of the founder, died in 1148.[2]

Isabella, daughter of Richard de Clare (Strongbow) and wife of William Marshall, earl of Pembroke, died in 1221.

Walter, fourth son of the above William Marshall, died in 1246.

Anselm, fifth son of the above William, died in 1246.[3]

Maud, wife of Hugh Bigod and daughter of the above William, died in 1248, and was buried in the quire.[4]

Of these no memorials are left, but there is in the vestry an effigy of a knight in armour, said to be Gilbert de Clare, called Strongbow, the conqueror of Ireland. He died in 1177, and is claimed to have been buried in the chapter-house at Gloucester.[5]

The representation of the tomb of the first earl of Pembroke, who was beheaded after the battle of Banbury in 1469, is from a coloured drawing in the manuscript book by sir Thomas Herbert called *Prosapia Herbertorum*, and preserved in the free library at Cardiff.[6] The artist has, however, made a mistake in placing the arms of the wives on the wrong side of the impaled shields.

On the top of the tomb were effigies of the earl and countess with coronets on their heads, and their hands in an attitude of prayer. Below are six of the daughters who married peers, with coronets on their heads, followed by the eldest son William, afterwards earl of Huntingdon, also with a coronet, and then the younger sons sir Walter and sir George.

The lady at the dexter end and the blank space at the sinister end were, by the way in which they are drawn, at the two ends of the tomb.

The first shield is for Cecily, wife of Ralph, lord Greystoke—the impalement being *Barry of 6 arg. and az., 3 chaplets gu.*

The second—Maud, wife of Henry Percy, earl of Northumberland, *Quarterly 1 and 4, Or, a lion ramp. az.; 2, Gu., 3 lucies haurient arg.; 3, Az., 5 fusils conjoined in fesse or.*

The third—Catherine, wife of George Grey, earl of Kent, *Barry of 6 arg. and az., in chief 3 torteaux.*

The fourth—Anne, wife of John Grey, lord Powis, the same shield as above without the torteaux.

The fifth—The impalement is blank; this is probably for Crisley, wife of . . . . Cornwall of Burford.

The sixth—Margaret, wife of Thomas Talbot, viscount Lisle, *Gu., a lion ramp. or, a bordure engrailed of the last.*

The seventh—William, earl of Huntingdon, HERBERT impaling *Arg., a fesse and a canton conjoined gu.* (WOODVILLE).

The eighth—Sir Walter Herbert, HERBERT impaling *Or, a chevron gu.* (STAFFORD).

The ninth—Sir George Herbert. The impalement here seems to be *Sa., 3 bulls' heads couped arg.*,[1] but the artist has made a mistake in copying the coat which, it is more than probable, was much defaced at the time. Sir George's wife was Sibyl, daughter of sir Richard Croft of Croft, and the impaled coat ought therefore to be *Quarterly, per fesse indented az. and arg., in the first quarter a lion pass. guard. or.* There were two other daughters who do not appear on the tomb—Jane, wife of sir Thomas Bulkeley, to whom the coat abovementioned would have belonged, and Isabel, wife of sir Thomas Cokesey.

Below these coats is the shield of Herbert impaling Devereux, surrounded by the garter. Underneath is written—

> Gulielmus Herbert Comes Pembrochie obijt 28º die Julij, A.D. 1469 et D'na Anna uxor eius Sororis Walteri Deuereux Baronis fferrers de Chartley Sepulti in Abbatia de Tinterne.

William Herbert, earl of Huntingdon, which earldom he accepted in lieu of Pembroke, son of the above earl, was also with his wife buried in the abbey. Their tomb is also illustrated in the same MS. Above the effigies is a shield of Herbert impaling Woodville, surmounted by an earl's coronet, the tomb being surrounded by iron railings. Underneath is written—

> Willi'mus Herbert Comes Huntindon sepultus est in Abba Monaster' Bᵗᵃᵉ Mariae Virginis de Tynterne una cum Uxore Sua Dⁿᵃ Maria Wideuille filia et coh' Ric' Com' Riuers obijt 15º Apr' AD 1491 relinquens Eliza. H. filliam et Heredem.

There are remains on the floor of the church of several memorial stones, few of which are legible.[2]

Within iron rails :

Ladi	help
Mercy	Ihefu
Jenkyn	ap Hoell

Around a slab is :

Nunc [mi]chi miserere. Hic jacet Numat' Philipus . . . . vocatus . . . . obiit . . . .

A slab within rails :

Hic jacet Will'mus wemted

A slab within rails :

Hic jacet Joh'n's miserere . . . .

I H S.

---

[1] *Itinerarium*, edited by James Nasmith.
[2] Dugdale's *Baronage*, I., 208.
[3] *Ibid.*, 207. [4] *Ibid.*, 134.
[5] *Ibid.*, p., 210. Rudder's *Gloucestershire*, p. 127.
[6] *Vide* p. 249.

[1] It may, however, be that the artist, unable to distinguish the defaced coats, assigned to sir George Herbert the impalement which would have belonged to his son sir Walter, viz., *Arg., 3 bulls' heads cabossed sa.*, for Morgan of Pen-coed.
[2] In *Remarks on Christian Grave Stones*, by the rev. Eccles Carter, 1847, are drawings of five crosses taken from stones here, but these are not faithful representations, but are elaborated in order to describe various styles of the cross.

L L 2

A stone with a cross floreated at the top and bottom has around it and a crosier :

.... IACET HENRICVS DE LANCAVT
QVONDAM ABBAS DE VOTO.

This is assigned by Cutts to the fourteenth century, who gives a drawing of it.[1]

He also has a drawing of a similar cross assigned to the same century, with the wording :

HIC IACET IOHANNES DE LYVNS.

The Iron and Wire Works.

For some centuries iron and wire works have been carried on at Tintern. These were doubtless first established by the monks at the abbey, and were afterwards carried on by the earls of Worcester and their lessees.

Queen Elizabeth in the seventh year of her reign granted by Letters Patent to the *Governor, Assistants and Society of Mineral and Battery Works* the privilege of pre-emption of woods at Monkswood and elsewhere for the purpose of making what was called Osmond iron for the wire works at Tintern.[2] This company sublet the works to John Wheeler and Andrew Palmer, whose lease expired in 1577. Sir Richard Marten in 1580 had a lease of the same, which four or five years afterwards he sublet to Richard Hanbury at the rent of 400*l.* per annum. Hanbury was the subject of law suits,[3] and it does not appear how long he continued the works here.

In 1630 John Gwyn, whose great-grandfather came first to the abbey of Tintern, as is stated in his great-grandson's note-book,[4] was steward to Anne, dowager countess of Worcester, and managed the works. In that year for the half-year ending the 27th March the total receipts were 668*l.* 6*s.* 2*d.*, while the working expenses, " fforge accompts " and " ffornace accompt," were 490*l.* 17*s.*, leaving a profit of 177*l.* 9*s.* 2*d.* Heath states that later the iron works were leased to Mr. Hanbury of Pontypool, who was succeeded by Richard White, on whose death in 1752 his nephew, Edward Jorden of Shropshire, succeeded. The wire works were a separate concern, and Heath quotes articles of agreement between Thomas Farmer and Rowland Pitt, lessees of the wire works, and their workmen, dated 15 October, 1747. On the death of Rowland Pitt[5] the works were leased to David Tanner of Monmouth, who in 1799 was succeeded by Robert Thompson.

The manufacturing of wire was done by Germans[6] or Swedes, of whom there must have been a considerable colony. Heath[7] gives an account of the

drawing of wire as carried out in the seventeenth century, which it is best to quote in his own words. Referring to the foreign workmen, he says :—

Their dwellings, which obtained the name of SEATS—probably from their being seated when at work—were made copyholds of inheritance; gave them a vote for members of parliament for the county; and were exempted from all kinds of taxes. Their wages were also permanently fixed; nor could their masters either eject or remove them from their employment.

The assistance of the mechanic powers to the operations of labour appear to have been in a very infantile state at that period. . . . A large beam was erected across the building in which were affixed as many seats (in the form of large wood scales) as there were men employed, who were fastened in them by means of a girdle that went round their bodies. The men were placed opposite each other, while between them stood a piece of iron filled with holes of different bores for reducing the wire to the various sizes. When the iron to be worked was heated the beam was put in motion by means of a water wheel that moved it, with the workmen in their seats, regularly backwards and forwards, who, with a large pair of tongs, passed and repassed the iron through the holes till by force they reduced it to the sizes required. The motion was as regular as the pendulum of a clock; and if any of the men missed seizing the iron with his tongs he suffered a considerable shock in the return of the beam.

For a number of years did the colony continue in the uninterrupted enjoyment of their seats . . . .

When the present method of making wire was introduced, by which means less than one half of the former number of hands became necessary, the proprietors of these works were placed in a very unpleasant position. Though the improvement was known which enabled their competitors to undersell them at markets, they could not immediately adopt the same system; for by their charter the masters could not lessen their wages nor displace them from their employment. . . . At that period John Pytt, esq., of Persfield held the works, and to his exertions the surrender of these privileges are chiefly to be attributed.

The iron-works at Tintern were an industry established for many years. Richard White, the son of George White who had iron-works at the New Weir in Whitchurch, was the proprietor, and dying in 1752, was succeeded here by his nephew Edward Jorden. In 1775 David Tanner of Monmouth, who also had the iron-works at Blaendare near Pontypool, and at Lydbrook and Redbrook, took over the iron and wire works at Tintern. He served the office of sheriff in 1792, and in 1799 he failed for a large sum of money. He resided at the Elms near the gaol in Monmouth. Robert Thompson then had the works at Tintern till his death in 1822, when messrs. Briggs and Rowbotham took them, who were succeeded by messrs. Brown, who closed the works in 1828.

The iron and wire works continued with a smaller degree of success till recently. In 1850 John Hughes had them; in 1871 messrs. Morrall and Stothert; in 1884 a company called *The Abbey Tintern Wire and Tinplate Co.,* with John Rowland

1 *A Manual of Sepulchral Slabs,* by rev. Edward Cutts, 1849, plate lxi. *De Voto* refers to the Tintern founded in Ireland in 1219 by William Marshall, earl of Pembroke (*vide* p. 258). Henry of Llancaut, the abbot there, was presumably a native of Llancaut on the Gloucestershire side of the river Wye.

2 Exchequer Special Commission, No. 1519, 32 Eliz.

3 Vol. I., p. 432.

4 Note-book of John Gwyn *penes* his descendant Uriah Gwynne Watkins of Yorkshire.   5 For his pedigree, *vide* p. 74.

6 *Memoirs of Monmouthshire,* by Nathan Rogers, 1708, p. 34.

7 *Account of Tintern Abbey,* by Charles Heath, 1810.

Griffiths as manager, which later was known as *Griffiths and Co.* It is now about ten years since the works ceased, and there seems no probability of this ancient industry being revived here. The large pond in the village is now used to turn a circular saw for a firm of timber dealers.

The site of the ancient works can be seen up the picturesque valley down which the Angidy brook, diverted into several ponds, descends rapidly from Pont-Seison (*the Englishmen's bridge*), perhaps so-called from having been erected by English workmen, to the river Wye. Many cottages, a large number uninhabited, remain, and among them is a large house known as Gwyn-house, from being the residence of the manager John Gwyn in the seventeenth century, which has always till recently been occupied by the manager of the works.

Richard White, mentioned above as proprietor of the iron-works, was the son of George White, who established the iron-works at the New Weir in Whitchurch, Herefordshire. George White, senior, purchased an estate at Goodrich from the duke of Kent, the then owner of Goodrich castle, the priory farm in Monmouth, and the *Weir Head* from the Company of Haberdashers. This latter was probably so called as being the ruins of ancient works. George White, junior, carried on his father's works at the New Weir, and built the house near the church of Goodrich.[1] These estates have descended to John Conway Lloyd of Dinas, Breconshire. As the family have been much connected with this county, I give their pedigree.

---

[1] This was on the site of an ancient house called Goodrich Court. The house is now called Goodrich House, the name *Court* having been remitted to sir Samuel Meyrick when he built the present mansion, since known as Goodrich Court.

Pedigree of the family of White of Goodrich.

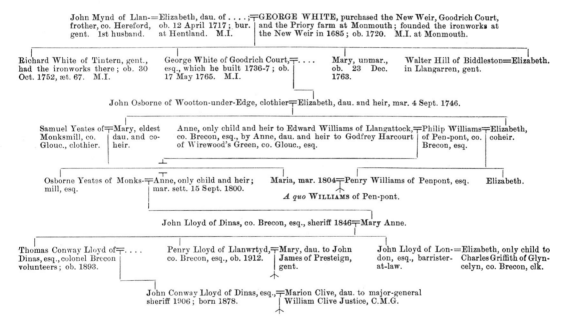

The Church.

The church is situated on a steep bank overlooking the monastic buildings, and was probably first built by the monks. The present edifice was rebuilt on the old site in the year 1866, and contains no features of particular interest.

The living has been a perpetual curacy, and has been held in connection with neighbouring churches. By an order in council in 1903 it was annexed to Tintern Parva. The advowson has always been in the hands of the owners of the abbey.

The church is dedicated to St. Andrew, and is called in Welsh Llanandras, this Andras being probably the son of Rhun and grandson of Brychan Brycheiniog, and not the apostle.[2]

INCUMBENTS.

24 Mar. 1717 Thomas Rodd, to officiate as curate of Chapel Hill and Llandogo.

6 Mar. 1766 John Williams, with Llanishen and Trelech Grange.

---

[2] Rees' *Welsh Saints*, p. 146.

19 Oct. 1768   Lewis Thomas, with the above.
25 June 1781   Thomas Hughes, with the above ; died
               1801-2.
18 Feb. 1803   John Rumsey, M.A. University College,
               Oxford, son of John Rumsey of Tre-
               lech, esq.¹ (patron, Henry, 5th duke
               of Beaufort, K.G.).
. . . 1851   George Jones.
. . . 1872   Henry John Williams ; also rector of
               Tintern Parva.
. . . 1879   Joseph Frederick Jones ; also rector of
               Tintern Parva.
. . . 1882   Edward Richard Godley ; also Tintern
               Parva.
. . . . . William Elitto Rosedale.
. . . 1889   Charles Henry Piggott.
. . . 1893   Harold Barclay Hennell ; also rector of
               Tintern Parva.
. . . . . William Donald Instance Mackintosh ;
               also rector of Tintern Parva.
8 Oct. 1903   Alfred William Washington Palmer ; also
               rector of Tintern Parva.

Monumental Inscriptions.

FLAT STONES IN THE PORCH, FORMERLY IN THE CHURCH.

HERE LYETH THE BODY OF ANNE
ALLDE. SHEE BURIED THREE
HUSBANES FRANCIS BRADFORD,
AND HENRY THOMAS, AND RAGER
ALLDE, GENT. SHEE DEPARTED
THIS . . DAY OF JANUARY
1670.

HERE LYETH THE . . . .
OF JOHN GROVAR
DECESED THE 17
OF MAY 1677.

Here lyeth the Body of
Francis Bradford, Clarke
of the Wire Works, who
decesed the first day of
October in the yeare of
our Lord God, 1657.²

HERE LYETH Yᴱ BODY OF FRANCIS,
Yᴱ WIFE OF PHILIP EUANES OF Yᴱ
PARISH OF CHAPELHILL, WHO DEPARTED
THIS LIFE Yᴱ 23ᵀᴴ DAY OF DECEMBER
IN Yᴱ YEAR OF OUR LORD GOD
1703.

Here lyeth the body of
Richard Laslat (?) of this
parish, Gent., who departed
this life the . . day of June
in the year of our Lord
God 1679.

1 For his pedigree, *vide* p. 139.
2 ffrancis Bradford Deceafsed on Thursday the first October 1657
by a fall from his horse goeinge to whitebrook fallinge hedlonge in a
sound [swoon] forward, vpon the horse neck, wᵗʰ his two feet fast in
the stirops, his wife was wᵗʰ hym, and she present alighted of her
hor[s]e, & cried for help, soe he was Carryed downe in a Trow to
Abbey and was sick about a week. Burried on the saterday followinge.
(Gwyn note-book referred to on p. 260.)

In the churchyard :

HERE LYETH THE BODY OF
MARY THE WIFE OF
GEORGE GWIN OF PVRCHASEGG, THE ONLY
DAVGHTER OF JOHN WILLIAMS OF ABBY AND
MARY HIS WIFE, WHO DEPARTED THIS LIFE THE
J DAY OF MARCH ANNO DOMINI 1696
AGED 25 YEARS AND 8 MONTHES.

HERE LIETH THE BODY OF CHARLES, Yᴱ SON
OF IOHN AND BRIDGETT RICHARDS,
WHO DEPARTED THIS LIFE Yᴱ 28 DAY OF
MARCH 1722.
Also here lieth yᵉ Body of Henry
the son of Henry and Mary . . . .
and Grandson of John Richards
who departed this life . . . . of
April 1735 Aged . . . . months.
Also here lieth yᵉ Body of Martha
yᵉ Daughter of George & Martha
Richards who departed this life
August 17, 1731, Aged 5 years
& 7 months.
Also here lieth the Body of Bridgett
the wife of Edward Tamplin who
departed this life September the
2, 1770, aged 34 years & 6 months.

In memory of
Ann Gwin of Porthcafseg
who died the 20 of October 1739 (?)
aged . . . . years.

A large altar-tomb :
Richard White
son of George White of New Wear
in the County of Hereford, Gent.,
Died Oct. 30, 1765, Aged 67 years.

An altar-tomb :
Sacred | to the memory of Prudentia | Relict of the
late John Flower | Fisher who died the 13ᵗʰ of April |
1789, Aged 49 years.
In Memory of | Susanna Fisher died the | 16 of Aug.
1814, Aged 41 years.
Prudentia, Daughter of | John Flower Fisher and
Prudentia | his wife died May 4ᵗʰ, 1847 | aged 70 years.
Mary, daughter of | John Flower Fisher | and Prudentia
his wife | Died Feb. 7, 1855 | in the 88 year of her age.
Flower, Son of | John Flower Fisher | and Prudentia
his wife | Died July 24, 1851 | Aged 76 years.

Near the vestry door, formerly in the chancel :
HERE LYETH THE BODY OF
WILLIAM THE SON OF
WILLIAM LEWIS OF WHITBROOK
WHO DEPARTED THIS LIFE
THE 16 DAY OF NOVEMBER
AN'O DOM. 1687
AGED 27 WEEKES.

Here lyeth interred the body of Mary, the wife of
Mist. Nicholas Williams of Tyntern, who departed this
life the 5 day of June in the year of our Lord God 1684.

Here lyeth the body of Mʳˢ Mary, the wife of Hugh
Williams, gent., of Tyntern, who departed this life the
18 day of July Anno Domini 1671.

Ann, the wife of John Hughes of Brockweir, ob.
21 Jan. 1697.

John Hughes, ob. 22 March 1716.

Charities.

Francis Bradford of Chapel, by his will dated 18 June, 1656, desired that lands amounting to the yearly value of 6l. should be purchased first for apprenticing a poor boy of his own kindred, and failing that, for placing out a boy belonging to Chapel Hill. There is no record of any land having been purchased, but the sum of 6l. per annum was paid by William Dinwoody, the owner of the Upper Court in Llangattock nigh Usk, who in 1786 disputed it, but subsequently allowed it. The farm was sold in 1806 by the trustees of Dinwoody to one Michael Phillips,[1] when the charge was confirmed.

The above Francis Bradford was, as his monument states, clerk of the wire works. He had a brother William of Bristol, who had two sons, Francis and William. His wife was Anne, daughter of Richard Bond of Redbrook, and sister of George Bond of Wyeseal, and, after the death of Francis, married Henry Thomas of Chapel Hill (will proved 1661), and on his death married Roger Aldey of Hardwick, esq.

Hackett's charity in 1898 produced 21l. per annum. This is for the benefit of the poor of Chapel Hill and Tintern Parva. In 1634 Thomas Hackett, whose son Philip of London, deceased, had given 15l., gave another 5l., making it in all 20l., and afterwards in satisfaction of the said 20l. gave twelve acres of land called Monk Reading in the parish of Mounton, then of the annual value of 3l. 13s. 4d., William Catchmay and others being the trustees. In 1831 and previously, the lands were let at 42l. per annum; at the time of the charity commission 1819—34 to Richard Watkins at 36l.; in 1898 at 21l.; in 1910 at 20l.

Samuel Pritchard, by his will dated 27 December, 1810, left 1000l. for the benefit of the poor. This was invested in the consolidated funds, and in 1898 produced 18l. 15s. per annum; in 1910, 15l. 12s.

There is also a field in Penterry comprising four acres, the rent of which is distributed among twelve poor females. This in 1898 produced 2l. per annum;[1] in 1910, 2l.

There is no account of any school being established until recent times, but there was doubtless a private institution for the benefit of the large number of people employed in the wire-works. On 2 May, 1704, Thomas Richards was admitted by the bishop to exercise the office of schoolmaster in the parish of Chapel Hill.

---

[1] Mr. Michael Phillips, grandson of the above Michael, is now the occupier and owner of the Upper Court.

[1] Report of Lord Brougham's Commission, 1819—37.

A History

OF

Monmouthshire

FROM THE COMING OF THE NORMANS INTO WALES
DOWN TO THE PRESENT TIME.

BY

JOSEPH ALFRED BRADNEY, *C.B., M.A., F.S.A.*

VOLUME II.

TITLE, INDICES, AND CORRIGENDA

TO

Part I.—The Hundred of Raglan.

Part II.—The Hundred of Trelech.

LONDON :

MITCHELL HUGHES AND CLARKE, 140 WARDOUR STREET, W.

1914.

Index Nominum.

An asterisk (*) signifies that the name occurs more than once on the page indicated.

A

Abbotts, Dr., Archbishop of Canterbury, 15.
A'Becket, Thomas, 237.
Aberdare, Lord, 120.
Abergavenny, George. Lord, 107* ; Henry, Earl, 107* ; Henry, Lord, 149 ; Mary, Lady, 149 ; William, Marquis of, 107 ; —, Marquis of, 85, 103* ; —, Earl of, 82 ; —, Lord, 82, 91, 111.
Abingdon, James, Earl of, 167 n. ; —, Earl of, 120 n.
Abrahall, Cecil, 56 ; John, 220* ; William, 56.
Adam, Morgan, 11.
Adams, Constance Lawson, 211 ; Henry, 211 ; John, 127 ; William, 73, 134*.
Adamthwaite, —, 28.
Addis, Edmund, 96.
Æddan ap Gwaethfoed, 105, 111, 115*.
Aiken, Chetwood-, Edward Hamilton Chetwode, 139 ; Eric Edward, 139 ; Nina, 139.
Aldey or Alde, Jane, 262 ; John, 208 ; Roger, 262, 263.
Aleston, Edward, 233.
Alexander, Arms of, 250.
Alexander, Lucy, 250, 251 ; Sir Walter, 251 ; Walter, 251.
Allen, Frances, 62 ; Joseph, 62 ; Thomas, 71 ; —, 71.
Alston, Thomas, 124.
Amberley, Lady, 147* ; Lord, 147*, 148.
Ambrose or Ambros, Elizabeth, 166, 177 ; John, 166, 177, 225* ; William, 225*.
Amorgan, Morgan, 203.
Amphlett, Richard, 51.
Anderson, John, 242.
Anderton, Elizabeth, Lady, 26, 231, 232 ; Sir Francis, Bart., 26, 231, 232.
Andrews or Andrew, Alice, 79 ; Anne, 16 ; Eleanor, 16 : George, 46, 175 ; John, 16* ; Katherine, 16 ; Margaret, 16 ; Rachael, 46 ; Robert, 16* ; Sara, 16* ; Susan, 46 ; Rev. Thomas, 175 ; Thomas, 16 ; William, 16 ; Mr., 15, 16 ; Mrs., 16.
Angle, Richard, 168.
Anne, John, 98.
Annesley, Arthur, Earl of Mountmorris, 27 ; Lady Catherine, 27.
Anthony, Jane, Viscountess Southwell, 116 ; Thomas, Viscount Southwell, 116.
Apperley, Elizabeth, 172 ; Thomas, 172.
Appletree, Francis, 178 ; James, 134*, 169, 178 ; John, 178* ; Mary, 178.
Arkwright, John, 59 ; Mary, 59.
Arney, Rev. William, 228.
Arnold or Arnald, Barbara, 188, 189* ; Edward, 244 ; James, 188*, 189 ; John, 72* ; Marie, 189 ; Mary, 188, 189 ; Thomas, 79, 112.
Arnott, Rev. Edward, 175 ; Edward, 157, 164, 174, 175* ; Mr., 170, 171.
Arthenus, 115.
Arthrwys, 213.
Arthur, Ann. 119 ; William, 103, 119 ; Family of, 112.
Arundel, Blanche, Lady, 26 ; Daniel, 232 ; Henry, Earl of, 27 ; Jane, 138 ; Sir John, 138 ; Hon. Mary, 27 ; Thomas, Lord, 26, 27 ; —. Earl of, 22.
Ashfield, Lieut.-Col., 19.
Aston, Ann, 27 ; Mary, 211 ; Walter, Lord, 27 ; Sir Willoughby, 211.
Atte Wall, John, 136.
Attley or Attlay, Stephen Oakley, 51 ; Mr., 169.
Attwood, Anthony, 139.
Aubrey or Awbrey, Ann, 218 ; Herbert, 78, 218 ; Jane, 27, 128 ; Rebecca, 78 ; —, 27, 128.
Austin, Rev. Frank Ernest, 100 ; William, 146*.
Avenal, Adam, 188 ; Dulcia, 196 ; Sir Morris, 188 ; Ralph, 196 ; Robert, 188 n., 196* ; William, 196.
Awbrey, see Aubrey.
A Wood, see Wood.
Awsell, Williamson alias, see Williamson alias Awsell.
Aylway or Ayleway, Elizabeth, 215 ; Joan, 172 ; John, 172, 215.

Aylworth of Trecastle, Pedigree of. 202.
Aylworth (Ailworth or Ayleworth), Ann, 204 ; Elizabeth, 201*, 202 ; Hannah=Edward Philpot, 202 ; John, 30, 31, 98*, 134*, 185*, 201*, 202, 204* ; John=Anne . . ., 202 ; John =Elizabeth . . ., 202 ; John=Martha Nelson, 202 ; Martha, 98, 204 ; Mathewe, 98, 202 ; Thomas, 98, 202, 243 ; William, 98*, 201, 202 ; Winifred, 98, 202 ; Winifred=John Gosling, 202.
Ayskew, Mr., 167.
Aythan, 116.

B

Babington, Gervais, Bishop of Llandaff, 149 ; Rev. Zachary, 134, 149*, 150, 152 ; Zachary, 152.
Bacheler, Nicholas, 219* ; Robert, 219* ; Thomas, 219 ; —, 219.
Backwell, Alderman, 124.
Badam, William, 38*.
Bagnall. Katherine, 170 ; John, 170* ; Mary Elizabeth, 170 ; Mrs., 249 n.
Bailey or Bayly, Clara, 116 ; Crawshay, 41. 52, 116 ; Rev. Josephus, 39 ; Dr. Thomas, 15 n., 19 n., 20, 21.
Bainham, see Baynham.
Bainton, see Baynton.
Baker, Anne, 33 ; Bridget, 186 ; Eleanor, 143 ; Henry, 143 ; Jane, 184 n.; John, 72 ; John William, 184*, 186 ; Richard, 243 ; Thomas, 50 ; Thomas Jones, 33 ; Thomas Watkins, 33 ; Walter, 188, 212 ; Rev. William, 253 ; William, 18 ; Mr., 88.
Baldwin, Archbishop of Canterbury, 105, 105 n., 115, 115 n.
Ball, Dorothy, 153 ; Francis, 218 ; Rev. James, 152, 153* ; James, 152 ; Mary, 218 ; Rev. Peregrine, 152, 152 n., 165 ; Rev. Mr., 145.
Ballard, Sir David, 142 ; George, 181, 182* ; Jane, 142 ; John, 182.
Baltimore, Charles, Lord, 27*.
Banister, —, 143*.
Bankes, George Vernon, 170 ; Rhoda, 170.
Bardwlff or Rodolphus, 236.
Barnes. Rev. Henry, 51.
Barnold, Ann, 199 n. ; Arnold, 199*, 199 n. ; James, 199 n.; John, 199 n.; Mary, 199*, 199 n.*; Thomas, 199.
Barrow. Rev. Anthony, 253 ; Edward, 253.
Barry, Pedigree of, 64.
Barry, Arms of, 64.
Barry, Anne, 65 ; Arthur Awbrey, 65 ; Arthur Edmund=Frances Robertson, 65 ; Barbara, 211 ; Boothby, 65 ; Caroline=Edward Usher, 65 : Catherine Octavia, 65 ; Charles=Louisa Miles, 65 ; David, 12 ; Rev. Edmund=Margaret Shepheard, 65 ; Rev. Edmund Gibson =Emily Saunders, 65 ; Edward, 65 : Elizabeth. 63 ; Elizabeth=William Ellis, 65 ; Elizabeth Amy=Douglas Kilburn, 65 ; Emma=Charles John Newby, 65 ; Frances =John Newby, 65 ; Frances Elizabeth, 65 ; Frances Mary, 65 ; Gerald de, 64 ; Rev. Henry=Elizabeth King, 65 ; Henry Boothby, 65 ; Rev. Henry William=Catherine Roberts, 65 ; Hester, 65 ; Jeremy, 65 ; John, 16, 64, 65, 88 ; John=1st . . . Humphries, 2nd . . . Saunders, 3rd Ann Sainsbury, 4th Sarah Singer, 65 ; John=. . ., 65 ; John Barry=1st . . ., 2nd . . ., 64 ; John Chamberlain, 65 ; Jonet, 12 ; Lilian=Arnold Hotham, 65 ; Margaret, 65 ; Rev. Martin=1st . . . Harris, 2nd . . . Ellis, 3rd Barbara Rooke, 4th . . . Driver, 65 ; Rev. Martin=Mary Perkins, 65 ; Rev. Martin, 64, 211 ; Martin, 65 ; Martin= Eleanor James. 65 ; Maud, 65 ; Mary, 65*, 107 ; Mary=John Honour, 65 ; Mary=John Price, 65 ; Mary=William Jones, 65 ; Phillis, 63, 64 ; Phillis=Joseph Meredith, 65 ; Richard, 65 ; Richard=. . ., 65 ; Susanna, 65 ; Thomas, 11, 65* ; William, 63, 64, 65*, 90 ; William=Elizabeth . . ., 65 ; William=Mary

Parry, 65 ; William=Phillis Roberts, 65 ; William=. . ., 65, 107* ; William Whittaker, 65 ; Family of, 64*.
Barton, Rev. Nicholas, 198.
Baryman, see Perryman.
Baskerville, Catherine, 27, 128 ; Margaret, 138 ; Walter, 27, 128 ; —, 138.
Basset or Bassett, Thomas, 124, 125 ; William, 22 n.
Bateman, Rev. Mallet, 253 ; Richard, 253.
Bates, Francis, 119 ; Mary Eleanor, 119.
Bath, John, Earl of, 27.
Batman, —, 227.
Batstone, Thomas, 39.
Batten, —, 87.
Baxter, Rev. Nathaniel, 175.
Bayly, see Bailey.
Baynham, Arms of, 141 n.
Baynham or Bainham, Alice, 163 ; Sir Christopher, 141 n., 142 ; Christopher, 162, 189 ; Cicely, 163* ; Dorothy, 141 n., 142, 163 ; Sir George, 163*, 163 n.; George, 163* ; Jane, 163* ; Joan, 142 ; Mary, 163 ; Philippa, 163* ; Thomas, 163* ; —, 189.
Baynton or Bainton, Daniel, 146, 244 ; Mr., 184.
Beale, Charles, 216 ; Rebecca, 216* ; William, 98 ; Winifred, 98.
Bean, William John, 90.
Beauchamp or de Beauchamp, Lady Eleanor, 26 ; Elizabeth, Countess of Warwick, 3 ; Henry, Earl, 43 ; Henry, Lord, 43 ; Joan, Lady of Abergaveny, 5* ; John, Lord of Abergaveny, 4* ; Sir John, 26 ; Margaret, 26 ; Mary, Lady, 27 ; Richard, Earl of Warwick, 3, 26 ; Richard, 3* ; Lady, 3*.
Beaufort, Arms of, 35.
Beaufort, Anne, 26 ; Charles, Duke of, 35* ; Charles Noel, Duke of, 24, 27 ; Edmund, Duke of Somerset, 7, 14 n. ; Edmund, Earl of Somerset, 14 n. ; Edward, Duke of. 23, 25 ; Eleanor, Duchess of Somerset, 26 ; Eleanor, 26 ; Elizabeth, Duchess of, 24, 27* ; Elizabeth, 26 ; Henry, Duke of, 13, 14 n., 24, 25*, 26, 27*, 31 n., 34, 35*, 35 n., 36, 41, 127, 132, 163, 165, 167 n., 168, 175, 176, 221, 225, 228, 243, 245*, 262 ; Henrv. Bishop of Winchester, 25 ; Henry, 26 ; Henry Charles, 25*, 28, 34*, 136, 137, 175*, 228, 245 ; Joan, Duchess of, 26 ; Joan, 25, 26* ; John, Duke of Somerset, 26 ; John Plantagenet, Duke of, and Somerset, 22 ; John, Earl of Somerset, 25 ; John, 26 ; Margaret, Duchess of Exeter, 25 ; Margaret, Duchess of Somerset, 25 ; Margaret, 26* ; Mary, Duchess of, 27, 34 ; Thomas, Duke of Exeter, 25 ; Thomas, 26* ; —, Duke of, 2, 13 n., 24, 31*, 32*, 34, 35, 38, 40, 48, 50, 52, 53, 71, 86*. 87, 104, 108, 111*, 115, 123 n., 125, 132, 137*, 157, 164, 166*, 167* n., 170, 177 n., 178, 179*, 180, 184, 230, 232, 237, 240, 243, 244, 247*, 255.
Beck, Maria, 217* ; —, 217.
Beddowe, Mary, 170.
Bedford, Francis. Duke of, 27 ; Francis, Earl of Bedford, 127, 127 n.; John, Earl of Bedford, 89.
Beever, Holt-, Adria Hannah, 139 ; Amy, 139 ; Vincent Morshead, 139.
Belchier or Belcher, John, 180* ; Mary, 60 ; Thomas, 60.
Bell, Edward, 213*, 214* ; William, 213*, 214*.
Bellamont, Lord, 18.
Bellamy, Frances, 50.
Bellasis, Lord, 18.
Bellew, Edward, 2nd Lord, 119 ; Gwendoline, 119 ; The Hon. Richard Eustace, 119.
Belson, Elizabeth, 194 ; John, 194 ; Maurice, 194.
Bengough, John Charles, 126 ; Mr., 122.
Bennett, Thomas, 187.
Benning, Adam, 124.
Benwyn, Dafydd, 12, 12 n., 14, 141, 230*, 231.
Berkeley, Arms of, 115.
Berkeley or Berkley, Apollonia, 116, 118 ;

Water, 98 ; William, 78, 86, 98, 127, 203 ; William John, 183 ; —, 13, 41, 61.
Howorth, Blanch, 81 ; Humphrey, 81 ; Susan, 81 ; —, 81.
Hoyskins, Hoyskin, see Hoskins.
Huddleston, Edward, 119 ; Frances, 119.
Hughes or Hugh, Ann, 52, 262 ; Charles, 41, 42, 93, 124 ; Deborah, 38, 38 n. ; Evan, 81 ; Evelyn, 95 ; Isabel, 152 ; James, 88, 88 n., 232 ; Jane, 42 ; Rev. John, 152 ; John, 65, 89, 134, 178, 260, 262* ; Mary, 14, 26, 38 n., 178 ; Maud, 134 ; Phillis or Philadelphia, 65 ; Richard, 41 ; Robert, 73, 145 ; Rev. Robert Vaughan, 253 n. ; Robert Vaughan, 95, 252 ; Col. Thomas, 123 ; Rev. Thomas, 245, 262 ; Thomas, 31*, 32, 38 n., 127, 232 ; Walter, 134 ; William, 14 n., 26, 65* ; —, 111, 175 n., 217.
Humphries or Humphreys, Jane, 201 ; Susan, 78 ; Thomas, 67, 78 ; William, 201 ; —, 65*.
Hunter, Eleanor, 59*, 68* ; Henry Lannoy, 59*, 68*.
Huntingdon, Francis, Earl of, 26, 35 ; William, Earl of, 14 n., 26, 35, 162, 258, 259 ; —, Earl of, 12, 13*, 14.
Huntley, Arms of, 42.
Huntley, Hugh, 9.
Huntley, Tomlyn alias, see Tomlyn alias Huntley.
Hustwaite, John de, 99.
Hutchins, Rev. Charles, 130, 152 ; Elizabeth, 152 ; Jane, 152 ; John, 152 ; Thomas, 152*.
Hutchinson, John, 81.
Huyske, Johanne, 123.
Hyde, Samuel, 44.
Hyett, Dorothy, 138 ; Rev. Edward, 240 ; Elizabeth, 37* ; Jane, 94 ; Mary, 37 ; Richard, 94, 138 ; Samuel, 37*.

I

Imary, Maud, 170.
Ingledew, Anne Mary, 218 ; —, 218.
Ingram, John, 38.
Innis, Jeremy, 146*.
Iorwerth, 142, 241.
Iorwerth, John ap, Arms of, 209.
Isan or Nissien, 241*.
Isgar, Jacob, 146.
Ithel, 48, 248.
Ithel, son of Arthrwys, 213.
Ithel, son of Morgan, 240.

J

Jackson, Elizabeth, 126 ; Sir Henry Mather, Bart., 84*, 90 ; Philip, 126 ; Rev. Robert, 52.
Jacob, Hannah, 201, 202* ; Robert, 201, 202.
James, Alice, 169 ; Rev. Andrew, 34 ; Ann, 57 ; Catherine, 245 n. ; Catring, 183 ; Charles, 163 ; David, 233 ; Rev. Edward, 175 ; Edward, 242 ; Eleanor, 65 ; Elizabeth, 80, 215 ; Enoch, 39 ; Henry, 169 ; Herbert, 81, 96* ; Howel, 75 ; James, 76*, 127* ; Jane, 55, 57 ; Joan, 56 ; John, 56, 80, 156, 200, 261 ; John Richard, 89*, 90 ; John Thomas, 92 ; John William, 31 ; J., 46 ; Rev. Lewis, 175 ; Margaret, 158, 169 ; Mary, 166, 168, 261 ; Maud, 89 ; Peter, 215 ; Richard, 103 ; Susanna, 39 ; Rev. Thomas, 34, 233, 245, 245 n. ; Thomas, 50, 75, 87, 92, 96, 98, 166, 237* ; Walter or Water, 54, 65, 96, 169 ; Walter John, 233 ; William, 31, 44, 86, 158, 168, 169 ; —, 180, 198.
Jayne, Elizabeth, 248 ; Jane, 32 ; John, 32, 103, 169 ; Margaret, 210 ; William, 210.
Jefferies or Jeffreys, Benjamin, 38, 38 n. ; Charles, 157 ; Edward, 38 n., 109* ; James, 36, 38*, 109* ; John, 38*, 87 ; Mary, 73, 109 ; Sarah, 36 ; Susanna, 109* ; Thomas, 36*, 73, 109 ; William, 38 n., 109.
Jenkin (Jenkyn or Jankin), Alice, 183 ; Bridget, 203 ; Charlotte, 38 ; Gwenllian, 203 ; Gwilym, 6 n. ; Hugh, 233 ; Rev. John, 233 ; John, 81*, 203*, 233 ; John William, 81*, 90 ; Katherine, 203 ; Maude, 81 ; Richard Pryce, 32 ; Susan, 203 ; Thomas, 160, 183 ; Thomas Gwilym, 6 n. ; Thomas John, 90 ; William, 91*, 109, 183.
Jenkins of Llidiart-Melyn, Pedigree of, 46.
Jenkins, Ann, 46*, 49, 143* ; Benjamin, 46, 49* ; Benjamin=Mary, 46 ; Cadwalader, 233 ; David, 44, 46, 210 ; Eleanor, 46*, 49* ; Elizabeth, 49, 95, 109, 120*, 243 ; Elizabeth=Thomas Lewis, 46 Elizabeth=. . . Stubs, 46 ; Frances, 32 ; Francis, 143*, 144* ; Hector, 90 ; James, 50 ; Jane, 36 ; Rev. John Rees, 223 ; Lewis, 32 ; Margaret, 210 ; Mary, 46, 234 ; Mary=Thomas Turner, 32 ; Mary= Reynold Williams, 32 ; Nathaniel, 46, 120 ; Nathaniel=Elizabeth Davies, 46 ; Rachael, 143, 144 ; Richard, 46, 55, 120 ; Thomas, 32, 36*, 46*, 49*, 109* ; Thomas=Winifred Lewis, 32 ; Thomas=Elinor . . ., 46* ; William, 32*, 33, 90, 95 ; William=Winifred Holmes, 32 ; William=Sarah . . ., 32 ; William Kinniard, 51 ; Winifred, 32*, 46.

Jepson, William, 124.
John, Anne, 98 ; Blanche, 98 ; Catherine, 61 ; Catring, 183 ; David, 213 ; Eleanor, 189 ; Elizabeth, 183, 227 ; Jane, 98*, 202, 227 ; Jenkin, 92 ; John William, 175, 242 ; Maud, 203 ; Rachel, 192 ; Rice, 227 ; Richard, 61 ; Richard William, 242 ; Saunder, 202, 203 ; Thomas, 183, 190 ; Walter, 67* ; Walter John, 242 ; William, 61, 237, 242.
John of Monmouth, 86, 89, 122, 219 n.
Johns or Johnes, Rev. Adam, 152 ; Rev. Alexander, 174 ; Alice, 92 ; Elizabeth, 226 ; Sir Harry, 92 ; Harry, 92 ; Maria, 168 ; Rice, 92 ; Col. Thomas, 168 ; Thomas, 168 ; William, 92, 213.
Johnson or Johnston, Rev. Benjamin, 39 ; Edith, 170 ; John, 75, 76, 91 ; Thomas, 170 ; William, 86 ; William Breer, 91.
Jones of Buckland, Pedigree of, 42.
Jones of Dingestow, Pedigree of, 56.
Jones of Tre Geirog, Pedigree of, 243.
Jones of the Waen, 218.
Jones, Arms of, 42, 56, 218, 242.
Jones, Adam, 185, 224 ; Rev. Alexander, 192 ; Alexander, 32*, 120 ; Alfred Edwin, 166 n. ; Alice, 216 ; Amos, 166 ; Amos Edwin, 166 ; Ann, 37, 47, 57, 80, 108, 134, 166, 184*, 189, 193, 202, 216*, 218, 226, 242 ; Ann=Richard Fitz-Gerard, 218 ; Ann=John Watkins, 57 ; Aron, 98 ; Benjamin, 31, 98 ; Blanche, 134, 159, 189 ; Bridget, 216 ; Bridget=. . . Howell, 243 ; Caroline, 47 ; Catherine, 42, 55*, 57, 118, 143, 144 n., 234* ; Cecil, 55, 57, 119 ; Cecil=Edward Jones, 57 ; Cecily, 55 ; Sir Charles, 30, 53*, 54*, 67, 80, 81, 133, 200*, 203, 243 ; Sir Charles=Elizabeth Jones, 55 ; Charles, 43, 47, 53, 54*, 57, 77, 90, 104, 125, 179, 181 ; Charles Gwillim, 47* ; Charlotte, 47 ; Christian, 125 ; Damaris, 42 ; Daniel, 44 ; Rev. David, 223, 239 ; David, 242* ; David= . . ., 243 ; David=. . ., 243 ; Dorothy=John Spencer Woollett, 218 ; Edmund, 31, 38, 38 n., 41, 42*, 103*, 103 n., 118, 134, 143, 144, 144 n., 166, 234*, 237, 242* ; Edmund=Gwladys Games, 42 ; Edmund Philip Herbert, 116 ; Edward, 30, 32, 41*, 42, 51, 95, 103, 103 n. ; Edward=Margaret Oates, 42 ; Edward Catchmayd, 218 ; Edward Decimus, 47 ; Eleanor, 41, 95 ; Eleanor=William Powell, 57 ; Elizabeth, 42, 47, 54, 56, 70*, 95, 104*, 118, 119, 125, 138, 166, 179, 242, 243 ; Elizabeth= Walter Bunting, 56 ; Elizabeth Margaret, 47 ; Emily, 170 ; Esther, 46, 120*, 159, 234 ; E., 145, 168 ; Florence, 95, 118, 145 ; Frances, 47, 229 ; Frances Catherine, 116 ; Games, 42* ; Rev. George, 262 ; George, 133*, 234* ; Rev. Griffith, 100 ; Gwenllian, 171, 189 ; Hannah, 171 ; Lady Harriet, 119 ; Harriet, 47 ; Harry, 81* ; Henry, 81, 124, 125*, 202, 216, 218 ; Rev. Henry Prowse, 233 ; Hugh, 16*, 75, 179, 183, 186 ; Inigo, 165 ; Isaac, 64 ; James, 72, 159* ; Jane, 53, 54*, 56, 57*, 69, 75, 81, 95, 115, 145, 159, 200, 208, 209, 215, 242 ; Jane=William Powell, 56 ; Joan, 54, 56, 125, 142, 233*, 242, 243* ; Joan=Sir John Herbert, 57 ; Job, 129 n., 147 n. ; Rev. John, 39, 47*, 120*, 239, 240 ; John, 30, 31, 39, 41, 42, 51, 52, 54*, 55*, 56*, 57, 66*, 69, 76, 79*, 81*, 95, 116*, 118*, 119, 123, 132, 133*, 144, 145*, 146, 149, 166, 168, 170*, 180, 181*, 184*, 189, 192, 193* 198, 200*, 215 n., 216*, 218*, 226*, 233, 234*, 242*, 243, 244, 245 ; Capt. John=Lydia Burgh, 57 ; John=Catherine Gibson, 57 ; John=Mary Vaughan, 57 ; John=. . ., 243 ; Rev. John Theodosius, 120 ; Rev. Joseph Frederick, 253, 262 ; Joyce, 77 ; Lewis, 80 ; Lucy, 145 ; Lydia, 168 ; Magdalen=. . . Long, 243 ; Margaret, 41, 42, 47*, 55*, 56, 138 ; Margaret=David Prichard, 243 ; Margaret= John Duncombe, 57 ; Margery, 63 ; Marmaduke, 87* ; Mary, 47, 54, 56, 57, 65, 68*, 79, 80, 81, 116, 118*, 125, 166, 170, 181, 216, 217, 218, 226 ; Mary=Herbert Morgan, 57 ; Mary =Edward Powell, 57 ; Mary=Edward Rouse, 218 ; Matthew, 189, 216* ; Matthew=Alice Prichard, 218 ; Rev. Matthew Henry, 51 ; Maud, 26 ; Maurice, 132 ; Meredith, 75 ; Merrick, 37* ; Rev. Morgan, 228 ; Moses, 42* ; Penelope, 216* ; Sir Philip, 15, 20, 69, 75, 88, 125* ; Philip, 51, 66, 76, 118, 119, 134*, 184, 190, 226 ; Philippa, 59 ; Rachel, 41*, 42* ; Rees, 39, 84 ; Rice, 216* ; Rice=Ann . . ., 218 ; Richard, 47, 54, 55*, 56, 57*, 66, 68*, 69, 81, 118, 126, 181*, 218 ; Richard=1st Margaret Gwillim, 2nd Mary Throgmorton, 57 ; Rev. Richard Ebenezer, 245 ; Richard Jermyn, 57, 69 ; Rev. Robert, 233* ; Robert, 165, 166, 214, 216*, 217, 218*, 225 ; Robert=Mary Catchmayd, 218 ; Roger, 41*, 244 ; Roger=Eleanor Evans, 42 ; Samuel, 138, 146 ; 216* ; Sarah, 47*, 86* ; Solomon, 81 ; Susan, 229 ; Susanna, 95, 229 n. ; Theophilus, 41 n., 231 ; Theresa, 55 ; Theresa=Peter Duncombe, 57 ; Rev. Thomas, 233 ; Thomas=Cecil Edward, 56 ; Thomas, 31, 32*, 41*, 42*, 53, 54*, 55*, 95, 97, 108, 119, 121, 124*, 125, 127, 132, 133, 134*, 166, 200, 225, 229, 242*, 243* ; Walter,

26, 31*, 53*, 56*, 60, 75, 104, 120, 138, 142, 218, 233*, 242*, 243 ; Walter=Joan Probert, 56 ; Walter=. . ., 243 ; Rev. William, 70, 98, 100, 107, 228, 233 ; William, 15, 30, 47, 51, 53, 56, 61*, 65, 67, 69, 81*, 87*, 88, 95, 96, 104*, 106*, 110, 115, 116*, 117*, 118*, 119*, 120, 121*, 123, 123 n., 124, 127*, 127 n., 145, 159*, 160, 178, 181, 182, 184, 185*, 189, 199, 200*, 209, 215, 215 n., 216*, 218, 224, 226, 242*, 243*, 245 ; William=Elinor . . ., 243 ; William=Elizabeth Morgan, 118 ; William =Penelope Prichard, 218 ; William=. . ., 243 ; William=. . ., 243 ; William Bence, 59 ; William Seys, 95 ; Winifred, 54, 56, 57 ; W., 83 ; —, Capt., 242 ; . . .=. . ., 218 ; —, Lady, 20 ; —, 117, 118, 119, 146, 164, 166, 170, 171*, 242 ; . . .=Watkin Herbert, 56.
Jones alias Evans, Johan, 75, 77 ; John, 75, 77 ; William, 75.
Jones alias High, Charles, 183.
Jones alias Morgan, see Morgan alias Jones.
Jones alias Robert, see Robert alias Jones.
Jorden, Edward, 260* ; Thomas, 62.
Joyce, Arms of, 214.
Joyce, —, 214*.
Justice, Marion Clive, 261 ; William, 14 ; William Clive, 261.

K

Kaltoff, Caspar, 23.
Kane, Clement, 146, 147, 147 n. ; Frances, 147 ; Grace, 146, 147 ; John Joseph, 52 ; Mary, 146*, 147*, 147 n., 244 ; Theresa, 147 ; Mrs., 147, 147 n.
Kearney, Rev. John, 207.
Keate, Dr., 58* n.
Keath, Morgan, 135.
Keene, —, 139*.
Kelly, —, 253 n.
Kemble, George, 90.
Kemeys, Sir Charles, Bart., 124*, 167*, 167 n. ; Dorothy, 169, 169 n., 190* ; Edward, 40, 41, 42, 167*, 169 ; George, 41, 42 ; Margaret, 42, 169 ; Lady Mary, 124 ; Sir Nicholas, Bart., 15* ; Rachael, 41*, 42 ; William, 132, 134*, 169, 169 n., 190* ; —, 17, 181, 193.
Kemp, Edward, 126 ; Elizabeth, 229* ; Margaret, 126 ; Jane Highings, 229 ; Robert, 229*.
Kennard, James, 168* ; Jane, 86 ; John, 86, 90 ; Susanna, 86.
Kent, Catherine Grey, Countess of, 13, 259 ; George Grey, Earl of, 13, 259 ; —, Duke of, 44, 45 ; —, Earl of, 221*.
Kerny, Rev. John, 223 ; John, 208.
Kerwood, Mary, 123, 125 ; Nicholas, 123, 125.
Kes, Bridget, 189 ; John, 189.
Keyes or Keyse, Anne, 113 ; Daniel, 113* ; Elizabeth, 113 ; Emma Evans, 113 ; James, 113* ; Joseph, 113 ; Mary, 113.
Kidson, William, 50.
Kilburn, Douglas, 65 ; Elizabeth, 65.
King, Daniel, 65 ; Elizabeth, 65 ; Gilbert, 210 ; Harriet, 210 ; James Bryan, 170* ; James Pearce, 170 ; Katherine, 170 ; —, 170.
Kingscote, Lady Isabella Anne, 28 ; Thomas Henry, 28.
Kingston or Kingstone, George, 159 ; Jane, 159 ; John, 135 ; Sarah, 159.
Kinnoul, Emily Blanch Charlotte, Countess of, 28 ; George, Earl of, 28.
Kinvin, Richard James, 89*, 90.
Knight or Knite, Emma, 210 ; Rev. Robert, 210 ; Robert, 88 n., 225 ; Mrs., 88.
Knovill, de, Gilbert, 99, 99 n.
Kupar or Kuper, Rev. Charles Augustus Frederick, 52, 152 ; Rev. William, 152.
Kyrle, Col., 19.

L

Lace, Rev. Richard, 175, 175 n., 189 ; Robert, 191 ; Thomas, 61 ; William, 31.
Lachlan, Dr., 131.
Lacon, Sir Francis, 128 ; Mary, 128.
Lake, Elizabeth, 140 ; —, 140.
Lambert, Rachael, 143 ; William, 52, 143.
Lambton, Susan, 251 ; —, 251.
Lane, William, 183.
Lancaster or Lancastre, Henry Plantagenet, Duke of, 25* ; Henry, Earl of, 219 ; Thomas, 4, 5 ; —, Earls and Dukes, 220.
Lane, Alice, 238 ; Cecil, 210 ; Francis, 238 ; Nathaniel, 210 ; William, 181*, 182.
Langattock, see Llangattock.
Langford, Abraham, 58 ; Louisa, 58.
Langley, Rev. Thomas, 223.
Larkin, Josiah, 200.
Lascelles, 253 n.
Laslat, Richard, 262.
Lasse, William, 61.
Latimer or de Latimer, John, Lord, 26 ; Lucy, Lady, 26 ; Philip, 240.
Laurence, see Lawrence.

Index Locorum.

174, 176, 177, 182, 184, 188, 212, 226, 243, 244.
Troy House, 167, 176, 195, 243.
Troy Park, 164, 165.
Troy Parva, 161, 162, 168.
Trylec Bechan, 206.
Trylec Lann Mainuon, 247.
Tuebrook, Liverpool, 176.
Tump, The, 56, 57, 111, 112, 121.
Tump, The, at The Pitt, Llanarth, 168.
Tump Terrett, 130, 137, 140.
Tunstall, Worcestershire, 211, 212 n.
Tutnall, 218.
Tutshill, Gloucestershire, 95.
Twickenham, 139.
Twr-melyn Gwent, 23, 29.
Twyford in Middlesex, 75, 76.
Twyn-tirret, 136, 137, 149.
Twyn-y-ceirios, 28.
Twyn-y-daley-du, 225.
Ty-bach, 234.
Ty-coch, 30, 104, 121.
Tydenham, Gloucestershire, 21, 24, 145.
Tydu, 39, 46, 119.
Ty-gwyn, 119, 120, 237.
Ty-Harry, 57, 196, 198 n.
Ty-isha, 180.
Tyle-glas, Brecnockshire, 56.
Ty-mawr, 63, 66, 74, 88 n., 93, 95, 104, 105, 224, 236.
Tyr-Cutta, 242.
Tyre-abellyer, 241.
Tyre-gwern-y-saint, 178.
Tyre-Newydd, 105, 133, 133 n.
Tyre-pelley-yssa, 203.
Tyre-Singlas, 134.
Tyre-y-valley, 90.
Tyr-feglyn, 242.
Tyr-Lucas, 242.
Tyr-mynach, 104.
Tyrone, Ireland, 58.
Tyr-pant-Jenkin, 242.
Tyr-y-coed, 146.
Tyr-y-coydner, 145.
Tyr-y-glynn, 133, 133 n.
Tyr-y-pant, 242.
Ty-Sewyn, 114.
Ty-Shaw, 81.
Ty-Shenkin, 90, 97.
Tythegston, Glamorganshire, 210.

U

Uley, Gloucestershire, 197.
Undy, 21, 257.
Unnis, The, 134.
Upper Court in Llangattock nigh Usk, 263.
Upton on Severn, 154.
Upton Warren, Worcestershire, 218.
Urchenfield, 7, 9.
Usk, 2*, 8, 9, 13, 19, 32, 39, 40, 41, 44 n., 45, 46, 47, 48, 55, 56, 57, 60, 66, 79, 97, 100, 107, 114, 114 n., 115, 120, 121, 124 n., 129, 131, 132, 133, 135 n., 136, 138, 138 n., 140, 155, 161, 166, 170, 173, 174 n., 180, 183, 190, 191, 192, 196, 200, 201, 204, 207, 218, 225, 226, 233, 236, 239, 241, 242, 243, 245.
Usk Castle, 166, 183, 186, 244, 257.

V

Vanhaddlog, 242.
Vauxhall, 23.
Velindre, 91.
Vibon Avel, 88.
Victoria, Australia, 65.
Vinters, Kent, 59.
Virginia, 146, 186.
Virtuous Well, The, 148, 206.
Vorland Vawr, 66.
Vowchurch, 27, 81.

W

Waen (Wayne), The, 80, 216, 218.
Waen (Wayne) Mill, 88, 88 n.
Wainway, 132.
Waldingespall, 257.
Wales, University of, 245.
Walford, Herefordshire, 19, 62, 78.
Walk, The, 92, 96.
Walker's Farm, 124.
Walweir, 219, 257.
Walwyn's Castle, 7.
Wandsworth, 156.
Wanstead, Essex, 27.
Wardour, 26.
Warham, co. Heref., 96.
Warrage, 19, 30, 71, 82.
Warwick, 149, 193.
Warwickshire, 57.
Wasing, Berks, 44.
Waterloo, 208, 211, 237.
Watermoor, co. Glouc., 119.
Waun-y-parc, 206, 206 n.
Wayfhers, 257.
Weir Head in Abbey Tintern, 261.
Welsh Bicknor, 166.
Welsh Newton, 146, 210.
Wem, 25.
Wenarth hedge, 132, 132 n.
Wenge, 27.
Wenhalt, 257.
Wentllwg, 142.
Wentsland, 56, 103.
Wenvoe, 215.
Weobley, 18, 96.
Wern, The, 172.
Wern-ddu, 10 n., 196, 197.
Wern-gochen, 236.
Wern Obrey, 200.
Wern-y-cleppa, 18, 18 n.
Wern-y-cwm, 88 n.
Wern-y-cwrt, 103.
Wern-y-felin, 216.
Wern-y-melyn, 78, 79, 80, 83.
Wern-yr-heolydd, 97.
West Bromwich, Staffordshire, 170.
Westerham, Kent, 26.
Westhide, Herefordshire, 168 n.
Westminster, 220, 248.
 Abbey, 27.
 Bruar St., Piccadilly, 124.
 St. Giles' in the Fields, 171.
 St. James', 251.
 St. John's, 100.
 St. Margaret's, 211.
 Treleck Terrace, Pimlico, 154.
 Worcester House, Strand, 15, 16, 21, 27.
Weston under Penyard, Herefordshire, 47, 146.
Weun, 206.
Whechan, 66.
Whechan Brook, 2, 85, 87, 91, 133 n.
Whiligh, Sussex, 59.
Whitchurch, Herefordshire, 34, 57, 91, 126, 142, 172, 210, 221, 260, 261.
Whitebridge, 87.
Whitebrook (Whitbrook), 129, 134, 155, 206, 222, 241, 262.
Whitebrook's Mill, 134.
Whitebrook's Slip, 132, 133.
White Castle, 6, 78, 119, 122.
Whitehall, 15, 53, 56.
Whitehaven, Cumberland, 44, 45.
Whitehouse, 190.
 near the Carn, 132.
 Farm, 134.
 in Skenfrith, 75.
 in Vowchurch, 81.
Whitland, Carmarthenshire, 215.
Whitson, 95, 141.
Wickwick, Gloucestershire, 125.
Wigmore, 7 n.

Wilcae (Wilsbrook), 2, 30, 32, 37, 48, 105.
Wilchcome, Wiltshire, 233.
Wilcrick (Wilgrig), 95, 201, 216.
Willersley, Gloucestershire, 175.
Wilton, 26.
Winchester, 26, 149.
Windsor, 10, 13, 21, 24, 26, 27, 211.
Windy Hole, 182 n.
Winkfield, 98.
Wirewood's Green in Tyddenham, 95, 145.
Withington, Gloucestershire, 62.
Withington, Herefordshire, 47.
Wonastow (Wynastowe), 27, 74, 76, 77, 86, 91, 121, 122, 123, 123 n., 125, 126, 128, 133 n., 146, 162, 162 n., 163, 164, 166, 170, 175, 175 n., 178, 179, 195, 198, 215, 213 n., 231.
Wonastow, New, 179.
Wondy (Undy), 257.
Wonton in Much Marcle, 218.
Woodhall, 8.
Woolaston, Gloucestershire, 31, 175, 257.
Woolaston Grange, Gloucestershire, 168.
Woolvesnewton, 133, 135, 138, 140, 145, 146, 147, 183, 198, 229, 233, 234, 236, 237, 238, 239, 240, 242.
Woolvesnewton, The Great House in, 140.
Wooton under Edge, 26, 34.
Wootton, Gloucestershire, 172.
Worcester, 18, 19, 24 n., 55, 57, 68, 216, 218.
 St. Oswald's Hospital in, 218.
Worthy brook, 178, 179.
Wraheen, Kilkenny, 178.
Writtle, 26.
Wye, 51, 78 n., 129, 132, 133, 134, 147, 155, 157, 160, 206, 212, 213, 219, 220, 221, 241, 247, 248, 255, 256, 256 n., 261.
Wye Bridge, 51.
Wyelands, 95.
Wyeseal, 215, 263.
Wyesham (Wysham), 21, 78 n.
Wyespool, 241.
Wyes Wood, 135, 136.
Wyes Wood Chase, 134.
Wymondley, Little, Hertfordshire, 211.

Y

Y-Coome, 242.
Y-Croft, 183.
Y-Croft-beeth, 62, 62 n.
Y-darn-isaf, 183.
Y-ddwy-errowe-dion, 93, 93 n.
Y-ddwy-worlod-y-pysgodlyn, 78.
Yewtree field, 200.
Yewtree ford, 66.
Y-ffos-fach, 196.
Y-gerddinen, 190.
Y-gyderowe, 242.
Ynys, 181.
Ynys Fawr, 93.
Ynys Iarll, 141.
Ynys-Kelling, 243.
Ynys-Nichol, 244.
Ynys-Pwll-Melyn, 40.
Ynys-Tair-Erw, 241.
Ynys-ysgallog, 60.
York, 139, 249, 251.
 Petergate, 249.
 St. Crux, 249, 251.
 St. Mary le Belfrey, 251.
Yorkshire, 251.
Youghall, Ireland, 175.
Y-palsie-bach, 200.
Yr-erw, 182.
Yr-hafod, 243.
Yr-ynys, 244.
Yr-ynys-fawr, 84, 93.
Ysgubor-newydd in Rockfield, 65.
Ystern Llewern, 8 n.
Y teynhalog, 60.

CORRIGENDA.

Page 2, col. 2, line 31.   Henry VII. should be *Henry II.*

Page 26.   The wife of William, 3rd earl of Worcester, should be *Christian* (not Catherine).

Page 26, seventh generation of pedigree.   Gwernogs should be *Gwernoga.*

Page 43.   An earl's coronet appears in error for a baron's.

Page 48, col. 1, line 14.   Fferwael should be *Ffernwael.*

Page 79, col. 2, line 32, should read *John Watkins, grandson of the above John* (not Charles).

Page 93, col. 1, line 9.   Mr. Godfrey Seys died in *1905* (*not* 1895).

Page 107, list of rectors.   1805.   John Cooke was son of John Cooke of Goitre, whose pedigree is in Vol. I., p. 419.   John Cooke the rector is there erroneously called *gent.*

Page 140, pedigree.   The name Winslow should be *Winsloe.*   Of the daughters of Sidney Tudor Evans, Isabella should be *Isabel,* and Florence should be *Flora Winsloe.*

Page 141, col. 2, line 39, read *inferioris* (not interioris).

Id., line 40, read *desideratissimus* (not desiderantissimus).

Page 175, line 60.   Ginting should be *Guiting.*

Page 204, col. 2, line 41.   Said should be *Laid.*

Page 209, line 5.   Glorydd should be *Glodrydd.*